INTRODUCTION TO
SOCIOLOGY

FIFTH EDITION

W. W. Norton & Company, Inc.
New York • London

INTRODUCTION TO SOCIOLOGY

FIFTH EDITION

Anthony Giddens
LONDON SCHOOL OF ECONOMICS

Mitchell Duneier
CITY UNIVERSITY OF NEW YORK
GRADUATE CENTER

PRINCETON UNIVERSITY

Richard P. Appelbaum
UNIVERSITY OF CALIFORNIA,
SANTA BARBARA

Copyright © 2005, 2003 by Anthony Giddens, Mitchell Duneier, and Richard P. Appelbaum.
Copyright © 2000 by Anthony Giddens and Mitchell Duneier.
Copyright © 1996, 1991 by Anthony Giddens.

Editor: Karl Bakeman
Project editor: Lory Frenkel
Editorial assistant: Sarah Solomon
Photo research: Stephanie Romeo
Page layout: Brad Walrod, High Text Graphics
Composition by GGS Book Services, Atlantic Highlands
Manufacturing by Courier Kendallville
Book design by Rubina Yeh
Production manager: JoAnn Simony

Library of Congress Cataloging-in-Publication Data

Giddens, Anthony.
    Introduction to sociology / Anthony Giddens, Mitchell Duneier, Richard P. Appelbaum.—5th ed.
        p. cm.
    Includes bibliographical references.
    ISBN 0-393-92553-6 (pbk.)
    1. Sociology.   I. Duneier, Mitchell.   II. Appelbaum, Richard P.   III. Title.

HM585.G53 2005
301—dc22   2004063646

W. W. Norton & Company, Inc., 500 Fifth Avenue, New York, N.Y. 10110 www.wwnorton.com

W. W. Norton & Company Ltd., Castle House, 75/76 Wells Street, London W1T 3QT

4 5 6 7 8 9 0

W. W. Norton & Company has been independent since its founding in 1923, when William Warder Norton and
Mary D. Herter Norton first published lectures delivered at the People's Institute, the adult education division
of New York City's Cooper Union. The Nortons soon expanded their program beyond the Institute, publishing
books by celebrated academics from America and abroad. By mid-century, the two major pillars of Norton's
publishing program—trade books and college texts—were firmly established. In the 1950s, the Norton family
transferred control of the company to its employees, and today—with a staff of four hundred and a comparable
number of trade, college, and professional titles published each year—W. W. Norton & Company stands as the
largest and oldest publishing house owned wholly by its employees.

CONTENTS

Part Two: The Individual and Society 49

Chapter 3: Culture and Society 51

Chapter 4: Socialization and the Life Cycle 87

Chapter 5: Social Interaction and Everyday Life 109

Chapter 6: Groups, Networks, and Organizations 131

Chapter 7: Conformity, Deviance, and Crime 167

Part Three: Structures of Power 201

Chapter 8: Stratification, Class, and Inequality 203

Chapter 17: Religion in Modern Society 505

Part Five: Social Change in the Modern World 543

Chapter 18: The Sociology of the Body: Health and Illness and Sexuality 545

Chapter 19: Urbanization, Population, and the Environment 579

Chapter 20: Globalization in a Changing World 617

t his book was written in the belief that sociology has a key role to play in modern intellectual culture and a central place within the social sciences. Our aim has been to write a book that combines some originality with an analysis of the basic issues that interest sociologists today. In some places, we attempt to bring the reader into a subject through the use of ethnographies written for this book. The book does not try to introduce overly sophisticated notions; nevertheless, ideas and findings drawn from the cutting edge of the discipline are incorporated throughout. We hope it is not a partisan treatment; we endeavored to cover the major perspectives in sociology and the major findings of contemporary American research in an evenhanded, although not indiscriminate, way.

Major Themes

The book is constructed around a number of basic themes, each of which helps to give the work a distinctive character. The newest theme is *public sociology*, reflected in a series of boxes inspired by the 2004 annual meeting of the American Sociological Association. At this meeting, Michael Burawoy's pathbreaking presidential address called for the discipline to draw on the insights and methods of sociology to involve ordinary people in studying and solving the social problems that afflict them. The book features thirteen boxes that profile sociologists engaged in public sociology in diverse arenas: for example, Boston sociology professor Diane Vaughan's influential research on the *Challenger* shuttle disaster, which helped shape subsequent governmental investigations; a report on the working conditions of the University of California-Berkeley's service staff by three Berkeley grad students, which garnered wide spread publicity; and an essay by Brandeis professor David Cunningham about his annual social movements course, in which he takes students around the country to visit different communities and participate in various social and political movements. It is our hope that the Public Sociology boxes will inspire students to draw on their sociological imaginations to become more publicly involved and will provide some useful ideas for instructors who wish to generate class projects that directly engage students in the real world. In his speech, Burawoy also emphasized that public sociology cannot exist without a professional sociology that develops a body of theoretical knowledge and empirical findings. The central task of the book is to explain what the discipline of sociology has to offer along these lines.

A second theme of the book is that of the *world in change*. Sociology was born of the transformations that wrenched the industrializing social order of the West away from the ways of life characteristic of earlier societies. The world that was created by these changes is the primary object of concern of sociological analysis. The pace of social change has continued to accelerate, and it is possible that we stand on the threshold of transitions as significant as those that occurred in the late eighteenth and nineteenth centuries. Sociology has prime responsibility for charting the transformations of the past and for grasping the major lines of development taking place today.

Another fundamental theme of the book is the *globalizing of social life*. For far too long, sociology has been dominated by the view that societies can be studied as independent entities. But even in the past, societies never really existed in isolation. In current times, we can see a clear acceleration in processes of global integration. This is obvious, for example, in the expansion of international trade across the world. The emphasis on globalization also connects closely with the weight given to the interdependence of the industrialized and developing worlds today.

The book also focuses on the importance of *comparative* study. Sociology cannot be taught solely by understanding the institutions of any one particular society. While we have slanted the discussion toward the United States, we have also balanced it with a rich variety of materials drawn from other cultures. These include research carried out in other Western countries, as well as Russia and the Eastern European societies, which are currently undergoing substantial changes. The book also includes much more material on developing countries than has been usual in introductory texts. In addition, we strongly emphasize the relationship between sociology and anthropology, whose concerns overlap comprehensively. Given the close connections that now mesh societies across the world with one another, and the virtual disappearance of traditional social systems, sociology and anthropology have increasingly become indistinguishable.

A fifth theme is the necessity of taking a *historical approach* to sociology. This involves more than just filling in the historical context within which events occur. One of the most important developments in sociology over the past few years has been an increasing emphasis on historical analysis. This should be understood not solely as applying a sociological outlook to the past, but as a way of contributing to our understanding of institutions in the present. Recent work in historical sociology is discussed throughout the text and provides a framework for the interpretations offered in the chapters.

Throughout the text, particular attention is given to *issues of gender*. The study of gender is ordinarily regarded as a specific field within sociology as a whole—and this volume contains a chapter that specifically explores thinking and research on the subject (Chapter 10). However, questions about gender relations are so fundamental to sociological analysis that they cannot simply be considered a subdivision. Thus, many chapters contain sections concerned with issues of gender.

A seventh theme is the *micro and macro link*. At many points in the book, we show that interaction in micro-level contexts affects larger social processes and that such macro-level processes influence our day-to-day lives. We emphasize that one can better understand a social situation by analyzing it at both the micro and macro levels.

The final major theme is the relation between the *social* and the *personal*. Sociological thinking is a vital help to self-understanding, which in turn can be focused back on an improved understanding of the social world. Studying sociology should be a liberating experience: The field enlarges our sympathies and imagination, opens up new perspectives on the sources of our own behavior, and creates an awareness of cultural settings different from our own. Insofar as sociological ideas challenge dogma, teach appreciation of cultural variety, and allow us insight into the working of social institutions, the practice of sociology enhances the possibilities of human freedom.

All of the chapters in the book have been updated and revised to reflect the most recent available data. Additionally, four chapters have received special attention: Chapter 7 (*Conformity, Deviance, and Crime*) has significant new material on the increasing trend to use the criminal justice system to regulate poverty in the United States. Since the 1970s, the U.S. penal system has grown continuously to the point where today nearly two million people are in prison or jail. We examine the effect of incarceration on the future life chances of inmates and on inequality trends in the United States. Increasingly, we recognize that penal institutions are also stratification institutions. Chapter 11 (*Ethnicity and Race*) works toward new definitions of race and ethnicity that take account of the need to transcend simple folk understandings. In particular, we no longer accept at face value the clear-cut distinction between race and ethnicity, which has been forcefully challenged by many scholars in recent years. The chapter also includes new research on mixed race identity, which is included to illustrate clearly the complexities associated with definitions of race and ethnicity. Chapter 13 (*Government, Political Power, and Social Movements*) has significant new material on the Internet and democratization, including an expanded discussion of censorship and Internet surveillance. The discussion of politics and voting has been revised to reflect recent trends (through the 2004 election) in party identification and voter turnout, including an examination of some possible reasons for voter apathy. There is also an expanded discussion of interest groups, Political Action Committees, and campaign finance reform. Finally, the analysis of social movements has been recast, with expanded attention being paid to New Social Movements. Chapter 17 (*Religion in Modern Society*) now begins by addressing the September 11 attacks on the World Trade Center and the Pentagon, placing religious terrorism as a central concern. While there is expanded discussion of the spread of Islamic revivalism, particularly al Qaeda, the examination of religious nationalism and violence draws on recent research to argue that under certain conditions, ordinary conflicts can be recast as "cosmic wars" that must be won at all costs. The chapter shows that religious violence is found today among all major religious groups—Muslims, Sikhs, Jews, Hindus, Christians, and even Buddhists.

Organization

There is very little abstract discussion of basic sociological concepts at the beginning of this book. Instead, concepts are explained when they are introduced in the relevant chapters, and we have sought throughout to illustrate them by means of concrete examples. While these are usually taken from sociological research, we have also used material from other sources (such as newspaper articles). We have tried to keep the writing style as simple and direct as possible, while endeavoring to make the book lively and full of surprises.

The chapters follow a sequence designed to help achieve a progressive mastery of the different fields of sociology, but we have taken care to ensure that the book can be used flexibly and is easy to adapt to the needs of individual courses. Chapters can be deleted or studied in a different order without much loss. Each has been written as a fairly autonomous unit, with cross-referencing to other chapters at relevant points.

Study Aids

The pedagogy in this book has been completely reconfigured in the Fifth Edition in order to facilitate critical thinking and reinforce important concepts. Each chapter begins with a chapter organizer, which highlights the learning objectives of each section and allows students to preview that chapter's discussion. *Introduction to Sociology* includes significantly expanded chapter review material, including keyword and concept-review questions and data exercises linking material in the text to real-world data on the Web.

Another helpful aid is the use of a global icon to indicate examples of the changing world or the globalization process, or comparisons of U.S. society with other societies. Social change, the globalization of social life, and comparative analysis are all important themes of this text. The icon will help alert readers to discussions of these themes.

Further Research: Reading and Libraries

Libraries contain abundant sources of information that can be used to follow up or expand on issues discussed here. References are given throughout the text and are listed fully in the bibliography at the end. We have also included a short appendix that provides a guide to library resources and how to use them.

Acknowledgments

During the writing of all five editions of this book, many individuals offered comments and advice on particular chapters, and, in some cases, large parts of the text. They helped us see issues in a different light, clarified some difficult points, and allowed us to take advantage of their specialist knowledge in their respective fields. We are deeply indebted to them.

Anthony Troy Adams, Eastern Michigan University
Angelo A. Alonzo, Ohio State University
Michael Blain, Boise State University
Deirdre Boden, Washington University, St. Louis
Richard J. Bord, Pennsylvania State University
Gerard A. Brandmeyer, University of South Florida
Phil Brown, Brown University
Annette Burfoot, Queen's University
Lee Clarke, Rutgers University, New Brunswick
Stephen E. Cornell, University of California, San Diego
Steven P. Dandaneau, University of Dayton
Lynn Davidman, University of Pittsburgh
Judith F. Dunn, Pennsylvania State University
Mark Eckel, McHenry County College
John V. A. Ehle, Jr., Northern Virginia Community College
Eliot Freidson, New York University
J. William Gibson, California State University, Long Beach
Richard H. Hall, University at Albany, SUNY
John Hartman, University at Buffalo, SUNY
Rick Helmes-Hayes, University of Waterloo
Wanda Kaluza, Camden County College
Paul Kingston, University of Virginia
Janet Koenigsamen, West Virginia University
Cora B. Marrett, University of Wisconsin
Garth Massey, University of Wyoming
Greg Matoesian, Fontbonne College
William H. McBroom, University of Montana
Katherine McClelland, Franklin and Marshall College
Greg McLauchlan, University of Oregon
Angela O'Rand, Duke University
Celia J. Orona, San Jose State University

Thomas Petee, Auburn University
Jennifer L. Pierce, University of Minnesota
Brian Powell, Indiana University
Allan Pred, University of California, Berkeley
Tomi-Ann Roberts, Colorado College
Roland Robertson, University of Pittsburgh
Martin Sanchez-Jankowski, University of California, Berkeley
Jack Sattel, Normandale Community College
Andrew Scull, University of California, San Diego
David R. Segal, University of Maryland, College Park
Peter Singelmann, University of Missouri, Kansas City
Craig St. John, University of Oklahoma
Judith Stepan-Norris, University of California, Irvine
Joel C. Tate, Germanna Community College
France Winddance Twine, University of California, Santa Barbara
Christopher K. Vanderpool, Michigan State University
Henry A. Walker, Cornell University
Chaim I. Waxman, Rutgers University, New Brunswick
Timothy P. Wickham-Crowley, Georgetown University
Paul Root Wolpe, University of Pennsylvania
Dennis H. Wrong, New York University
Irving M. Zeitlin, University of Toronto

We would like to thank the numerous readers of the text who have written with comments, criticisms, and suggestions for improvements. We have adopted many of their recommendations in this new edition.

We have many others to thank as well. We are especially grateful to Barbara Gerr, who did a marvelous job of copyediting the book, and offered numerous suggestions for alterations and improvements that have contributed in important ways to the final form of the volume. We are also extremely grateful to project editor Lory Frenkel, production manager JoAnn Simony, and editorial assistant Sarah Solomon for managing the myriad details involved in producing this book.

We are also grateful to our editors at Norton, Steve Dunn, Melea Seward, and Karl Bakeman, who have made many direct contributions to the various chapters, and have ensured that we have made reference to the very latest research. Particular thanks are due also to Deborah Carr of Rutgers University and Neil Gross of Harvard University, two of the most outstanding young sociologists in the United States. Both had a tremendous influence on many chapters in the book. We would also like to register our thanks to a number of graduate students whose contributions have proved invaluable: Alair MacLean, Sharmila Rudrappa, Susan Munkres, Blackhawk Hancock, Ann Meier, Katherina Zippel, Paul LePore, Wendy Carter, Josh Rossol, and David Yamane. Joe Conti, UCSB graduate student in sociology, proved to be a tireless and creative researcher, ferreting out the most recent data on every conceivable topic. He also provided his considerable expertise on the World Trade Organization for the discussion in Chapter 20. Denise Shanks, our electronic media editor, deserves special thanks for creating the elegant new Web site to accompany the book. Finally, Neil Hoos and Stephanie Romeo showed unusual flair and originality in the selections made for illustrating the book.

PART ONE

THE STUDY OF SOCIOLOGY

We live in a world today that is increasingly more complex. Why are the conditions of our lives so different from those of earlier times? How will our lives change in the future? These are the types of questions that lead us to the study of sociology. Throughout your reading of this text, you will encounter examples from different people's lives that will help us to answer these important questions.

In Chapter 1, we begin to explore the scope of sociology and learn what sort of insights the field can bring to our lives. Among these insights are the development of a global perspective and an understanding of social change. Sociology is not a subject with a body of theories everyone agrees on. As in any complex field, the questions we raise allow for different answers. In this chapter, we compare and contrast differing theoretical traditions.

Chapter 2 is an exploration of the tools of the trade and how sociologists set about doing research. A number of basic methods of investigation are available to help us find out what is going on in the social world. We must be sure that the information on which sociological reasoning is based is as reliable and accurate as possible. The chapter examines the problems with gathering such information and indicates how they are best dealt with.

Developing a Sociological Perspective

Learn what sociology covers as a field and how everyday topics like love and romance are shaped by social and historical forces.

Recognize that sociology is more than just acquiring knowledge; it also involves developing a sociological imagination. Learn that studying sociology leads us to see that we construct society through our actions and are constructed by it. Understand that two of the most important components of the sociological imagination are developing a global perspective and understanding social change.

The Development of Sociological Thinking

Learn how sociology originated and how it developed. Think about the theoretical issues that frame the study of sociology. Be able to name some of the leading social theorists and the concepts they contributed to the study of sociology. Learn the different theoretical approaches modern sociologists bring to the field.

Is Sociology a Science?

Learn how sociology is similar to and different from natural sciences.

How Can Sociology Help Us in Our Lives?

See the practical implications that sociology has for our lives.

CHAPTER ONE

WHAT IS SOCIOLOGY?

from the tragic terrorist attacks on the World Trade Center and the Pentagon to the mass murder at Columbine High School in Littleton, Colorado, the world today is intensely worrying, yet full of the most extraordinary promise for the future. It is a world awash with change, marked by deep conflicts, tensions, and social divisions, as well as by the destructive onslaught of modern technology on the natural environment. Yet we have possibilities of controlling our destiny and shaping our lives for the better that would have been unimaginable to earlier generations.

How did this world come about? Why are our conditions of life so different from those of our parents and grandparents? What directions will change take in the future? These questions are the prime concern of sociology, a field of study that consequently has a fundamental role to play in modern intellectual life.

Sociology is the scientific study of human social life, groups, and societies. It is a dazzling and compelling enterprise, as its subject matter is our own behavior as social beings. The scope of sociological study is extremely wide, ranging from the analysis of passing encounters between individuals on the sidewalk to the investigation of global social processes such as the rise of Islamic fundamentalism. A brief example will provide an initial taste of the nature and objectives of sociology.

Have you ever been in love? Almost certainly you have. Most people who are in their teens or older know what being in love is like. Love and romance provide, for many of us, some of the most intense feelings we ever experience. Why do people fall in love? The answer at first sight seems obvious. Love expresses a mutual physical and personal attachment two individuals feel for one another. These days, we might be skeptical of the idea that love is "forever," but falling in love, we tend to think, is an experience arising from universal human emotions. It seems natural for a couple who fall in love to want personal and sexual fulfillment in their relationship, perhaps in the form of marriage.

Yet this situation, which seems so self-evident to us today, is in fact very unusual. Falling in love is *not* an experience most people across the world have—and where it does happen, it is rarely thought of as having any connection to marriage. The idea of romantic love did not become widespread until fairly recently in our society and has never even existed in most other cultures.

Only in modern times have love and sexuality come to be seen as closely connected. In the Middle Ages and for centuries afterward, men and women married mainly in order to keep property in the hands of family or to raise children to work the family farm. Once married, they may have become close companions; this happened after marriage, however, rather than before. People sometimes had sexual affairs outside marriage, but these inspired few of the emotions we associate with love. Romantic love was regarded as at best a weakness and at worst a kind of sickness.

Romantic love first made its appearance in courtly circles as a characteristic of extramarital sexual adventures indulged in by members of the aristocracy. Until about two centuries ago, it was wholly confined to such circles and kept specifically separate from marriage. Relations between husband and wife among aristocratic groups were often cool and distant—certainly compared to our expectations of marriage today. The wealthy lived in large houses, each spouse having his or her own bedroom and servants; they may rarely have seen each other in private. Sexual compatibility was a matter of chance and was not considered relevant to marriage. Among both rich and poor, the decision of whom to marry was made by family and kin, not by the individuals concerned, who had little or no say in the matter.

This remains true in many non-Western countries today. In Afghanistan under the rule of the Taliban, where Islam underwent a major revival and became the basis of an important political movement, men were prohibited from speaking to women they were not related or married to, and marriages were arranged by parents. If a girl and boy were seen by authorities to be speaking with one another, they would be whipped so severely that one or both of them could be left seriously injured, if not dead. The ruling Taliban government saw romantic love as deeply offensive, so much so that one of its first acts as a new power in 1996 was to outlaw music and films.

Like many in the non-Western world, the ruling Taliban believed Afghanistan was being inundated by Hollywood movies and American rock music and videos, filled as they are with sexual images. Osama bin Laden launched his terrorist attacks against the United States from Afghanistan, and the rhetoric of his followers has partly been aimed at criticizing such kinds of Western influences.

It is not only in those sections of the world where Islamic fundamentalism has taken root that romantic love is considered unnatural. In India, for example, the vast majority of marriages are arranged by parents or other relatives. The opinions of prospective marriage partners are quite often—but by no means always—taken into account. A study of marriage in Kerala, a state in India, showed that just over half the young people thought that meeting the prospective spouse before marriage was relevant to marital happiness. Among parents, only 1 percent were willing to let their children choose their own marriage partners. Romantic love is recognized to exist there, but it is equated with temporary infatuation, or actually seen as a barrier to a happy marriage.

Neither romantic love, then, nor its association with marriage can be understood as natural features of human life. Rather, it has been shaped by broad social and historical influences. These are the influences sociologists study.

Most of us see the world in terms of the familiar features of our own lives. Sociology demonstrates the need to take a much broader view of why we are as we are, and why we act as we do. It teaches us that what we regard as inevitable, good, or true may not be such, and that the "natural" in our life is strongly influenced by historical and social forces. Understanding the subtle yet complex and profound ways in which our individual lives reflect the contexts of our social experience is basic to the sociological outlook.

Developing a Sociological Perspective

In the aftermath of the attack by suicide terrorists on the World Trade Center and the Pentagon on September 11, 2001, many Americans asked themselves how such an event could have occurred and why anyone would want to carry it out. You undoubtedly encountered many explanations for this event in the mass media, and some of the inescapable ones were sociological. The war that America and its allies have had to fight has not been merely against the country of Afghanistan, whose former Taliban government supported the terrorists. The war is also against groups, networks, and organizations that stretch around the world. A key sociological question has to do with how human beings coordinate their activities in groups, networks, and organizations. In order to understand how the World Trade Center and Pentagon attacks were possible, many analysts have focused on understanding the kinds of coordinated activity that culminated in the attack of September 11. Over time, they came to see that events on September 11 did not occur through the efforts of a loose network or group, but were carried out by a single hierarchical organization whose leaders planned the attack, coordinated all the activities, and received financial support from Osama bin Laden.

One of the things we have seen in discussions of the September 11 attacks is that our lives are connected to other societies that extend around the world. The people who worked in the World Trade Center did not imagine that their lives had very much to do with events being coordinated in Afghanistan. They also might not have imagined that their lives would come to an end due to large-scale global processes that have drawn different societies into interrelation with one another. The world in which we live today makes us much more *interdependent* with others, even those thousands of miles away, than people have ever been previously.

Likewise, in the aftermath of the 1999 mass murder at Columbine High School in Littleton, Colorado, many Americans asked themselves how and why two high school students could murder thirteen of their classmates and teachers and then take their own lives. One explanation focused on the social cliques at Columbine High, which divided into "jocks," "preps," "geeks," "goths," and other groups. It was well known that the two murderers, part of a group called the "Trenchcoat Mafia," were teased and embarrassed by their classmates, especially the "jocks." It was also reported that the two teens were obsessed with the video game *Doom,* in which each player tries to make the most kills. Many saw this as the embodiment of American culture's glorification of violence. The police also investigated how the two killers procured the guns and bombs used in the massacre. Many commentators denounced the easy availability of these weapons in American society. Others saw the tragedy as a symbol of the emptiness of suburban life, where young people have few public places to go and socialize with others.

While explanations like these focus on the social causes of violence in the United States, sociology can provide an even deeper understanding of events such as mass murder. Sociology shows us the need to look beyond the surface of people's actions and study the social context in order to understand what happened. Sociology can also teach us to try to identify general patterns of behavior in particular individuals and to be systematic in explaining the social influences on these behavioral patterns (Berger, 1963). A sociologist must look at a wide array of evidence before accepting any single explanation. Thus, a sociologist studying the Columbine High killings might

In an image from airport surveillance tape, two men identified by authorities as suspected hijackers Mohammed Atta (*right*) and Abdulaziz Alomari (*center*) pass through airport security on September 11, 2001, at Portland International Jetport in Maine. The two men took a commuter flight to Boston before boarding American Airlines Flight 11, which was one of four jetliners hijacked on September 11, and one of two that were crashed into New York's World Trade Center.

study other mass murders and look to see if there was a pattern in the group characteristics—such as social class, race, gender, age, or cultural background—of the murderers and victims. This might lead a sociologist to ask why mass murders like the one at Columbine High seem to be mostly the doing of young, middle-class, white men and then explain why this is the case (Patterson, 1999). In other words, a sociologist would not simply ask, "What led these two students at Columbine High to commit mass murder?" but also, "What social factors explain why mass murders have occurred in the United States?"

Another question sociologists ask is, "What holds society together?" When you think of it, the very existence of an orderly society is remarkable. Take as an example the use of anthrax to kill innocent citizens in the United States. Isn't it amazing how rarely such terrorism has been attempted in the United States? The existence of order in the country is something we have long taken for granted. When you think of it, though, living is partly an act of faith that order will be maintained from minute to minute in skyscrapers and on sidewalks and everywhere in between. It is the faith that incidents such as the bioterrorism of sending anthrax through the mail, or the September 11 attacks, or the acts of the Trenchcoat Mafia will be few. But though we must take this order for granted in order to live our lives, sociologists seek to understand how such order comes about. For the sociologist who wants to know how society is possible in the first place, the interesting question is not merely why someone sends anthrax through the mail or why someone shoots up a high school. It is, more important, why such acts happen so infrequently. Why are so many willing

Three businessmen relax and chat over coffee. A group of workers on a hashish plantation smoke hash during a break. In both instances, the socially acceptable consumption of a drug serves as an occasion to socialize.

to work together to maintain the social order? And isn't it unsettling that in a society where so many work to maintain this order, just nineteen hijackers or two high school students are capable of doing so much harm?

Learning to think sociologically—looking, in other words, at the broader view—means cultivating the imagination. As sociologists, we need to imagine, for example, what the experience of sex and marriage is like for people—the majority of humankind until recently—to whom ideals of romantic love appear alien or even absurd. Or we need to image what life was like for the victims and the murderers in the 2001 terrorist attacks and at Columbine High. Studying sociology *cannot* be just a routine process of acquiring knowledge. A sociologist is someone who is able to break free from the immediacy of personal circumstances and put things in a wider context. Her work depends on what the American sociologist C. Wright Mills, in a famous phrase, called the **sociological imagination** (Mills, 1959).

The sociological imagination requires us, above all, to *"think ourselves away" from the familiar routines of our daily lives in order to look at them anew.* Consider the simple act of drinking a cup of coffee. What could we find to say, from a sociological point of view, about such an apparently uninteresting piece of behavior? An enormous amount. We could point out first of all that coffee is not just a refreshment. It possesses *symbolic value* as part of our day-to-day social activities (see the accompanying "Globalization and Everyday Life"). Often the ritual associated with coffee drinking is much more important than the act of consuming the drink itself. Two people who arrange to meet for coffee are probably more interested in getting together and chatting than in what they actually drink. Drinking and eating in all societies, in fact, provide occasions for social interaction and the enactment of rituals—and these offer a rich subject matter for sociological study.

Second, coffee is a *drug* containing caffeine, which has a stimulating effect on the brain. Coffee addicts are not regarded by most people in Western culture as drug users. Like alcohol, coffee is a socially acceptable drug, whereas marijuana, for instance, is not. Yet there are societies that tolerate the consumption of marijuana or even cocaine but frown on both coffee and alcohol. Sociologists are interested in why these contrasts exist.

Third, an individual who drinks a cup of coffee is caught up in a complicated set of *social and economic relationships* stretching across the world. The production, transport, and distribution of coffee require continuous transactions between people thousands of miles away from the coffee drinker. Studying such global transactions is an important task of sociology, since many aspects of our lives are now affected by worldwide social influences and communications.

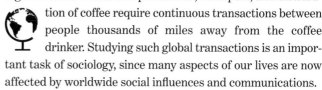

Finally, the act of sipping a cup of coffee presumes a whole process of *past social and economic development.* Along with other now-familiar items of Western diets—like tea, bananas, potatoes, and white sugar—coffee only began to be widely consumed in the late 1800s. Although the drink originated in the Middle East, its mass consumption dates from the period of Western colonial expansion about a century and a half ago. Virtually all the coffee we drink in the Western countries today comes from areas (South America and Africa) that were colonized by Europeans; it is in no sense a "natural" part of the Western diet.

Studying Sociology

As individuals, we all know a great deal about ourselves and about the societies in which we live. We tend to think we have a good understanding of why we act as we do, without needing sociologists to tell us! And to some degree this is true. We do many of the things in our day-to-day lives because we understand the social requirements involved. Yet there are definite boundaries to such self-knowledge, and it is one of the main tasks of sociology to show us what these are.

The sociological imagination allows us to see that many events that seem to concern only the individual actually reflect larger social issues. Divorce, for instance, may be a very difficult process for someone who goes through it—what Mills calls a personal trouble. But divorce, he points out, is also a public issue in a society like the present-day United States, where over half of all marriages break up within ten years. Unemployment, to take another example, may be a personal tragedy for someone thrown out of a job and unable to find another. Yet it is much more than only a matter for private despair when millions of people in a society are in the same situation: It is a public issue expressing large social trends.

Try applying this sort of outlook to your own life. It isn't necessary to think only of troubling events. Consider, for instance, why you are turning the pages of this book at all—why you have decided to study sociology. You might be a reluctant sociology student, taking the course only to fulfill a requirement. Or you might be enthusiastic to find out more about the subject. Whatever your motivations, you are likely to have a good deal in common, without necessarily knowing it, with others studying sociology. Your private decision reflects your position in the wider society.

Do the following characteristics apply to you? Are you young? White? From a professional or white-collar background? Have you done, or do you still do, some part-time work to boost your income? Do you want to find a good job when you leave school but are not especially dedicated to studying? Do you not really know what sociology is but think it has something to do with how people behave in groups? More than three quarters of you will answer yes to all these questions. College students are not typical of the population as a whole but tend to be drawn from more privileged backgrounds. And their attitudes usually reflect those held by friends and acquaintances. The social backgrounds from which we come have a great deal to do with what kinds of decisions we think appropriate.

But suppose you answered "no" to one or more of these questions. You might come from a minority-group background or one of poverty. You may be someone in midlife or older. If so, however, further conclusions probably follow. You will likely have had to struggle to get where you are; you might have had to overcome hostile reactions from friends and others when you told them you were intending to go to college; or you might be combining school with full-time parenthood and/or work.

Although we are all influenced by the social contexts in which we find ourselves, none of us is simply *determined* in his or her behavior by those contexts. We possess, and create, our own individuality. It is the business of sociology to investigate the connections between *what society makes of us and what we make of ourselves.* Our activities both structure—give shape to—the social world around us and at the same time are structured *by* that social world.

The concept of **social structure** is an important one in sociology. It refers to the fact that the social contexts of our lives do not just consist of random assortments of events or actions; they are structured, or *patterned,* in distinct ways. There are regularities in the ways we behave and in the relationships we have with one another. But social structure is not like a physical structure, such as a building, which exists independently of human actions. Human societies are always in the process of **structuration.** They are reconstructed at every moment by the very "building blocks" that compose them—human beings like you and me.

As an example, consider again the case of coffee. A cup of coffee does not automatically arrive in your hands. You choose, for example, to go to a particular café, whether to drink your coffee black or light, and so forth. As you make these decisions, along with millions of other people, you shape the market for coffee and affect the lives of coffee producers living perhaps thousands of miles away on the other side of the world.

"How would you like me to answer that question? As a member of my ethnic group, educational class, income group, or religious category?"

The Sociology of Coffee

The world drinks about 2.25 billion cups [of coffee] per day—the United States alone drinks one fifth of this. Coffee drinking is a cultural fixture that says as much about us as it does about the bean itself. Basically a habit forming stimulant, coffee is nonetheless associated with relaxation and sociability. In a society that combines buzzing overstimulation with soul-aching meaninglessness, coffee and its associated rituals are, for many of us, the lubricants that make it possible to go on.

Perhaps for this reason coffee occupies a distinctive niche in our cultural landscape. Along with alcohol, it is the only beverage to engender public houses devoted to its consumption. . . . Uniquely, though, coffee is welcome in almost any situation, from the car to the boardroom, from the breakfast table to the public park, alone or in company of any kind. Since its adoption as a beverage, coffee has been offered as an antipode to alcohol—more so even than abstinence, perhaps in recognition of a human need for joyfully mood-altering substances and the convivial social interactions that go along with them.

Only a handful of consumer goods has fueled the passions of the public as much as coffee. . . . [C]offee has inspired impassioned struggles on the battlefields of economics, human rights, politics, and religion, since its use first spread. Coffee

Developing a Global Perspective

As we just saw in our discussions of the terrorist attacks and of the sociological dimensions of drinking a cup of coffee, all our local actions—the ways in which we relate to one another in face-to-face contexts—form part of larger social settings that extend around the globe. These connections between the *local* and the *global* are quite new in human history. They have accelerated over the past thirty or forty years as a result of the dramatic advances in communications, information technology, and transportation. The development of jet planes, large, speedy container ships, and other means of fast travel has meant that people and goods can be continuously transported across the world. And our worldwide system of satellite communication, established only some thirty years ago, has made it possible for people to get in touch with each other instantaneously.

American society is influenced every moment of the day by **globalization,** the growth of world interdependence, a social phenomenon that will be discussed throughout this book. Globalization should not be thought of simply as the development of worldwide networks—social and economic systems that are remote from our individual concerns. It is a local phenomenon, too. For example, only a few years ago, when they dined out, most Americans were faced with a limited choice. In many U.S. towns and cities today, a single street might feature Italian, Chinese, Japanese, Thai, French, and other types of restaurants next door to each other. In turn, the dietary decisions we make are consequential for food producers who might live on the other side of the world. Another everyday aspect of global-

may be a drink for sharing, but as a commodity it invites protectionism, oppression, and destruction. Its steamy past implicates the otherwise noble bean in early colonialism, various revolutions, the emergence of the bourgeoisie, international development, technological hubris, crushing global debt, and more. These forces, in turn, have shaped the way coffee has been incorporated into our culture and economy. Colonialism, for example, served as the primary reason for and vehicle of coffee's expansion throughout the globe; colonial powers dictated where coffee went and where it did not and established trading relationships that continue to this day.

The story of coffee also reveals how (and why) we interact with a plethora of other commodities, legal or not. Surprising similarities exist, for example, between coffee's early history and the current controversy over marijuana. Today's national debate over the merits of marijuana, although young by comparison, is the modern version of the strife surrounding coffee in other ages. The social acceptability of each has been affected by religious and political opinion, conflicting health claims, institutionalized cultural norms, and the monied interests of government and private industry. The evolution of coffee's social acceptability highlights the delicate dance of interests and "truths" that governs the ways in which we structure our societies.

Coffee is consumed with great fervor in rich countries such as the United States yet is grown with few exceptions in the poorest parts of the globe. In fact, it is the second most valuable item of legal international trade (after petroleum), and the largest food import of the United States by value. It is the principal source of foreign exchange for dozens of countries around

the world. The coffee in your cup is an immediate, tangible connection with the rural poor in some of the most destitute parts of the planet. It is a physical link across space and cultures from one end of the human experience to the other.

The coffee trading system that has evolved to bring all this about is an intricate knot of economics, politics, and sheer power—a bizarre arena trod . . . by some of the world's largest transnational corporations, by enormous governments, and by vast trading cartels. The trip coffee takes from the crop to your cup turns out not to be so straightforward after all, but rather a turbulent and unpredictable ride through the waves and eddies of international commodity dynamics, where the product itself becomes secondary to the wash of money and power.

SOURCE: Gregory Dicum and Nina Luttinger, *The Coffee Book: Anatomy of an Industry from Crop to the Last Drop* (New York: The New Press, 1999), pp. ix–xi. Used with permission.

ization can be found in your closet and drawers. If you take a look at the labels of your clothes and see the many various countries in which they were manufactured, then you are experiencing globalization firsthand.

Do college students today have a global perspective? By at least one measure, the answer is yes. Furthermore, their activist values suggest that many students also possess a sociological imagination. According to an annual survey of more than 281,064 first-year college students, a record 47.5 percent of all students who entered U.S. colleges in 2001 reported that they had "participated in organized demonstrations" concerned with social, political, and economic issues during the previous year. This was the highest percentage since the UCLA survey began asking the question in 1966 (Sax, L. J., Lindholm, J. A., Astin, A. W., Korn, W. S., and Mahoney, K. M., 2001). This

upsurge in activist values suggests that many entering college students possess a sociological imagination: They recognize that their private lives are shaped by larger social forces, and they are seeking to do something about it. The demonstrations these students participated in were concerned with a wide range of issues, including the growing power of global institutions such as the World Trade Organization and the World Bank, the production of clothing in overseas sweatshops, global warming, environmental destruction, and the right of workers to be paid a living wage (Meatto, 2000). Concern with these issues reflects an awareness that globalization has a direct effect on our daily, private lives. As University of California, Berkeley, student Joanna Evelan said at one anti-sweatshop rally, "We want to raise awareness among students that they wear Cal clothes from manufacturers that are socially responsible."

Columbine High School Shootings

It is the perfect suburban shrine, sprawling, growing without boundaries and taking on a life of its own.

The Columbine High School memorial is piled under tents and draped along fences. It crawls up and over hills in Clement Park, interrupted by parking lots filled with news media trucks, satellite dishes and the other trappings of the communications machine.

After days of rain, the mud is trying to win, though straw and bark chips have been spread on the ground.

The memorial has become a place where there is little sense of place. It is a color-drenched sea of teddy bears, flowers, butterfly balloons, poetry and paper chains in a neighborhood of gray and beige houses.

From a distance, the memorial looks like a fair.

People wander around the site, some with video cameras recording every bit of the experience, others handing out flowers to those who visit empty handed. You can hear the tears. One woman seemed to recoil when approached to take a bouquet. The young woman toting an armload of wrapped blossoms reassured her: "No, it's free."

That sense of material culture and its effect on attitudes toward the mystery of death are part of what emerges from the experience of the shrine. So does the tension on the hill where 15 crosses have been hoisted, a provocative act in all definitions of the word.

"Sleep baby sleep" was one of the first phrases scrawled on 13 of those crosses, but "hate breeds hate" was the message on the two erected for the young men who died at their own hand. "How can anyone forgive you?" someone has written on those two crosses. "I forgive you" is below, over and over. On the cross carrying Dylan Klebold's picture: "No one is to blame";

on the side of the cross carrying Eric Harris' picture: "You died over a year ago . . . and no one noticed."

On student Steven Curnow's cross, someone has scrawled, "Although I never met you, when you died, I died." At the foot of Rachel Scott's cross is a book about the Holocaust, *The Rescuers.*

Other mementos are spontaneous and heartbreaking; after all, each new loss brings back the memory of each past loss. The note attached to a fuzzy stuffed bunny, with pink bows around its ears, says: "My daughter died on Aug. 10, 1987. Her name was Heather and she was 19 years old. Her animals have been a great source of comfort to me and I hope that they will comfort you also. Be at peace."

John Tomlin's brown truck has become a parking lot shrine—Colorado tag 93922RS. There is a letter jacket with the notation: "To all the people of CHS. You are all creations of God. You are beautiful people."

Questions

- What can you learn about our society from the shrine?
- What religious, cultural, political, and social messages can you detect from the photographs and the article?
- What do people gain from public displays of grief?
- One of the crosses bore the inscription, "Although I never met you, when you died, I died." In our society, do we only feel this kind of empathy when we witness death? How does the presence of death change or intensify our emotions and alter our actions?

Growing daily, flowers crushed and decaying, the memorial at Columbine is a signal of a shifting cultural approach to death and how people participate in their society, says an American studies professor immersed in researching shrines, memorials and grieving.

"Spontaneous eruption" is how Erika Doss [a professor at the University of Colorado] describes the wave of memorials springing up across America, from the gifts left at the Vietnam Veterans Memorial in Washington, D.C., to the fence at the site of the Oklahoma City bombing.

SOURCE: Reprinted from Mary Voelz Chandler, "Heartbreak, Mystery Shroud Shrine," *Rocky Mountain News,* May 2, 1999, http://denver.rockymountainnews.com/shooting/0502shr51.shtml.

Developing a global perspective has great importance for sociology. A global perspective not only allows us to become more aware of the ways that we are connected to people in other societies; it also makes us more aware of the many problems the world faces at the beginning of the twenty-first century. The global perspective opens our eyes to the fact that our interdependence with other societies means that our actions have consequences for others and that the world's problems have consequences for us.

Understanding Social Change

The changes in human ways of life in the last two hundred years, such as globalization, have been far-reaching. We have become accustomed, for example, to the fact that most of the population does not work on the land and lives in towns and cities rather than in small rural communities. But this was *never* the case until the middle of the nineteenth century. For virtually all of human history, the vast majority of people had to produce their own food and shelter and lived in tiny groups or in small village communities. Even at the height of the most developed traditional civilizations—such as ancient Rome or traditional China—less than 10 percent of the population lived in urban areas; everyone else was engaged in food production in a rural setting. Today, in most of the industrialized societies, these proportions have become almost completely reversed. Quite often, more than 90 percent of the people live in urban areas, and only 2 to 3 percent of the population work in agricultural production.

It is not only the environment surrounding our lives that has changed; these transformations have radically altered, and continue to alter, the most personal and intimate side of our daily existence. To extend a previous example, the spread of ideals of romantic love was strongly conditioned by the transition from a rural to an urban, industrialized society. As people moved into urban areas and began to work in industrial production, marriage was no longer prompted mainly by economic motives—by the need to control the inheritance of land and to work the land as a family unit. "Arranged" marriages—fixed through the negotiations of parents and relatives—became less and less common. Individuals increasingly began to initiate marriage relationships on the basis of emotional attraction and in order to seek personal fulfillment. The idea of "falling in love" as a basis for contracting a marriage tie was formed in this context.

Sociology had its beginnings in the attempts of thinkers to understand the initial impact of these transformations that accompanied industrialization in the West. Our world today is radically different from that of former ages; it is the task of sociology to help us understand this world and what future it is likely to hold for us.

The Development of Sociological Thinking

When they first start studying sociology, many students are puzzled by the diversity of approaches they encounter. Sociology has never been a discipline having a body of ideas that everyone accepts as valid. Sociologists often quarrel among themselves about how to go about studying human behavior and how research results might best be interpreted. Why should this be so? Why can't sociologists agree with one another more consistently, as natural scientists seem able to do? The answer is bound up with the very nature of the field itself. Sociology is about our own lives and our own behavior, and studying ourselves is the most complex and difficult endeavor we can undertake.

Theories and Theoretical Approaches

Trying to understand something as complex as the impact of industrialization on society raises the importance of theory to sociology. Factual research shows *how* things occur. Yet sociology does not just consist of collecting facts, however important and interesting they may be. We also want to know *why* things happen, and in order to do so we have to learn to construct explanatory theories. For instance we know that industrialization has had a major influence on the emergence of modern societies. But what are the origins and preconditions of industrialization? Why do we find differences between societies in their industrialization processes? Why is industrialization associated with changes in ways of criminal punishment, or in family and marriage systems? To respond to such questions, we have to develop theoretical thinking.

Theories involve constructing abstract interpretations that can be used to explain a wide variety of situations. A theory about industrialization, for example, would be concerned with identifying the main features that processes of industrial development share in common and would try to show which of these are most important in explaining such development. Of course, factual research and theories can never completely be separated. We can only develop valid theoretical approaches if we are able to test them out by means of factual research.

We need theories to help us make sense of facts. Contrary to popular assertion, facts do not speak for themselves. Many sociologists work primarily on factual research, but unless they are guided by some knowledge of theory, their work is unlikely to explain the complexity of modern societies. This is true even of research carried out with strictly practical objectives.

"Practical people" tend to be suspicious of theorists and may like to see themselves as too "down to earth" to need to pay attention to more abstract ideas, yet all practical decisions have some theoretical assumptions lying behind them. A manager of a business, for example, might have scant regard for "theory." Nonetheless, every approach to business activity involves theoretical assumptions, even if these often remain unstated. Thus, the manager might assume that employees are motivated to work hard mainly for money—the level of wages they receive. This is not only a theoretical interpretation of human behavior, it is also a mistaken one, as research in industrial sociology tends to demonstrate.

Without a **theoretical approach**, we would not know what to look for in beginning a study or in interpreting the results of research. However, the illumination of factual evidence is not the only reason for the prime position of theory in sociology. Theoretical thinking must respond to general problems posed by the study of human social life, including issues that are philosophical in nature. Deciding to what extent sociology should be modeled on the natural sciences are questions that do not yield easy solutions. They have been handled in different ways in the various theoretical approaches that have sprung up in the discipline.

Early Theorists

We human beings have always been curious about the sources of our own behavior, but for thousands of years our attempts to understand ourselves relied on ways of thinking passed down from generation to generation, often expressed in religious terms. (For example, before the rise of modern science, many people believed that natural events such as earthquakes were caused by gods or spirits.) Although writers from earlier periods provided insights into human behavior and society, the systematic study of society is a relatively recent development whose beginnings date back to the late 1700s and early 1800s. The background to the origins of sociology was the series of sweeping changes ushered in by the French Revolution of 1789 and the emergence of the Industrial Revolution in Europe. The shattering of traditional ways of life wrought by these changes resulted in the attempts of thinkers to develop a new understanding of both the social and natural worlds.

A key development was the use of science instead of religion to understand the world. The types of questions these nineteenth-century thinkers sought to answer—What is human nature? Why is society structured like it is? How and why do societies change?—are the same questions sociologists try to answer today. Our modern world is radically different from that of the past; it is sociology's task to help us understand this world and what the future is likely to hold.

August Comte (1798–1857).

AUGUSTE COMTE

There were many contributors to early sociological thinking. Particular prominence, however, is usually given to the French author Auguste Comte (1798–1857), if only because he invented the word *sociology*. Comte originally used the term *social physics,* but some of his intellectual rivals at the time were also making use of that term. Comte wanted to distinguish his own views from theirs, so he introduced *sociology* to describe the subject he wished to establish.

Comte believed that this new field could produce a knowledge of society based on scientific evidence. He regarded sociology as the last science to be developed—following physics, chemistry, and biology—but as the most significant and complex of all the sciences. Sociology, he believed, should contribute to the welfare of humanity by using science to understand and therefore predict and control human behavior. In the later part of his career, Comte drew up ambitious plans for the reconstruction of French society in particular and for human societies in general, based on scientific knowledge.

ÉMILE DURKHEIM

The works of another French writer, Émile Durkheim (1858–1917), have had a much more lasting impact on modern sociology than those of Comte. Although he drew on aspects of Comte's work, Durkheim thought that many of his predecessor's ideas were too speculative and vague and that Comte had not successfully carried out his program—to establish sociology on a scientific basis. To become scientific, according to Durkheim, sociology must study **social facts,** aspects of social life that shape our actions as individuals, such as the state of the economy or the influence of religion. Durkheim believed that we must study social life with the same objectivity as scientists study the natural world. His famous first principle of sociology was "Study social facts as *things!*" By this he meant

Émile Durkheim
(1858–1917).

that social life can be analyzed as rigorously as objects or events in nature.

Like a biologist studying the human body, Durkheim saw society as a set of independent parts, each of which could be studied separately. A body consists of various specialized parts (such as the brain, the heart, the lungs, the liver, and so forth), each of which contributes to sustaining the continuing life of the organism. These necessarily work in harmony with one another; if they do not, the life of the organism is under threat. So it is, according to Durkheim, with society. For a society to have a continuing existence over time, its specialized institutions (such as the political system, the religion, the family, and the educational system) must work in harmony with each other and function as an integrated whole. Durkheim referred to this social cohesion as **"organic solidarity."** He argued that the continuation of a society thus depends on cooperation, which in turn presumes a general consensus, or agreement, among its members over basic values and customs.

Another major theme pursued by Durkheim, and by many others since, is that the societies of which we are members exert **social constraint** over our actions. Durkheim argued that society has primacy over the individual person. Society is far more than the sum of individual acts; when we analyze social structures, we are studying characteristics that have a "firmness" or "solidity" comparable to those of structures in the physical world. Think of a person standing in a room with several doors. The structure of the room constrains the range of her or his possible activities. The position of the walls and the doors, for example, defines the routes of exit and entry. Social structure, according to Durkheim, constrains our activities in a parallel way, setting limits on what we can do as individuals. It is "external" to us, just as the walls of the room are.

Like the other major founders of sociology, Durkheim was preoccupied with the changes transforming society in his own lifetime. His analysis of social change was based on the development of the **division of labor** (the growth of complex dis-

tinctions among different occupations). Durkheim argued that the division of labor gradually replaced religion as the basis of social cohesion and provided organic solidarity to modern societies. He argued that as the division of labor expands, people become more and more dependent on each other, because each person needs goods and services that those in other occupations supply. Another of Durkheim's most famous studies was concerned with the analysis of suicide (Durkheim, 1966; orig. 1897). Suicide seems to be a purely personal act, the outcome of extreme personal unhappiness. Durkheim showed, however, that social factors exert a fundamental influence on suicidal behavior—**anomie**, a feeling of aimlessness or despair provoked by modern social life being one of these influences. Suicide rates show regular patterns from year to year, he argued, and these patterns must be explained sociologically. Many objections can be raised against Durkheim's study, but it remains a classic work whose relevance to sociology today is by no means exhausted. According to Durkheim, processes of change in the modern world are so rapid and intense that they give rise to major social difficulties, which he linked to anomie. Traditional moral controls and standards, which used to be supplied by religion, are largely broken down by modern social development, and this leaves many individuals in modern societies feeling that their daily lives lack meaning. Later in his life, Durkheim came to be especially concerned with the role of religion in social life. In his study of religious beliefs, practices, and rituals—*The Elementary Forms of the Religious Life* (1912)—he focused particularly on the importance of religion in maintaining moral order in society.

KARL MARX

The ideas of Karl Marx (1818–1883) contrast sharply with those of Comte and Durkheim, but like them, he sought to explain the changes in society that took place over the time of the industrial revolution. When he was a young man, Marx's political

Karl Marx
(1818–1883).

activities brought him into conflict with the German authorities; after a brief stay in France, he settled permanently in exile in Britain. His writings covered a diversity of areas. Even his sternest critics regard his work as important for the development of sociology. Much of his writing concentrates on economic issues, but since he was always concerned to connect economic problems to social institutions, his work was, and is, rich in sociological insights.

Marx's viewpoint was founded on what he called the **materialist conception of history.** According to this view, it is not the ideas or values human beings hold that are the main sources of social change, as Durkheim claimed. Rather, social change is prompted primarily by economic influences. The conflicts between classes—the rich versus the poor—provide the motivation for historical development. In Marx's words, "All human history thus far is the history of class struggles."

Though he wrote about various phases of history, Marx concentrated on change in modern times. For him, the most important changes were bound up with the development of capitalism. **Capitalism** is a system of production that contrasts radically with previous economic systems in history, involving as it does the production of goods and services sold to a wide range of consumers. Those who own capital, or factories, machines, and large sums of money, form a ruling class. The mass of the population make up a class of wage workers, or a working class, who do not own the means of their livelihood but must find employment provided by the owners of capital. Capitalism is thus a class system in which conflict between classes is a commonplace occurrence because it is in the interests of the ruling class to exploit the working class and in the interests of the workers to seek to overcome that exploitation.

According to Marx, in the future capitalism will be supplanted by a society in which there are no classes—no divisions between rich and poor. He didn't mean by this that all inequalities between individuals will disappear. Rather, societies will no longer be split into a small class that monopolizes economic and political power and the large mass of people who benefit little from the wealth their work creates. The economic system will come under communal ownership, and a more equal society than we know at present will be established.

Marx's work had a far-reaching effect on the twentieth-century world. Until recently, before the fall of Soviet communism, more than a third of the earth's population lived in societies whose governments claimed to derive their inspiration from Marx's ideas. In addition, many sociologists have been influenced by Marx's ideas about class divisions.

MAX WEBER

Like Marx, Max Weber (pronounced "Vaber," 1864–1920) cannot be labeled simply a sociologist; his interests and concerns

Max Weber
(1864–1920).

ranged across many areas. Born in Germany, where he spent most of his academic career, Weber was an individual of wide learning. His writings covered the fields of economics, law, philosophy, and comparative history as well as sociology, and much of his work was also concerned with the development of modern capitalism. Like other thinkers of his time, Weber sought to understand social change. He was influenced by Marx but was also strongly critical of some of Marx's major views. He rejected the materialist conception of history and saw class conflict as less significant than did Marx. In Weber's view, economic factors are important, but ideas and values have just as much impact on social change.

Some of Weber's most influential writings were concerned with analyzing the distinctiveness of Western society as compared with other major civilizations. He studied the religions of China, India, and the Near East, and in the course of these researches made major contributions to the sociology of religion. Comparing the leading religious systems in China and India with those of the West, Weber concluded that certain aspects of Christian beliefs strongly influenced the rise of capitalism. He argued that the capitalist outlook of Western societies did not emerge, as Marx supposed, only from economic changes. In Weber's view, cultural ideas and values help shape society and affect our individual actions.

One of the most persistent concerns of Weber's work was the study of bureaucracy. A **bureaucracy** is a large organization that is divided into jobs based on specific functions and staffed by officials ranked according to a hierarchy. Industrial firms, government organizations, hospitals, and schools are all examples of bureaucracies. Weber believed the advance of bureaucracy to be an inevitable feature of our era. Bureaucracy makes it possible for these large organizations to run efficiently, but at the same time it poses problems for effective democratic participation in modern societies. Bureaucracy involves the rule of experts, whose decisions are made without much consultation with those whose lives are affected by them.

Interpreting Modern Development

DURKHEIM
1. The main dynamic of modern development is the **division of labor** as a basis for social cohesion and **organic solidarity.**
2. Durkheim believed that sociology must study **social facts** as things, just as science would analyze the natural world. His study of suicide led him to stress the important influence of social factors, qualities of a society external to the individual, on a person's actions. Durkheim argued that society exerts **social constraint** over our actions.

MARX
1. The main dynamic of modern development is the expansion of **capitalism.** Rather than being cohesive, society is divided by class differences.
2. Marx believed that we must study the divisions within a society that are derived from the economic inequalities of capitalism.

WEBER
1. The main dynamic of modern development is the **rationalization** of social and economic life.
2. Weber focused on why Western societies developed so differently from other societies. He also emphasized the importance of cultural ideas and values on social change.

Weber's contributions range over many other areas, including the study of the development of cities, systems of law, types of economy, and the nature of classes. He also produced a range of writings concerned with the overall character of sociology itself. Weber was more cautious than either Durkheim or Marx in proclaiming sociology to be a science. According to Weber, it is misleading to imagine that we can study people using the same procedures that are applied to investigate the physical world. Humans are thinking, reasoning beings; we attach meaning and significance to most of what we do, and any discipline that deals with human behavior must acknowledge this.

Neglected Founders

Although Comte, Durkheim, Marx, and Weber are, without doubt, foundational figures in sociology, other important thinkers from the same period made contributions that must also be taken into account. Sociology, like many academic fields, has not always lived up to its ideal of acknowledging the importance of every thinker whose work has intrinsic merit. Very few women or members of racial minorities were given the opportunity to become professional sociologists during the "classical" period of the late nineteenth and early twentieth centuries. In addition, the few that were given the opportunity

to do sociological research of lasting importance have frequently been neglected by the field. These individuals deserve the attention of sociologists today.

HARRIET MARTINEAU

Harriet Martineau (1802–1876) was born and educated in England. She has been called the "first woman sociologist," but, like Marx and Weber, she cannot be thought of simply as a sociologist. She was the author of over fifty books, as well as numerous essays. Martineau is now credited with introducing

Harriet Martineau (1802–1876).

sociology to England through her translation of Comte's founding treatise of the field, *Positive Philosophy* (Rossi, 1973). In addition, Martineau conducted a firsthand systematic study of American society during her extensive travels throughout the United States in the 1830s, which is the subject of her book *Society in America*. Martineau is significant to sociologists today for several reasons. First, she argued that when one studies a society, one must focus on all its aspects, including key political, religious, and social institutions. Second, she insisted that an analysis of a society must include an understanding of women's lives. Third, she was the first to turn a sociological eye on previously ignored issues, including marriage, children, domestic and religious life, and race relations. As she once wrote, "The nursery, the boudoir, and the kitchen are all excellent schools in which to learn the morals and manners of a people" (Martineau, 1962). Finally, she argued that sociologists should do more than just observe, they should also act in ways to benefit a society. As a result, Martineau was an active proponent of both women's rights and the emancipation of slaves.

W. E. B. DU BOIS

W. E. B. Du Bois (1868–1963) was the first African American to earn a doctorate at Harvard University. Du Bois's contributions to sociology were many. Perhaps most important is the concept of "double consciousness," which is a way of talking about identity through the lens of the particular experiences of African Americans. He argued that American society let African Americans see themselves only through the eyes of others: "It is a particular sensation, this double consciousness, this sense of always looking at one's soul by the tape of a world that looks on in amused contempt and pity. One ever feels his two-ness—an American, a Negro, two souls, two thoughts, two unreconciled strivings, two warring ideals in one dark body, whose dogged strength alone keeps it from being torn asunder" (Du Bois, 1903). Du Bois made a persuasive claim that one's sense of self and one's identity are greatly influenced by historical experiences and social circumstances—in the case of African Americans, the impact of slavery, and following emancipation, segregation and prejudice. Throughout his career, Du Bois focused on race relations in the United States; as he said in an often repeated quote, "the problem of the twentieth century is the problem of the color line." His influence on sociology today is evidenced by continued interest in the questions that he raised, particularly his concern that sociology must explain "the contact of diverse races of men." Du Bois was also the first social researcher to trace the problems faced by African Americans to their social and economic underpinnings, a connection that most sociologists now widely accept. Finally, Du Bois became known for connecting social analysis to social reform. He was one of the founding members of the

W. E. B. Du Bois
(1868–1963).

National Association for the Advancement of Colored People (NAACP) and a long-time advocate for the collective struggle of African Americans. Later in his life, Du Bois became disenchanted by the lack of progress in American race relations and moved to the African nation of Ghana, where he died in 1963.

Understanding the Modern World: The Sociological Debate

From Marx's time to the present day, many sociological debates have centered on the ideas that Marx set out about the influence of economics on the development of modern societies. According to Marx, as was mentioned earlier, modern societies are *capitalistic*—the driving impulse behind social change in the modern era is to be found in the pressure toward constant economic transformation produced by the spread of capitalist production. Capitalism is a vastly more dynamic economic system than any other that preceded it in history. Capitalists compete with each other to sell their goods to consumers, and to survive in a competitive market, firms have to produce their wares as cheaply and efficiently as possible. This leads to constant technological innovation, because increasing the effectiveness of the technology used in a particular production process is one way in which companies can secure an edge over their rivals.

There are also strong incentives to seek out new markets in which to sell goods, acquire cheap raw materials, and make use of cheap labor power. Capitalism, therefore, according to Marx, is a restlessly expanding system, pushing outward across the world. This is how Marx explains the global spread of Western industry.

Marx's interpretation of the influence of capitalism has found many supporters. Subsequent Marxist authors have considerably refined Marx's own portrayal. On the other hand, numerous critics have set out to rebut Marx's view, offering alternative analyses of the influences shaping the modern world. Virtually everyone accepts that capitalism *has* played a major part in creating the world in which we live today. But other sociologists have argued both that Marx exaggerated the impact of purely *economic* factors in producing change, and that capitalism is *less central* to modern social development than he claimed. Most of these writers have also been skeptical of Marx's belief that a socialist system would eventually replace capitalism.

One of Marx's earliest and most acute critics was Max Weber. Weber's writings, in fact, have been described as involving a lifelong struggle with "the ghost of Marx"—with the intellectual legacy that Marx left. The alternative position that Weber worked out remains important today. According to Weber, noneconomic factors have played the key role in modern social development. Weber's celebrated and much discussed work *The Protestant Ethic and the Spirit of Capitalism* (1977; orig. 1904) proposes that religious values—especially those associated with Puritanism—were of fundamental importance in creating a capitalistic outlook. This outlook did not emerge, as Marx supposed, only from economic changes.

Weber's understanding of the nature of modern societies, and the reasons for the spread of Western ways of life across the world, also contrasts substantially with that of Marx. According to Weber, capitalism—a distinct way of organizing economic enterprise—is one among other major factors shaping social development in the modern period. Underlying capitalistic mechanisms, and in some ways more fundamental than them, is the impact of *science* and *bureaucracy*. Science has shaped modern technology and will presumably continue to do so in any future society, whether socialist or capitalist. Bureaucracy is the only way of organizing large numbers of people effectively and therefore inevitably expands with economic and political growth. The development of science, modern technology, and bureaucracy are examples of a general social process that Weber refers to collectively as **rationalization.** Rationalization means the organization of social, economic, and cultural life according to principles of efficiency, on the basis of technical knowledge.

Which interpretation of modern societies, that deriving from Marx or that coming from Weber, is correct? Again, scholars are divided on the issue. It must be remembered that within each camp there are variations, so not every theorist will agree with all the points of one interpretation. The contrasts between these two standpoints inform many areas of sociology.

Modern Theoretical Approaches

While the origins of sociology were mainly European, in this century the subject has become firmly established worldwide, and some of the most important developments have taken place in the United States. The following sections explore these developments.

SYMBOLIC INTERACTIONISM

The work of George Herbert Mead (1863–1931), a philosopher teaching at the University of Chicago, had an important influence on the development of sociological thought, in particular through a perspective called **symbolic interactionism.** Mead placed particular importance on the study of *language* in analyzing the social world. According to him, language allows us to become self-conscious beings—aware of our own individuality. The key element in this process is the **symbol,** something that *stands for* something else. For example, the word *tree* is a symbol by means of which we represent the object tree. Once we have mastered such a concept, Mead argued, we can think of a tree even if none is visible; we have learned to think of the object symbolically. Symbolic thought frees us from being limited in our experience to what we actually see, hear, or feel.

Unlike animals, according to Mead, human beings live in a richly symbolic universe. This applies even to our very sense of self. Each of us is a self-conscious being because we learn to look at ourselves as if from the outside—we see ourselves as others see us. When a child begins to use "I" to refer to that object (herself) whom others call "you," she is exhibiting the beginnings of self-consciousness.

Virtually all interactions between individuals, symbolic interactionists say, involve an exchange of symbols. When we interact with others, we constantly look for clues to what type of behavior is appropriate in the context and how to interpret what others are up to. Symbolic interactionism directs our attention to the detail of interpersonal interaction and how that detail is used to make sense of what others say and do. For instance, suppose two people are out on a date for the first time. Each is likely to spend a good part of the evening sizing the other up and assessing how the relationship is likely to develop, if at all. Neither wishes to be seen doing this too openly, although each recognizes that it is going on. Both individuals are careful about their own behavior, being anxious to present themselves in a favorable light; but, knowing this, both are likely to be looking for aspects of the other's behavior that would reveal his or her true opinions. A complex and subtle process of symbolic interpretation shapes the interaction between the two.

FUNCTIONALISM

Symbolic interactionism is open to the criticism that it concentrates too much on things that are small in scope. Symbolic interactionists have found difficulty in dealing with larger-scale structures and processes—the very thing that a rival tradition of thought, **functionalism,** tends to emphasize. Functionalist thinking in sociology was originally pioneered by Comte, who saw it as closely bound up with his overall view of the field.

To study the *function* of a social activity is to analyze the contribution that that activity makes to the continuation of the society as a whole. The best way to understand this idea is by analogy to the human body, a comparison Comte, Durkheim, and other functionalist authors made. To study an organ such as the heart, we need to show how it relates to other parts of the body. When we learn how the heart pumps blood around the body, we then understand that the heart plays a vital role in the continuation of the life of the organism. Similarly, analyzing the function of some aspect of society, such as religion, means showing the part it plays in the continued existence and health of a society. Functionalism emphasizes the importance of *moral consensus* in maintaining order and stability in society. Moral consensus exists when most people in a society share the same values. Functionalists regard order and balance as the normal state of society—this social equilibrium is grounded in the existence of a moral consensus among the members of society. According to Durkheim, for instance, religion reaffirms people's adherence to core social values, thereby contributing to the maintenance of social cohesion.

Functionalism became prominent in sociology through the writings of Talcott Parsons and Robert K. Merton, each of whom saw functionalist analysis as providing the key to the development of sociological theory and research. Merton's version of functionalism has been particularly influential.

Merton distinguished between manifest and latent functions. **Manifest functions** are those known to, and intended by, the participants in a specific type of social activity. **Latent functions** are consequences of that activity of which participants are unaware. To illustrate this distinction, Merton used the example of a rain dance performed by the Hopi Tribe of Arizona and New Mexico. The Hopi believe that the ceremony will bring the rain they need for their crops (manifest function). This is why they organize and participate in it. But using Durkheim's theory of religion, Merton argued that the rain dance also has the effect of promoting the cohesion of the Hopi society (latent function). A major part of sociological explanation, according to Merton, consists in uncovering the latent functions of social activities and institutions.

Merton also distinguished between functions and dysfunctions. To look for the dysfunctional aspects of social behavior means focusing on features of social life that challenge the existing order of things. For example, it is mistaken to suppose that religion is always functional—that it contributes only to social cohesion. When two groups support different religions or even different versions of the same religion, the result can be major social conflicts, causing widespread social disruption. Thus, wars have often been fought between religious communities—as can be seen in the struggles between Protestants and Catholics in European history.

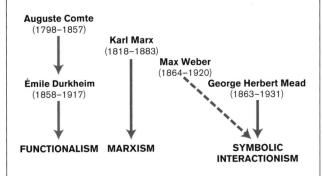

FIGURE 1.1

Theoretical Approaches in Sociology

The unbroken lines indicate direct influence, the dotted line an indirect connection. Mead is not indebted to Weber, but Weber's views—stressing the meaningful, purposive nature of human action—have affinities with the themes of symbolic interactionism.

Auguste Comte (1798–1857)

Karl Marx (1818–1883)

Max Weber (1864–1920)

Émile Durkheim (1858–1917)

George Herbert Mead (1863–1931)

FUNCTIONALISM   **MARXISM**   **SYMBOLIC INTERACTIONISM**

For a long while, functionalist thought was probably the leading theoretical tradition in sociology, particularly in the United States. In recent years, its popularity has declined as its limitations have become apparent. While this was not true of Merton, many functionalist thinkers (Talcott Parsons is an example) unduly stressed factors leading to social cohesion at the expense of those producing division and conflict. In addition, it has seemed to many critics that functional analysis attributes to societies qualities they do not have. Functionalists often wrote as though societies have "needs" and "purposes," even though these concepts make sense only when applied to individual human beings. Figure 1.1 shows how functionalism relates to other theoretical approaches in sociology.

MARXISM AND CLASS CONFLICT

Functionalism and symbolic interactionism are not the only modern theoretical traditions of importance in sociology. A further influential approach is **Marxism.** Marxists, of course, all trace their views back in some way to the writings of Karl Marx. But numerous interpretations of Marx's major ideas are possible, and there are today schools of Marxist thought that take very different theoretical positions.

In all of its versions, Marxism differs from non-Marxist traditions of sociology in that its authors see it as a combination of sociological analysis and political reform. Marxism is supposed to generate a program of radical political change. Moreover,

Marxists lay more emphasis on conflict, class divisions, power, and ideology than many non-Marxist sociologists, especially most of those influenced by functionalism. The concept of **power**—and a closely associated notion, that of **ideology**—are of great importance to Marxist sociologists and to sociology in general. By *power* is meant the capability of individuals or groups to make their own concerns or interests count, even when others resist. Power sometimes involves the direct use of force but is almost always accompanied by the development of ideas (ideologies), which are used to *justify* the actions of the powerful. Power, ideology, and conflict are always closely connected. Many conflicts are *about* power, because of the rewards it can bring. Those who hold most power may depend mainly on the influence of ideology to retain their dominance but are usually able also to use force if necessary.

FEMINISM AND FEMINIST THEORY

Feminist theory is one of the most prominent areas of contemporary sociology. This is a notable development, since issues of gender are scarcely central in the work of the major figures who established the discipline. Sociologists did not add the study of women and gender inequality to their concerns without a pitched battle. The success of feminism's entry into sociology required a fundamental shift in the discipline's approach.

Many feminist theorists brought their experiences in the women's movement of the 1960s and 1970s to their work as sociologists. Like Marxism, feminism makes a link between sociological theory and political reform. Many feminist sociologists have been advocates for political and social action to remedy the inequalities between women and men in both the public and private spheres.

Feminist sociologists argue that women's lives and experiences are central to the study of society. Sociology, like most academic disciplines, has presumed a male point of view. Driven by a concern with women's subordination in American society, feminist sociologists highlight gender relations and gender inequality as important determinants of social life in terms of both social interaction and social institutions such as the family, the workplace, and the educational system. Feminist theory emphasizes that gendered patterns and gendered inequalities are not natural, but socially constructed. (We will cover this point in more detail in Chapter 10.)

Today, feminist sociology is characterized by a focus on the intersection of gender, race, and class. A feminist approach to the study of inequality has influenced new fields of study, like men's studies, sexuality studies, and gay and lesbian studies.

RATIONAL CHOICE THEORY

The sociologist Max Weber had a very interesting way of dividing up the actions of human beings. He thought that all behavior could be divided into four categories: (1) behavior that is oriented toward higher values, such as politics; (2) behavior that is oriented toward habit, such as walking to school on a path you have taken before; (3) behavior that is oriented toward affect (emotions), such as falling in love; and (4) behavior that is oriented toward self-interest, such as making money. Behavior that falls into the last of these categories is often called "instrumental" or "rational action." In recent years, many sociologists have come to follow an approach that focuses on the last of these categories. This has led numerous scholars to ask under what conditions the behavior of human beings can be said to be rational responses to opportunities and constraints.

The **rational choice approach** to human behavior posits that if you could have only a single variable to explain society, self-interest would be the best one to work with. A person who believes in this approach might even try to use it to explain things that seem irrational. One popular rational choice theory sees decisions to marry as maximizing self-interest in a marriage market. This theory has been used to explain why marriage has declined the most in poor African American communities where rates of employment have been low. The explanation is that it is not in the self-interest of women to marry men who cannot support them (Wilson, 1987). Such an explanation goes against other, competing explanations suggesting that poor African Americans don't marry because they don't share mainstream values. The rational choice argument is that this decline in marriage has little to do with values and much to do with self-interest under existing conditions. According to this theory, if employment rates for black men changed, so too would the number of "eligible" men and the desire of women to marry them.

Rational choice theorists tend to believe that there are few irrational mysteries in life. One of the few some note is love, which they define as the irrational act of substituting another person's self-interest for one's own (Becker, 1991). But with such a definition, it is quite difficult to distinguish among basic altruism, friendship, and romantic love. Indeed, although a rational choice approach is often quite useful, there are some aspects of life that it would have trouble explaining. Consider, for example, an angry driver who tries to teach a lesson to other offending drivers by, for instance, tailgating a tailgater. Self-interest does not make this action sensible. Even if the lesson is well learned, the "teacher" is unlikely to reap personally the benefits of the student's progress (Katz, 1999).

POSTMODERN THEORY

Advocates of the idea of **postmodernism** claim that the classic social thinkers took their inspiration from the idea that history has a shape—it "goes somewhere" and leads to

New York's Times Square serves as the backdrop for live television programs such as MTV's *TRL* and ESPN's *SportsCenter*. Covered with advertisements and constantly in flux, it epitomizes Baudrillard's theories of postmodern society.

progress—and that now this notion has collapsed. There are no longer any "grand narratives," or metanarratives—overall conceptions of history or society—that make any sense (Lyotard, 1985). Not only is there no general notion of progress that can be defended, there is no such thing as history. The postmodern world is not destined, as Marx hoped, to be a socialist one. Instead, it is one dominated by the new media, which "take us out" of our past. Postmodern society is highly pluralistic and diverse. In countless films, videos, TV programs, and Web sites, images circulate around the world. We come into contact with many ideas and values, but these have little connection with the history of the areas in which we live, or indeed with our own personal histories. Everything seems constantly in flux. As one group of authors expressed things:

> Our world is being remade. Mass production, the mass consumer, the big city, big-brother state, the sprawling housing estate, and the nation-state are in decline: flexibility, diversity, differentiation, and mobility, communication, decentralization and internationalization are in the ascendant. In the process our own identities, our sense of self, our own subjectivities are being transformed. We are in transition to a new era (Hall et al., 1988).

One of the important theorists of postmodernity is the French author Jean Baudrillard, who believes that the electronic media have destroyed our relationship to our past and created a chaotic, empty world. Baudrillard was strongly influenced by Marxism in his early years. However, he argues, the spread of electronic communication and the mass media have reversed the Marxist theorem that economic forces shape society. Instead, social life is influenced above all by signs and images.

In a media-dominated age, Baudrillard says, meaning is created by the flow of images, as in TV programs. Much of our world has become a sort of make-believe universe in which we are responding to media images rather than to real persons or places. Thus, when Diana, Princess of Wales, died in 1997, there was an enormous outpouring of grief, not only in Britain but all over the world. Yet were people mourning a real person? Baudrillard would say not. Diana existed for most people only through the media. Her death was more like an event in a soap opera than a real event in the way in which people experienced it. Baudrillard speaks of "the dissolution of life into TV."

Theoretical Thinking in Sociology

So far in this chapter we have been concerned with theoretical approaches, which refer to broad, overall orientations to the subject matter of sociology. However, we can draw a distinction between theoretical approaches and theories. Theories are more narrowly focused and represent attempts to explain particular social conditions or types of event. They are usually formed as part of the process of research and in turn suggest problems to which research investigations should be devoted. An example would be Durkheim's theory of suicide, referred to earlier in this chapter.

Innumerable theories have been developed in the many different areas of research in which sociologists work. Sometimes theories are very precisely set out and are even occasionally expressed in mathematical form—although this is more common in other social sciences (especially economics) than in sociology.

Some theories are also much more encompassing than others. Opinions vary about whether it is desirable or useful for sociologists to concern themselves with very wide-ranging theoretical endeavors. Robert K. Merton (1957), for example, argues forcefully that sociologists should concentrate their attention on what he calls *theories of the middle range*. Rather than attempting to create grand theoretical schemes (in the manner of Marx, for instance), we should be concerned with developing more modest theories.

Middle-range theories are specific enough to be tested directly by empirical research, yet sufficiently general to cover a range of different phenomena. A case in point is the theory of *relative deprivation*. This theory holds that how people evaluate their circumstances depends on whom they compare themselves to. Thus, feelings of deprivation do not conform directly to the level of material poverty individuals experience. A family living in a small home in a poor area, where everyone is in more or less similar circumstances, is likely to feel less deprived than a family living in a similar house in a neighborhood where the majority of the other homes are much larger and the other people more affluent.

It is indeed true that the more wide ranging and ambitious a theory is, the more difficult it is to test empirically. Yet there seems no obvious reason why theoretical thinking in sociology should be confined to the "middle range."

Assessing theories, and especially theoretical approaches, in sociology is a challenging and formidable task. Theoretical debates are by definition more abstract than controversies of a more empirical kind. The fact that there is not a single theoretical approach that dominates the whole of sociology might seem to be a sign of weakness in the subject. But this is not the case at all: The jostling of rival theoretical approaches and theories is an expression of the vitality of the sociological enterprise. In studying human beings—ourselves—theoretical variety rescues us from dogma. Human behavior is complicated and many sided, and it is very unlikely that a single theoretical perspective could cover all of its aspects. Diversity in theoretical thinking provides a rich source of ideas that can be drawn on in research and stimulates the imaginative capacities so essential to progress in sociological work.

Levels of Analysis: Microsociology and Macrosociology

One important distinction between the different theoretical perspectives we have discussed in this chapter involves the level of analysis each is directed at. The study of everyday behavior in situations of face-to-face interaction is usually called **microsociology**. **Macrosociology** is the analysis of large-scale social systems, like the political system or the economic order. It also includes the analysis of long-term processes of change, such as the development of industrialism. At first glance, it might seem as though micro analysis and macro analysis are distinct from one another. In fact, the two are closely connected (Knorr-Cetina and Cicourel, 1981; Giddens, 1984).

Macro analysis is essential if we are to understand the institutional background of daily life. The ways in which people live their everyday lives are greatly affected by the broader institutional framework, as is obvious when the daily cycle of activities of a culture such as that of the medieval period is compared with life in an industrialized urban environment. In modern societies, as has been pointed out, we are constantly in contact with strangers. This contact may be indirect and impersonal. However, no matter how many indirect or electronic relations we enter into today, even in the most complex societies, the presence of other people remains crucial. While we may choose just to send an acquaintance an e-mail message on the Internet, we can also choose to fly thousands of miles to spend the weekend with a friend.

Micro studies are in turn necessary for illuminating broad institutional patterns. Face-to-face interaction is clearly the main basis of all forms of social organization, no matter how large scale. Suppose we are studying a business corporation. We could understand much about its activities simply by looking at face-to-face behavior. We could analyze, for example, the interaction of directors in the boardroom, people working in the various offices, or the workers on the factory floor. We would not build up a picture of the whole corporation in this way, since some of its business is transacted through printed materials, letters, the telephone, and computers. Yet we could certainly contribute significantly to understanding how the organization works.

In later chapters, we will see further examples of how interaction in micro contexts affects larger social processes, and how macro systems in turn influence more confined settings of social life.

Is Sociology a Science?

Durkheim, Marx, and the other founders of sociology thought of it as a science. But can we really study human social life in a scientific way? To answer this question, we must first understand what the word means. What is science?

Science is the use of *systematic methods of empirical investigation, the analysis of data, theoretical thinking, and the logical assessment of arguments* to develop a body of knowledge about a particular subject matter. Sociology is a scientific endeavor, according to this definition. It involves systematic methods of empirical investigation, the analysis of data, and the assessment of theories in the light of evidence and logical argument.

Studying human beings, however, is different from observing events in the physical world, and sociology shouldn't be seen as directly like a natural science. Unlike objects in nature, humans are self-aware beings who confer sense and purpose on what they do. We can't even describe social life accurately unless we first grasp the concepts that people apply in their behavior. For instance, to describe a death as a suicide means knowing what the person in question was intending when he died. Suicide can only occur when an individual actively has self-destruction in mind. If he accidentally steps in front of a car and is killed, he cannot be said to have committed suicide.

The fact that we cannot study human beings in exactly the same way as objects in nature is in some ways an advantage to sociology. Sociological researchers profit from being able to pose questions directly to those they study—other human beings. In other respects, sociology creates difficulties not encountered by natural scientists. People who are aware that their activities are being scrutinized frequently will not behave in the same way as they do normally. They may consciously or unconsciously portray themselves in a way that differs from their usual attitudes. They may even try to "assist" the researcher by giving the responses they believe she wants.

Is Sociology Merely a Restatement of the Obvious?

Because sociologists study things that you have some personal experience with, you will sometimes wonder if what this subject has to teach you is merely "a painful elaboration of the obvious" (Wright, 2000). Is sociology merely the restatement, in more abstract jargon, of things we already know? Is it simply the tedious definition of social phenomena with which we are already familiar? Sociology at its worst can be all of these things, but it is never appropriate to judge any discipline by what its worst practitioners do. In fact, good sociology either sharpens our understanding of the obvious (Berger, 1963), or it completely transforms our common sense. In either event, good sociology is neither tedious nor a restatement of the obvious. In this text, we will sometimes begin with definitions of things that you may already understand. It is necessary for any academic discipline to define its terms. But when, for example, we define a family as a unit of people who are related to one another, we do so not as an endpoint but instead as a beginning. We know that you may not need a sociology text to tell you the definition of a family, yet we also know that if we do not begin by defining our terms, we cannot move forward to sharper levels of understanding later on. Good sociology never defines terms as an end in itself.

How Can Sociology Help Us in Our Lives?

Sociology has several practical implications for our lives, as C. Wright Mills emphasized when developing his idea of the sociological imagination.

Awareness of Cultural Differences

First, sociology allows us to see the social world from many perspectives. Quite often, if we properly understand how others live, we also acquire a better understanding of what their problems are. Practical policies that are not based on an informed awareness of the ways of life of people they affect have little chance of success. Thus, a white social worker operating in an African American community won't gain the confidence of its members without developing a sensitivity to the differences in social experience that often separate white and black in the United States.

Assessing the Effects of Policies

Second, sociological research provides practical help in assessing the results of policy initiatives. A program of practical reform may simply fail to achieve what its designers sought or may produce unintended consequences of an unfortunate kind. For instance, in the years following World War II, large public-housing blocks were built in city centers in many countries. These were planned to provide high standards of accommodation for low-income groups from slum areas and offered shopping amenities and other civic services close at hand. However, research later showed that many people who had moved from their previous dwellings to large apartment blocks felt isolated and unhappy. High-rise apartment blocks and shopping malls in poorer areas often became dilapidated and provided breeding grounds for muggings and other violent crimes.

Self-Enlightenment

Third, and in some ways most important, sociology can provide us with self-enlightenment—increased self-understanding. The more we know about why we act as we do and about the overall workings of our society, the more likely we are to be able to influence our own futures. We should not see sociology as assisting only policy makers—that is, powerful groups—in making informed decisions. Those in power cannot be assumed always to consider the interests of the less powerful or under-privileged in the policies they pursue. Self-enlightened groups can often benefit from sociological research by using the information gleaned to respond in an effective way to government policies or form policy initiatives of their own. Self-help groups such as Alcoholics Anonymous and social movements like the environmental movement are examples of social groups that have directly sought to bring about practical reforms, with some degree of success.

The Sociologist's Role in Society

Finally, it should be mentioned that many sociologists concern themselves directly with practical matters as professionals. People trained in sociology are to be found as industrial consultants, urban planners, social workers, and personnel managers, as well as in many other jobs. An understanding of society can also help one in careers in law, journalism, business, and medicine.

Those who study sociology also frequently develop a social conscience. Should sociologists themselves actively advocate and agitate for programs of reform or social change? Some argue that sociology can preserve its intellectual independence only if sociologists are studiously neutral in moral and political controversies. Yet are scholars who remain aloof from current debates necessarily more impartial in their assessment of sociological issues than others? There is often a connection between studying sociology and the prompting of social conscience. No sociologically sophisticated person can be unaware of the inequalities that exist in the world today, the lack of social justice in many social situations, and the deprivations suffered by millions of people. It would be strange if sociologists did not take sides on practical issues, and it would be illogical to try to ban them from drawing on their expertise in so doing.

In this chapter, we have seen that sociology is a discipline in which we often set aside our personal view of the world to look more carefully at the influences that shape our lives and those of others. Sociology emerged as a distinct intellectual endeavor with the development of modern societies, and the study of such societies remains its principal concern. But sociologists are also preoccupied with a broad range of issues about the nature of social interaction and human societies in general.

Sociology isn't just an abstract intellectual field but has major practical implications for people's lives. Learning to become a sociologist shouldn't be a dull academic endeavor! The best way to make sure it doesn't become so is to approach the subject in an imaginative way and to relate sociological ideas and findings to situations in your own life.

Study Outline

www.wwnorton.com/giddens5

Developing a Sociological Perspective

* *Sociology* can be identified as the systematic study of human societies giving special emphasis to modern, industrialized systems. The subject came into being as an attempt to understand the far-reaching changes that have occurred in human societies over the past two to three centuries.
* Major social changes have also occurred in the most intimate and personal characteristics of people's lives. The development of romantic love as a basis for marriage is an example of this.
* The practice of sociology involves the ability to think imaginatively and to detach oneself as far as possible from preconceived ideas about social relationships.

Modern Theoretical Approaches

* A diversity of theoretical approaches is found in sociology. The reason for this is not particularly puzzling. Theoretical disputes are difficult to resolve even in the natural sciences, and in sociology we face special difficulties because of the complex problems involved in subjecting our own behavior to study.
* Important figures in the early development of sociological theory include Auguste Comte (1798–1857), Émile Durkheim (1858–1917), Karl Marx (1818–1883), and Max Weber (1864–1920). Many of their ideas remain important in sociology today.
* The main theoretical approaches in sociology are *symbolic interactionism, functionalism, Marxism, feminism, rational choice approach,* and *postmodernism.* To some extent, these approaches complement each other. However, there are also major contrasts between them, which influence the ways in which theoretical issues are handled by authors following different approaches.

Levels of Analysis

* The study of face-to-face interaction is usually called *microsociology—* as contrasted to *macrosociology,* which studies larger groups, institutions, and social systems. Micro and macro analyses are in fact very closely related and each complements the other.

How Can Sociology Help Us in Our Lives?

* Sociology is a *science* in that it involves systematic methods of investigation and the evaluation of theories in the light of evidence and logical argument. But it cannot be modeled directly on the nat-

ural sciences, because studying human behavior is in fundamental ways different from studying the world of nature.

- Sociology is a subject with important practical implications. Sociology can contribute to social criticism and practical social reform in several ways. First, the improved understanding of a given set of social circumstances often gives us a better chance of controlling them. Second, sociology provides the means of increasing our cultural sensitivities, allowing policies to be based on an awareness of divergent cultural values. Third, we can investigate the consequences (intended and unintended) of the adoption of particular policy programs. Finally, and perhaps most important, sociology provides self-enlightenment, offering groups and individuals an increased opportunity to alter the conditions of their own lives.

Key Concepts

anomie (p. 14)
bureaucracy (p. 15)
capitalism (p. 15)
division of labor (p. 14)
feminist theory (p. 20)
functionalism (p. 18)
globalization (p. 8)
ideology (p. 20)
latent functions (p. 19)
macrosociology (p. 22)
manifest functions (p. 19)
Marxism (p. 19)
materialist conception of history (p. 15)
microsociology (p. 22)
organic solidarity (p. 14)
postmodernism (p. 20)
power (p. 20)
rational choice approach (p. 20)
rationalization (p. 18)
science (p. 22)
social constraint (p. 14)
social facts (p. 13)
social structure (p. 7)
sociological imagination (p. 6)
sociology (p. 3)
structuration (p. 7)
symbol (p. 18)
symbolic interactionism (p. 18)
theory (p. 12)
theoretical approach (p. 13)

Review Questions

1. What is the definition of sociology?
   a. Sociology is the study of individuals.
   b. Sociology is the study of group interaction, from the family to the system of nation.
   c. Sociology is the study of human social life, groups, and societies, focusing on the modern world.
   d. Sociology is a branch of the social reform movement. It is dedicated to providing a scientific underpinning for the liberal and social democratic political agendas.

2. What is the sociological imagination?
   a. It is the ability to "think ourselves away" from the familiar routines of our daily lives in order to look at them anew.
   b. It is the study of the way private troubles aggregate into public issues.
   c. It is the world view of Karl Marx.
   d. It is the application of liberal and socialist political values to social scientific inquiry.

3. What is the definition of *functionalism?*
   a. It is the study of the function of a social activity to determine the contribution that the activity makes to society as a whole.
   b. It is the study of the way people function in groups.
   c. It is the study of the way social institutions reproduce social systems.
   d. It was the conservative response to the social reform movement.

4. Structuration is considered to be a double process because
   a. social structure patterns human activity and is created by it.
   b. human societies are complex and often contradictory.
   c. human beings operate in both a personal and a social sphere.
   d. social structures are both biological and social.

5. Why is Weber's study *The Protestant Ethic and the Spirit of Capitalism* important to sociology?
   a. It showed that capitalism is the only major factor of social development in the modern period.
   b. It was the first major study validating Marx's materialist conception of history.
   c. It demonstrated the importance of ideas, such as religious values, in creating a capitalistic outlook.
   d. It created the sociology of religion.

6. Sociology can be considered a science because it
   a. uses systematic methods to study a phenomenon.
   b. uses systematic methods of theoretical thinking.
   c. involves the logical assessment of arguments.
   d. All of the above.

7. Who developed the idea of symbolic interactionism in human social life?
   a. Émile Durkheim
   b. Karl Marx
   c. Max Weber
   d. George Herbert Mead

8. According to Karl Marx, the most important changes that occurred in the modern period were tied to the development of
   a. democracy.
   b. socialism.
   c. historical materialism.
   d. capitalism.

9. Why is Émile Durkheim's study of suicide important to sociology?

a. It introduced Durkheim's concept of social facts.

b. It showed that suicide, seemingly the most individual of acts, is socially influenced. Suicide rates vary according to the social cohesion of groups.

c. It showed that the meaning of suicide varies across social groups. It is not the same for Catholics as it is for Protestants.

d. It started the field known as the sociology of death.

10. Which of the following is true about good sociology?

a. It is merely a restatement of the obvious.

b. It reinforces our common sense.

c. It sharpens our understanding of the obvious.

d. It defines sociological terms only for the purpose of defining.

Thinking Sociologically Exercises

1. Healthy older Americans often encounter exclusionary treatment when younger people assume that they are feeble-minded and thus overlook them for jobs they are fully capable of doing. How would each of the popular theoretical perspectives presented in Chapter 1—functionalism, conflict theory, and symbolic interactionism—explain the dynamics of prejudice against the elderly?

2. Your text discusses the sociology of coffee, suggesting that the consumption of coffee is more than a simple product designed to quench a person's thirst and to help fend off drowsiness. Mention and adequately discuss **five** sociological features of coffee that clearly show its "sociological" nature.

Data Exercises

www.wwnorton.com/giddens5
Keyword: Data1

In this chapter you read about some of the early sociological theorists who made important contributions to the development of sociology as a social science, and to our understanding of human behavior. The first data exercise will allow you to become more familiar with the important social theorists in this field, and get some practice using your sociological imagination. After completing this exercise you will understand how broader social forces shape individual experiences.

Sociological Questions

Be able to name the different types of questions sociologists try to answer in their research—factual, theoretical, comparative, and developmental.

The Research Process

Learn the steps of the research process, and be able to complete the process yourself.

Understanding Cause and Effect

Be able to differentiate between causation and correlation.

Research Methods

Familiarize yourself with all the different methods available to sociological research, and know the advantages and disadvantages of each.

Research in the Real World: Methods, Problems, and Pitfalls

See how research methods were combined in a real study, and recognize the problems the researcher faced.

CHAPTER TWO

ASKING AND ANSWERING SOCIOLOGICAL QUESTIONS

t oward the end of a working day, the public restroom of a particular St. Louis park is suddenly busier than one might expect. One man walks in clad in a gray suit; another has on a baseball cap, tennis shoes, shorts, and a T-shirt; a third is wearing the mechanic's uniform from the gas station where he has fixed cars all day. What are these men doing here? Surely there are more convenient places to use a restroom. Is there some common interest besides the restroom itself that brings them to this place?

Believe it or not, none of these men has come to the public toilet for the official use to which a toilet is usually put. Instead, they are searching for "instant sex." Many men—married and unmarried, those with straight identities and those whose self-image is as gay men—seek sex with people they do not know. They are hoping to experience sexual excitement, but they want to avoid involvement. They don't want any commitments that extend beyond the particular encounters they will have in this public bathroom.

Until the 1970s, the phenomenon of impersonal sex persisted as a widespread but rarely studied form of human interaction. In the gay community, such public bathrooms were called "tearooms." Laud Humphreys, a sociologist, went to these public restrooms to be part of these scenes and then conducted surveys of the participants. He wrote about them in his book *Tearoom Trade* (1970). On the basis of his research in the tearooms, Humphreys was able to cast a new light on the struggles of men who were forced to keep their sexual proclivities secret. He showed that many

Laud Humphreys's groundbreaking study of anonymous gay sex in public bathrooms led to a deeper understanding of the consequences of the social stigma and legal persecution associated with gay lifestyles.

men who otherwise live "normal" lives—the people next door—find ways to engage in embarrassing behaviors that will not harm their careers or family lives. Humphreys's research was conducted more than three decades ago, when a much greater stigma was associated with gay and lesbian identities and when police were vigilant in enforcing laws against such behavior. Many lives were ruined in the process of harsh enforcement.

Why Hang Out in Public Bathrooms?

Humphreys spent an extended period of time in such public bathrooms because an excellent way to understand social processes is to participate in and observe them. He also conducted survey interviews that enabled him to gather more information than he would have obtained by simply observing the bathrooms. Humphreys's research opened a window on an aspect of life that many people would be shocked to know existed at all and that certainly needed to be understood at a deeper level. His work was based on systematic research, but it also carried a note of passion.

Humphreys argued that persecution against gay lifestyles leads men to live anguished existences in which they must re-

sort to extreme secrecy and often dangerous activities. His study was conducted before the onset of AIDS; such activity would be much more dangerous today. He argued that tolerance for a gay subculture would put gays in a position where they could provide one another with self-esteem, mutual support, and relief from torment.

Sociological Questions

The bathrooms under study in *Tearoom Trade* are perfect examples of phenomena that are subjects of many of the kinds of questions that sociologists ask. For example, in looking at the surprising uses to which bathrooms are put, Humphreys was asking how society works in ways that are different from the official versions of how it should work and how what we take to be natural—a public bathroom—is actually *socially constructed* depending on how it is used.

It is also interesting to note that elements of modern theoretical approaches can help us understand the issues addressed by Humphreys's study. A *rational choice* approach would ask: How is this behavior in the tearooms a rational response to opportunities and constraints? The answer is that the men who go to the tearooms have few other ways to fulfill their needs, so they must engage in behavior with intense risks. An *interactionist* might ask: How does this behavior take place through processes of interaction? What kinds of interaction take place? Humphreys found that people who go into the tearooms learn from others to be silent. This is a response to the demand for privacy without involvement. Another finding is that men who go into the restroom and do not respond to initial sexual advances will not be approached any further. Each party must cooperate to make a sexual situation occur. A *functionalist* approach might ask: What contribution does the tearoom make to the continuation of society as a whole? The answer is that it provides an outlet for sexual activity that, when carried out in secret, enables the participants and other members of society to carry on as "normal" people in their everyday lives without challenging the accepted order of things. A *Marxist* approach might ask: Is thinking about economic class relations apparent in the tearooms? Humphreys found that the impersonal sex of the tearooms had a democratic quality. Men of all social classes and races would come together in these places for sexual contact, a finding that has been verified by a study of Times Square in New York City (Delany, 1999). Finally, a *feminist* approach might ask: How can women's lives be considered in this study of an all-male group? This approach was not dominant at the time Humphreys conducted his study, but a feminist today would ask how women—

perhaps wives who know nothing about the activity of their male partners—are affected by this secret behavior in the tearooms.

It has been thirty years since *Tearoom Trade* was published, and in the interim society has become more tolerant of gay identities and gay sex. After the publication of his important book, Humphreys became part of the political movement—the gay rights movement—that made this change possible. He used his findings to convince courts and police to ease up on prosecuting men for engaging in gay sex so as to alleviate the damaging side effects of covert sexual activity.

It is the business of sociological research in general to go beyond surface-level understandings of ordinary life, as Humphreys did. Good research should help us understand our social lives in a new way. It should take us by surprise, in the questions that it asks and in the findings it comes up with. The issues that concern sociologists, in both their theorizing and their research, are often similar to those that worry other people. But the results of such research frequently run counter to our commonsense beliefs.

What are the circumstances in which racial or sexual minorities live? How can mass starvation exist in a world that is far wealthier than it has ever been before? What effects will the increasing use of the Internet have on our lives? Is the family beginning to disintegrate as an institution? Sociologists try to provide answers to these and many other questions. Their findings are by no means conclusive. Nevertheless, it is always the aim of sociological theorizing and research to break away from the speculative manner in which the ordinary person usually considers such questions. Good sociological work tries to make the questions as precise as possible and seeks to gather factual evidence before coming to conclusions. To achieve these aims, we must know the most useful **research methods** to apply in a given study and how to best analyze the results.

Some of the questions that sociologists ask in their research studies are largely **factual,** or empirical, **questions.** For example, many aspects of sexual behavior, such as the aspects Humphreys studied, need direct and systematic sociological investigation. Thus, we might ask: What kinds of occupations and domestic arrangements are most common among men who go to the tearooms? What proportion of tearoom participants are caught by the police? Factual questions of this kind are often difficult to answer. Official statistics on tearooms would not exist. Even official statistics on crime are of dubious value in revealing the real level of criminal activity. Researchers who have studied crime levels have found that only about one half of all serious crimes are reported to the police.

Factual information about one society, of course, will not always tell us whether we are dealing with an unusual case or a general set of influences. Sociologists often want to ask comparative questions, relating one social context within a society to another or contrasting examples drawn from different societies. There are significant differences, for example, between the social and legal systems of the United States and Canada. A typical comparative question might be: How much do patterns of criminal behavior and law enforcement vary between the two countries?

In sociology, we need not only to look at existing societies in relation to one another but also to compare their present and past. The questions sociologists ask in this case are **developmental questions.** To understand the nature of the modern world, we have to look at previous forms of society and also study the main direction that processes of change have taken. Thus, we can investigate, for example, how the first prisons originated and what they are like today.

Factual—or what sociologists usually prefer to call **empirical**—**investigations** concern how things occur. Yet sociology does not consist of just collecting facts, however important and interesting they may be. We always need to interpret what facts mean, and to do so we must learn to pose **theoretical questions.** Many sociologists work primarily on empirical questions, but unless they are guided in research by some knowledge of theory their work is unlikely to be illuminating (see Table 2.1).

At the same time, sociologists strive not to attain theoretical knowledge for its own sake. A standard view is that although values should not be permitted to bias conclusions, social research should be relevant to real-world concerns. In this chapter, we look further into such issues by asking whether it is possible to produce objective knowledge. First, we examine the stages involved in sociological research. We then compare the most widely used research methods as we consider some actual investigations. As we shall see, there are often significant differences between the way research should ideally be carried out and real-world studies.

The Research Process

Let us first look at the stages normally involved in research work. The research process takes in a number of distinct steps, leading from when the investigation is begun to the time its findings are published or made available in written form.

Defining the Research Problem

All research starts from a research problem. This is sometimes an area of factual ignorance: We may simply wish to improve

TABLE 2.1

A Sociologist's Line of Questioning

Factual question	What happened?	During the 1980s, there was an increase in the proportion of women in their thirties bearing children for the first time.
Comparative question	Did this happen everywhere?	Was this a global phenomenon, or did it occur just in the United States, or only in a certain region of the United States?
Developmental question	Has this happened over time?	What have been the patterns of childbearing over time?
Theoretical question	What underlies this phenomenon?	Why are more women now waiting until their thirties to bear children? What factors would we look at to explain this change?

our knowledge about certain institutions, social processes, or cultures. A researcher might set out to answer such questions as: What proportion of the population holds strong religious beliefs? Are people today really disaffected with "big government"? How far does the economic position of women lag behind that of men?

The best sociological research, however, begins with problems that are also puzzles. A puzzle is not just a lack of information, but a *gap in our understanding*. Much of the skill in producing worthwhile sociological research consists in correctly identifying puzzles.

Rather than simply answering the question "What is going on here?" puzzle-solving research tries to contribute to our understanding of *why* events happen as they do. Thus, we might ask: Why are patterns of religious belief changing? What accounts for the decline in the proportions of the population voting in presidential elections in recent years? Why are women poorly represented in high-status jobs?

No piece of research stands alone. Research problems come up as part of ongoing work; one research project may easily lead to another because it raises issues the researcher had not previously considered. A sociologist may discover puzzles by reading the work of other researchers in books and professional journals or by being aware of specific trends in society. For example, over recent years, an increasing number of programs seek to treat the mentally ill while they continue to live in the community rather than confining them in asylums. Sociologists might be prompted to ask: What has given rise to this shift in attitude toward the mentally ill?

What are the likely consequences both for the patients themselves and for the rest of the community?

Reviewing the Evidence

Once the problem is identified, the next step taken in the research process is usually to review the available evidence in the field; it might be that previous research has already satisfactorily clarified the problem. If not, the sociologist will need to sift through whatever related research does exist to see how useful it is for his purpose. Have previous researchers spotted the same puzzle? How have they tried to resolve it? What aspects of the problem has their research left unanalyzed? Drawing upon others' ideas helps the sociologist to clarify the issues that might be raised and the methods that might be used in the research.

Making the Problem Precise

A third stage involves working out a clear formulation of the research problem. If relevant literature already exists, the researcher might return from the library with a good notion of how to approach the problem. Hunches about the nature of the problem can sometimes be turned into definite **hypotheses**—educated guesses about what is going on—at this stage. If the research is to be effective, a hypothesis must

In looking at this painting by Brueghel, we can observe the number of people, what each is doing, the style of the buildings, or the colors the painter chose. But without the title, *Netherlandish Proverbs*, these facts tell us nothing about the picture's meaning. In the same way, sociologists need theory as a context for their observations.

be formulated in such a way that the factual material gathered will provide evidence either supporting or disproving it.

Working Out a Design

The researcher must then decide just *how* the research materials are to be collected. A range of different research methods exists, and which one the researcher chooses depends on the overall objectives of the study as well as the aspects of behavior to be analyzed. For some purposes, a survey (in which questionnaires are normally used) might be suitable. In other circumstances, interviews or an observational study such as that carried out by Laud Humphreys might be appropriate. We shall learn more about various research methods later.

Carrying Out the Research

At the point of actually proceeding with the research, unforeseen practical difficulties can easily crop up. It might prove impossible to contact some of those to whom questionnaires are to be sent or those whom the researcher wishes to interview. A business firm or government agency may be unwilling to let the researcher carry out the work planned. Difficulties such as these could potentially bias the result of the study and give her a false interpretation. For example, if the researcher is studying how business corporations have complied with affirmative

action programs for women, then companies that have not complied might not want to be studied. The findings could be biased as a result.

Interpreting the Results

Once the material has been gathered to be analyzed, the researcher's troubles are not over—they may be just beginning! Working out the implications of the data collected and relating these back to the research problem are rarely easy. Although it may be possible to reach a clear answer to the initial questions, many investigations are in the end less than fully conclusive.

Reporting the Findings

The research report, usually published as a journal article or book, provides an account of the nature of the research and seeks to justify whatever conclusions are drawn. In Humphreys's case, this report was the book *Tearoom Trade*. This is a final stage only in terms of the individual research project. Most reports indicate questions that remain unanswered and suggest further research that might profitably be done in the future. All individual research investigations are part of the continuing process of research taking place within the sociological community. Other scholars have built on Humphreys's research findings.

Reality Intrudes!

The preceding sequence of steps is a simplified version of what happens in actual research projects (see Figure 2.1). In real sociological research, these stages rarely succeed each other so neatly, and there is almost always a certain amount of sheer muddling through. The difference is a bit like that between the recipes outlined in a cookbook and the actual process of preparing a meal. Experienced cooks often don't work from recipes at all, yet they might cook better than those who do. Following fixed schemes can be unduly restricting; much outstanding sociological research could not in fact be fitted rigidly into this sequence, although most of the steps would be there.

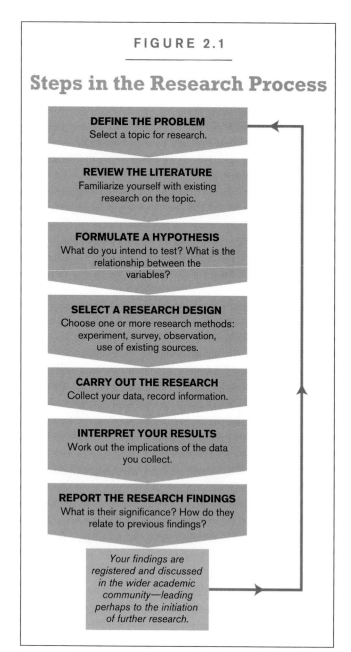

FIGURE 2.1

Steps in the Research Process

DEFINE THE PROBLEM
Select a topic for research.

REVIEW THE LITERATURE
Familiarize yourself with existing research on the topic.

FORMULATE A HYPOTHESIS
What do you intend to test? What is the relationship between the variables?

SELECT A RESEARCH DESIGN
Choose one or more research methods: experiment, survey, observation, use of existing sources.

CARRY OUT THE RESEARCH
Collect your data, record information.

INTERPRET YOUR RESULTS
Work out the implications of the data you collect.

REPORT THE RESEARCH FINDINGS
What is their significance? How do they relate to previous findings?

Your findings are registered and discussed in the wider academic community—leading perhaps to the initiation of further research.

Understanding Cause and Effect

One of the main problems to be tackled in research methodology is the analysis of cause and effect. A **causal relationship** between two events or situations is an association in which one event or situation produces another. If the parking brake is released in an automobile pointing down a hill, it will roll down the incline, gathering speed progressively as it does so. Taking the brake off *caused* this to happen; the reasons for this can readily be understood by reference to the physical principles involved. Like natural science, sociology depends on the assumption that all events have causes. Social life is not a random array of occurrences, happening without rhyme or reason. One of the main tasks of sociological research—in combination with theoretical thinking—is to identify causes and effects.

Causation and Correlation

Causation cannot be directly inferred from **correlation.** Correlation means the existence of a regular relationship between two sets of occurrences or **variables.** A variable is any dimension along which individuals or groups vary. Age, differences in income, crime rates, and social-class differences are among the many variables sociologists study. It might seem as though when two variables are found to be closely correlated, one must be the cause of another; such is often not the case. There are many correlations without any causal relationship between the variables. For example, over the period since World War II, a strong correlation can be found between a decline in pipe smoking and a decrease in the number of people who regularly go to the movies. Clearly one change does not cause the other, and we would find it difficult to discover even a remote causal connection between them.

There are many instances, however, in which it is not so obvious that an observed correlation does not imply a causal relationship. Such correlations are traps for the unwary and easily lead to questionable or false conclusions. In his classic work *Suicide,* Émile Durkheim (1966; orig. 1897) found a correlation between rates of suicide and the seasons of the year. In the societies Durkheim studied, levels of suicide increased progressively from January to around June or July. From that time onward they declined through the end of the year. It might be supposed that this demonstrates that temperature or climatic change is causally related to the propensity of individuals to kill themselves. Perhaps as temperatures increase, people become more impulsive and hot headed? However, the causal relation here has nothing directly to do with temperature or climate at all. In spring and summer most people engage in a more intensive social life than they do in winter. Individuals who are isolated or unhappy tend to experience an intensification of these feelings as the activity level of other people rises. Hence they are likely to experience acute suicidal tendencies more in spring and summer than in autumn and winter, when the pace of social activity slackens. We always have to be on our guard both in assessing whether correlation involves causation and in deciding in which direction causal relations run.

CAUSAL MECHANISM

Working out causal connections involved in correlations is often a difficult process. There is a strong correlation, for instance, between level of educational achievement and occupational success in modern societies. The better the grades an individual gets in school, the better paying the job he or she is likely to get. What explains this correlation? Research tends to show that it is not mainly school experience itself; levels of school attainment are influenced much more by the type of home from which the person comes. Children from better-off homes, whose parents take a strong interest in their learning skills and where books are abundant, are more likely to do well than those coming from homes where these qualities are lacking. The causal mechanisms here are the attitudes of parents toward their children, together with the facilities for learning that a home provides.

Causal connections in sociology should not be understood in too mechanical a way. The attitudes people have and their subjective reasons for acting as they do are causal factors in relationships between variables in social life.

CONTROLS

In assessing the cause or causes that explain a correlation, we need to distinguish **independent variables** from **dependent variables.** An independent variable is one that produces an effect on another variable. The variable affected is the dependent one. In the example just mentioned, academic achievement is the independent variable and occupational income the dependent variable. The distinction refers to the direction of the causal relation we are investigating. The same factor may be an independent variable in one study and a dependent variable in another. It all depends on what causal processes are being analyzed. If we were looking at the effects of differences in occupational income on lifestyles, occupational income would then be the independent variable rather than the dependent one.

To find out whether a correlation between variables is a causal connection we use **controls,** which means we hold some variables constant in order to look at the effects of others. By doing this, we are able to judge between explanations of observed correlations, separating causal from noncausal relationships. For example, researchers studying child development have claimed that there is a causal connection between maternal deprivation in infancy and serious personality problems in adulthood. ("Maternal deprivation" means that an infant is separated from its mother for a long period—several months or more—during the early years of its life.) How might we test whether there really is a causal relationship between maternal deprivation and later personality disorders? We would do so by trying to control, or "screen out," other possible influences that might explain the correlation.

One source of maternal deprivation is the admission of a child to a hospital for a lengthy period, during which it is separated from its parents. Is it attachment to the mother, however, that really matters? Perhaps if a child receives love and attention from *other* people during infancy, she might subsequently be a stable person. To investigate these possible causal connections, we would have to compare cases where children were deprived of regular care from anyone with other instances in which children were separated from their mothers but received love and care from someone else. If the first group developed severe personality difficulties but the second group did not, we would suspect that regular care from *someone* in infancy is what matters, regardless of whether or not it is the mother. (In fact, children do seem to prosper normally as long as they have a loving, stable relationship with someone looking after them; this person does not have to be the mother herself.)

IDENTIFYING CAUSES

A large number of possible causes could be invoked to explain any given correlation. How can we ever be sure that we have covered them all? The answer is that we cannot be sure. We would never be able to carry out and interpret the results of a piece of sociological research satisfactorily if we were compelled to test for the possible influence of every causal factor we could imagine as potentially relevant. Identifying causal relationships is normally guided by previous research into the area in question. If we do not have some reasonable idea beforehand of the causal mechanisms involved in a correlation we would probably find it very difficult to discover what the real causal connections are. We would not know what to test *for*.

A good example of how difficult it is to be sure of the causal relations involved in a correlation is given by the long history of studies of smoking and lung cancer. Research has consistently demonstrated a strong correlation between the two. Smokers are more likely to contract lung cancer than nonsmokers, and very heavy smokers are more likely to do so than light smokers. The correlation can also be expressed the other way around. A high proportion of those who have lung cancer are smokers or have smoked for long periods in their past. So many studies have confirmed these correlations that it is generally accepted that a causal link is involved, but the exact causal mechanisms are thus far largely unknown.

However much correlational work is done on any issue, there always remains some doubt about possible causal relationships. Other interpretations of the correlation are possible. It has been proposed, for instance, that people who are predisposed to get lung cancer are also predisposed to smoke. In this view it is not smoking that causes lung cancer but rather some built-in biological disposition to smoking and cancer.

Research Methods

Let's now look at the various research methods sociologists commonly employ in their work (see Table 2.2).

Ethnography

Humphreys used **ethnography** (or firsthand studies of people, using **participant observation** or interviewing) as his main research method. Here, the investigator hangs out or works or lives with a group, organization, or community and perhaps takes a direct part in its activities. An ethnographer cannot usually just be present in the place she studies, but must explain and justify her presence to its members. She must gain the cooperation of the community and sustain it over a period of time, if any worthwhile results are to be achieved.

For a long while, it was usual for research based on participant observation to exclude any account of the hazards or problems that had to be overcome, but more recently the published reminiscences and diaries of field workers have been more open about them. Frequently, field workers must cope with feelings of loneliness—it isn't easy to fit into a social context or community where you don't really belong. The researcher may be constantly frustrated because the members of the group refuse to talk frankly about themselves; direct queries may be welcomed in some contexts but meet with a chilly silence in others. Some types of fieldwork may even be physically dangerous; for instance, a researcher studying a delinquent gang might be seen as a police informer or might become unwittingly embroiled in conflicts with rival gangs.

In traditional works of ethnography, accounts were presented without very much information about the observer. This was because it was believed that an ethnographer could present objective pictures of the things they studied. More recently, ethnographers have increasingly tended to talk about themselves and the nature of their connection to the people under study. Sometimes, for example, it might be a matter of trying to consider how one's race, class, or gender affected the work, or how the power differences between observer and observed distorted the dialogue between them.

ADVANTAGES AND LIMITATIONS OF FIELDWORK

Where it is successful, ethnography provides information on the behavior of people in groups, organizations, and communities, and also how those people understand their own behavior. Once we see how things look from inside a given group, we are likely to develop a better understanding not only of that group, but of social processes that transcend the situation under study.

But fieldwork also has major limitations. Only fairly small groups or communities can be studied. And much depends on the skill of the researcher in gaining the confidence of the individuals involved; without this skill, the research is unlikely to get off the ground at all. The reverse is also possible. A researcher could begin to identify so closely with the group that she becomes too much of an "insider" and loses the perspective of an outside observer. Or a researcher may interpret the situation she is studying and reach conclusions that are more about her own effects on the situation than she or her readers ever realize.

Surveys

Interpreting field studies usually involves problems of generalization. Since only a small number of people are under study, we cannot be sure that what is found in one context will apply in other situations as well, or even that two different researchers would come to the same conclusions when studying the same group. This is usually less of a problem in survey research. In a **survey,** questionnaires are either sent or administered directly in interviews to a selected group of people—sometimes as many as several thousand. This group of people is referred to by sociologists as a **population.** Fieldwork is best suited for in-depth studies of small slices of social life; survey research tends to produce information that is less detailed but that can usually be applied over a broad area.

TABLE 2.2

Three of the Main Methods Used in Sociological Research

RESEARCH METHOD	STRENGTHS	LIMITATIONS
Ethnography	Usually generates richer and more in-depth information than other methods.	Can only be used to study relatively small groups or communities.
	Ethnography can provide a broader understanding of social processes.	Findings might only apply to groups or communities studied; not easy to generalize on the basis of a single fieldwork study.
Surveys	Make possible the efficient collection of data on large numbers of individuals.	Material gathered may be superficial; if questionnaire is highly standardized, important differences between respondents' viewpoints may be glossed over.
	Allow for precise comparisons to be made between the answers of respondents.	Responses may be what people profess to believe rather than what they actually believe.
Experiments	Influence of specific variables can be controlled by the investigator.	Many aspects of social life cannot be brought into the laboratory.
	Are usually easier for subsequent researchers to repeat.	Responses of those studied may be affected by their experimental situation.

STANDARDIZED AND OPEN-ENDED QUESTIONNAIRES

Two sorts of questionnaires are used in surveys. Some contain a standardized, or fixed-choice, set of questions, to which only a fixed range of responses is possible—for instance, *"Yes/No/Don't know"* or *"Very likely/Likely/Unlikely/Very unlikely."* Such surveys have the advantage that responses are easy to compare and count up, since only a small number of categories are involved. On the other hand, because they do not allow for subtleties of opinion or verbal expression, the information they yield is likely to be restricted in scope, if not misleading.

Other questionnaires are open ended: respondents have more opportunity to express their views in their own words; they are not limited to making fixed-choice responses. Open-ended questionnaires typically provide more detailed information than standardized ones. The researcher can follow up answers to probe more deeply into what the respondent thinks. On the other hand, the lack of standardization means that responses may be more difficult to compare statistically.

Questionnaire items are normally listed so that a team of interviewers can ask the questions and record responses in the same predetermined order. All the items must be readily understandable to interviewers and interviewees alike. In the large national surveys undertaken regularly by government agencies and research organizations, interviews are carried out more or less simultaneously across the whole country. Those who conduct the interviews and those who analyze the results could not do their work effectively if they constantly had to be checking with each other about ambiguities in the questions or answers.

Questionnaires should also take into consideration the characteristics of respondents. Will they see the point the researcher has in mind in asking a particular question? Have they enough information to answer usefully? Will they answer at all? The terms of a questionnaire might be unfamiliar to the respondents. For instance, the question "What is your marital status?" might baffle some people. It would be more appropriate to ask, "Are you single, married, separated, or divorced?" Most surveys are preceded by **pilot studies** in order to pick up problems not anticipated by the investigator. A pilot study is a trial run in which a questionnaire is completed by just a few people. Any difficulties can then be ironed out before the main survey is done.

SAMPLING

Often sociologists are interested in the characteristics of large numbers of individuals—for example, the political attitudes of the American population as a whole. It would be impossible to study all these people directly, so in such situations researchers engage in **sampling**—they concentrate on a **sample,** or small proportion of the overall group. One can usually be confident that results from a population sample, as long as it was properly chosen, can be generalized to the total population. Studies of only two to three thousand voters, for instance, can give a very accurate indication of the attitudes and voting intentions of the entire population. But to achieve such accuracy, a sample must be **representative:** The group of individuals studied must be typical of the population as a whole. Sampling is more complex than it might seem, and statisticians have developed rules for working out the correct size and nature of samples.

A particularly important procedure used to ensure that a sample is representative is **random sampling,** in which a sample is chosen so that every member of the population has the same probability of being included. The most sophisticated way of obtaining a random sample is to give each member of the population a number and then use a computer to generate a random list, from which the sample is derived—for instance, by picking every tenth number.

"THE PEOPLE'S CHOICE?"

One of the most famous early examples of survey research was "The People's Choice?" a study carried out by Paul Lazarsfeld and a number of colleagues about half a century ago (Lazarsfeld, Berelson, and Gaudet, 1948). This study, which investigated the voting intentions of residents of Erie County, Ohio, during the 1940 campaign for the U.S. presidency, pioneered several of the main techniques of survey research in use to this day. In order to probe a little more deeply than a single questionnaire would do, the investigators interviewed each member of a sample of voters on seven separate occasions. The aim was to trace and understand the reasons for changes in voting attitudes.

The research was set up with a number of definite hypotheses in view. One was that relationships and events close to voters in a community influence voting intentions more than distant world affairs, and the findings on the whole confirmed this. The researchers developed sophisticated measurement techniques for analyzing political attitudes; yet their work also made significant contributions to theoretical thinking. Among the concepts they helped to introduce were those of "opinion leaders" and the "two-step flow of communication." The study showed that some individuals—opinion leaders—tend to shape the political opinions of those around them. People's views are not formed in a direct fashion, but in a two-step process. In the first step, opinion leaders react to political events; in the second step, those leaders influence people around them—relatives, friends, and colleagues. The views expressed by opinion leaders, filtered through personal relationships, then influence the responses of other individuals toward political issues of the day.

ADVANTAGES AND DISADVANTAGES OF SURVEYS

Surveys are widely used in sociological research, for several reasons. Questionnaire responses can be more easily quantified and analyzed than material generated by most other research methods; large numbers of people can be studied; and given sufficient funds, researchers can employ an agency specializing in survey work to collect the responses. The scientific method is the model for this kind of research, as surveys give researchers a statistical measure of what they are studying.

However, many sociologists are critical of the survey method. They argue that an appearance of precision can be given to findings whose accuracy may be dubious, given the relatively shallow nature of most survey responses. Levels of nonresponse are sometimes high, especially when questionnaires are sent and returned through the mail. It is not uncommon for studies to be published based on results derived from little over half of those in a sample, although normally an effort is made to recontact nonrespondents or to substitute other people. Little is known about those who choose not to respond to surveys or refuse to be interviewed, but survey research is often experienced as intrusive and time consuming.

Experiments

An **experiment** can be defined as an attempt to test a hypothesis under highly controlled conditions established by an investigator. Experiments are often used in the natural sciences, as they offer major advantages over other research procedures. In an experimental situation, the researcher directly controls the circumstances being studied. As compared with the natural sciences, the scope for experimentation in sociol-

In Philip Zimbardo's make-believe jail, tension between students playing guards and students playing prisoners became dangerously real. From his experiment Zimbardo concluded that behavior in prisons is influenced more by the nature of the prison itself than the individual characteristics of those involved.

ogy is quite restricted. We can bring only small groups of individuals into a laboratory setting, and in such experiments, people know that they are being studied and may behave unnaturally.

Nevertheless, experimental methods can occasionally be applied in a helpful way in sociology. An example is the ingenious experiment carried out by Philip Zimbardo, who set up a make-believe jail, randomly assigning some student volunteers to the role of guards and other volunteers to the role of prisoners (Zimbardo, 1972). His aim was to see how far playing these different parts led to changes in attitude and behavior. The results shocked the investigators. Students who played at being guards quickly assumed an authoritarian manner; they displayed real hostility toward the prisoners, ordering them around and verbally abusing and bullying them. The prisoners, by contrast, showed a mixture of apathy and rebelliousness—a response often noted among inmates in real prisons. These effects were so marked and the level of tension so high that the experiment had to be called off at an early stage. The results, however, were important. Zimbardo concluded that behavior in prisons is more influenced by the nature of the prison situation itself than by the individual characteristics of those involved.

Life Histories

In contrast to experiments, **life histories** belong purely to sociology and the other social sciences; they have no place in natural science. Life histories consist of biographical material assembled about particular individuals—usually as recalled by the individuals themselves. Other procedures of research don't usually yield as much information as the life-history method does about the development of beliefs and attitudes over time. Life-historical studies rarely rely wholly on people's memories, however. Normally, sources such as letters, contemporary reports, and newspaper descriptions are used to expand on and check the validity of the information individuals provide. Sociologists' views differ on the value of life histories: Some feel they are too unreliable to provide useful information, but others believe they offer sources of insight that few other research methods can match.

Life histories have been successfully employed in studies of major importance. A celebrated early study was *The Polish Peasant in Europe and America,* by W. I. Thomas and Florian Znaniecki, the five volumes of which were first published between 1918 and 1920 (Thomas and Znaniecki, 1966). Thomas and Znaniecki were able to provide a more sensitive and subtle account of the experience of migration than would have been possible without the interviews, letters, and newspaper articles they collected.

Comparative Research

Each of the research methods described above is often applied in a comparative context. **Comparative research** is of central importance in sociology, because making comparisons allows us to clarify what is going on in a particular area of research. Let's take the American rate of divorce—the number of divorces granted each year—as an example. Divorce rates rose rapidly in the United States after World War II, reaching a peak in the early 1980s. Current trends suggest that as many as 60 percent of couples marrying today will divorce before their tenth wedding anniversary—a statistic that expresses profound changes taking place in the area of sexual relations and family life. Do these changes reflect specific features of American society? We can find out by comparing divorce rates in the United States with those of other countries. Such a comparison reveals that although the U.S. rate is higher than in

Studying the Homeless

Since the 1980s, there has been a remarkable growth in the number of homeless people in the United States. But how big is the problem? How can we know whom to count as homeless? These are questions that social scientists have sought to answer, often coming up with dramatically different results.

Until the mid-1980s, the conventional wisdom was that there were over 1 million homeless people, but the statistics were essentially undocumented. Why was it so difficult to know? The reason is that it is difficult to count people living in bus stations, subways, abandoned buildings, doorways, or Dumpsters. In the absence of hard data, politicians relied on estimates provided by "homeless activists." For instance, one prominent activist, Mitch Snyder, told Ted Koppel on ABC's *Nightline* that the number was between 2 and 3 million. When asked where his numbers came from, he responded, "We got on the phone, we made a lot of calls, we talked to a lot of people, and we said, 'Okay, here are some numbers.' "

In his 1994 book *The Homeless,* the sociologist Christopher Jencks stressed how important it is to look at hard data based on documented research instead of political numbers chosen to have the maximum impact on government policy. Jencks's research strategy was to assess carefully data and research collected by other social scientists or government agencies and come up with a more precise definition and count of the homeless. His definition excluded a number of people generally counted as homeless, such a those living in welfare hotels at the expense of social welfare programs, and therefore produced a number far smaller than the rough guesses of journalists and activists.

The sociologist Elliot Liebow studied homelessness entirely differently and wrote about it in his book *Tell Them Who I Am* (1993). Liebow went out on the streets of Washington, D.C., and observed homelessness firsthand. He befriended the homeless women he was studying, volunteered to work in shelters, and helped them get along with their lives. Some would argue that in doing so, Liebow breached the rules of research discussed in this chapter, allowing himself to identify too closely with the group he was studying. But Liebow was able to learn something about homelessness that other research failed to illuminate: What do homeless people do all day? What are their most immediate concerns? What do they do with their limited possessions? Why do they think they are homeless?

The differences between Jencks's and Liebow's studies illustrate the differences between quantitative and qualitative research and between macrosociology and microsociology. By carefully scrutinizing the known data on the homeless, Jencks contributed a better knowledge of the extent of homelessness. By learning more about the day-to-day experiences of being homeless, Liebow contributed a better understanding of the everyday life conditions of the homeless. Both are crucial for coming to grips with the problem and developing more informed welfare policies.

Questions

- What are the benefits of a quantitative method of talking about homelessness or about any social problem? What are the disadvantages of these methods?
- How and why is it advantageous for sociologists to distance themselves from their subjects? How can identifying with one's subject help one's research?

most other Western societies, the overall trends are similar. Virtually all Western countries have experienced steadily climbing divorce rates over the past half century.

Historical Analysis

As was mentioned in Chapter 1, a historical perspective is often essential in sociological research. For we frequently need a *time perspective* to make sense of the material we collect about a particular problem.

Sociologists commonly want to investigate past events directly. Some periods of history can be studied in a direct way, when there are still survivors alive—such as in the case of the Holocaust in Europe during World War II. Research in **oral history** means interviewing people about events they witnessed at some point earlier in their lives. This kind of research work, obviously, can only stretch at the most some sixty or seventy years back in time. For historical research on an earlier period, sociologists are dependent on the use of documents and written records, often contained in the special collections of libraries or the National Archives.

An interesting example of the use of historical documents is sociologist Anthony Ashworth's study of trench warfare during World War I (Ashworth, 1980). Ashworth was concerned with analyzing what life was like for men who had to endure being under constant fire, crammed in close proximity for weeks on end. He drew on a diversity of documentary sources: official histories of the war, including those written about different military divisions and battalions; official publications of the time; the notes and records kept informally by individual soldiers; and personal accounts of war experiences. By drawing on such a variety of sources, Ashworth was able to develop a rich and detailed description of life in the trenches. He discovered that most soldiers formed their own ideas about how often they intended to engage in combat with the enemy and often effectively ignored the commands of their officers. For example, on Christmas Day, German and Allied soldiers suspended hostilities, and in one place the two sides even staged an informal soccer match.

Combining Comparative and Historical Research

Ashworth's research concentrated on a relatively short time period. As an example of a study that investigated a much longer one and that also applied comparative research in a historical context, we can take Theda Skocpol's *States and Social Revolutions* (1979), one of the best-known studies of social change. Skocpol set herself an ambitious task: to produce a theory of the origins and nature of revolution grounded in detailed empirical study. She looked at processes of revolution in three different historical contexts: the 1789 revolution in France, the 1917 revolution in Russia (which brought the communists to power and established the Soviet Union, which was eventually dissolved in 1989), and the revolution of 1949 in China (which created communist China).

By analyzing a variety of documentary sources, Skocpol was able to develop a powerful explanation of revolutionary change, one that emphasized the underlying social structural conditions. She showed that social revolutions are largely the result of unintended consequences. Before the Russian Revolution, for instance, various political groups were trying to overthrow the preexisting regime, but none of these—including the Bolsheviks (communists), who eventually came to power—anticipated the revolution that occurred. A series of clashes and confrontations gave rise to a process of social transformation much more radical than anyone had foreseen.

Research in the Real World: Methods, Problems, and Pitfalls

All research methods, as was stressed earlier, have their advantages and limitations. Hence, it is common to combine several methods in a single piece of research, using each to supplement and check on the others in a process known as **triangulation.** We can see the value of combining methods—and, more generally, the problems and pitfalls of real sociological research—by looking once again at Laud Humphreys's *Tearoom Trade.*

One of the questions that Humphreys wanted to answer was: What kinds of men came to the tearooms? But it was very hard for him to find this out, because all he could really do in the bathrooms was observe. The norm of silence in the restrooms made it difficult to ask any questions, or even to talk. Plus, it would have been very odd if he had begun to ask personal questions of people who basically wanted to be anonymous.

Humphreys's solution was to try to find out more about the men in the tearooms using survey methods. Standing by the door of the restrooms, he would write down the license plate numbers of people who pulled up to the parking lot and then went into the restrooms for the purpose of engaging in sexual

Statistical Terms

Research in sociology often makes use of statistical techniques in the analysis of findings. Some are highly sophisticated and complex, but those most often used are easy to understand. The most common are **measures of central tendency** (ways of calculating averages) and **correlation coefficients** (measures of the degree to which one variable relates consistently to another).

There are three methods of calculating averages, each of which has certain advantages and shortcomings. Take as an example the amount of personal wealth (including all assets such as houses, cars, bank accounts, and investments) owned by thirteen individuals. Suppose the thirteen own the following amounts:

1	$ 000 (zero)	8	$ 80,000
2	$ 5,000	9	$ 100,000
3	$10,000	10	$ 150,000
4	$20,000	11	$ 200,000
5	$40,000	12	$ 400,000
6	$40,000	13	$10,000,000
7	$40,000		

The **mean** corresponds to the average, arrived at by adding together the personal wealth of all thirteen people and dividing the result by 13. The total is $11,085,000; dividing this by 13, we reach a mean of $852,692.31. This mean is often a useful calculation because it is based on the whole range of data provided. However, it can be misleading where one or a small number of cases are very different from the majority. In the above example, the mean is not in fact an appropriate measure of central tendency, because the presence of one very large figure, $10,000,000, skews the picture. One might get the impression when using the mean to summarize this data that most of the people own far more than they actually do.

In such instances, one of two other measures may be used.

The **mode** is the figure that occurs most frequently in a given set of data. In our example, it is $40,000. The problem with the mode is that it doesn't take into account the *overall distribution* of the data, i.e., the range of figures covered. The most frequently occurring case in a set of figures is not necessarily representative of their distribution as a whole and thus may not be a useful average. In this case, $40,000 is too close to the lower end of the figures.

The third measure is the **median,** which is the middle of any set of figures; here, this would be the seventh figure, again $40,000. Our example gives an odd number of figures, thirteen. If there had been an even number—for instance, twelve—the median would be calculated by taking the mean of the two middle cases, figures 6 and 7. Like the mode, the median gives no idea of the actual *range* of the data measured.

Sometimes a researcher will use more than one measure of central tendency to avoid giving a deceptive picture of the average. More often, he will calculate the **standard deviation** for the data in question. This is a way of calculating the **degree of dispersal,** or the range, of a set of figures—which in this case goes from zero to $10,000,000.

Correlation coefficients offer a useful way of expressing how closely connected two (or more) variables are. Where two variables correlate completely, we can speak of a perfect positive correlation, expressed as 1.0. Where no relation is found between two variables—they have no consistent connection at all—the coefficient is zero. A perfect negative correlation, expressed as −1.0, exists when two variables are in a completely inverse relation to one another. Perfect correlations are never found in the social sciences. Correlations of the order of 0.6 or more, whether positive or negative, are usually regarded as indicating a strong degree of connection between whatever variables are being analyzed. Positive correlations on this level might be found between, say, social class background and voting behavior.

---

relations. He then gave those license plate numbers to a friend who worked at the Department of Motor Vehicles, securing the addresses of the men.

Months later, Washington University in St. Louis was conducting a door-to-door survey of sexual habits. Humphreys asked the principal investigators in that survey if he could add the names and addresses of his sample of tearoom partici-

pants. Humphreys then disguised himself as one of the investigators and went to interview these men at their homes, supposedly just to ask only the survey questions but actually to also learn more about their social backgrounds and lives. He found that most of these men were married and otherwise led very conventional lives. He often interviewed wives and other family members as well.

Reading a Table

You will often come across tables in reading sociological literature. They sometimes look complex, but are easy to decipher if you follow a few basic steps, listed below; with practice, these will become automatic. (See Table 2.3 as an example.) Do not succumb to the temptation to skip over tables; they contain information in concentrated form, which can be read more quickly than would be possible if the same material were expressed in words. By becoming skilled in the interpretation of tables, you will also be able to check how far the conclusions a writer draws actually seem justified.

1. Read the title in full. Tables frequently have longish titles, which represent an attempt by the researcher to state accurately the nature of the information conveyed. The title of Table 2.3 gives first the *subject* of the data, second the fact that the table provides material for comparison, and third the fact that data are given only for a limited number of countries.

2. Look for explanatory comments, or *notes,* about the data. A note at the foot of Table 2.3 linked to the main column heading indicates that the data cover only licensed cars. This is important, because in some countries the proportion of vehicles properly licensed may be lower than in others. Notes may say how the material was collected, or why it is displayed in a particular way. If the data have not been gathered by the researcher but are based on findings originally reported elsewhere, a **source** will be included. The source sometimes gives you some insight into how reliable the information is likely to be, as well as showing where to find the original data. In our table, the source note makes clear that the data have been taken from more than one source.

3. Read the *headings* along the top and left-hand side of the table. (Sometimes tables are arranged with "headings" at the foot rather than the top.) These tell you what type of information is contained in each row and column. In reading the table, keep in mind each set of headings as you scan the figures. In our example, the headings on the left give the countries involved, while those at the top refer to the levels of car ownership and the years for which they are given.

4. Identify the units used; the figures in the body of the table may represent cases, percentages, averages, or other measures. Sometimes it may be helpful to convert the figures to a form more useful to you: if percentages are not provided, for example, it may be worth calculating them.

5. Consider the conclusions that might be reached from the information in the table. Most tables are discussed by the author, and what he or she has to say should of course be borne in mind. But you should also ask what further issues or questions could be suggested by the data.

TABLE 2.3

Automobile Ownership: Comparisons of Several Selected Countries

Several interesting trends can be seen in the figures in this table. First, the level of car ownership varies considerably between different countries. The number of cars per 1,000 people is more than eight times greater in the United States than in Brazil, for example. Second, there is a clear connection between car ownership ratios as a rough indicator of differences in prosperity. Third, in all the countries represented, the rate of car ownership has increased between 1971 and 2001, but in some the rate of increase is higher than others—probably indicating differences in the degree to which countries have successfully generated economic growth or are catching up.

NUMBER OF CARS PER 1,000 OF THE ADULT POPULATION[a]

	1971	1981	1984	1989	1993[d]	1996[d]	2001[e]
Brazil	12	78	84	98	96	79	95[e]
Chile	19	45	56	67	94	110	NA
Ireland	141	202	226	228	290	307	347[f]
France	261	348	360	475	503	524	585[e]
Greece	30	94	116	150	271	312	NA
Italy	210	322	359	424	586	674	638[e]
Japan	100	209	207	286	506	552	576[e]
Sweden	291	348	445	445	445	450	418[c]
U.K.	224	317	343	366	386	399	554[e]
U.S.	448	536	540	607	747	767	785[e]
West Germany	247	385	312	479	470[b]	528	583[e]

[a] Includes all licensed cars.

[b] Germany as a whole in 1993.

[c] Figure is for the year 1999. Baltic 21 Secretariat, "Passenger Car Density," www.baltic21.org/reports/indicators/tr08.htm.

[d] From World Bank, *World Development Indicators 1999.*

[e] www.toyota.co.jp/IRweb/corp_info/and_the_world/pdf/2003_c07.pdf.

[f] Figure is for the year 2000. For Ireland, see United Nations Economic Commission for Europe, www.unece.org/stats/trend/irl.pdf.

SOURCES: International Road Federation, *United Nations Annual Bulletin of Transport Statistics,* reported in *Social Trends* (London: HMSO, 1987), p. 68; Statistical Office of the European Community, *Basic Statistics of the Community* (Luxembourg: European Union, 1991); data for 1993 from *The Economist, Pocket World in Figures,* 1996; Baltic 21 Secretariat, "Passenger Car Density," www.baltic21.org/reports/indicators/tr08.htm; International Bank for Reconstruction and Development/The World Bank, *World Development Indicators 1999;* Toyota Corporation, "2001 Number and Diffusion Rate for Motor Vehicles in Major Countries," www.toyota.co.jp/IRweb/corp_info/and_the_world/pdf/2003_c07.pdf; United Nations Economic Commission for Europe, "Ireland," www.unece.org/stats/trend/irl.pdf.

Human Subjects and Ethical Problems

All research concerned with human beings can pose ethical dilemmas. A key question that sociologists agree must be asked is whether the research poses risks to the subjects that are greater than the risks they face in their everyday lives.

In writing *Tearoom Trade,* Humphreys said he was less than truthful to those whose behavior he was studying. He said he didn't reveal his identity as a sociologist when observing the tearoom. People who came into the tearoom assumed he was there for the same reasons they were and that his presence could be accepted at face value. While he did not tell any direct lies while observing the tearoom, he also did not reveal the real reason for his presence there. Was this particular aspect of his behavior ethical? The answer is that, on balance, this particular aspect of his study did not put any of his subjects at risk. On the basis of what he observed in the tearoom, Humphreys did not collect information about the participants that would have identified them. What he knew about them was similar to what all the other people in the tearoom knew. In this way, his presence did not subject them to any more risk than they already encountered in their everyday lives. At the same time, had Humphreys been completely frank at every stage, the research might not have gotten as far as it did. Indeed, some of the most valuable data that have been collected by sociologists could have never been gathered if the researcher had first explained the project to each person encountered in the research process.

If this were the only dilemma posed by Humphreys's research project, it would not stand out as a notable problem in the ethics of social research. What raised more eyebrows was that Humphreys wrote down the license plate numbers of the people who came into the tearooms, obtained their home addresses from a friend who worked at the Department of Motor Vehicles, and visited their homes in the guise of conducting a neutral survey. Even though Humphreys did not reveal to the men's families anything about their activities in the tearooms, and even though he took great pains to keep the data confidential, the knowledge he gained could have been damaging. Since the activity he was documenting was illegal, police officers might have demanded that he release information about the identities of the subjects. It is also possible that a less skilled investigator could have slipped up when interviewing the subjects' families or that Humphreys could have lost his notes, which could then have been found later by someone else. Considering the number of things that could go wrong in the research process, researchers do not consider projects of this kind to be legitimate.

Humphreys was one of the first sociologists to study the lives of gay men. His account was a humane treatment that went well beyond the existing stock of knowledge on sexual communities. Although none of his research subjects actually suffered as a result of his book, Humphreys himself later agreed with his critics on the key ethical controversy. He said that were he to do the study again, he would not trace license plates or go to people's homes. Instead, after gathering his data in the public tearooms, he might try to get to know a subset of the people well enough to inform them of his goals for the study and then ask them to talk about the significance of these activities in their lives.

In recent years, the federal government has become increasingly strict with universities that make use of government grant money for research purposes. The National Science Foundation and the National Institutes of Health have strict requirements outlining how human subjects must be treated. In response to these requirements, American universities now routinely review all research that involves human subjects. The result of these review procedures has been both positive and negative. On the one hand, researchers are more aware of ethical considerations than ever before. On the other hand, many sociologists are finding it increasingly difficult to get their work done when institutional review boards required them to secure informed consent from their research subjects before they are able to establish a rapport with the subjects. There will likely never be easy solutions to problems of this kind.

The Influence of Sociology

Sociological research is rarely of interest only to the intellectual community of sociologists. Its results are often disseminated throughout society. Sociology, it must be emphasized, is not just the *study* of modern societies; it is a significant element *in the continuing life* of those societies. Take the transformations taking place in the United States in marriage, sexuality, and the family. Few people living in a modern society do not have some knowledge of these changes, as a result of the filtering down of sociological research. Our thinking and behavior are affected by sociological knowledge in complex and often subtle ways, thus reshaping the very field of sociological investigation. A way of describing this phenomenon, using the technical concepts of sociology, is to say that sociology stands in a reflexive relation to the human beings whose behavior is studied. **Reflexivity** describes the interchange between sociological research and human behavior. We should not be surprised that sociological findings often correlate closely with common sense. The reason is not simply that sociology comes up with findings we knew already; it is rather that sociological research continually influences what our common-sense knowledge of society actually *is*.

Study Outline

www.wwnorton.com/giddens5

The Research Process

- Sociologists investigate social life by posing distinct questions and trying to find the answers to these by systematic research. These questions may be *factual, comparative, developmental,* or *theoretical.*
- All research begins from a *research problem,* which interests or puzzles the investigator. Research problems may be suggested by gaps in the existing literature, theoretical debates, or practical issues in the social world. There are a number of clear steps in the development of research strategies—although these are rarely followed exactly in actual research.

Understanding Cause and Effect

- A *causal relationship* between two events or situations is one in which one event or situation brings about the other. This is more problematic than it seems at first. *Causation* must be distinguished from *correlation,* which refers to the existence of a regular relationship between two *variables.* A variable can be differences in age, income, crime rates, etc. We need to also distinguish *independent variables* from *dependent variables.* An independent variable is a variable that produces an effect on another. Sociologists often use *controls* to ascertain a causal relationship.

Research Methods

- In fieldwork, or *participant observation,* the researcher spends lengthy periods of time with a group or community being studied. A second method, *survey research,* involves sending or administering questionnaires to samples of a larger *population.* Documentary research uses printed materials, from archives or other resources, as a source for information. Other research methods include *experiments,* the use of *life histories,* historical analysis, and *comparative research.*
- Each of these various methods of research has its limitations. For this reason, researchers will often combine two or more methods in their work, each being used to check or supplement the material obtained from the others. This process is called *triangulation.*

The Influence of Sociology

- Sociological research often poses ethical dilemmas. These may arise either where deception is practiced against those who are the subjects of the research, or where the publication of research findings might adversely affect the feelings or lives of those studied. There is no entirely satisfactory way to deal with these issues, but all researchers have to be sensitive to the dilemmas they pose.

Key Concepts

causal relationship (p. 34)
causation (p. 34)
comparative questions (p. 31)
comparative research (p. 39)
control (p. 35)
correlation (p. 34)
dependent variable (p. 35)
developmental questions (p. 31)
empirical investigation (p. 31)
ethnography (p. 36)
experiment (p. 38)
factual questions (p. 31)
hypothesis (p. 32)
independent variable (p. 35)
life history (p. 39)
oral history (p. 42)
participant observation (p. 36)
pilot study (p. 37)
population (p. 36)
random sample (p. 38)
reflexivity (p. 46)
representative sample (p. 38)
research methods (p. 31)
sample (p. 38)
sampling (p. 38)
survey (p. 36)
theoretical questions (p. 31)
triangulation (p. 42)
variable (p. 34)

Review Questions

1. Which of the following are the stages in the sociological research process?
   a. Defining the problem / making the problem precise / reviewing the evidence / working out a design / carrying out research / interpreting the results / reporting the findings
   b. Defining the problem / reviewing the evidence / making the problem precise / working out a design / carrying out research / interpreting the results / reporting the findings
   c. Defining the problem / reviewing the evidence / making the problem precise / working out a design / interpreting the results / carrying out research / reporting the findings
   d. Making the problem precise / defining the problem / reviewing the evidence / working out a design / carrying out research / interpreting the results / reporting the findings

2. What is the standard deviation?
   a. A measure of the degree of concentration around the arithmetic mean
   b. A measure of the degree of dispersal, or range, of a set of figures
   c. The median divided by the mode
   d. The degree of variation in respect of group norms
3. What are the main steps that must be taken to administer a social survey?
   a. Making the problem precise enough to study, deciding whether to use fixed-choice or open-ended questions, and generating a representative sample
   b. Doing a pilot study, generating a representative sample of respondents, and calculating correlation coefficients
   c. Deciding whether to use fixed-choice or open-ended questions, doing a pilot study, and generating a representative sample of respondents
   d. Generating a representative sample of respondents, calculating correlation coefficients, and writing up the study
4. What are the main limitations of using documents in sociological research?
   a. They may be partial and difficult to interpret.
   b. They are not as useful as interviews with those who wrote them.
   c. They are quickly outdated by subsequent events.
   d. They do not lend themselves to statistical analysis.
5. Which type of sociological method is exemplified by Thomas and Znaniecki's *Polish Peasant in Europe and America* (1966)?
   a. Life histories
   b. Oral history
   c. Historical analysis
   d. Comparative analysis
6. What does it mean to say that, unlike the natural sciences, sociology stands in reflexive relationship to its subject of study?
   a. The findings of sociology can reflect the behavior of those studied.
   b. The findings of sociology can be understood by those studied, whereas the findings of the natural sciences cannot.
   c. The findings of sociology can affect the behavior of those studied and influence our collective understanding of what society actually is.
   d. The findings of sociology are the subject of public debate, whereas those of the natural sciences are not.
7. All research begins with
   a. a hypothesis.
   b. conclusions.
   c. the research design.
   d. a research problem.
8. The process in which researchers often combine two or more methods in their work, each being used to check or supplement the material obtained from the others, is called
   a. sampling.
   b. correlation.

c. triangulation.
d. control.
9. How does the text suggest sociologists can conduct good sociological research?
   a. By working in teams, sociologists are less likely to let personal bias influence their research.
   b. By asking subjects numerous questions, including trick questions, sociologists can make sure a subject is telling the truth.
   c. There is no standard for conducting sociological research.
   d. The best results can be obtained by making the questions posed as precise as possible and by gathering factual evidence before making a conclusion.
10. Which of the following research methods tests a hypothesis in a highly controlled environment?
    a. experiment
    b. survey
    c. life history
    d. participant observation

Thinking Sociologically Exercises

1. Let's suppose the dropout rate in your local high school increased dramatically. Faced with such a serious problem, the board offers you a $500,000 grant to do a study to explain the sudden increase. Following the recommended study procedures outlined in your text, explain how you would go about doing your research. What might be some of the hypotheses to test in your study? How would you prove or disprove them?
2. Explain in some detail the advantages and disadvantages of doing documentary research. What will it yield that will be better than experimentation, surveys, and ethnographic field work? What are its limitations compared with those approaches?

Data Exercises

www.wwnorton.com/giddens5
Keyword: Data2

Now that you have read about the research process in sociology, it is time to gain some experience of your own. This Data Exercise will be an opportunity for you to apply the sociological perspective as you analyze data and draw conclusions about Americans' attitudes toward abortion.

PART TWO

THE INDIVIDUAL AND SOCIETY

We start our exploration of sociology by looking at the connections between individual development and culture and by analyzing types of society from the past and present. Our personalities and outlooks are strongly influenced by the culture and society in which each of us exists. However, we actively recreate and reshape the cultural and social contexts in which our activities occur.

In Chapter 3, we examine the unity and diversity of human culture. We consider how human beings resemble and differ from animals, and analyze the range of variations among human cultures.

Chapter 4 discusses socialization, concentrating on how the human infant develops into a social being. Socialization continues through the life span, so studying it also means analyzing the relationships among young, middle-aged, and older people.

In Chapter 5, we discuss how people interact in everyday life. We look at the mechanisms individuals use to interpret what others say and do. The study of social interaction can tell us a great deal about the larger social environment in which we live.

In Chapter 6, we study social groups, networks, and organizations and how individuals interact in various settings. Chapter 7 moves on to look at deviance and crime. We can learn much about the way a population behaves by studying people whose behavior deviates from generally accepted patterns.

The Sociological Study of Culture

Know what culture consists of, and recognize how it differs from society.

The Development of Human Culture

Begin to understand how both biological and cultural factors influence our behavior. Learn the ideas of sociobiology and how others have tried to refute them by emphasizing cultural differences.

Disappearing World: Premodern Societies and Their Fate

Learn how societies have changed over time.

Societies in the Modern World

Recognize the factors that changed premodern societies, particularly how industrialization and colonialism influenced global development. Know the differences between the First World, the Second World, and the developing world (Third World) and how they developed.

The Impact of Globalization

Recognize the impact of globalization on your life and the lives of people around the world. Think about the impact of a growing global culture.

CHAPTER THREE

CULTURE AND SOCIETY

just eight years ago, the French president Jacques Chirac was visiting France's new National Library, where he reportedly viewed for the first time a computer mouse. Chirac expressed wonderment at the new technology (Cairncross, 1997). The United States at that time ranked first among major countries in terms of Internet servers; France was not even among the top twenty-five (Starrs, 1997).

France is no less modern than the United States. Why was it so reluctant to come online? Could it be that in 1997, as today, the Internet was dominated by the United States and was thus a powerful source for spreading American culture, along with the English language?

The unofficial language of the Internet is English. Nearly half of all Internet users worldwide are Americans (Nua Online, 2000), and one study (published in French) concluded that 82 percent of all Web sites are in English—even though 94 percent of the world's population speaks some other language (ISOC, 1997; Wallraff, 2000). The French are especially sensitive about the threat of American culture and the English language to their way of life. The French government spends $100 million a year promoting the country's language and culture (Jones, 1998) and has actively sought to curb the "invasion" of English words such as *software* and *computer*. Many French people resent what they call American "cultural imperialism," seen as a form of conquest—one of values and attitudes—and including such unwelcome imports as McDonald's restaurants. McDonald's, their high golden arches a visible symbol of American cultural domination, have even been attacked and burned down in France.

France is not alone in resisting the inroads of American culture. In Germany, for example, the Club for the Preservation of the German Language was founded to combat, in the words of its founder, "the colonization of German by English" (quoted in Jones, 1998). As American culture spreads around the world through film, television, and now the Internet, many people fear the erosion of their own cultures—even as they tune in to *The Simpsons*, sip Coke or Pepsi, and download music from the Web. Is modern technology an irresistible force that will eventually press the world's diverse cultures into a single mold? Or will it permit local cultures to flourish? These are some of the questions we explore in this chapter.

First, however, we look at what culture is and its role in encouraging conformity to shared ways of thinking and acting. We then consider the early development of human culture, emphasizing features that distinguish human behavior from that of other species. After assessing the role of biology in shaping human behavior, we examine the different aspects of culture that make it essential for human society. This leads to a discussion of cultural diversity, examining not only the cultural variations across different societies but also the cultural variations within a society such as the United States.

Cultural variations among human beings are linked to differing types of society, and we will compare and contrast the main forms of society found in history. The point of doing this is to tie together closely the two aspects of human social existence—the different cultural values and products that human beings have developed and the contrasting types of society in which such cultural development has occurred. Too often, culture is discussed separately from society as though the two were disconnected, whereas in fact, as we've already emphasized, they are closely meshed. Throughout the chapter, we will concentrate on how social change has affected cultural development. One instance of this is the impact of technology and globalization on the many cultures of the world, a topic we will explore in the conclusion to this chapter.

The Sociological Study of Culture

The sociological study of culture began with Durkheim in the nineteenth century and soon became the basis of *anthropology,* a social science specifically focused on the study of cultural differences and similarities among the world's many peoples. The work of early sociologists and anthropologists was strongly biased toward the beliefs and values of highly educated Europeans. These early social scientists assumed that "primitive" cultures were inferior, lagging far behind modern European "civilization." However, two destructive world wars, fought largely between European countries that claimed to be the most "civilized" cultures on earth, helped to discredit that belief. Sociologists and anthropologists now recognize that there are many different cultures, each with its own distinctive characteristics. The task of social science is to understand this cultural diversity, which is best done by avoiding value judgments.

What Is Culture?

Culture consists of the values the members of a given group hold, the languages they speak, the symbols they revere, the norms they follow, and the material goods they create, from tools to clothing. Some elements of culture, especially the beliefs and expectations people have about each other and the world they inhabit, are a component of all social relations. **Values** are abstract ideals. For example, monogamy—being faithful to a single marriage partner—is a prominent value in most Western societies. In other cultures, on the other hand, a person may be permitted to have several wives or husbands simultaneously. **Norms** are definite principles or rules people are expected to observe; they represent the dos and don'ts of social life. Norms of behavior in marriage include, for example, how husbands and wives are supposed to behave toward their in-laws. In some societies, they are expected to develop a close relationship with parents-in-law; in others, they keep a clear distance from each other.

Norms, like the values they reflect, vary widely across cultures. Among most Americans, for example, one norm calls for direct eye contact between persons engaged in conversation; completely averting one's eyes is usually interpreted as a sign of weakness or rudeness. Yet, among the Navajo, a cultural norm calls for averting one's eyes as a sign of respect. Direct eye contact, particularly between strangers, is seen as violating a norm of politeness and consequently as insulting. When a Navajo and a Western tourist encounter one another for the first time, the Navajo's cultural norm calls for averting the eyes, while the tourist's cultural norm calls for direct eye contact. The result is likely to be a misunderstanding: The Navajo may see the tourist as rude and vulgar, while the tourist may see the Navajo as disrespectful or deceptive. Such cultural misunderstandings may lead to unfair generalizations and stereotypes and even promote outright hostility. Values and norms work together to shape how members of a culture behave within their surroundings. For example, in cultures that value learning highly, cultural norms would encourage students to devote great energy to studying and would support parents in making sacrifices for children's education. In a culture that places great value on hospitality, cultural norms might guide expectations about gift giving or about the social behaviors of both guests and hosts.

Finally, **material goods** refer to the physical objects that a society creates, which influence the ways in which people live. They include the goods we consume, from the clothes we wear to the cars we drive to the houses we live in; the tools and technologies we use to make those goods, from sewing machines to computerized factories; and the towns and cities that we build as places in which to live and work. A central aspect of a society's material culture is technology.

Today material culture is rapidly becoming globalized, thanks in large part to modern information technology such as the computer and the Internet. As noted at the beginning of this chapter, the United States has been in the forefront of this technological revolution, although most other industrial countries are rapidly catching up. In fact, it no longer makes sense to speak of an exclusively "U.S. technology" any more than it makes sense to speak of a U.S. car. The "world car," with parts manufactured across the planet in a global assembly line, embodies technology developed in Japan, the United States, and Europe. Automobiles have increasingly come to resemble each other, so that it is difficult to distinguish a car made in Japan from one made in Detroit. Another example of the globalization of material culture is the way classrooms the world over have increasingly come to resemble each other, as have department stores, and the fact that McDonald's restaurants are now found on nearly every continent.

When we use the term *culture* in ordinary daily conversation, we often think of the higher things of the mind—art, literature, music, dance. As sociologists employ it, the concept includes these activities but also far more. Culture refers to the ways of life of the individual members or groups within a society: how they dress, their marriage customs and family life, their patterns of work, their religious ceremonies, and their leisure pursuits. The concept also covers the goods they create and the goods that become meaningful for them—bows and arrows, plows, factories and machines, computers, books, dwellings. We should think of culture as a "design for living" or "tool kit" of practices, knowledge, and symbols acquired—as we shall see later—through learning rather than by instinct (Kluckhohn, 1949; Swidler, 1986).

How might we describe American culture? It involves, first, a particular range of values shared by many, if not all, Americans—such as the belief in the merits of individual achievement or in equality of opportunity. Second, these values are connected to specific norms: For example, it is usually expected that people will work hard in order to achieve occupational success (Parsons, 1964; Bellah et al., 1985). Third, it involves the use of material artifacts created mostly through modern industrial technology, such as cars, mass-produced food, clothing, and so forth.

Values and norms vary enormously across cultures. Some cultures value individualism highly, whereas others place great emphasis on shared needs. A simple example makes this clear. Most pupils in the United States would be outraged to find another student cheating on an examination. In the United States, copying from someone else's paper goes against core values of individual achievement, equality of opportunity, hard work, and respect for the rules. Russian students, however, might be puzzled by this sense of outrage among their American peers. Helping each other to pass an examination reflects the value Russians place on equality and on collective problem solving in the face of authority. Think of your own reaction to this example. What does it say about the values of your society?

Even within one society or community, values may conflict: Some groups or individuals might value traditional religious beliefs, whereas others might favor progress and science. Some people might prefer material comfort and success, whereas others might favor simplicity and a quiet life. In our changing age—filled with the global movement of people, ideas, goods, and information—it is not surprising that we encounter instances of cultural values in conflict. Sociological research suggests that such conflicts foster a sense of frustration and isolation in American society (Bellah et al., 1985).

Social norms change over time. When medical evidence linked smoking with serious health problems, a strong social norm in the United States favoring smoking turned toward a strong antismoking social norm.

Norms, like the values they reflect, also change over time. Between 1964 and 1999, for example, smoking in the United States declined by over one third (National Center for Health Statistics, 2000). Beginning in 1964, with the U.S. Surgeon General's report "Smoking and Health," which reported definitive medical evidence linking smoking with a large number of serious health problems, the U.S. government waged a highly effective campaign to discourage people from smoking. A strong social norm favoring smoking—once associated with independence, sex appeal, and glamour—has increasingly given way to an equally strong antismoking social norm that depicts smoking as unhealthful, unattractive, and selfish. Today, the percentage of American adults who smoke is only 25 percent, half the rate of 1964, when the Surgeon General's Report was issued (U.S. Surgeon General's Office, 2000).

Many norms that people now take for granted in their personal lives—such as premarital sexual relations and unmarried couples' living together—contradict commonly held values even from only several decades ago. The values that guide our intimate relationships have evolved gradually and naturally over a period of many years. But what about instances in which cultural norms and behaviors are altered in a deliberate way?

In January 2000, a Japanese government commission published a report that outlined the main goals for Japan in the twenty-first century. In the face of economic recession, rising crime rates, and high unemployment, the commission was established by the prime minister and given the task of charting a new course for the country in the coming decades. The commission's main findings surprised many people: It found that Japanese citizens need to loosen their hold on some of their core values if their country is to address its current social ills successfully. The commission first concluded that the Japanese culture places too much value on conformity and equality and then called for action to reduce the excessive degree of homogeneity and uniformity in society. The commission pointed to some basic facets of Japanese life that reflect this conformity: For example, almost all schoolchildren in Japan wear identical dark-blue uniforms that mask signs of individuality, and employees generally stay late at the office even if they don't need to because of an unspoken rule that proscribes leaving early. These values, the commission concluded, were preventing Japanese people from embracing notions of individual achievement that would be essential in the coming years. Cultural norms and values are deeply embedded, and it is too early to say whether a government mandate will succeed in altering traditional Japanese values. Yet a common Japanese expression—"the nail that sticks up must be hammered down"—suggests that it may take some time and effort before the Japanese cultural values of conformity and self-effacement are weakened.

The uniforms worn by these Tokyo schoolboys reflect the traditional Japanese value of conformity. A government commission proposed that holding on to such traditional values would prevent the Japanese people from aiming for the individual goals they believe will be necessary for success in the twenty-first century.

Many of our everyday behaviors and habits are grounded in cultural norms. As we shall see in Chapter 5, movements, gestures, and expressions are strongly influenced by cultural factors. A clear example of this can be seen in the way people smile—particularly in public contexts—across different cultures.

Among the Inuit (Eskimos) of Greenland, for example, one does not find the strong tradition of public smiling that exists in many areas of Western Europe and North America. This does not mean that the Inuit are cold or unfriendly; it is simply not their common practice to smile at or exchange pleasantries with strangers. As the service industry has expanded in Greenland in recent years, however, some employers have made efforts to instill smiling as a cultural value in the belief that smiling and expressing "polite" attitudes toward customers are essential to competitive business practices. Clients who are met with smiles and told to "Have a nice day" are more likely to become repeat customers. In many supermarkets in Greenland, shop assistants are now shown training videos on friendly service techniques; the staff at some have even been sent abroad on training courses. The opening of fast-food restaurants like McDonald's in Greenland has introduced Western-style service approaches for the first time. McDonald's employees have been taught to greet customers, introduce themselves, and smile frequently. Initially these requirements were met with some discomfort by staff who found the style insincere and artificial. Over time, however, the idea of public smiling—at least in the workplace—has become more accepted.

Culture and Society

"Culture" can be distinguished from "society," but these notions are closely connected. A **society** is a *system of interrelationships* that connects individuals together. No culture could exist without a society; and, equally, no society could exist without culture. Without culture, we would not be human at all, in the sense in which we usually understand that term. We would have no language in which to express ourselves, no sense of self-consciousness, and our ability to think or reason would be severely limited.

Culture also serves as a society's glue, because culture is an important source of conformity, since it provides ready-made ways of thinking and acting for its members. For example, when you say that you subscribe to a particular value, such as formal learning, you are probably voicing the beliefs of your family members, friends, teachers, or others who are significant in your life. When you choose a word to describe some personal experience, that word acquires its meaning in a language you learned from others. When you buy a seemingly

unique article of clothing to express your individuality, that garment was very likely created by the design department of a global manufacturer that carefully studied the current tastes of consumers and then ordered the mass production of your "unique" garment. When you listen to music, it is most likely the same kind of music that your friends listen to.

Cultures differ, however, in how much they value conformity. Research based on surveys of more than one hundred thousand adults in over sixty countries shows that Japanese culture lies at one extreme in terms of valuing conformity (Hofstede, 1997), while at the other extreme lies American culture, one of the least conformist, ranking among the world's highest in cherishing individualism. Americans pride themselves on their independence of spirit, represented by the lone bald eagle, the U.S. national symbol. The assertion "that government is best which governs least" and Hollywood's version of the maverick lawman reinforce as positive the image of the person standing alone, revered and emulated for his independence and individuality.

American high school and college students often see themselves as especially nonconformist. Like the body piercers of today, the hippies of the 1960s and the punks of the 1980s all sported distinctive clothing styles, haircuts, and other forms of bodily adornment. Yet how individualistic are they? Are young people with dyed hair or nose rings or studs in their tongues or tattoos really acting independently? Or are their

Members of a 1960s commune pose together for a group portrait (left). Punks gather on the street in 1989 (right). Though their distinctive styles set them apart from mainstream society, these people are not as nonconformist as they may think they are. Both the hippies and the punks pictured above conform to the norms of their respective social groups.

The Amish and Cell Phones

[***]

Amish settlements have become a cliché for refusing technology. Tens of thousands of people wear identical, plain, homemade clothing, cultivate their rich fields with horse-drawn machinery, and live in houses lacking that basic modern spirit called electricity. But the Amish do use such 20th-century consumer technologies as disposable diapers, in-line skates, and gas barbecue grills. Some might call this combination paradoxical, even contradictory. But it could also be called sophisticated, because the Amish have an elaborate system by which they evaluate the tools they use; their tentative, at times reluctant use of technology is more complex than a simple rejection or a whole-hearted embrace. What if modern Americans could possibly agree upon criteria for acceptance, as the Amish have? Might we find better ways to wield technological power, other than simply unleashing it and seeing what happens? What can we learn from a culture that habitually negotiates the rules for new tools?

Last summer, armed with these questions and in the company of an acquaintance with Amish contacts, I traveled around the countryside of Lancaster County, Pennsylvania. [***] At one farm we passed, a woman was sitting a hundred yards from her house on the edge of a kitchen garden. She wore the traditional garb of the conservative Old Order—a long, unadorned dress sheathed by an apron, her hair covered by a prayer bonnet. She was sitting in the middle of the garden, alone, the very image of technology-free simplicity. But she was holding her hand up to her ear. She appeared to be intent on something, strangely engaged.

"Whenever you see an Amish woman sitting in the field like that," my guide said, "she's probably talking on a cell phone."

"It's a controversy in the making," he continued. A rather large one, it turns out—yet part of the continuum of determining whether a particular technology belongs in Amish life. They've adopted horses, kerosene lamps, and propane refrigerators; should they add cell phones?

Collective negotiations over the use of telephones have ignited intense controversies in the Amish community since the beginning of the 20th century. In fact, a dispute over the role of the phone was the principal issue behind the 1920s division of the Amish church, wherein one-fifth of the membership broke away to form their own church.

Eventually, certain Amish communities accepted the telephone for its aid in summoning doctors and veterinarians, and in calling suppliers. But even these Amish did not allow the telephone into the home. Rather, they required that phones be used communally. Typically, a neighborhood of two or three extended families shares a telephone housed in a wooden shanty, located either at the intersection of several fields or at the end of a common lane. These structures look like small bus shelters or privies; indeed, some phones are in outhouses. Sometimes the telephone shanties have answering machines in them. (After all, who wants to wait in the privy on the off chance someone will call?)

The first Amish person I contacted, I reached by answering machine. He was a woodworker who, unlike some of his brethren, occasionally talked to outsiders. I left a message on his phone, which I later learned was located in a shanty in his neighbor's pasture. The next day the man, whom I'll call Amos, returned my call. We agreed to meet at his farmstead a few days later.

I couldn't help thinking it was awfully complicated to have a phone you used only for calling back—from a booth in a meadow. Why not make life easier and just put one in the house?

"What would that lead to?" another Amish man asked me. "We don't want to be the kind of people who will interrupt a conversation at home to answer a telephone. It's not just how you use the technology that concerns us. We're also concerned about what kind of person you become when you use it."

[***]

I asked another Amish workshop owner whom I'll call Caleb what he thought about technology. He pulled some papers out of a file cabinet, handed them to me, and said, "I share some of this fellow's opinions," pointing to a magazine interview with virtual reality pioneer Jaron Lanier. Asked for an opinion he shared with the dreadlocked-and-dashikied Jaron, he replied, "I agree with his statement that you can't design foolproof machines, because fools are so clever."

Caleb also discussed the Amish resistance to becoming "modern." They're not worried about becoming people without religion or people who use lots of technology, he explained; rather, the Amish fear assimilating the far more dangerous ideas that "progress" and new technologies are usually beneficial, that individuality is a precious value, that the goal of life is to "get ahead." This mind-set, not specific technologies, is what the Amish most object to.

"The thing I noticed about the telephone is the way it invades who you are," Caleb said. "We're all losing who we are because of the telephone and other machines—not just the Amish."

[***]

Donald Kraybill, who is also provost of Messiah College, on the outskirts of Amish country, believes taboos about telephones are "a symbolic way of keeping the technology at a distance and making it your servant, rather than the other way around."

[***]

It's a pretty safe prediction that when the bishops get around to their formal ruling, cell phones will not be deemed appropriate for personal use. In the 1910s, when the telephone was only begin-

ning to change the world at large, the Old Order Amish recognized that the caller at the other end of the line was an interloper, someone who presumed to take precedence over the family's normal, sacred communications. Keeping the telephone in an unheated shanty in a field, or even an outhouse, was keeping the phone in its proper place.

[***] I appreciate the deliberation put into their decision. In fact, similar reflection might highlight conflicts between our own practices and values. How often do we interrupt a conversation with someone who is physically present in order to answer the telephone? Is the family meal enhanced by a beeper? Who exactly is benefiting from call waiting? Is automated voicemail a dark hint about the way our institutions value human time and life? Can pagers and cell phones that vibrate instead of ring solve the problem? Does the enjoyment of virtual communities by growing numbers of people enhance or erode citizen participation in the civic life of geographic communities?

[***]

I never expected the Amish to provide precise philosophical yardsticks that could guide the use of technological power. What drew me in was their long conversation with their tools. We technology-enmeshed "English" don't have much of this sort of discussion. And yet we'll need many such conversations, because a modern heterogeneous society is going to have different values, different trade-offs, and different discourses. It's time we start talking about the most important influence on our lives today.

I came away from my journey with a question to contribute to these conversations: If we decided that community came first, how would we use our tools differently?

SOURCE: Howard Rheingold, "Look Who's Talking," *Wired* 7.01 (Jan. 1999).

Questions

- Do you think cell phones have drastically changed life in Amish communities?
- Why do the Amish believe that telephones change the people that use them?
- How could the use of cellular technology make people more isolated?

styles perhaps as much the "uniforms" of their group as are navy blue suits or basic black among conservative business people? There is an aspect of conformity to their behavior—conformity to their own group.

Since some degree of conformity to norms is necessary for any society to exist, one of the key challenges for all cultures is to instill in people a willingness to conform. This is accomplished in two ways (Parsons, 1964). First, members of all cultures learn the norms of their culture. While this occurs throughout one's life, the most crucial learning occurs during childhood, and parents play a key role. When learning is successful, the norms are so thoroughly ingrained that they become unquestioned ways of thinking and acting; they come to appear "normal." (Note the similarity between the words *norm* and *normal*.) Chapter 4 covers the important topic of learning social norms, also known as "socialization."

When the learning of social norms falls short of what is deemed desirable by a society—that is, when a person fails to adequately conform to a culture's norms—a second way of instilling cultural conformity comes into play: *social control*. Social control often involves punishing rule breaking. Punishment includes such informal behavior as rebuking friends for minor breaches of etiquette, gossiping behind their backs, or ostracizing them from the group. Official, formal forms of discipline might range from parking tickets to imprisonment (Foucault, 1979). Émile Durkheim, one of the founders of sociology (introduced in Chapter 1), argued that punishment serves not only to help guarantee conformity among those who would violate a culture's norms and values, but also to vividly remind others what the norms and values are.

Culture and Change: A "Cultural Turn" in Sociology?

Because of the power of culture in our lives, it is easy to assume that culture determines everything about us, that we are so thoroughly shaped by a more or less uniform culture from the day we are born until the day we die that we never escape its influence. In fact, that is how most sociologists thought about culture until recently, if they thought about culture at all (DiMaggio, 1997). Most sociologists simply took for granted the importance of culture, without stopping to study seriously how culture works in daily life.

Today, a growing number of sociologists are studying culture, once primarily the domain of anthropologists. The phrase **cultural turn** is often used to describe sociology's recent emphasis on the importance of understanding the role of culture in daily life. One result has been to challenge the assumption that culture blindly determines our values and

behaviors. Instead, the sociologist Ann Swidler (1986) has characterized culture as a "tool kit," from which people can select different understandings and behaviors, enabling them to choose among different courses of action rather than constraining them to conform to a single one. Thus, some people can choose to dye their hair and wear nose rings and adorn their bodies with tattoos but still accept their parents' traditional ideas about sexual restraint. Since people participate in many different (and often conflicting) cultures, the "tool kit" can be quite large and its contents varied (Bourdieu, 1990; Sewell, 1992; Tilly, 1992).

Our cultural "tool kits" include a variety of "scripts" that we can draw on to shape our beliefs, values, and actions. Like the written script of a stage play, cultural scripts help to determine our actions as well as our words. As actors in real life, however, we are not bound by a single script, but are able to choose the scripts we want to follow, as well as improvise along the way. The more appropriate the script to a particular set of circumstances, the more likely we will be to follow it—and recall events that conform to it long after they have occurred (D'Andrade, 1995; DiMaggio, 1997). For example, imagine that you are a woman walking alone in an unfamiliar city late at night and suddenly encounter a male stranger who begins to cross the street, stating as he approaches, "Excuse me, but may I ask you a question?" Your choice of cultural script will shape how you respond to this situation. A popular cultural script, honed by film and television entertainment, reality TV, and politicians, is to fear such encounters, especially if you are female (Glassner, 1999). As a result, instead of hearing him out, you quickly turn and head for the safety of a nearby all-night restaurant. Later, when retelling the story, you might recall the stranger as taller and more dangerous than he was—perhaps even that he was brandishing a weapon—traits consistent with American cultural scripts about such encounters.

On the other hand, imagine that you are the male in this brief encounter—perhaps an out-of-town businessman trying to find your hotel in an unfamiliar neighborhood. You see a woman walking on the other side of the street, and as you cross to ask directions, she immediately turns and disappears into a restaurant. Your experience of this encounter would be very different from that of the woman: You are concerned about the late hour, worried about being lost, and stunned by her sudden actions. Perhaps when you return home you will describe this event as evidence that people in this city are cold and indifferent to strangers, if not downright unfriendly.

The "cultural turn" calls on sociologists to examine the many meanings of such behavior in order to better understand the ways people interpret their social worlds and thereby choose appropriate courses of action. In studying this case, sociologists would go beyond merely reporting the circumstances of the late-night encounter. Instead, they would attempt to understand the different cultural scripts each person was following and why he or she might have chosen those scripts. How did physical appearance influence their different experiences? What words, if any, were spoken, and what meanings did they convey? What did the two people's "body language" communicate? Sociologists would also be interested in examining alternating scripts that might have been available and how these scripts could have altered the experience of each participant. For example, the woman might have chosen the script of "good Samaritan," viewing the approaching stranger as potentially in need of assistance and thereby offering to lend a helping hand. Or the stranger might have recognized that a lone woman might feel threatened by the situation and instead chosen a less confrontational, more empathetic script—perhaps remaining on his side of the street and beginning his sentence with a soft-spoken, "Excuse me, can you please tell me the way to my hotel? I seem to be lost."

The "cultural turn" in sociology reveals that there is no single "reality" to social encounters and that there are multiple cultural scripts that can be applied and followed in any one situation. The challenge of sociology is to seek to understand people's differing "realities," the various scripts that they follow, and the reasons they choose one set of scripts over another (Chaney, 1994; Long, 1997; Seidman, 1997b; Bonnell and Hunt, 1999; Glassner, 1999; Sewell, 1999; Hays, 2000; Smith and West, 2000; Swidler, 2001).

The Development of Human Culture

Human culture and human biology are closely intertwined. Understanding how culture is related to the physical evolution of the human species can help us better understand the central role that culture plays in shaping our lives.

Early Human Culture: Adaptation to Physical Environment

Given the archaeological evidence, as well as knowledge of the close similarities in blood chemistry and genetics between chimpanzees and humans, scientists believe that the first humans evolved from apelike creatures on the African continent some 4 million years ago. The first evidence of human-like culture dates back only 2 million years. In these early cultures, early humans fashioned stone tools, derived sustenance by hunting animals and gathering nuts and berries, harnessed the use of fire, and established a highly cooperative way of life. Because early humans planned their hunts, they must also have had some ability for abstract thought.

Culture enabled early humans to compensate for their physical limitations, such as lack of claws, sharp teeth, and running speed, relative to other animals (Deacon, 1998). In particular, culture freed humans from dependence on the instinctual and genetically determined set of responses to the environment characteristic of other species. The larger, more complex human brain permitted a greater degree of adaptive learning in dealing with major environmental changes such as the Ice Age. For example, humans figured out how to build fires and sew clothing for warmth. Through greater flexibility, humans were able to survive unpredictable challenges in their surroundings and shape the world with their ideas and their tools. In a mere instant of geological time, we became the dominant species on the planet.

Yet early humans were closely tied to their physical environment, since they still lacked the technological ability to modify their immediate surroundings significantly (Harris, 1975, 1978, 1980; Bennett, 1976). Their ability to secure food and make clothing and shelter depended largely on the physical resources that were close at hand. Cultures in different environments varied widely as a result of adaptations by which people fashioned their cultures to be suitable to specific geographic and climatic conditions. For example, the cultures developed by desert dwellers, where water and food were scarce, differed significantly from the cultures that developed in rain forests, where such natural resources abounded. Similarly, people who lived in the frozen Arctic created cultures that varied greatly from those that evolved in more temperate climates. Human inventiveness spawned a rich tapestry of cultures around the world. As you will see at the conclusion of this chapter, however, modern technology and other forces of globalization pose both challenges and opportunities for future global cultural diversity.

Nature or Nurture?

Because humans evolved as a part of the world of nature, it would seem logical to assume that human thinking and behavior are the result of biology and evolution. In fact, one of the oldest controversies in the social sciences is the "nature/nurture" debate: Are we shaped by our biology, or are we products of learning through life's experiences, that is, of "nurture"? Biologists and some psychologists emphasize biological factors in explaining human thinking and behavior. Sociologists, not surprisingly, stress the role of learning and culture. They are also likely to argue that since human beings are capable of making conscious choices, neither biology nor culture wholly determines human behavior.

Decoding the New Cues in Online Society

A sociologist among geeks and a geek among sociologists, Danah Boyd has 278 friends who link her to 1.1 million others.

So says Friendster.com, whose millions of members have transformed it from a dating site into a free-for-all of connectedness where new social rules are born of necessity. A 25-year-old graduate student at the University of California at Berkeley, Ms. Boyd studies Friendster, hovering above the fray with a Web log called Connected Selves (www.zephoria.org/snt) and interviewing Friendster users. Her irrepressible observations have made her a social-network guru for the programmers and venture capitalists who swarm around Friendster and its competitors.

[***]

Ms. Boyd explained Friendster this way: "It allows you to purposely say who the people in your world are and to allow them to see each other, through a connection of you." An individual registered at Friendster has a home page with photos, a brief profile and photos of people to whom they have agreed to link. That person can then browse his or her network or search it for dates or activity partners.

Ms. Boyd says that the real world has a set of properties, which she calls architectures. With its deceptively simple set of features, her thinking goes, Friendster bends or replaces all of the real-world architectures.

For instance, when two people speak to each other, they assume their conversation is fleeting, but e-mail and instant messaging, by making that conversation persistent, offer a new architecture. When two people greet each other on the street, neither can see (nor hope to grasp) the range of the other's social network. For that matter, no individual can see information about his or her own social network: who knows whom, and how.

[***] The basic idea behind Friendster and other social networking sites is not new. Neither is the technology, which is based on a business process patent from a 1997 site called SixDegrees.com that failed because too few people were online at the time.

[***]

Ms. Boyd has found the site populated by a variety of subcultures: a large contingent of gay men from New York City, the Bay Area's Burning Man scene, ravers in Baltimore. Porn queens and venture capitalists share the site with neo-Nazis

and garden-variety hipsters. Most users are in their 20s and 30s. Many are overseas, particularly in Asia.

Bringing all those worlds together is not without its perils. "What social software like Friendster does is collapse our networks in ways we're not used to," Ms. Boyd said.

Devon Lake, 25, a high school teacher, discovered that this fall when she was bombarded with requests from former students to accept them into her Friendster circle, which she uses to keep in touch with her friends from Burning Man, the annual primal gathering in the Nevada desert. The potential costs of putting one part of her network in contact with the other part were too high, so she rebuffed her students and cleaned up her profile by removing anything that could be interpreted as a reference to drugs. "I'm a young teacher, so drawing that line is already a careful balancing act," Ms. Lake said. "It made me feel on my guard about what I posted to the site."

[***]

A lively speaker sometimes inclined to pink hair, Ms. Boyd is part of a cohort of young scholars who are trying to come up with ways to describe these new social behaviors in the online environments in which they have grown up. She and her peers "are talking about this from an inside, embedded perspective," said Genevieve Bell, an anthropologist at Intel Research who was a co-director of Ms. Boyd's master's thesis at M.I.T. "One of the challenges for them is, how do they analyze this thing they have grown up inside of?"

Ms. Boyd grew in up in Lancaster, Pa., and was introduced to far-flung virtual communities in the early 1990s by her younger brother. Soon afterward, their mother wisely signed up for two Compuserve accounts. "It gave me an opportunity to talk to people who were far more like me than anybody I knew in real life," Ms. Boyd said.

She said she comes to her research through experiences as a perpetual outsider. "I didn't grow up in an elite community," she said. "I was the daughter of a single mother. I grew up queer in a rural environment. I grew up as a woman in computer science. I grew up constantly negotiating these spaces where they didn't exactly welcome me with open arms."

After studying computer science as an undergraduate at Brown, she turned to the social side of things at M.I.T., studying at the Media Lab and producing a project that visualized people's e-mail networks.

Taking a year off from school, Ms. Boyd found herself in the Bay Area, hanging out with many of the people who were developing Friendster and other social-network sites. She began a blog to document what she saw; her critiques became useful; people began asking her—and hiring her—to do more.

The chief executive of one social-networking site, tribe.net, Mark Pincus, has sought her advice because she is involved in some of the groups to which his site tries to appeal. "Danah's this researcher, but she also lives the whole thing—the Burning Man scene, the rave scene, the techno music scene," he said.

Her academic supervisors are envious of her advantage. "I look at cyberspace the way a deep-sea diver looks at the sea: through a glass plate," said Ms. Boyd's academic adviser, Peter Lyman, a professor at Berkeley's School of Information Management and Systems. "She is out there swimming in it."

[***]

SOURCE: Michael Erard, "Decoding the New Cues in Online Society," *New York Times,* 27 November, 2003.

The "nature/nurture" debate has raged for more than a century, opinion swinging first one way and then the other. For example, in the 1930s and 1940s, many social scientists tended to focus on biological factors, with some researchers seeking (unsuccessfully), for example, to prove that a person's physique determined his or her personality. In the 1960s and 1970s, scholars in different fields emphasized culture. For example, social psychologists argued that even the most severe forms of mental illness were the result of the labels that society attaches to unusual behavior rather than of biochemical processes (Scheff, 1966). Today, partly because of new understandings in genetics and brain neurophysiology, the pendulum is again swinging toward the side of biology.

The resurgence of biological explanations for human behavior began more than twenty-five years ago, when the evolutionary biologist Edward O. Wilson of Harvard University published *Sociobiology: The New Synthesis* (1975). The term **sociobiology** refers to the application of biological principles to explain the social activities of animals, including human beings. Using studies of insects and other social creatures, Wilson argued that genes influence not only physical traits, but behavior as well. For instance, some species of animals engage in elaborate courtship rituals, whereby sexual union and reproduction are achieved. Human courtship and sexual behavior, according to sociobiologists, generally involve similar rituals, based also on inborn characteristics. In most species, to take a second example, males are larger and more aggressive than females and tend to dominate the "weaker sex." Some suggest that genetic factors explain why, in all human societies that we know of, men tend to hold positions of greater authority than women.

One way in which sociobiologists have tried to illuminate the relations between the sexes is by means of the idea of "reproductive strategy." A reproductive strategy is a pattern of behavior, arrived at through evolutionary selection, that favors the chances of survival of offspring. The female body has a larger investment in its reproductive cells than the male—a fertilized egg takes nine months to develop. Thus, according to sociobiologists, women will not squander that investment and are not driven to have sexual relations with many partners; their overriding aim is the care and protection of children. Men, on the other hand, tend toward promiscuity. Their wish to have sex with many partners is sound strategy from the point of view of the species; to carry out their mission, which is to maximize the possibility of impregnation, they move from one partner to the next. In this way, it has been suggested, we can explain differences in sexual behavior and attitudes between men and women.

Sociobiologists do not argue that our genes determine 100 percent of our behavior. For example, they note that depending on the circumstances, men can choose to act in nonaggressive ways. Yet even though this argument would seem to open up the field of sociobiology to culture as an additional explanatory factor in describing human behavior, social scientists have roundly condemned sociobiology for claiming that a propensity for particular behaviors such as violence, is somehow "genetically programmed" into our brains ("Seville Statement on Violence," 1990).

How Nature and Nurture Interact

Most sociologists today would acknowledge a role for nature in determining attitudes and behavior, but with strong qualifications. For example, no one questions that newborn babies come into the world with certain basic human reflexes, such as the automatic ability to "root" for the mother's nipple without being taught to do so. There is also evidence that babies are born with the ability to recognize faces: Babies a few minutes old turn their heads in response to patterns that resemble human faces but not in response to other patterns (Johnson and Morton, 1991; Cosmides and Tooby, 1997). But it is a large leap to conclude that because babies are born with basic reflexes, the behavior of adults is governed by **instincts,** inborn, biologically fixed patterns of action found in all cultures.

Sociologists no longer pose the question as one of nature *or* nurture. Instead they ask how nature and nurture interact to produce human behavior. But their main concern is with how our different ways of thinking and acting are learned in interactions with family, friends, schools, television, and every other facet of the social environment. For example, sociologists argue that it's not some inborn biological disposition that makes American males feel attracted to a *particular* type of woman. Rather, it is the exposure they've had throughout their lives to tens of thousands of magazine ads, TV commercials, and film stars that emphasize specific cultural standards of female beauty. Any American male who is at all uncertain about just what constitutes an "attractive" woman need only reach into his "cultural tool kit" and pull out the latest *Sports Illustrated* swimsuit issue for an answer.

Early child rearing is especially relevant to this kind of learning. Human babies have a large brain, requiring birth relatively early in their fetal development, before their heads have grown too large to pass through the birth canal. As a result, human babies are totally unequipped for survival on their own, compared with the young of other species, and must spend a number of years in the care of adults. This need, in turn, fosters a lengthy period of learning, during which the child is taught its society's culture.

Because humans think and act in so many different ways, sociologists do not believe that "biology is destiny." If biology were all-important, we would expect all cultures to be highly similar, if not identical. Yet this is hardly the case. For example, pork is forbidden to religious Jews and Muslims, but it is a dietary staple in China. Americans are likely to greet one another with a casual "How are you?" On the other hand, the Yanomamö, a tribe that lives in the rain forests of Venezuela and Brazil, greet each other with an exchange of gifts and would find the casual American greeting an insult.

This is not to say that human cultures have nothing in common. Surveys of thousands of different cultures have concluded that all known human cultures have such common characteristics as language, forms of emotional expression, rules that tell adults how to raise children or engage in sexual behavior, and even standards of beauty (Brown, 1991). But there is enormous variety in exactly *how* these common characteristics play themselves out.

All cultures provide for childhood socialization, but what and how children are taught vary greatly from culture to culture. An American child learns the multiplication tables from a classroom teacher, while a child born in the forests of Borneo learns to hunt with older members of the tribe. All cultures have standards of beauty and ornamentation, but what is regarded as beautiful in one culture may be seen as ugly in another (Elias, 1987; Elias and Dunning, 1987; Foucault, 1988). The half-starved body of a typical *Vogue* model or the bulked-up body of a weight lifter would be regarded as grossly unattractive to the Borneo forest dweller.

Cultural Diversity

The study of cultural differences highlights the importance of cultural learning as an influence on our behavior. However, not only cultural beliefs vary across cultures; human behavior and practices also vary widely from culture to culture and often contrast radically with what people from Western societies consider "normal." For example, in the modern West, we regard the deliberate killing of infants or young children as one of the worst of all crimes. Yet in traditional Chinese culture, female children were sometimes strangled at birth because a daughter was regarded as a liability rather than an asset to the family. In the West, we eat oysters but we do not eat kittens or puppies, both of which are regarded as delicacies in some parts of the world. Jews and Muslims don't eat pork, whereas Hindus eat pork but avoid beef. Westerners regard kissing as a normal part of sexual behavior, but in other cultures the practice is either unknown or regarded as disgusting. All these different kinds of behavior are aspects of broad cultural differences that distinguish societies from one another.

SUBCULTURES

Small societies tend to be culturally uniform, but industrialized societies are themselves culturally diverse or multicultural, involving numerous different **subcultures.** As you will discover in the discussion of global migration in Chapter 11, processes such as slavery, colonialism, war, migration, and contemporary globalization have led to populations dispersing across borders and settling in new areas. This, in turn, has led to the emergence of societies that are cultural composites, meaning that the population is made up of a number of groups from diverse cultural and linguistic backgrounds. In modern cities, for example, many subcultural communities live side by side. For example, over ninety different cultural groups can be found in New York City today.

Subcultures do not refer only to people from different cultural backgrounds, or who speak different languages, within a larger society. They concern any segments of the population that are distinguishable from the rest of society by their cultural patterns. Subcultures are very broad in scope and might include Goths, computer hackers, hippies, Rastafarians, and fans of hip-hop. Some people might identify themselves clearly with a particular subculture, whereas others might move fluidly among a number of different ones.

Culture plays an important role in perpetuating the values and norms of a society, yet it also offers important opportunities for creativity and change. Subcultures and countercultures—groups that largely reject the prevailing values and norms of society—can promote views that represent alternatives to the dominant culture. Social movements or groups of people sharing common lifestyles are powerful forces of change within societies. In this way, subcultures allow freedom for people to express and act on their opinions, hopes, and beliefs.

U.S. schoolchildren are frequently taught that the United States is a vast melting pot, into which various subcultures are assimilated. **Assimilation** is the process by which different cultures are absorbed into a single mainstream culture. Although it is true that virtually all peoples living in the United States take on many common cultural characteristics, many groups strive to retain some subcultural identity. In fact, identification based on race or country of origin in the United States persists and even grows, particularly among African Americans and immigrants from Asia, Mexico, and Latin America (Totti, 1987).

Given the immense cultural diversity and number of subcultures in the United States, a more appropriate metaphor than the assimilationist "melting pot" might be the culturally diverse "salad bowl," in which all the various ingredients, though mixed together, retain some of their original flavor and integrity, contributing to the richness of the salad as a whole. This viewpoint, termed **multiculturalism,** calls for respecting cultural diversity and promoting equality of different cultures. Adherents to multiculturalism acknowledge that certain central cultural values are shared by most people in a society but also that certain important differences deserve to be preserved (Anzaldua, 1990).

Young people also have their own subcultures in many modern industrial nations. Examples of youth subcultures can be found in college dorms or neighborhoods near major universities, with pop music blaring from seemingly every window late into the night. Youth subcultures typically revolve around particular musical preferences (for example, hip-hop, techno, heavy metal, reggae) and somewhat distinctive style of dress, language (especially slang), and behavior. Like all subcultures, however, they still accept most of the norms and values of the dominant culture.

Consider the patchwork that is hip-hop. Although it emerged as a subculture in the Bronx, New York, in the mid-1970s, hip-hop owes much of its original identity to Jamaica. The first important hip-hop DJ, Kool Herc, was a Jamaican immigrant, and rapping, or rhythmic talk, derives from the Jamaican disc jockey tradition of "toasting": chanting stories into microphones over records. From these origins, hip-hop gradually spread across the world. Its story is a contemporary lesson in the fluidity of contemporary cultural identity. The music is built around beats often taken from other records. But in "sampling" from recordings, hip-hop artists often do something considerably more significant. They and their fans sample identities, taking on the characteristics of subcultures that can be considerably foreign to them.

The origins of hip-hop culture can be traced back to DJ Kool Herc, who brought the Jamaican disc jockey tradition of "toasting" to New York in the mid-1970s.

Hip-hop's reach has widened over time. Rappers from Queens and Long Island—like Run-D.M.C., LL Cool J, and Public Enemy—recorded some of the first great hip-hop albums. By the end of the 1980s, the music had a national presence in the United States, as Los Angeles artists like N.W.A. and Ice-T developed gangsta rap, which soon had outposts in Oakland, New Orleans, Houston, and elsewhere. White rappers like Kid Rock and Eminem, belatedly following in the footsteps of the Beastie Boys, pioneered a rap-rock synthesis, and a Filipino-American crew known as the Invisible Skratch Piklz revolutionized turntable techniques. Hip-hop became a global form, with British trip-hop artists like Tricky, French rappers like MC Solaar, and record spinners like Japan's DJ Krush.

The sampled beats of hip-hop can contain nearly anything. In "I'll Be Missing You," for example, Puff Daddy (Sean "Puffy" Combs), a master at finding unlikely sources of inspiration, liberally drew from the middle-of-the-road, Top 40 Police song "Every Breath You Take" to mourn the slain rapper Notorious B.I.G. The secret is transformation: A portion of an earlier song, recast to fit a new context, can take on an entirely different meaning while still retaining just enough of its former essence to create a complicated and richly meaningful finished product. In many ways, hip-hop is a music of echoes: rappers revisiting the funk music and "blaxploitation" films of the 1970s (black action movies, often criticized for glorifying violence and presenting blacks in negative stereotypes); suburban fans romanticizing inner-city "street" styles.

These borrowings have often proved controversial. The militant politics of Public Enemy, for example, were in many ways "sampled" from the Black Panther revolutionaries of the 1960s. The outrage stirred by Eminem's offensive language about women and gay people owes much to the fact that this rapper is white and blond, and raps in a style that is easy to follow for those unfamiliar with street slang. Hip-hop is the soundtrack to an emerging global culture that treats the looks, sounds, and byways of particular subcultures, or particular moments in time, as raw material for the creation of new styles.

What does hip-hop tell us about cultural diversity? On the one hand, its history of incorporating an ever-wider circle of influences and participants demonstrates that what is "normal" in one community can quickly be adopted and become "normal" in another community far away, through the dissemination of ideas and styles and so on through records and other forms of media. On the other hand, the controversies that hip-hop has generated suggest that these cultural crossings are marked by a great deal of uncertainty, misperception, and fear. Finally, hip-hop's evolution suggests that even in a global culture, subcultural distinctions retain an important aura of authenticity. Even today, hip-hop remains stamped with the mark of its origins in social realities that most Americans would prefer not to contemplate.

Eminem represents one aspect of the widening appeal of hip-hop across cultural lines, arguably for better and for worse.

Subcultures also take shape around different types of work often associated with unique cultural features. Long-distance truckers, coal miners, Wall Street stockbrokers, computer programmers, professional athletes, corporate lawyers, and artists, for example, form subcultures that differ by the degree of importance they attach to such values as physical strength, bravery, shrewdness, speed, knowledge, material wealth, and creativity. However, they seldom stray far from the dominant culture. For example, even professional thieves who make their living engaging in such illegal activities as robbing banks, burglarizing grocery stores, or passing bad checks, share most of the values of U.S. society. Professional thieves often marry and raise children. Like most Americans, they want to "make it" by accumulating wealth, power, and prestige. They eat with knives and forks, drive on the right side of the road, and try to avoid trouble as much as possible. Indeed, the subculture of thieves comprises people who believe in *almost* all of the values and norms of U.S. society (Chambliss, 1988).

CULTURAL IDENTITY AND ETHNOCENTRISM

Every culture displays its own unique patterns of behavior, which seem alien to people from other cultural backgrounds. If you have traveled abroad, you are probably familiar with the sensation that can result when you find yourself in a new culture. Aspects of daily life that you unconsciously take for granted in your own culture may not be part of everyday life in other parts of the world. Even in countries that share the same language, you might find their everyday habits, customs, and behaviors to be quite different. The expression "culture shock" is an apt one! Often people feel disoriented when they become immersed in a new culture. This is because they have lost the familiar reference points that help them understand the world around them and have not yet learned how to navigate in the new culture.

As an example of the uniqueness of each culture's patterns of behavior, we can take the Nacirema, a group described by Horace Miner. Miner concentrated his attention on the strange and exotic body rituals in which the Nacirema engage. His discussion is worth quoting at length:

The fundamental belief underlying the whole system appears to be that the human body is ugly and that its natural tendency is to debility and disease. Incarcerated in such a body, man's only hope is to avert these characteristics through the use of the powerful influences of ritual and ceremony. Every household has one or more shrines devoted to this purpose. . . . The focal point of the shrine is a box or chest which is built into the wall. In the chest are kept the many charms and magical potions without which no native believes he could live. These preparations are secured from a variety of specialized practitioners. The most powerful of these are the medicine men, whose assistance must be rewarded with substantial gifts. However, the medicine men do not provide the curative potions for their clients, but decide what the ingredients should be and then write them down in an ancient and secret language. This writing is understood only by the medicine man and by the herbalists who, for another gift, provide the required charm. . . .

The Nacirema have an almost pathological horror of and fascination with the mouth, the condition of which is believed to have a supernatural influence on all social relationships. Were it not for the rituals of the mouth, they believe that their teeth would fall out, their gums bleed, their jaws shrink, their friends desert them, and their lovers reject them. They also believe that a strong relationship exists between oral and moral characteristics. For example, there is a ritual ablution of the mouth for children which is supposed to improve their moral fibre.

The daily body ritual performed by everyone includes a mouth-rite. Despite the fact that these people are so punctilious about care of the mouth, this rite involves a practice which strikes the uninitiated stranger as revolting. . . . [T]he ritual consists of inserting a small

Reggae Music

When those knowledgeable about popular music listen to a song, they can often pick out the stylistic influences that helped shape it. Each musical style, after all, represents a unique way of combining rhythm, melody, harmony, and lyrics. And though it doesn't take a genius to notice the differences among grunge, hard rock, techno, and hip-hop, musicians

often combine a number of styles in composing songs. Identifying the components of these combinations can be difficult. But for sociologists of culture, the effort is often rewarding. Different musical styles tend to emerge from different social groups, and studying how styles combine and fuse is a good way to chart the cultural contacts between groups.

Some sociologists of culture have turned their attention to reggae music because it exemplifies the process whereby contacts between social groups result in the creation of new musical forms. Reggae's roots can be traced to West Africa. In the seventeenth century, large numbers of West Africans were enslaved by the British and brought by ship to work in the sugarcane fields of the West Indies. Although the British attempted to prevent slaves from playing traditional African music, for fear it would serve as a rallying cry to revolt, the slaves managed to keep alive the tradition of African drumming, sometimes by integrating it with the European musical styles imposed by the slave owners. In Jamaica, the drumming of one group of slaves, the Burru, was openly tolerated by slaveholders because it helped meter the pace of work.

bundle of hog hairs into the mouth, along with certain magical powders, and then moving the bundle in a highly formalized series of gestures. (1956)

Who are the Nacirema, and in which part of the world do they live? You can answer these questions for yourself, as well as identify the body ritual described, simply by spelling "Nacirema" backward. The Nacirema, in other words, are Americans (and other Westerners), and the ritual described is the brushing of teeth. Almost any familiar activity will seem strange if described out of context. Western cleanliness rituals are no more or less bizarre than the customs of some Pacific groups who knock out their front teeth to beautify themselves, or of certain South American tribal groups who place discs inside their lips to make them protrude, believing that this enhances their attractiveness.

We cannot understand these practices and beliefs separately from the wider cultures of which they are a part. A culture must be studied in terms of its own meanings and values—a key presupposition of sociology. Sociologists endeavor as far as possible to avoid **ethnocentrism,** which is judging other cultures in terms of the standards of one's own. Since human cultures vary so widely, it is not surprising that people belonging to one culture frequently find it difficult to sympathize with the ideas or behavior of those from a different culture. In studying and practicing sociology, we must remove our own cultural blinkers in order to see the ways of life of different peoples in an unbiased light. The practice of judging a society by its own standards is called **cultural relativism.**

Applying cultural relativism—that is, suspending your own deeply held cultural beliefs and examining a situation according to the standards of another culture—can be fraught with uncertainty and challenge. Not only can it be hard to see things from a completely different point of view, but sometimes troubling questions are raised. Does cultural relativism mean that all customs and behavior are equally legitimate? Are there any universal standards to which all humans should adhere? Consider, for example, the

Slavery was finally abolished in Jamaica in 1834, but the tradition of Burru drumming continued, even as many Burru men migrated from rural areas to the slums of Kingston.

It was in these slums that a new religious cult began to emerge—one that would prove crucial for the development of reggae. In 1930, a man who took the title Haile Selassie ("Power of the Trinity") was crowned emperor of the African country of Ethiopia. While opponents of European colonialism throughout the world cheered his accession to the throne, a number of people in the West Indies came to believe that Haile Selassie was a god, sent to earth to lead the oppressed of Africa to freedom. Haile Selassie's original name was Ras Tafari Makonnen, and the West Indians who worshiped him

called themselves "Rastafarians." The Rastafarian cult soon merged with the Burru, and Rastafarian music came to combine Burru styles of drumming with biblical themes of oppression and liberation. In the 1950s, West Indian musicians began mixing Rastafarian rhythms and lyrics with elements of American jazz and black rhythm and blues. These combinations eventually developed into "ska" music, and then, in the late 1960s, into reggae, with its relatively slow beat, its emphasis on the bass, and its stories of urban deprivation and of the power of collective social consciousness. Many reggae artists, such as Bob Marley, became commercial successes, and by the 1970s, people the world over were listening to reggae music. In the 1980s, reggae was first fused with hip-hop (or rap) to produce new sounds, as can be heard today in the dance hall music of the Jamaican rapper Sean Paul.

The history of reggae is thus the history of contact between different social groups and of the meanings—political, spiritual, and personal—that those groups expressed through their music. Globalization has intensified these contacts. It is now possible for a young musician in Scandinavia, for example, to grow up listening to music produced by men and women in the ghettos of Los Angeles and to be deeply influenced as well by, say, a mariachi performance broadcast live via satellite from Mexico City. If the number of contacts between groups is an important determinant of the pace of musical evolution, we can predict that a veritable profusion of new styles will flourish in the coming years as the process of globalization continues to unfold.

ritual acts of what opponents have called "genital mutilation" practiced in some societies. Numerous young girls in certain African, Asian, and Middle Eastern cultures undergo clitoridectomies. This is a painful cultural ritual in which the clitoris and sometimes all or part of the vaginal labia of young girls are removed with a knife or a sharpened stone and the two sides of the vulva are partly sewn together as a means of controlling sexual activity and increasing the sexual pleasure of the man.

In cultures where clitoridectomies have been practiced for generations, they are regarded as normal, even expected practice. A study of two thousand men and women in two Nigerian communities found that nine out of ten women interviewed had undergone clitoridectomies in childhood and that the large majority favored the procedure for their own daughters, primarily for cultural reasons. Yet a significant minority believed that the practice should be stopped (Ebomoyi, 1987). Clitoridectomies are regarded with abhorrence by most people from other cultures and by a growing number of women in

the cultures where they are practiced (El Dareer, 1982; Lightfoot-Klein, 1989; Johnson-Odim, 1991). These differences in views can result in a clash of cultural values, especially when people from cultures where clitoridectomies are common migrate to countries where the practice is actually illegal.

France is an example. France has a large North African immigrant population, in which many African mothers arrange for traditional clitoridectomies to be performed on their daughters. Some of these women have been tried and convicted under French law for mutilating their daughters. These African mothers have argued that they were only engaging in the same cultural practice that their own mothers had performed on them, that their grandmothers had performed on their mothers, and so on. They complain that the French are ethnocentric, judging traditional African rituals by French customs. Feminists from Africa and the Middle East, while themselves strongly opposed to clitoridectomies, have been critical of Europeans and Americans who sensationalize the practice by calling it "backward" or "primitive," without seeking any understanding of the cultural and economic circumstances that sustain it (Accad, 1991; Johnson-Odim, 1991; Mohanty, 1991). In this instance, globalization has led to a fundamental clash of cultural norms and values that has forced members of both cultures to confront some of their most deeply held beliefs. The role of the sociologist is to avoid knee-jerk responses and to examine complex questions carefully from as many different angles as possible.

Cultural Universals

Amid the diversity of human behavior, there are some common features. Where these are found in virtually all societies, they are called **cultural universals.** For example, there is no known culture without a grammatically complex **language.** All cultures possess some recognizable form of family system, in which there are values and norms associated with the care of the children. The institution of **marriage** is a cultural universal, as are religious rituals and property rights. All cultures, also, practice some form of incest prohibition—the banning of sexual relations between close relatives, such as father and daughter, mother and son, or brother and sister. A variety of other cultural universals have been identified by anthropologists, including art, dancing, bodily adornment, games, gift giving, joking, and rules of hygiene.

Yet there are variations within each category. Consider, for example, the prohibition against incest. Most often, incest is regarded as sexual relations between members of the immediate family; but among some peoples, it includes cousins, and in some instances all people bearing the same family name. There have also been societies in which a small proportion of the population have been permitted to engage in incestuous practices. This was the case, for instance, within the ruling class of ancient Egypt, when brothers and sisters were permitted to have sex with each other.

Among the cultural characteristics shared by all societies, two stand out in particular. All cultures incorporate ways of expressing meaning and communication, and all depend on material means of production. In all cultures, *language* is the primary vehicle of meaning and communication. It is not the only such vehicle, however. Material culture itself carries meanings, as we shall show in what follows.

LANGUAGE

Language is one of the best examples for demonstrating both the unity and the diversity of human culture, because there are no cultures without language, yet there are thousands of different languages spoken in the world. Anyone who has visited a foreign country armed with only a dictionary knows how difficult it is either to understand anything or to be understood. Although languages that have similar origins have words in common with one another—as do, for example, German with English—most of the world's major language groups have no words in common at all.

Language is involved in virtually all of our activities. In the form of ordinary talk or speech, it is the means by which we organize most of what we do. (We will discuss the importance of talk and conversation in social life at some length in Chapter 5.) However, language is involved not just in mundane, everyday activities, but also in ceremony, religion, poetry, and many other spheres. One of the most distinctive features of human language is that it allows us to extend vastly the scope of our thought and experience. Using language, we can convey information about events remote in time or space and can discuss things we have never seen. We can develop abstract concepts, tell stories, and make jokes.

In the 1930s, the anthropological linguist Edward Sapir and his student Benjamin Lee Whorf advanced the **linguistic relativity hypothesis,** which argues that the language we use influences our perceptions of the world. That is because we are much more likely to be aware of things in the world if we have words for them (Haugen, 1977; Witkowski and Brown, 1982; Malotki, 1983). Expert skiers or snowboarders, for example, uses terms such as *black ice, corn, powder,* and *packed powder* to describe different snow and ice conditions. Such terms enable them to more readily perceive potentially life-threatening situations that would escape the notice of a novice. In a sense, then, experienced winter athletes have a different perception of the world—or at least, a different perception of the alpine slopes—than do novices.

Language also helps give permanence to a culture and an identity to a people. Language outlives any particular speaker or writer, affording a sense of history and cultural continuity, a feeling of "who we are." In the beginning of this chapter, we argued that the English language is becoming increasingly global in its use, as a primary language of both business and the Internet. One of the central paradoxes of our time is that despite this globalization of the English language, local attachments to language persist, often out of cultural pride. For example, the French-speaking residents of the Canadian province of Quebec are so passionate about their linguistic heritage that they often refuse to speak English, the dominant language of Canada, and periodically seek political independence from the rest of Canada. Minority languages are sometimes even outlawed by the majority government: Turkey restricts the use of the Kurdish language spoken by one of its minority populations, and the "English-only" movement in the United States seeks to restrict the language of education and government to English, even though numerous other languages are spoken throughout the country.

Languages—indeed, all symbols—are representations of reality. The symbols we use may signify things we imagine, such as mathematical formulas or fictitious creatures, or they may represent (that is, "re-present," or make present again in our minds) things initially experienced through our senses. Human behavior is oriented toward the symbols we use to represent "reality," rather than to the reality itself—and these symbols are determined within a particular culture. Since symbols are representations, their cultural meanings must be interpreted when they are used. When you see a four-footed furry animal, for example, you must determine which cultural symbol to attach to it. Do you decide to call it a dog, a wolf, or something else? If you determine it is a dog, what cultural meaning does that convey? In American culture, dogs are typically regarded as household pets and lavished with affection. In Guatemalan Indian culture, on the other hand, dogs are more likely to be seen as watchdogs or scavengers and treated with an indifference that might strike many Americans as bordering on cruelty. Among the Akha of northern Thailand, dogs are seen as food and treated accordingly. The diversity of cultural meanings attached to the word *dog* thus requires an act of interpretation. In this way, human beings are freed, in a sense, from being directly tied to the physical world around us. For example, whereas a cat instinctively recoils when a dog appears, the response of human beings is not so inflexible. Humans, depending on their culture, will have different interpretations, seeing the dog as a neighbor's household pet, a wild dog scrounging for food, or tonight's meal.

SPEECH AND WRITING

All societies use speech as a vehicle of language. However, there are other ways of "carrying," or expressing, language—most notably, writing. The invention of writing marked a major transition in human history. Writing first began as the drawing up of lists. Marks would be made on wood, clay, or stone to keep records about significant events, objects, or people. For example, a mark, or sometimes a picture, might be drawn to represent each tract of land possessed by a particular family or set of families (Gelb, 1952). Writing began as a means of storing information and as such was closely linked to the administrative needs of the early civilizations. A society that possesses writing can locate itself in time and space. Documents can be accumulated that record the past, and information can be gathered about present-day events and activities.

Writing is not just the transfer of speech to paper or some other durable material. It is a phenomenon of interest in its own right. Written documents or *texts* have qualities in some ways quite distinct from the spoken word. The impact of speech is always by definition limited to the particular contexts in which words are uttered. Ideas and experiences can be passed down through generations in cultures without writing, but only if they are regularly repeated and passed on by word of mouth. Texts, on the other hand, can endure for thousands of years, and through them those from past ages can in a certain sense address us directly. This is, of course, why documentary research is so important to historians. Through interpreting the texts that are left behind by past generations, historians can reconstruct what their lives were like.

SEMIOTICS AND MATERIAL CULTURE

The symbols expressed in speech and writing are the chief ways in which cultural meanings are formed and expressed. But they are not the only ways. Both material objects and aspects of behavior can be used to generate meanings. A **signifier** is any vehicle of meaning—any set of elements used to communicate. The sounds made in speech are signifiers, as are the marks made on paper or other materials in writing. Other signifiers, however, include dress, pictures or visual signs, modes of eating, forms of building or architecture, and many other material features of culture (Hawkes, 1977). Styles of dress, for example, normally help signify differences between the sexes. In our culture, at least until relatively recently, women used to wear skirts and men pants. In other cultures, this is reversed: women wear pants and men skirts (Leach, 1976).

Semiotics—the analysis of nonverbal cultural meanings—opens up a fascinating field for both sociology and anthropology. Semiotic analysis can be very useful in comparing one culture with another. Semiotics allows us to contrast the ways in which different cultures are structured by looking at the cultural meanings of symbols. For example, the buildings in

Regensburg Cathedral, built in the Middle Ages, stands at the center of Regensburg, Germany, and towers over the city, symbolizing the central role Christianity played in medieval European life.

Prior to the terrorist attacks of September 11, 2001, the World Trade Center dominated the New York City skyline. Today, the buildings of lower Manhattan's financial district still stand significantly taller than those in other areas of the city. Commerce and business occupy the symbolic center of contemporary American culture.

cities are not simply places in which people live and work. They often have a symbolic character. In traditional cities, the main temple or church was usually placed on high ground in or near the city center. It symbolized the all-powerful influence that religion was supposed to have over the lives of the people. In modern societies, by contrast, the skyscrapers of big business often occupy that symbolic position.

Of course, material culture is not simply symbolic; it is also vital for catering to physical needs—in the tools or technology used to acquire food, make weaponry, construct dwellings, and so forth. We have to study both the practical and the symbolic aspects of material culture in order to understand it completely.

Culture and Social Development

Cultural traits are closely related to overall patterns in the development of society. The level of material culture reached in a given society influences, although by no means completely determines, other aspects of cultural development. This is easy to see, for example, in the level of technology. Many aspects of culture characteristic of our lives today—cars, telephones, computers, running water, electric light—depend on technological innovations that have been made only very recently in human history.

The same is true at earlier phases of social development. Prior to the invention of the smelting of metal, for example, goods had to be made of organic or naturally occurring materials like wood or stone—a basic limitation on the artifacts that

could be constructed. Variations in material culture provide the main means of distinguishing different forms of human society, but other factors are also influential. Writing is an example. As has been mentioned, not all human cultures have possessed writing—in fact, for most of human history, writing was unknown. The development of writing altered the scope of human cultural potentialities, making different forms of social organization possible from those that had previously existed.

We now turn to analyzing the main types of society that existed in the past and that are still found in the world today. In the present day, we are accustomed to societies that contain many millions of people, many of them living crowded together in urban areas. But for most of human history, the earth was much less densely populated than it is now, and it is only over the past hundred years or so that any societies have existed in which the majority of the population were city dwellers. To understand the forms of society that existed prior to modern industrialism, we have to call on the historical dimension of the sociological imagination.

Disappearing World: Premodern Societies and Their Fate

The explorers, traders, and missionaries sent out during Europe's great age of discovery met with many different peoples. As the anthropologist Marvin Harris has written in his work *Cannibals and Kings:*

> In some regions—Australia, the Arctic, the southern tips of South America and Africa—they found groups still living much like Europe's own long-forgotten stone age ancestors: bands of twenty or thirty people, sprinkled across vast territories, constantly on the move, living entirely by hunting animals and collecting wild plants. These hunter-collectors appeared to be members of a rare and endangered species. In other regions—the forests of eastern North America, the jungles of South America, and East Asia—they found denser populations, inhabiting more or less permanent villages, based on farming and consisting of perhaps one or two large communal structures, but here too the weapons and tools were relics of prehistory....
>
> Elsewhere, of course, the explorers encountered fully developed states and empires, headed by despots and ruling classes, and defended by standing armies. It

was these great empires, with their cities, monuments, palaces, temples and treasures, that had lured all the Marco Polos and Columbuses across the oceans and deserts in the first place. There was China—the greatest empire in the world, a vast, sophisticated realm whose leaders scorned the "red-faced barbarians," supplicants from puny kingdoms beyond the pale of the civilised world. And there was India—a land where cows were venerated and the unequal burdens of life were apportioned according to what each soul had merited in its previous incarnation. And then there were the native American states and empires, worlds unto themselves, each with its distinctive arts and religions: the Incas, with their great stone fortresses, suspension bridges, over-worked granaries, and state-controlled economy; and the Aztecs, with their bloodthirsty gods fed from human hearts and their incessant search for fresh sacrifices. (Harris, 1978)

This seemingly unlimited variety of premodern societies can actually be grouped into three main categories, each of which is referred to in Harris's description: hunters and gatherers (Harris's "hunter-collectors"); larger agrarian or pastoral societies (involving agriculture or the tending of domesticated animals); and nonindustrial civilizations or traditional states. We shall look at the main characteristics of these societies in turn (see Table 3.1).

The Earliest Societies: Hunters and Gatherers

For all but a tiny part of our existence on this planet, human beings have lived in **hunting and gathering societies,** small groups or tribes often numbering no more than thirty or forty people. Hunters and gatherers gain their livelihood from hunting, fishing, and gathering edible

---

TABLE 3.1

Types of Human Society

TYPE	PERIOD OF EXISTENCE	CHARACTERISTICS
Hunting and gathering societies	50,000 B.C.E. to the present. Now on the verge of complete disappearance.	Consist of small numbers of people gaining their livelihood from hunting, fishing, and the gathering of edible plants. Few inequalities. Differences of rank limited by age and gender.
Agrarian societies	12,000 B.C.E. to the present. Most are now part of larger political entities and are losing their distinct identity.	Based on small rural communities, without towns or cities. Livelihood gained through agriculture, often supplemented by hunting and gathering. Stronger inequalities than among hunters and gatherers. Ruled by chiefs.
Pastoral societies	12,000 B.C.E. to the present. Today mostly part of larger states; their traditional ways of life are being undermined.	Size ranges from a few hundred people to many thousands. Dependent on the tending of domesticated animals for their subsistence. Marked by distinct inequalities. Ruled by chiefs or warrior kings.
Traditional societies or civilizations	6000 B.C.E. to the nineteenth century. All traditional states have disappeared.	Very large in size, some numbering millions of people (though small compared with larger industrialized societies). Some cities exist, in which trade and manufacture are concentrated. Based largely on agriculture. Major inequalities exist among different classes. Distinct apparatus of government headed by a king or emperor.

plants growing in the wild. Hunting and gathering cultures continue to exist in some parts of the world, such as in a few arid parts of Africa and the jungles of Brazil and New Guinea. Most such cultures, however, have been destroyed or absorbed by the spread of Western culture, and those that remain are unlikely to stay intact for much longer. Currently, less than a quarter of a million people in the world support themselves through hunting and gathering—only 0.004 percent of the world's population (see Global Map 3.1).

Compared with larger societies—particularly modern societies, such as the United States—little inequality was found in most hunting and gathering groups. The material goods they needed were limited to weapons for hunting, tools for digging and building, traps, and cooking utensils. Thus, there was little difference among members of the society in the number or kinds of material possessions—there were no divisions of rich and poor. Differences of position or rank tended to be limited to age and gender; men were almost always the hunters, while women gathered wild crops, cooked, and brought up the children.

The "elders"—the oldest and most experienced men in the community—usually had an important say in major decisions affecting the group. But just as there was little variation in wealth among members, differences of power were much less than in larger types of society. Hunting and gathering societies were usually participatory rather than competitive: all adult male members tended to assemble together when important decisions were to be made or crises were faced.

Hunters and gatherers moved about a good deal, but not in a completely erratic way. They had fixed territories, around which they migrated regularly from year to year. Since they were without animal or mechanical means of transport, they could take few goods or possessions with them. Many hunting and gathering communities did not have a stable membership; people often moved between different camps, or groups split up and joined others within the same overall territory.

Hunters and gatherers had little interest in developing material wealth beyond what was needed for their basic wants. Their main concerns were with religious values and ritual activities. Members participated regularly in elaborate ceremonials and often spent a great deal of time preparing the dress, masks, paintings, or other sacred objects used in such rituals.

Hunters and gatherers are not merely primitive peoples whose ways of life no longer hold any interest for us. Studying their cultures allows us to see more clearly that some of our institutions are far from being natural features of human life. We shouldn't idealize the circumstances in which hunters and gatherers lived; but the lack of major inequalities of wealth and power and the emphasis on cooperation rather than competition are instructive reminders that the world created by modern industrial civilization is not necessarily to be equated with progress.

Pastoral and Agrarian Societies

About fifteen thousand years ago, some hunting and gathering groups turned to the raising of domesticated animals and the cultivation of fixed plots of land as their means of livelihood. **Pastoral societies** relied mainly on domesticated livestock, while **agrarian societies** grew crops (practiced agriculture). Some societies had mixed pastoral and agrarian economies.

Depending on the environment in which they lived, pastoralists reared animals such as cattle, sheep, goats, camels, or horses. Some pastoral societies still exist in the modern world, concentrated especially in areas of Africa, the Middle East, and Central Asia. They are usually found in regions of dense grasslands or in deserts or mountains. Such regions are not amenable to fruitful agriculture but may support livestock.

At some point, hunting and gathering groups began to sow their own crops rather than simply collect those growing in the wild. This practice first developed as what is usually called "horticulture," in which small gardens were cultivated by the use of simple hoes or digging instruments. Like pastoralism, horticulture provided for a more reliable supply of food than was possible from hunting and gathering and therefore could support larger communities. Since they were not on the move, people whose livelihood was horticulture could develop larger stocks of material possessions than people in either hunting and gathering or pastoral communities. Some peoples in the world still rely primarily on horticulture for their livelihood (see Table 3.2).

Traditional Societies or Civilizations

From about 6000 B.C.E. onward, we find evidence of societies larger than any that existed before and that contrast in distinct ways with earlier types. These societies were based on the development of cities, led to pronounced inequalities of wealth and power, and were ruled by kings or emperors. Because writing was used and science and art flourished, they are often called "civilizations."

The earliest civilizations developed in the Middle East, usually in fertile river areas (see Global Map 3.2). The Chinese Empire originated in about 1800 B.C.E., at which time powerful states were also in existence in what are now India and Pakistan. By the fifteenth century, a number of large civiliza-

The Decline of Hunting and Gathering Societies

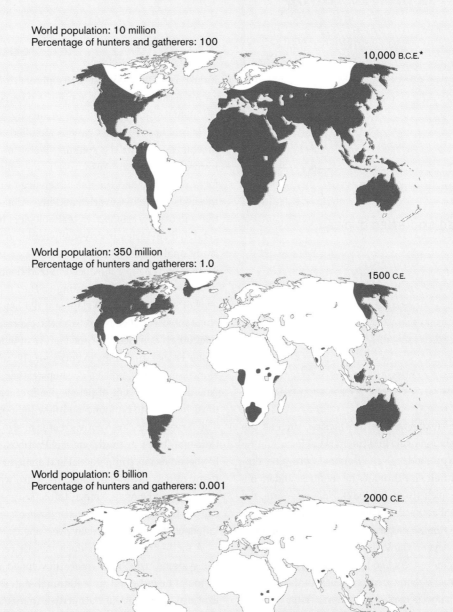

World population: 10 million
Percentage of hunters and gatherers: 100

10,000 B.C.E.*

World population: 350 million
Percentage of hunters and gatherers: 1.0

1500 C.E.

World population: 6 billion
Percentage of hunters and gatherers: 0.001

2000 C.E.

*Many historians now use B.C.E. (before the Common Era) and C.E. (Common Era) rather than B.C. and A.D.

SOURCE: Richard B. Lee and Irven De Vore, eds., *Man the Hunter* (Chicago: Aldine Press, 1968), and authors' update.

TABLE 3.2

Some Agrarian Societies Still Remain

COUNTRY	PERCENTAGE OF WORKFORCE IN AGRICULTURE
Nepal	91.1
Rwanda	90.1
Ethiopia	88.3
Uganda	82.1
Bangladesh	64.2
INDUSTRIALIZED SOCIETIES DIFFER	
Japan	6.2
Australia	5.0
Germany	3.8
Canada	3.4
United States	2.8
United Kingdom	2.0

tions also existed in Mexico and Latin America, such as the Aztecs of the Mexican peninsula and the Incas of Peru.

Most traditional (premodern) civilizations were also empires: They achieved their size through the conquest and incorporation of other peoples (Kautsky, 1982). This was true, for instance, of traditional Rome and China. At its height, in the first century C.E., the Roman empire stretched from Britain in northwest Europe to beyond the Middle East. The Chinese empire, which lasted for more than two thousand years, up to the threshold of the twentieth century, covered most of the massive region of eastern Asia now occupied by modern China.

Societies in the Modern World

What happened to destroy the forms of society that dominated the whole of history up to two centuries ago? The answer, in a word, is **industrialization**—the emergence of machine production, based on the use of inanimate power resources (such as steam or electricity). The industrialized, or modern, societies differ in several key respects from any previous type of social order, and their development has had consequences stretching far beyond their European origins (see Table 3.3).

The Industrialized Societies

Industrialization originated in eighteenth-century Britain as a result of the industrial revolution, a complex set of technological changes that affected the means by which people gained their livelihood. These changes included the invention of new machines (such as the spinning jenny for weaving yarn), the harnessing of power resources (especially water and steam) for production, and the use of science to improve production methods. Since discoveries and inventions in one field lead to more in others, the pace of technological innovation in **industrialized societies** is extremely rapid compared with that of traditional social systems.

In even the most advanced of traditional civilizations, most people were engaged in working on the land. The relatively low level of technological development did not permit more than a small minority to be freed from the chores of agricultural production. By contrast, a prime feature of industrialized societies today is that the large majority of the employed population work in factories, offices, or shops rather than in agriculture. And over 90 percent of people live in towns and cities, where most jobs are to be found and new job opportunities created. The largest cities are vastly greater in size than the urban settlements found in traditional civilizations. In the cities, social life becomes more impersonal and anonymous than before, and many of our day-to-day encounters are with strangers rather than with individuals known to us. Large-scale organizations, such as business corporations or government agencies, come to influence the lives of virtually everyone.

A further feature of modern societies concerns their political systems, which are more developed and intensive than forms of government in traditional states. In traditional civilizations, the political authorities (monarchs and emperors) had little direct influence on the customs and habits of most of their subjects, who lived in fairly self-contained local villages. With industrialization, transportation and communications became much more rapid, making for a more integrated "national" community.

The industrialized societies were the first nation-states to come into existence. **Nation-states** are political communities with clearly delimited borders dividing them from each other, rather than the vague frontier areas that used to separate traditional states. Nation-state governments have extensive powers

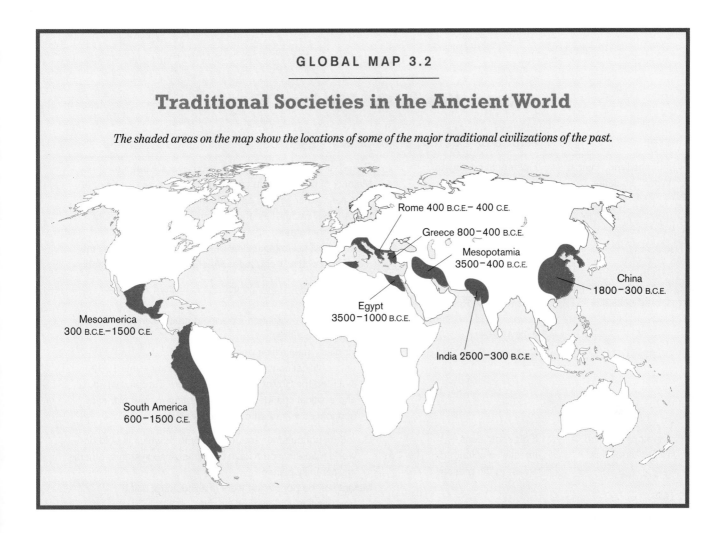

GLOBAL MAP 3.2

Traditional Societies in the Ancient World

The shaded areas on the map show the locations of some of the major traditional civilizations of the past.

Rome 400 B.C.E.– 400 C.E.

Greece 800–400 B.C.E.

Mesopotamia 3500–400 B.C.E.

China 1800–300 B.C.E.

Egypt 3500–1000 B.C.E.

India 2500–300 B.C.E.

Mesoamerica 300 B.C.E.–1500 C.E.

South America 600–1500 C.E.

over many aspects of citizens' lives, framing laws that apply to all those living within their borders. The United States is a nation-state, as are virtually all other societies in the world today.

The application of industrial technology has been by no means limited to peaceful processes of economic development. From the earliest phases of industrialization, modern production processes have been put to military use, and this has radically altered ways of waging war, creating weaponry and modes of military organization much more advanced than those of nonindustrial cultures. Together, superior economic strength, political cohesion, and military superiority account for the seemingly irresistible spread of Western ways of life across the world over the past two centuries.

Global Development

From the seventeenth to the early twentieth centuries, the Western countries established colonies in numerous areas previously occupied by traditional societies, using their supe-

rior military strength where necessary. Although virtually all these colonies have now attained their independence, the process of **colonialism** was central to shaping the social map of the globe as we know it today. In some regions, such as North America, Australia, and New Zealand, which were only thinly populated by hunting and gathering or pastoral communities, Europeans became the majority population. In other areas, including much of Asia, Africa, and South America, the local populations remained in the majority.

Societies of the first of these two types, including the United States, have become industrialized. Those in the second category are mostly at a much lower level of industrial development and are often referred to as less developed societies, or the **developing world.** Such societies include China, India, most of the African countries (such as Nigeria, Ghana, and Algeria), and those in South America (e.g., Brazil, Peru, and Venezuela). Since many of these societies are situated south of the United States and Europe, they are sometimes referred to collectively as the South, and contrasted to the wealthier, industrialized North.

You may often hear developing countries referred to as part of the Third World. The term **Third World** was originally

TABLE 3.3

Societies in the Modern World

TYPE	PERIOD OF EXISTENCE	CHARACTERISTICS
Industrialized "First World" societies	Eighteenth century to the present.	Based on industrial production and generally free enterprise. Majority of people live in towns and cities; a few live in rural areas and engage in agricultural pursuits. Major class inequalities, though less pronounced than in traditional states. Distinct political communities or nation-states, including the nations of the West, Japan, Australia, and New Zealand.
Communist "Second World" societies	Early twentieth century (following the Russian Revolution of 1917) to early 1990s.	Based on industry, but the economic system is centrally planned. Minority of the population work in agriculture; most live in the towns and cities. Major class inequalities persist. Distinct political communities or nation-states—until 1989, included the Soviet Union and Eastern Europe, but social and political changes began to transform their planned economies in free-enterprise economic systems.
Developing "Third World" societies	Eighteenth century (mostly as colonized areas) to the present.	Based on agricultural production, some of which is sold on world markets; some have free-enterprise systems, others are centrally planned. Majority of the population work in agriculture, using traditional methods of production. Most people live in poverty. Distinct political communities or nation-states, including China, India, and most African and South American nations.
Newly industrializing economies	1970s to the present.	Former developing societies now based on industrial production and generally free enterprise. Majority of people live in towns and cities; a few pursue agricultural production for their livelihood. Some have major class inequalities, more pronounced than in industrialized societies. Average per capita income considerably less than in industrialized societies, with the exception of Singapore. Include Hong Kong, South Korea, Singapore, Taiwan, Brazil, and Mexico.

part of a contrast drawn between three main types of society found in the early twentieth century. **First World** countries were (and are) the industrialized states of Europe, the United States, Canada, Australasia (Australia, New Zealand, and Melanesia), South Africa, and Japan. Nearly all First World societies have multiparty, parliamentary systems of government. **Second World** societies meant the communist countries of what was then the Soviet Union (USSR) and Eastern Europe, including for example Czechoslovakia, Poland, East Germany, and Hungary. Second World societies were centrally planned economies, which allowed little role for private property or competitive economic enterprise. They were also one-party states: The Communist party dominated both the political and economic systems. For some seventy-five years, world history was affected by a global rivalry between the Soviet Union and Eastern European countries on the one hand and the capitalistic societies of the West and Japan on the other. Today that rivalry is over. With the ending of the cold war and the disintegration of communism in the former USSR and Eastern Europe, the Second World has effectively disappeared.

Even though the three worlds distinction is still often used in sociology textbooks, today it has outlived whatever usefulness it might have once had as a way of describing the countries of the world. For one thing, the Second World of socialist and communist countries no longer exists, and even exceptions such as China are rapidly adopting capitalist economies. More important, the ranking of First, Second, and Third Worlds reflects a value judgment, in which "first" means "best" and "third" means "worst," and is therefore best avoided.

The Developing World

The large majority of less developed societies are in areas that underwent colonial rule in Asia, Africa, and South America. A few colonized areas gained independence early, such as Haiti, which became the first autonomous black republic in January 1804. The Spanish colonies in South America acquired their freedom in 1810, while Brazil broke away from Portuguese rule in 1822.

Some countries that were never ruled from Europe were nonetheless strongly influenced by colonial relationships, the most notable example being China. By force of arms, China was compelled from the seventeenth century on to enter into trading agreements with European powers, by which the Europeans were allocated the government of certain areas, including major seaports. Hong Kong was the last of these. Most nations in the developing world have become independent states only since World War II—often following bloody anticolonial struggles. Examples include India, which shortly after achieving self-rule split into India and Pakistan, a range of other Asian countries (like Myanmar, Malaysia, and Singapore), and countries in Africa (including, e.g., Kenya, Nigeria, the Democratic Republic of Congo, Tanzania, and Algeria).

Although they may include peoples living in traditional fashion, developing countries are very different from earlier forms of traditional society. Their political systems are modeled on systems first established in the societies of the West— that is to say, they are nation-states. Most of the population still live in rural areas, but many of these societies are experiencing a rapid process of city development. Although agriculture remains the main economic activity, crops are now often produced for sale in world markets rather than for local consumption. Developing countries are not merely societies that

have "lagged behind" the more industrialized areas. They have been in large part created by contact with Western industrialism, which has undermined the earlier, more traditional systems that were in place there.

Conditions in the more impoverished of these societies have deteriorated rather than improved over the past few years. It has been estimated that in 2000 1.5 billion people were living in poverty in the developing countries, nearly a quarter of the population of the world. Some half of the world's poor live in South Asia, in countries such as India, Myanmar, and Cambodia. About a third are concentrated in Africa. A substantial proportion, however, live on the doorstep of the United States—in Central and South America (see Global Map 3.3).

Once more, the existence of global poverty shouldn't be seen as remote from the concerns of Americans. Whereas in previous generations the bulk of immigrants into the United States came from the European countries, most now come from poor, developing societies (see Figure 3.1). Recent years have seen waves of Hispanic immigrants, nearly all from Latin America. Some U.S. cities near the entry points of much

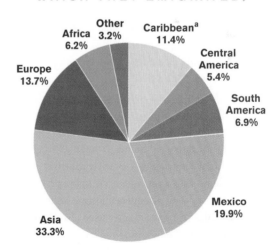

FIGURE 3.1

MOVING TO AMERICA: IMMIGRANTS TO THE UNITED STATES, 1998 (BY AREA FROM WHICH THEY EMIGRATED)

Africa 6.2%
Other 3.2%
Caribbean[a] 11.4%
Central America 5.4%
Europe 13.7%
South America 6.9%
Asia 33.3%
Mexico 19.9%

[a]Antigua and Barbuda, the Bahamas, Barbados, Cuba, Dominica, Dominican Republic, Grenada, Haiti, Jamaica, St. Kitts-Nevis, St. Lucia, St. Vincent and the Grenadines, and Trinidad and Tobago.

SOURCE: Immigration and Naturalization Service, *Annual Report: Legal Immigration, Fiscal Year 1998.*

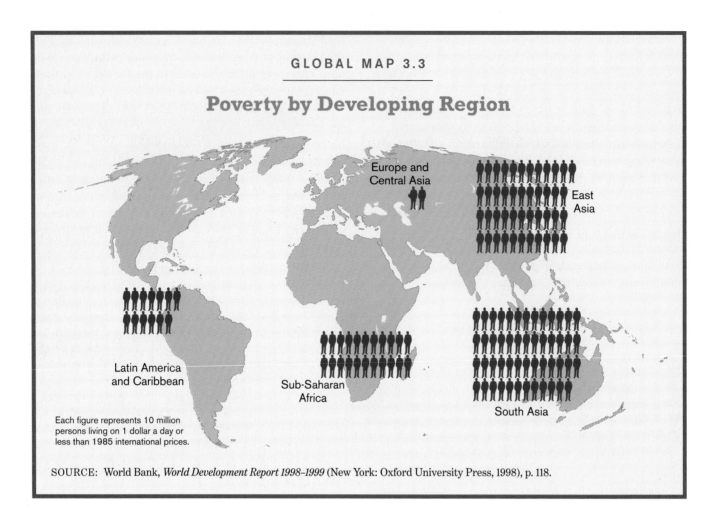

GLOBAL MAP 3.3

Poverty by Developing Region

Latin America
and Caribbean

Europe and
Central Asia

East
Asia

Sub-Saharan
Africa

South Asia

Each figure represents 10 million
persons living on 1 dollar a day or
less than 1985 international prices.

SOURCE: World Bank, *World Development Report 1998–1999* (New York: Oxford University Press, 1998), p. 118.

of this immigration, such as Los Angeles and Miami, are bursting with new immigrants and also maintain trading connections with developing countries.

In most developing societies, poverty tends to be at its worst in rural areas. Malnutrition, lack of education, low life expectancy, and substandard housing are generally most severe in the countryside. Many of the poor are to be found in areas where arable land is scarce, agricultural productivity low, and drought or floods common. Women are usually more disadvantaged than men. They encounter cultural, social, and economic problems that even the most underprivileged men do not. For instance, they often work longer hours and, when they are paid at all, earn lower wages. (See also Chapter 10 for a lengthier discussion of gender inequality.)

The poor in developing countries live in conditions almost unimaginable to Americans. Many have no permanent dwellings apart from shelters made of cartons or loose pieces of wood. Most have no running water, sewer systems, or electricity. Nonetheless, millions of poor people also live in the United States, and there are connections between poverty in America and global poverty. Almost half of the people living

in poverty in the United States immigrated from the global South. This is true of the descendants of the black slaves brought over by force centuries ago; and it is true of more recent, and willing, immigrants who have arrived from Latin America, Asia, and elsewhere.

The Newly Industrializing Economies

Although the majority of developing countries lag well behind societies of the West, some have now successfully embarked on a process of industrialization. These are sometimes referred to as **newly industrializing economies** (NIEs), and they include Brazil, Mexico, Hong Kong, South Korea, Singapore, and Taiwan. The rates of economic growth of the most successful NIEs, such as those in East Asia, are several times those of the Western industrial economies. No developing country figured among the top thirty exporters in the world in 1968, but twenty-five years later South Korea was in the top fifteen.

Two African American children play near their home and an open sewer. This poverty-stricken area of Tunica, Mississippi, is sometimes referred to as "Sugarditch."

Due to extreme poverty and the lack of land in El Salvador, many Salvadorans are forced to make their homes in public cemeteries.

The East Asian NIEs have shown the most sustained levels of economic prosperity. They are investing abroad as well as promoting growth at home. South Korea's production of steel has doubled in the last decade, and its shipbuilding and electronics industries are among the world's leaders. Singapore is becoming the major financial and commercial center of Southeast Asia. Taiwan is an important presence in the manufacturing and electronics industries. All these changes in the NIEs have directly affected the United States, whose share of global steel production, for example, has dropped significantly over the past thirty years.

The Impact of Globalization

In Chapter 1 it was pointed out that the chief focus of sociology has historically been the study of the industrialized societies. As sociologists, can we thus safely ignore the developing world, leaving this as the domain of anthropology? We certainly cannot. The industrialized and the developing societies have developed in *interconnection* with one another and are today more closely related than ever before. Those of us living in the industrialized societies depend on many raw materials and manufactured products coming from developing countries to sustain our lives. Conversely, the economies of most developing states depend on trading networks that bind them to the industrialized countries. We can only fully understand the industrialized order against the backdrop of societies in the developing world—in which, in fact, by far the greater proportion of the world's population lives.

Take a close look at the array of products on display the next time you walk into a local shop or supermarket. The diversity of goods we in the West have come to take for granted as available for anyone with the money to buy them depends on amazingly complex economic connections stretching across the world. The store products have been made in, or use ingredients or parts from, a hundred different countries. These parts must be regularly transported across the globe, and constant flows of information are necessary to coordinate the millions of daily transactions.

As the world rapidly moves toward a single, unified economy, businesses and people move about the globe in increasing numbers in search of new markets and economic opportunities. As a result, the cultural map of the world changes: Networks of peoples span national borders and even continents, providing cultural connections between their birthplaces and their adoptive countries (Appadurai, 1986). A handful of languages come to dominate, and in some cases replace, the thousands of different languages that were once spoken on the planet.

It is increasingly impossible for cultures to exist as islands. There are few, if any, places on earth so remote as to escape radio, television, air travel—and the throngs of tourists they bring—or the computer. A generation ago, there were still tribes whose way of life was completely untouched by the rest of the world. Today, these peoples use machetes and other tools made in the United States or Japan, wear T-shirts and shorts manufactured in garment factories in the Dominican Republic or Guatemala, and take medicine manufactured in Germany or Switzerland to combat diseases contracted

Two Masai natives proudly display T-shirts bearing the logos of American football teams. There is almost no place on earth untouched by the globalization of culture.

Does the Internet Promote a Global Culture?

Many believe that the rapid growth of the Internet around the world will hasten the spread of a global culture—one resembling the cultures of Europe and North America, currently home to nearly three-quarters of all Internet users (see Global Map 3.4). Belief in such values as equality between men and women, the right to speak freely, democratic participation in government, and the pursuit of pleasure through consumption are readily diffused throughout the world over the Internet. Moreover, Internet technology itself would seem to foster such values: Global communication, seemingly unlimited (and uncensored) information, and instant gratification are all characteristics of the new technology.

Yet it may be premature to conclude that the Internet will sweep aside traditional cultures, replacing them with radically new cultural values. As the Internet spreads around the world, evidence shows that it is in many ways compatible with traditional cultural values as well, perhaps even a means of strengthening them.

Consider, for example, the Middle Eastern country of Kuwait, a traditional Islamic culture that has recently experienced strong American and European influences. Kuwait, an oil-rich country on the Persian Gulf, has one of the highest average per-person incomes in the world. The government provides free public education through the university level, resulting in high rates of literacy and education for both men and women. Kuwaiti television frequently carries NFL football and other U.S. programming, although broadcasts are regularly interrupted for the traditional Muslim calls to prayer. Half of Kuwait's approximately 2 million people are under twenty-five years old, and, like their youthful counterparts in Europe and North America, many surf the Internet for new ideas, information, and consumer products.

Although Kuwait is in many respects a modern country, Kuwait law treats men and women differently. Legally, women have equal access to education and employment, yet they are barred from voting or running for political office. Cultural norms treating men and women differently are almost as strong: Women are generally expected to wear traditional clothing that leaves only the face and hands visible and are forbidden to leave home at night or be seen in public at any time with a man who is not a spouse or relative.

Deborah Wheeler (1998) spent a year studying the impact of the Internet on Kuwaiti culture. The Internet is increasingly popular in Kuwait; half of all Internet users in Middle Eastern Arab countries live in this tiny country. Kuwaiti newspapers frequently carry stories about the Internet and the Web, and Kuwait University was the first university in the Arab world to hook its students up to the Internet.

through contact with outsiders. These people also have their stories broadcast to people around the world through satellite television and the Internet. Within a generation or two at the most, all the world's once-isolated cultures will be touched and transformed by global culture, despite their persistent efforts to preserve their age-old ways of life.

The forces that produce a global culture will be discussed throughout this book. These include:

- television, which brings U.S. culture (through networks and shows such as MTV and *The Simpsons*) into homes throughout the world daily, while also adapting a Swedish cultural product (*Expedition: Robinson*) for a U.S. audience in the form of *Big Brother* and *Survivor*;
- the emergence of a unified global economy, with business whose factories, management structures, and markets often span continents and countries;
- "global citizens," such as managers of large corporations, who may spend as much time crisscrossing the globe as they do at home, identifying with a global, cosmopolitan culture rather than with their own nation's;
- a host of international organizations, including United Nations agencies, regional trade and mutual defense associations, multinational banks and other global financial institutions, international labor and health organizations, and global tariff and trade agreements, that are creating a global political, legal, and military framework; and
- electronic communications (telephone, fax, electronic mail, the Internet and the World Wide Web), which make instantaneous communication with almost any part of the planet an integral part of daily life in the business world.

Global Internet Connectivity: Number of Internet Servers, January 1999

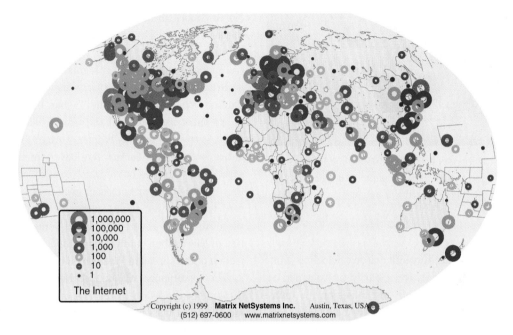

1,000,000
100,000
10,000
1,000
100
10
1

The Internet

Copyright (c) 1999 **Matrix NetSystems Inc.**   Austin, Texas, USA
(512) 697-0600   www.matrixnetsystems.com

SOURCE: John Quarterman and colleagues at Matrix Information Directory Services (MIDS), www.geog.ucl.ac.uk/casa/martin/atlas/mids_intrworld9901_large.gif.

Wheeler reports that Kuwait teenagers are flocking to Internet cafés, where they spend most of their time in chat rooms or visiting pornographic sites—two activities strongly frowned on by traditional Islamic culture. According to Wheeler,

Many young people told me of encounters they were having with the opposite sex in cyberspace. There are even keyboard symbols for kisses (*), kisses on the lips (:*), and embarrassed giggles (LOL)—all those interactions and reactions that make courtship exciting and, in this case, safe. (1998)

The new communications technologies are clearly enabling men and women to talk with each other, in a society where such communications outside of marriage are extremely limited. Wheeler also notes that ironically men and women are segregated in the Internet cafés. Furthermore, she finds that Kuwaitis are extremely reluctant to voice strong opinions or political views online. With the exception of discussing conservative Islamic religious beliefs, which are freely disseminated over the Internet, Kuwaitis are remarkably inhibited online. Wheeler attributes this to the cultural belief that giving out too much information about oneself is dangerous:

In Kuwait, information is more of a potential threat than a means for individual empowerment. It is a weapon to use against your enemies, a tool for keeping conformity, or a reinforcement of regulations of daily life. . . . Kuwait's transition to the information age is influenced by these attitudes and the desire to keep one's reputation protected. This keeps the Internet from registering significant political and social impacts, except for the rise in Kuwaiti Islamist discourses on the Internet. . . . In Kuwait, there is an ethos that states that having and/or pronouncing a political opinion publicly is bad. No one wants to talk on the record or to be quoted. The idea makes people scared or nervous. Only those who are elite feel they can speak freely and openly. (1998)

Using the Internet to connect with the world around them is common among young people across cultures. Here, an Iranian girl at a Tehran Internet café reads the latest news on the Iraq crisis.

Wheeler concludes that Kuwaiti culture, which is hundreds of years old, is not likely to be easily transformed by simple exposure to different beliefs and values on the Internet. The fact that a few young people are participating in global chat rooms does not mean that Kuwaiti culture is adopting the sexual attitudes of the United States or even the form of everyday relations found between men and women in the West. The culture that eventually emerges as a result of the new technologies will not be the same as American culture; it will be uniquely Kuwaiti.

Globalization and Local Cultures

The world has become a single *social system* as a result of growing ties of interdependence, both social and economic, that now affect virtually everyone. But it would be a mistake to think of this increasing interdependence, or globalization, of the world's societies simply as the growth of world unity. The globalizing of social relations should be understood primarily as the reordering of *time and distance* in social life. Our lives, in other words, are increasingly and quickly influenced by events happening far removed from our everyday activities.

Globalizing processes have brought many benefits to Americans: a much greater variety of goods and foodstuffs is available than ever before. At the same time, the fact that we are all now caught up in a much wider world has helped create some of the most serious problems American society faces, such as the threat of terrorism.

The influence of a growing global culture has provoked numerous reactions at the local level. Many local cultures remain strong or are experiencing a rejuvenation, partly as a response to the diffusion of global culture. Such a response grows out of the concern that a global culture, dominated by North American and European cultural values, will corrupt the local culture. For example, the Taliban, an Islamic movement that controlled most of Afghanistan, sought to impose traditional, tribal values throughout the country. Through its governmental "Ministry for Ordering What Is Right and Forbidding What Is Wrong," the Taliban banned music, closed movie theaters, abolished the use of alcohol, and required men to grow full beards. Women were ordered to cover their entire bodies with *burkas*, tentlike garments with a woven screen over the eyes, out of which to see. They were forbidden to work outside their homes, or even to be seen in public with men who were not their spouses or relations. Violations of these rules were severely punished, sometimes by death. The rise of the Taliban can be understood at least partly as a rejection of the spread of Western culture.

The resurgence of local cultures is sometimes seen throughout the world in the rise of **nationalism,** a sense of identification with one's people that is expressed through a common set of strongly held beliefs. Sometimes these include the belief that the people of a particular nation have historical or God-given rights that supersede those of other people. Nationalism can be strongly political, involving attempts to assert the power of a nation based on a shared ethnic or racial identity over people of a different ethnicity or race. The strife in the former Yugoslavia, as well as parts of Africa and the former Soviet Union, bear tragic witness to the power of nationalism. The world of the twenty-first century may well witness responses to globalization that celebrate ethnocentric nationalist beliefs, promoting intolerance and hatred rather than a celebration of diversity.

New nationalisms, cultural identities, and religious practices are constantly being forged throughout the world. When you socialize with students from the same cultural background or celebrate traditional holidays with your friends and family, you are sustaining your culture. The very technology that helps foster globalization also supports local cultures: The Internet enables you to communicate with others who share your cultural identity, even when they are dispersed around the world. American students who share a passion for a particular type of music can stay up all night in Internet chat rooms with like-minded people: if you are studying abroad you can stay connected with communities back home by logging on to the Web site of your hometown newspaper

(Wallraff, 2000). A casual search of the Web reveals thousands of pages devoted to different cultures and subcultures.

Although sociologists do not yet fully understand these processes, they often conclude that despite the powerful forces of globalization operating in the world today, local cultures remain strong and indeed flourish. But is it still too soon to tell whether and how globalization will transform our world, whether it will result in the homogenization of the world's diverse cultures, the flourishing of many individual cultures, or both.

Study Outline

www.wwnorton.com/giddens5

The Concepts of Culture

- *Culture* consists of the *values* held by a given group, the *norms* they follow, and the *material goods* they create.

Culture and Change

- In recent years the sociology of culture has attracted renewed interest, a phenomenon known as the *cultural turn.* Attention is being given both to culture as a set of scripts we draw on to shape our beliefs, values, and actions and to the many different meanings of cultural symbols.

The Development of Human Culture

- Human cultures have evolved over thousands of years and reflect both human biology and the physical environment where the cultures emerged. A defining feature of humankind is its inventiveness in creating new forms of culture.

How Nature and Nurture Interact

- Most sociologists do not deny that biology plays a role in shaping human behavior, especially through the interaction between biology and culture. Sociologists' main concern, however, is with how behavior is learned in the individual's interaction with society.
- Forms of behavior found in all, or virtually all, cultures are called *cultural universals.* *Language,* the prohibition against incest, institutions of *marriage,* the family, religion, and property are the main types of cultural universals—but within these general categories there are many variations in values and modes of behavior between different societies.
- We live in a world of symbols, or representations, and one of our most important forms of symbolization is language. The *linguistic relativity hypothesis* argues that language influences perception. Language is also an important source of cultural continuity, and the members of a culture are often passionate about their linguistic heritage.
- *Cultural diversity* is a chief aspect of modern culture, and in the United States it is seen in the large number of vibrant *subcultures* as well as in the existence of countercultures. Although some people feel that different subcultures should be *assimilated* into a single mainstream culture, others argue in favor of *multiculturalism.*
- Sociologists try to avoid *ethnocentrism* and instead adopt a stance of *cultural relativism,* attempting to understand a society relative to its own cultural norms and values.

Premodern Societies

- Several types of premodern society can be distinguished. In *hunting and gathering societies,* people do not grow crops or keep livestock but gain their livelihood from gathering plants and hunting animals. *Pastoral societies* are those that raise domesticated animals as their major source of subsistence. *Agrarian societies* depend on the cultivation of fixed plots of land. Larger, more developed, urban societies form traditional states or civilizations.

Societies in the Modern World

- The development of industrialized societies and the expansion of the West led to the conquest of many parts of the world through the process of *colonialism,* which radically changed long-established social systems and cultures.
- In industrialized societies, industrial production (whose techniques are also used in the production of food) is the main basis of the economy. Industrialized countries include the nations of the West, plus Japan, Australia, and New Zealand. They now include those industrialized societies ruled by communist governments. The *developing world,* in which most of the world's population live, is almost all formerly colonized areas. The majority of the population works in agricultural production, some of which is geared to world markets.

The Impact of Globalization

- The increase in global communications and economic interdependence represents more than simply the growth of world unity.

Time and distance are being reorganized in ways that bring us all closer together, but even as globalization threatens to make all cultures seem alike, local cultural identifications are resurging around the world. This is seen in the rise of *nationalism,* which can result in ethnic conflict as well as ethnic pride.

Key Concepts

agrarian society (p. 72)
assimilation (p. 63)
colonialism (p. 75)
cultural relativism (p. 66)
cultural turn (p. 58)
cultural universal (p. 68)
culture (p. 52)
developing world (p. 75)
ethnocentrism (p. 66)
First World (p. 76)
hunting and gathering society (p. 71)
industrialization (p. 74)
industrialized society (p. 74)
instinct (p. 62)
language (p. 68)
linguistic relativity hypothesis (p. 68)
marriage (p. 68)
material goods (p. 53)
multiculturalism (p. 64)
nation-state (p. 74)
nationalism (p. 82)
newly industrializing economy (NIE) (p. 78)
norm (p. 52)
pastoral society (p. 72)
Second World (p. 76)
semiotics (p. 69)
signifier (p. 69)
society (p. 57)
sociobiology (p. 62)
subculture (p. 63)
Third World (p. 75)
values (p. 52)

Review Questions

1. What are values?
   a. Values are those ideas that a culture holds in the highest esteem. They give people a purpose in life.
   b. Values are abstract ideals—for example, in most Western societies, monogamy is considered a virtue. In other cultures, a person may be permitted to have several wives or husbands simultaneously.
   c. Values are lists of "dos" and "don'ts" that regulate everyday behavior.
   d. Values depend on the development of a money economy and systems of credit.

2. What is a signifier?
   a. A signifier is the name given to the meaning of a spoken or written word.
   b. A signifier is any vehicle of meaning, such as speech, writing, dress, and buildings.
   c. A signifier is the meaning of a symbol.
   d. A signifier is an electronic sign.

3. Using one's own cultural values to judge another culture is called
   a. ethnocentrism.
   b. cultural relativism.
   c. cultural turn.
   d. cultural universals.

4. What is culture?
   a. Culture consists of the values, norms, and material goods of a people. Culture can be described as a "design for living."
   b. Culture is the sum total of a society's artistic expression—all the novels, poems, dance, theater, museums, and so on.
   c. Culture is the material apparatus of everyday life—the chairs, tables, cooking utensils, clothes, shoes, and coats that we use in our daily round.
   d. Culture consists of the values and norms of a society, its founding "myths" and ideals, and its beliefs about the kinds of conduct appropriate in everyday life.

5. What was the basis for the rise of modern societies?
   a. The fall of the Roman Empire
   b. The Renaissance
   c. The Industrial Revolution
   d. The cold war

6. Which of the following is not a cultural universal?
   a. The prohibition against incest
   b. Some form of religion
   c. A concept of property
   d. The idea of adolescence

7. What was colonialism?
   a. The creation by the European powers of a network of colonies in ports of call along their trade routes.
   b. The military conquest of African peoples by Europeans.
   c. The process by which industrial powers incorporated regions rich in natural resources into their economic and political systems.
   d. The impact of trade with the empire on the economies of the European powers.

8. What is the position of sociologists on the debate of nature vs. nurture?
   a. Sociologists believe that "biology is destiny."
   b. Sociologists ask how nature and nurture interact to produce human behavior.
   c. No sociologists today acknowledge a role for nature.
   d. Sociologists do not have a position.

9. Which of the following statements is true about developing countries?

  a. About one quarter of the world's population lives in developing countries.

  b. Very few of them are formerly colonized areas.

  c. The majority of the population works in manufacturing and service sectors.

  d. Some agricultural production in developing countries is geared to world markets.

10. Subcultures are:

  a. abstract ideals, such as American ideals of liberty and justice.

  b. systems of relationships that connect individuals who share the same culture.

  c. smaller segments of society distinguished by unique patterns of behavior.

  d. populations made up of a number of groups from diverse cultural, ethnic, and linguistic backgrounds.

Thinking Sociologically Exercises

1. Mention at least two cultural traits that you would claim are universals; mention two others you would claim are culturally specific traits. Use case study materials from different societies you are familiar with to show the differences between universal and specific cultural traits. Are the cultural universals you have discussed derivatives of human instincts? Explain your answer fully.

2. What does it mean to be ethnocentric? How is ethnocentrism dangerous in conducting social research? How is ethnocentrism problematic among nonresearchers in their everyday lives?

Data Exercises

www.wwnorton.com/giddens5
Keyword: Data3

Are you among the millions of Americans whose families have arrived in the United States in the past twenty-five years? Or have you noticed that your community, school, church, or workplace has become more diverse? In the data exercise for Chapter 3 you will learn more about the patterns of immigration to the United States, both historically and currently; how Americans feel about recent immigration; and how your own community has changed as a result of immigration.

Culture, Society, and Child Socialization

Learn about socialization (including gender socialization), and know the most important agencies of socialization.

Socialization Through the Life Course

Learn the various stages of the life course, and see the similarities and differences among different cultures.

CHAPTER FOUR

SOCIALIZATION AND THE LIFE CYCLE

t the start of J. K. Rowling's first Harry Potter adventure, *Harry Potter and the Sorcerer's Stone,* the shrewd wizard Albus Dumbledore leaves Harry, a newly orphaned infant, at the doorstep of his nonmagician (or "Muggle") uncle and aunt's house. Harry has already shown himself to have unique powers, but Dumbledore is concerned that if left in the wizarding world, Harry won't mature healthily. "It would be enough to turn any boy's head," he says. "Famous before he can walk and talk! Famous for something he won't even remember. Can't you see how much better off he'll be, growing up away from all that until he's ready to take it?" (Rowling, 1998).

The Harry Potter novels, each of which follows Harry through a single year of his life, are based on the premise that there is no adventure greater than that of growing up. Although Harry attends the Hogwarts School of Witchcraft and Wizardry, it's still a school, because everyone, even a young wizard with limitless power, needs help developing a set of values. We all pass through important life stages: the passage from childhood to adolescence, and then to adulthood. So, for example, as the Harry Potter series progresses, Harry feels the onset of sexual urges, to which he responds with an entirely common awkwardness. Since sports are an important place for many children to learn about camaraderie and ambition, Harry plays the wizard sport Quidditch. Rowling loves to use the paranormal to help us see the enchanting complexities behind the fundamentals of everyday life. In her universe, owls unerringly deliver letters; is this really any stranger than the postal system or e-mail? The function of all classic children's stories is to make the process of growing up more understandable, whether they're set in a fairy-tale universe, our own world, or—as with the innovation of the Harry Potter series—both.

Socialization is the process whereby the helpless infant gradually becomes a self-aware, knowledgeable person, skilled in the ways of the culture into which he or she was born. Socialization among the young allows for the more general phenomenon of **social reproduction**—the process whereby societies have structural continuity over time. During the course of socialization, especially in the early years of life, children learn the ways of their elders, thereby perpetuating their values, norms, and social practices. All societies have characteristics that endure over long stretches of time, even though their members change as individuals are born and die. American society, for example, has many distinctive social and cultural characteristics that have persisted for generations—such as the fact that English is the main language spoken.

Socialization connects the different generations to one another (Turnbull, 1983). The birth of a child alters the lives of those who are responsible for its upbringing—who themselves therefore undergo new learning experiences. Parenting usually ties the activities of adults to children for the remainder of their lives. Older people still remain parents when they become grandparents, of course, thus forging another set of relationships connecting the different generations with each other. Although the process of cultural learning is much more intense in infancy and early childhood than later, learning and adjustment go on through the whole life cycle.

In the sections to follow, we will continue the theme of "nature interacting with nurture," introduced in the previous chapter. We will first analyze the development of the human individual from infancy to early childhood, identifying the main stages of change involved. Different writers have put forward a number of theoretical interpretations about how and why children develop as they do, and we will describe and compare these, including theories that explain how we develop gender identities. Finally, we will move on to discuss the main groups and social contexts that influence socialization during the various phases of individuals' lives.

Culture, Society, and Child Socialization

"Unsocialized" Children

What would children be like if, in some way or another, they were raised without the influence of human adults? Obviously no humane person could bring up a child away from social in-

fluence. There are, however, a number of much-discussed cases of children who have spent their early years away from normal human contact.

THE "WILD BOY OF AVEYRON"

On January 9, 1800, a strange creature emerged from the woods near the village of Saint-Serin in southern France. In spite of walking erect, he looked more animal than human, although he was soon identified as a boy of about eleven or twelve. He spoke only in shrill, strange-sounding cries. The boy apparently had no sense of personal hygiene and relieved himself where and when he chose. He was brought to the attention of the local police and taken to a nearby orphanage. In the beginning he tried constantly to escape and was only recaptured with some difficulty. He refused to tolerate wearing clothes, tearing them off as soon as they were put on him. No parents ever came forward to claim him.

The child was subjected to a thorough medical examination, which turned up no major physical abnormalities. On being shown a mirror, he seemingly saw an image, but did not recognize himself. On one occasion, he tried to reach through the mirror to seize a potato he saw in it. (The potato in fact was being held behind his head.) After several attempts, without turning his head, he took the potato by reaching back over his shoulder. A priest who was observing the boy from day to day and who described this incident, wrote: "All these little details, and many others we could add prove that this child is not totally without intelligence, reflection, and reasoning power. However, we are obliged to say that, in every case not concerned with his natural needs or satisfying his appetite, one can perceive in him only animal behavior. If he has sensations, they give birth to no idea. He cannot even compare them with one another. One would think that there is no connection between his soul or mind and his body" (quoted in Shattuck, 1980; see also Lane, 1976).

Later the boy was moved to Paris and a systematic attempt was made to change him "from beast to human." The endeavor was only partly successful. He was toilet trained, accepted wearing clothes, and learned to dress himself. Yet he was uninterested in toys or games and was never able to learn or speak more than a few words. So far as anyone could tell, on the basis of detailed descriptions of his behavior and reactions, this was not because he was mentally retarded. He seemed either unwilling or unable to master human speech fully. He made little further progress and died in 1828.

GENIE

It cannot be proved how long the wild boy of Aveyron lived on his own in the woods or whether or not he suffered from some congenital defect that made it impossible for him to develop like a normal human being. However, more recent examples reinforce some of the observations made about his behavior. One case is provided by the life of Genie, a California girl who was locked in a room when she was about one and a half until she was over thirteen (Curtiss, 1977). Genie's father kept his wife, who was going blind, more or less completely confined to the house. The main connection between the family and the outside world was through a teenage son, who attended school and did the shopping.

Genie had a hip defect from birth that prevented her from walking properly. Her father frequently beat her. When Genie was twenty months old, her father apparently decided she was retarded and put her away in a closed room with the curtains drawn and the door shut. She stayed there for the next eleven years, seeing the other members of the family only when they came to feed her. Genie had not been toilet trained and spent part of her time harnessed, naked, to a toddler's potty chair. Sometimes at night she was removed, only to be put into another restraining garment, a sleeping bag within which her arms were imprisoned. Tied up in this way, she was also enclosed in an infant's crib with wire-mesh sides and a mesh cover overhead. Somehow, in these appalling circumstances she endured the hours, days, and years of her life. She had almost no opportunity to overhear any conversation between others in the house. If she attempted to make a noise, or to attract attention, her father would beat her. Her father never spoke to her, but instead made barking, animal-like sounds if she did anything to annoy him. She had no proper toys or other objects with which to occupy her time.

In 1970, the mother escaped from the house, taking Genie with her. The condition of the girl came to the notice of a social worker, and she was placed in the rehabilitation ward of a children's hospital. When she was first admitted to the hospital, she could not stand erect; could not run, jump, or climb; and was only able to walk in a shuffling, clumsy fashion. She was described by a psychiatrist as "unsocialized, primitive, hardly human." Once in a rehabilitation ward, however, Genie made fairly rapid progress. She learned to eat quite normally, was toilet trained, and tolerated being dressed like other children. Yet she was silent almost all of the time, except when she laughed, her laugh being high-pitched and unreal. She masturbated constantly in public situations, refusing to abandon the habit. Later she lived as a foster child in the home of one of the doctors from the hospital. She gradually came to develop a fairly wide vocabulary and could make a limited number of basic utterances, but her mastery of language never progressed beyond that of a three- or four-year-old.

Genie's behavior was studied intensively and she was given a variety of tests over a period of some seven years. These seemed to indicate that she was not retarded, nor did she suf-

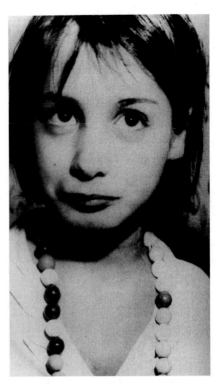

This is the only photograph of Genie to appear in the press upon her discovery in 1970. Having been deprived of almost all human contact for the first thirteen years of her life, Genie provided some sense of what an "unsocialized" child would be like.

fer from any other congenital defects. What seems to have happened to Genie, as to the wild boy of Aveyron, is that by the time she came into close human contact, she had grown beyond the age at which children readily accomplish the learning of language and other human skills. There is probably a "critical period" for the learning of language and other complex achievements, after which it is too late to master them fully. The wild boy and Genie provide some sense of what an "unsocialized" child would be like. Each retained many "nonhuman" responses. Yet, in spite of the deprivations they suffered, neither displayed any lasting viciousness. They responded quickly to others who treated them sympathetically and were able to acquire a certain minimum level of ordinary human capabilities.

Of course, we have to be cautious about interpreting cases of this sort. In each of these examples it is possible that there was a mental abnormality that remained undiagnosed. Alternatively, the experiences to which the children were subjected may have inflicted psychological damage that prevented them from gaining the skills most children acquire at a much earlier age. Yet there is sufficient similarity between these two case histories, and others that have been recorded, to suggest how limited our faculties would be in the absence of an extended period of early socialization.

Theories of Child Development

One of the most distinctive features of human beings, compared with other animals, is that humans are *self-aware*. How should we understand the emergence of a sense of self—the awareness that the individual has a distinct identity separate from others? During the first months of life, the infant possesses little or no understanding of differences between human beings and material objects in the environment, and has no awareness of self. Children do not begin to use concepts such as "I," "me," and "you" until the age of two or after. Only gradually do they then come to understand that others have distinct identities, consciousness, and needs separate from their own.

The problem of the emergence of self is much debated and is viewed rather differently in contrasting theoretical perspectives. To some extent, this is because the most prominent theories about child development emphasize different aspects of socialization. The American philosopher and sociologist George Herbert Mead gives attention mainly to how children learn to use the concepts of "I" and "me." Jean Piaget, the Swiss student of child behavior, worked on many aspects of child development, but his best-known writings concern **cognition**—the ways in which children learn to *think* about themselves and their environment.

G. H. MEAD AND THE DEVELOPMENT OF SELF

Since Mead's ideas form the main basis of a general tradition of theoretical thinking, *symbolic interactionism,* they have had a very broad impact in sociology. Symbolic interactionism emphasizes that interaction between human beings takes place through symbols and the interpretation of meanings (see Chapter 1). But in addition, Mead's work provides an account of the main phases of child development, giving particular attention to the emergence of a sense of self.

According to Mead, infants and young children first of all develop as social beings by imitating the actions of those around them. Play is one way in which this takes place, and in their play small children often imitate what adults do. A small child will make mud pies, having seen an adult cooking, or dig with a spoon, having observed someone gardening. Children's play evolves from simple imitation to more complicated games in which a child of four or five years old will act out an adult role. Mead called this "taking the role of the other"—learning what it is like to be in the shoes of another person. It is only at this stage that children acquire a developed sense of self. Children achieve an understanding of themselves as separate agents—as a "me"—by seeing themselves through the eyes of others.

Using their toy wheelbarrows to help their father with the gardening, these boys are, according to Mead, "taking on the role of the other" and achieving an understanding of themselves as separate social agents.

We achieve self-awareness, according to Mead, when we learn to distinguish the "me" from the "I." The "I" is the unsocialized infant, a bundle of spontaneous wants and desires. The "me," as Mead used the term, is the **social self.** Individuals develop **self-consciousness,** Mead argued, by coming to see themselves as others see them. A further stage of child development, according to Mead, occurs when the child is about eight or nine years old. This is the age at which children tend to take part in organized games, rather than unsystematic play. It is at this period that children begin to understand the overall *values* and *morality* according to which social life is conducted. To learn organized games, children must understand the rules of play and notions of fairness and equal participation. Children at this stage learn to grasp what Mead termed the **generalized other**—the general values and moral rules of the culture in which they are developing.

JEAN PIAGET AND THE STAGES OF COGNITIVE DEVELOPMENT

Piaget placed great emphasis on the child's active capability to make sense of the world. Children do not passively soak up information, but instead select and interpret what they see, hear, and feel in the world around them. Piaget described several distinct stages of cognitive development during which children learn to think about themselves and their environment. Each stage involves the acquisition of new skills and depends on the successful completion of the preceding one.

Piaget called the first stage, which lasts from birth up to about age two, the **sensorimotor stage,** because infants learn mainly by touching objects, manipulating them, and physically exploring their environment. Until about age four months or so, infants cannot differentiate themselves from their environment. For example, a child will not realize that her own movements cause the sides of her crib to rattle. Objects are not differentiated from persons, and the infant is unaware that anything exists outside her range of vision. Infants gradually learn to distinguish people from objects, coming to see that both have an existence independent of their immediate perceptions. The main accomplishment of this stage is that by its close children understand their environment to have distinct and stable properties.

The next phase, called the **preoperational stage,** is the one to which Piaget devoted the bulk of his research. This stage lasts from age two to seven. During the course of it, children acquire a mastery of language and become able to use words to represent objects and images in a symbolic fashion. A four-year-old might use a sweeping hand, for example, to represent the concept "airplane." Piaget termed the stage "preoperational" because children are not yet able to use their developing mental capabilities systematically. Children in this stage are **egocentric.** As Piaget used it, this concept does not refer to selfishness, but to the tendency of the child to interpret the world exclusively in terms of his own position. A child during this period does not understand, for instance, that others see objects from a different perspective from his own. Holding a book upright, the child may ask about a picture in it, not realizing that the other person sitting opposite can only see the back of the book.

Children at the preoperational stage are not able to hold connected conversations with another. In egocentric speech, what each child says is more or less unrelated to what the other speaker said. Children talk together, but not *to* one another in the same sense as adults. During this phase of development, children have no general understanding of categories of thought that adults tend to take for granted: concepts such as causality, speed, weight, or number. Even if the child sees water poured from a tall, thin container into a shorter, wider one, she will not understand that the volume of water remains the same—and conclude rather that there is less water because the water level is lower.

A third period, the **concrete operational stage,** lasts from age seven to eleven. During this phase, children master abstract, logical notions. They are able to handle ideas such as causality without much difficulty. A child at this stage of development will recognize the false reasoning involved in the idea that the wide container holds less water than the thin, narrow one, even though the water levels are different. She becomes capable of carrying out the mathematical operations of multiplying, dividing, and subtracting. Children by this stage are much less egocentric. In the preoperational stage, if a girl is asked, "How many sisters do you have?" she may correctly answer "one." But if asked, "How many sisters does your sister have?" she will probably answer "none," because she cannot see herself from the point of view of her sister. The concrete operational child is able to answer such a question with ease.

The years from eleven to fifteen cover what Piaget called the **formal operational stage.** During adolescence, the developing child becomes able to grasp highly abstract and hypothetical ideas. When faced with a problem, children at this stage are able to review all the possible ways of solving it and go through them theoretically in order to reach a solution. The young person at the formal operational stage is able to understand why some questions are trick ones. To the question, "What creatures are both poodles and dogs?" the individual might not be able to give the correct reply but will understand why the answer "poodles" is right and appreciate the humor in it.

According to Piaget, the first three stages of development are universal; but not all adults reach the formal operational stage. The development of formal operational thought depends in part on processes of schooling. Adults of limited educational attainment tend to continue to think in more concrete terms and retain large traces of egocentrism.

Agents of Socialization

Sociologists often speak of socialization as occurring in two broad phases, involving a number of different agents of socialization. **Agents of socialization** are groups or social contexts in which significant processes of socialization occur. Primary socialization occurs in infancy and childhood and is the most intense period of cultural learning. It is the time when children learn language and basic behavioral patterns that form the foundation for later learning. The family is the main agent of socialization during this phase. Secondary socialization takes place later in childhood and into maturity. In this phase, other agents of socialization take over some of the responsibility from the family. Schools, peer groups, organizations, the media, and eventually the workplace become socializing forces for individuals. Social interactions in these contexts help people learn the values, norms, and beliefs that make up the patterns of their culture.

THE FAMILY

Since family systems vary widely, the range of family contacts that the infant experiences is by no means standard across cultures. The mother everywhere is normally the most important individual in the child's early life, but the nature of the relationships established between mothers and their children is influenced by the form and regularity of their contact. This is, in turn, conditioned by the character of family institutions and their relation to other groups in society.

In modern societies, most early socialization occurs within a small-scale family context. The majority of American children spend their early years within a domestic unit containing mother, father, and perhaps one or two other children. In many other cultures, by contrast, aunts, uncles, and grandparents are often part of a single household and serve as caretakers even for very young infants. Yet even within American society there are many variations in the nature of family contexts. Some children are brought up in single-parent households; some are cared for by two mothering and fathering agents (divorced parents and stepparents). A high proportion of women with families are now employed outside the home and return to their paid work relatively soon after the births of their children. In spite of these variations, the family normally remains the major agency of socialization from infancy to adolescence and beyond—in a sequence of development connecting the generations.

Families have varying "locations" within the overall institutions of a society. In most traditional societies, the family into which a person was born largely determined the individual's social position for the rest of his or her life. In modern societies, social position is not inherited at birth in this way, yet the region and social class of the family into which an individual is born affects patterns of socialization quite distinctly. Children pick up ways of behavior characteristic of their parents or others in their neighborhood or community.

Varying patterns of child rearing and discipline, together with contrasting values and expectations, are found in different sectors of large-scale societies. It is easy to understand the influence of different types of family background if we think of what life is like, say, for a child growing up in a poor black family living in a run-down city neighborhood compared to one born into an affluent white family living in an all-white suburb (Kohn, 1977).

Of course, few if any children simply take over unquestioningly the outlook of their parents. This is especially true in the modern world, in which change is so pervasive. Moreover, the very existence of a range of socializing agents in modern societies leads to many divergences between the outlooks of children, adolescents, and the parental generation.

SCHOOLS

Another important socializing agency is the school. Schooling is a formal process: Students pursue a definite curriculum of subjects. Yet schools are agents of socialization in more subtle respects. Children are expected to be quiet in class, be punctual at lessons, and observe rules of school discipline. They are required to accept and respond to the authority of the teaching staff. Reactions of teachers also affect the expectations children have of themselves. These expectations in turn become linked to their job experience when they leave school. Peer groups are often formed at school, and the system of keeping children in classes according to age reinforces their impact.

PEER RELATIONSHIPS

Another socializing agency is the **peer group.** Peer groups consist of children of a similar age. In some cultures, particularly small traditional societies, peer groups are formalized as **age-grades** (normally confined to males). There are often specific ceremonies or rites that mark the transition of men from one age-grade to another. Those within a particular age-grade generally maintain close and friendly connections throughout their lives. A typical set of age-grades consists of childhood, junior warriorhood, senior warriorhood, junior elderhood, and senior elderhood. Men move through these grades not as individuals, but as whole groups.

The family's importance in socialization is obvious, since the experience of the infant and young child is shaped more or less exclusively within it. It is less apparent, especially to those of us living in Western societies, how significant peer groups are. Yet even without formal age-grades, children over four or five usually spend a great deal of time in the company of friends the same age. Given the high proportion of women now in the work force whose young children play together in day-care centers, peer relations are even more important today than before (Corsaro, 1997; Harris, 1998).

In her book *Gender Play* (1993), Barrie Thorne, a sociologist now at the University of California, Berkeley, looked at socialization in this way. As others had before her, she wanted to understand how children come to know what it means to be male and female (you will learn three classic theories of gender socialization later in this chapter). Rather than seeing children as passively learning the meaning of gender from their parents and teachers, she looked at the way in which children actively create and recreate the meaning of gender in their interactions with each other. The social activities that schoolchildren do together can be as important as other agents for their socialization.

Thorne spent two years observing fourth and fifth graders at two schools in Michigan and California, sitting in the classroom with them and observing their activities outside the classroom. She watched games such as "chase and kiss," "cooties," and "goin' with" and teasing to learn how children construct and experience gender meanings in the classroom and on the playground.

Thorne found that peer groups have a great influence on gender socialization, particularly as children talk about their changing bodies, a subject of great fascination. The social context created by these children determined whether a child's bodily change was experienced with embarrassment or worn with pride. As Thorne observed, "If the most popular women started menstruating or wearing bras (even if they didn't need to), then other girls wanted these changes too. But if the popular didn't wear bras and hadn't. . . . gotten their periods, then these developments were viewed as less desirable."

Thorne's research is a powerful reminder that children are social actors who help create their social world and influence their own socialization. Still, the impact of societal and cultural influences is tremendous, since the activities that children pursue and the values they hold are determined by influences such as their families and the media.

Peer relations are likely to have a significant impact beyond childhood and adolescence. Informal groups of people of similar ages, at work and in other situations, are usually of enduring importance in shaping individuals' attitudes and behavior.

THE MASS MEDIA

Newspapers, periodicals, and journals flourished in the West from the early 1800s onward, but they were confined to a fairly small readership. It was not until a century later that such printed materials became part of the daily experience of millions of people, influencing their attitudes and opinions. The spread of **mass media** involving printed documents was soon accompanied by electronic communication—radio, television, records, and videos. American children spend the equivalent of almost a hundred schooldays per year watching television.

Much research has been done to assess the effects of television programs on the audiences they reach, particularly children. Perhaps the most commonly researched topic is the impact of television on propensities to crime and violence.

The most extensive studies are those carried out by George Gerbner and his collaborators, who have analyzed samples of prime-time and weekend daytime TV for all the major American networks each year since 1967. The number and frequency of violent acts and episodes are charted for a range of programs. Violence is defined as physical force directed against the self or others, in which physical harm or death occurs. Television drama emerges as highly violent in character. On average, 80 percent of programs contain violence, with a rate of 7.5 violent episodes per hour. Children's programs show even higher levels of violence, although killing is less commonly portrayed. Cartoons depict the highest number of violent acts and episodes of any type of television program (Gerbner, 1985).

In general, research on the effects of television on audiences has tended to treat children as passive and undiscriminating in their reactions to what they see. Robert Hodge and David Tripp (1986) emphasized that children's responses to TV involve interpreting, or "reading," what they see, not just registering the content of programs. They suggested that

Video games have become a key part of the culture and experience of childhood today. Studies have indicated that playing video games might have a positive effect on children's social and intellectual development.

most research has not taken account of the complexity of children's mental processes. TV watching, even of trivial programs, is not an inherently low-level intellectual activity; children read programs by relating them to other systems of meaning in their everyday lives. According to Hodge and Tripp, it is not the violence alone that has effects on behavior, but rather the general framework of attitudes within which it is both presented and read.

In recent years home video games have come into widespread use. In his book *Video Kids* (1991), Eugene Provenzo analyzes the impact of Nintendo. There are currently some 19 million Nintendo, Sony, and Sega games in the United States and many more in other countries. Nearly all are owned and operated by children. Social codes and traditions have developed based on the games and their characters. Of the thirty best-selling toys in the United States in 1990, twenty-five were either video games or video equipment. The games are often directly linked to the characters or stories in films and TV programs; in turn, television programming has been based on Nintendo games. Video games, Provenzo concludes, have become a key part of the culture and experience of childhood today.

But is this impact a negative one? It is doubtful that a child's involvement with Nintendo harms her achievement at school. The effects of video games are likely to be governed by other influences on school performance. In other words, where strong pressures deflect students from an interest in their schoolwork, absorption with TV or video pursuits will tend to reinforce these attitudes. Video games and TV then can become a refuge from a disliked school environment.

But it is also possible that video games can act to develop skills that might be relevant both to formal education and to

"Complete Freedom of Movement": Video Games as Gendered Play Spaces

[In a recent essay, sociologist Henry Jenkins describes how video games are gendered play spaces. He suggests that games like Sega Saturn's *Nights into Dreams* represent a fusion of the boys' and girls' game genre.]

[***] In the frame stories that open [*Nights into Dreams*], we enter the mindscape of the two protagonists as they toss and turn in their sleep. Claris, the female protagonist, hopes to gain recognition on the stage as a singer, but has nightmares of being rejected and ridiculed. Elliot, the male character, has fantasies of scoring big on the basketball court yet fears being bullied by bigger and more aggressive players. They run away from their problems, only to find themselves in Nightopia, where they must save the dream world from the evil schemes of Wileman the Wicked and his monstrous minions. In the dreamworld, both Claris and Elliot may assume the identity of Nights, an androgynous harlequin figure, who can fly through the air, transcending all the problems below. *Nights'* complex mythology has players gathering glowing orbs which represent different forms of energy needed to confront Claris and Elliot's problems—purity (white), wisdom (green), hope (yellow), intelligence (blue) and bravery (red).

The tone of this game is aptly captured by one Internet game critic, Big Mitch (n.d.): "The whole experience of *Nights* is in soaring, tumbling, and freewheeling through colorful landscapes, swooping here and there, and just losing yourself in the moment. This is not a game you set out to win; the fun is in the journey rather than the destination." Big Mitch's response suggests a recognition of the fundamentally different qualities of this game—its focus on psychological issues as much as upon action and conflict, its fascination with aimless exploration rather than goal-driven narrative, its movement between a realistic world of everyday problems and a fantasy realm of great adventure, its mixture of the speed and mobility associated with the boys' platform games with the lush natural landscapes and the sculpted soundtracks associated with the girls' games. Spring Valley is a sparkling world of rainbows and waterfalls and emerald green forests. Other levels allow us to splash through cascading fountains or sail past icy mountains and frozen wonderlands or bounce on pillows and off the walls of the surreal Soft Museum or swim through aquatic tunnels. The game's 3-D design allows an exhilarating freedom of movement, enhanced by design features—such as wind resistance—which give players a stronger than average sense of embodiment. *Nights into Dreams* retains some of the dangerous and risky elements associated with the boys' games. There are spooky places in this game, including nightmare worlds full of day-glo serpents and winged beasties, and there are enemies we must battle, yet there is also a sense of unconstrained adventure, floating through the clouds. Our primary enemy is time, the alarm clock which will awaken us from our dreams. Even when we confront monsters, they don't fire upon us; we must simply avoid flying directly into their sharp teeth if we want to master them. When we lose Nights' magical, gender-bending garb, we turn back into boys and girls and must hoof it as pedestrians across the rugged terrain below, a situation which makes it far less likely we will achieve our goals. To be gendered is to be constrained; to escape gender is to escape gravity and to fly above it all.

Sociologist Barrie Thorne has discussed the forms of "borderwork" which occurs when boys and girls occupy the same play spaces: "The spatial separation of boys and girls [on the same playground] constitutes a kind of boundary, perhaps felt most strongly by individuals who want to join an activity con-

trolled by the other gender."[1] Boys and girls are brought together in the same space, but they repeatedly enact the separation and opposition between the two play cultures. In real world play, this "borderwork" takes the form of chases and contests on the one hand and "cooties" or other pollution taboos on the other. When "borderwork" occurs, gender distinctions become extremely rigid and nothing passes between the two spheres. [***]

As we develop digital playspaces for boys and girls, we need to make sure this same pattern isn't repeated, that we do not create blue and pink ghettos inside the playspace. On the one hand, the opening sequences of *Nights into Dreams*, which frame Elliot and Claris as possessing fundamentally different dreams (sports for boys and musical performance for girls, graffiti-laden inner city basketball courts for boys and pastoral gardens for girls), perform this kind of borderwork, defining the proper place for each gender. On the other hand, the androgenous Nights embodies a fantasy of transcending gender and thus achieving the freedom and mobility to fly above it all.

[1]Barrie Thorne, *Gender Play: Girls and Boys in School* (New Brunswick, NJ: Rutgers University, 1993), pp. 64–65.

To win the game, the player must become both the male and the female protagonists and they must join forces for the final level. The penalty for failure in this world is to be trapped on the ground and to be fixed into a single gender.

Thorne finds that aggressive "borderwork" is more likely to occur when children are forced together by adults than when they find themselves interacting more spontaneously, more likely to occur in prestructured institutional settings like the schoolyard than in the informal settings of the subdivisions and apartment complexes. All of this suggests that our fantasy of designing games which will provide common play spaces for girls and boys may be an illusive one, one as full of complications and challenges on its own terms as creating a "girls only" space or encouraging girls to venture into traditional male turf. We are not yet sure what such a gender neutral space will look like. Creating such a space would mean redesigning not only the nature of computer games but also the nature of society. The danger may be that in such a space, gender differences are going to be more acutely felt, as boys and girls will be repelled from each other rather than drawn together. There are reasons why this is a place where neither the feminist entrepreneurs nor the boys' game companies are ready to go, yet as the girls' market is secured, the challenge must be to find a way to move beyond our existing categories and to once again invent new kinds of virtual play spaces.

SOURCE: Henry Jenkins, *From Barbie to Mortal Kombat: Gender and Computer Games* (Cambridge, Mass.: MIT Press, 1998).

Questions

- Why should both girls and boys play video games?
- How does *Nights into Dreams* challenge real-world gender models?
- What do you think is the best strategy to break down gender distinctions in video games? Why?

wider participation in a society that depends increasingly on electronic communication. The sound and look of video games has been a major influence on the development of rave music, rockers like Trent Reznor of Nine Inch Nails, and even films like *The Matrix, Tomb Raider,* and *Final Fantasy*. According to Marsha Kinder, her son Victor's adeptness at Nintendo transferred fruitfully to other spheres. For example, the better he became at video games, the more interested and skillful he was at drawing cartoons. Patricia Greenfield has argued that "video games are the first example of a computer technology that is having a socializing effect on the next generation on a mass scale, and even on a world-wide basis" (Greenfield, 1993).

The mass media are an important influence on socialization, in all forms of society. There are few societies in current times, even among the more traditional cultures, that remain completely untouched by the media. Electronic communication is accessible even to those who are unable to read and write, and in the most impoverished parts of the world it is common to find people owning radios and television sets.

WORK

Work is in all cultures an important setting within which socialization processes operate, although it is only in industrial societies that large numbers of people go "out to work"—that is, go each day to places of work separate from the home. In traditional communities many people farmed the land close to where they lived or had workshops in their dwellings. "Work" in such communities was not so clearly distinct from other activities as it is for most members of the workforce in the modern West. In the industrialized countries, going "out to work" for the first time ordinarily marks a much greater transition in an individual's life than entering work in traditional societies. The work environment often poses unfamiliar demands, perhaps calling for major adjustments in the person's outlook or behavior.

Social Roles

Through the process of socialization, individuals learn about **social roles**—socially defined expectations that a person in a given social position follows. The social role of doctor, for example, encompasses a set of behaviors that should be enacted by all individual doctors, regardless of their personal opinions or outlooks. Because all doctors share this role, it is possible to speak in general terms about the professional role behavior of doctors, irrespective of the specific individuals who occupy that position.

Some sociologists, particularly those associated with the functionalist school, regard social roles as fixed and relatively unchanging parts of a society's culture. They are taken as social facts. According to such a view, individuals learn the expectations that surround social positions in their particular culture and perform those roles largely as they have been defined. Social roles do not involve negotiation or creativity. Rather, they are prescriptive in containing and directing an individual's behavior. Through socialization, individuals internalize social roles and learn how to carry them out.

This view, however, is mistaken. It suggests that individuals simply take on roles, rather than creating or negotiating them. In fact, socialization is a process in which humans can exercise agency; they are not simply passive subjects waiting to be instructed or programmed. Individuals come to understand and assume social roles through an ongoing process of social interaction.

Identity

The cultural settings in which we are born and come to maturity influence our behavior, but that does not mean that humans are robbed of individuality or free will. It might seem as though we are merely stamped into preset molds that society has prepared for us, and some sociologists do tend to write about socialization as though this was the case. But such a view is fundamentally flawed. The fact that from birth to death we are involved in interaction with others certainly conditions our personalities, the values we hold, and the behavior we engage in. Yet socialization is also at the origin of our very individuality and freedom. In the course of socialization each of us develops a sense of identity and the capacity for independent thought and action.

The concept of *identity* in sociology is a multifaceted one and can be approached in a number of ways. Broadly speaking, **identity** relates to the understandings people hold about who they are and what is meaningful to them. These understandings are formed in relation to certain attributes that take priority over other sources of meaning. Some of the main sources of identity include gender, sexual orientation, nationality or ethnicity, and social class. There are two types of identity often spoken of by sociologists: social identity and self-identity (or personal identity). These forms of identity are analytically distinct but are closely related to one another. **Social identity** refers to the characteristics that other people attribute to an individual. These can be seen as markers that indicate who, in a basic sense, that individual is. At the same time, they place that individual in relation to other individuals who share the same attributes. Examples of social identities might include student, mother, lawyer, Catholic, homeless, Asian, dyslexic, married, and so forth. Many individuals have social identities comprising more than one attribute. A person could simultaneously be a mother, an engineer, a Muslim, and a city council member. Multiple social identities reflect the many dimensions of people's lives. Although this plurality of social identities can be a potential source of conflict for people, most individuals organize meaning and experience in their lives around a primary identity that is fairly continuous across time and place.

Social identities therefore involve a collective dimension. They mark ways that individuals are the same as others. Shared identities—predicated on a set of common goals, values, or experiences—can form an important base for social movements. Feminists, environmentalists, labor unionists, and supporters of religious fundamentalist and/or nationalist movements are all examples of cases in which a shared social identity is drawn on as a powerful source of personal meaning or self-worth.

If social identities mark ways in which individuals are the same as others, **self-identity** (or personal identity) sets us apart as distinct individuals. Self-identity refers to the process of self-development through which we formulate a unique sense of ourselves and our relationship to the world around us. The notion of self-identity draws heavily on the work of symbolic interactionists. It is the individual's constant negotiation with the outside world that helps to create and shape his or her sense of self. The process of interaction between self and society helps to link an individual's personal and public worlds. Though the cultural and social environment is a factor in shaping self-identity, individual agency and choice are of central importance.

Tracing the changes in self-identity from traditional to modern societies, we can see a shift away from the fixed, inherited factors that previously guided identity formation. If at one time people's identities were largely informed by their membership in broad social groups, bound by class or nationality, they are now more multifaceted and less stable. The processes of urban growth, industrialization, and the breakdown of earlier social formations have weakened the impact of inherited rules and conventions. Individuals have become more socially and geographically mobile. This has freed people from the tightly knit, relatively homogeneous communities of the past in which patterns were passed down in a fixed way across generations. It has created the space for other sources of personal meaning, such as gender and sexual orientation, to play a greater role in people's sense of identity.

In today's world, we have unprecedented opportunities to make ourselves and to create our own identities. We are our own best resources in defining who we are, where we have come from, and where we are going. Now that the traditional

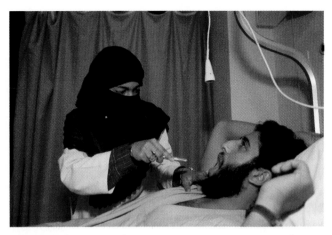

People often exhibit multiple social identities simultaneously, sometimes seemingly conflicting ones. Focusing on her primary identity as a medical professional in this context, a male patient at King Fahd Military Medical Complex in Saudi Arabia allows a doctor who is also a Muslim woman to examine him.

signposts of identity have become less essential, the social world confronts us with a dizzying array of choices about who to be, how to live, and what to do, without offering much guidance about which selections to make. The decisions we make in our everyday lives—about what to wear, how to behave, and how to spend our time—help make us who we are. The modern world forces us to find ourselves. Through our capacity as self-conscious, self-aware human beings, we constantly create and recreate our identities.

Gender Socialization

Agents of socialization play an important role in how children learn **gender roles.** Let's now turn to the study of **gender socialization,** the learning of gender roles through social factors such as the family and the media.

REACTIONS OF PARENTS AND ADULTS

Many studies have been carried out on the degree to which gender differences are the result of social influences. Studies of mother–infant interaction show differences in the treatment of boys and girls even when parents believe their reactions to both are the same. Adults asked to assess the personality of a baby give different answers according to whether or not they believe the child to be a girl or a boy. In one experiment, five young mothers were observed in interaction with a six-month-old called Beth. They tended to smile at her often and offer her dolls to play with. She was seen as "sweet," having a "soft cry."

The reaction of a second group of mothers to a child the same age, named Adam, was noticeably different. The baby was likely to be offered a train or other "male toys" to play with. Beth and Adam were actually the same child, dressed in different clothes (Will, Self, and Datan, 1976).

GENDER LEARNING

Gender learning by infants is almost certainly unconscious. Before a child can accurately label itself as either a boy or a girl, it receives a range of pre-verbal cues. For instance, male and female adults usually handle infants differently. The cosmetics women use contain scents different from those the baby might learn to associate with males. Systematic differences in dress, hairstyle, and so on provide visual cues for the infant in the learning process. By age two, children have a partial understanding of what gender is. They know whether they are boys or girls, and they can usually categorize others accurately. Not until five or six, however, does a child know that a person's sex does not change, that everyone has gender, and that sex differences between girls and boys are anatomically based.

The toys, picture books, and television programs with which young children come into contact all tend to emphasize differences between male and female attributes. Toy stores and mail-order catalogs usually categorize their products by gender. Even some toys that seem neutral in terms of gender are not so in practice. For example, toy kittens and rabbits are recommended for girls, while lions and tigers are seen as more appropriate for boys.

Vanda Lucia Zammuner studied the toy preferences of children aged between seven and ten in Italy and Holland (Zammuner, 1986). Children's attitudes toward a variety of toys were analyzed; stereotypically masculine and feminine toys as well as toys presumed not to be gender typed were included.

Toys play a major role in children's gender learning, as they often emphasize the difference between male and female attributes.

Both the children and their parents were asked to assess which toys were suitable for boys and which for girls. There was close agreement between the adults and the children. On average, the Italian children chose gender-differentiated toys to play with more often than the Dutch children—a finding that conformed to expectations, since Italian culture tends to hold a more traditional view of gender divisions than does Dutch society. As in other studies, girls from both societies chose gender-neutral or boys' toys to play with far more than boys chose girls' toys.

STORYBOOKS AND TELEVISION

Over twenty years ago, Lenore Weitzman and her colleagues carried out an analysis of gender roles in some of the most widely used preschool children's books and found several clear differences in gender roles (Weitzman et al., 1972). Males played a much larger part in the stories and pictures than females, outnumbering females by a ratio of 11 to 1. Including animals with gender identities, the ratio was 95 to 1. The activities of males and females also differed. The males engaged in adventurous pursuits and outdoor activities demanding independence and strength. Where girls did appear, they were portrayed as passive and confined mostly to indoor activities. Girls cooked and cleaned for the males or awaited their return. Much the same was true of the adult men and women represented in the storybooks. Women who were not wives and mothers were imaginary creatures like witches or fairy godmothers. There was not a single woman in all the books analyzed who held an occupation outside the home. By contrast, the men were depicted as fighters, policemen, judges, kings, and so forth.

More recent research suggests that things have changed somewhat but that the large bulk of children's literature remains much the same (Davies, 1991). Fairy tales, for example, embody traditional attitudes toward gender and toward the sorts of aims and ambitions girls and boys are expected to have. "Some day my prince will come"—in versions of fairy tales from several centuries ago, this usually implied that a girl from a poor family might dream of wealth and fortune. Today, its meaning has become more closely tied to the ideals of romantic love. Some feminists have tried to rewrite some of the most celebrated fairy tales, reversing their usual emphases: "I really didn't notice that he had a funny nose. And he certainly looked better all dressed up in fancy clothes. He's not nearly as attractive as he seemed the other night. So I think I'll just pretend that this glass slipper feels too tight" (Viorst, 1986). Like this version of "Cinderella," however, these rewrites are found mainly in books directed to adult audiences and have hardly affected the tales told in innumerable children's books.

Although there are some notable exceptions, analyses of television programs designed for children conform to the findings about children's books. Studies of the most frequently watched cartoons show that most of the leading figures are male and that males dominate the active pursuits. Similar images are found in the commercials that appear throughout the programs.

THE DIFFICULTY OF NONSEXIST CHILD REARING

June Statham studied the experiences of a group of parents committed to nonsexist child rearing. Thirty adults in eighteen families were involved in the research, which included children aged six months to twelve years. The parents were of middle-class background, mostly involved in academic work as teachers or professors. Statham found that most of the parents did not simply try to modify traditional gender roles by seeking to make girls more like boys, but wanted to foster new combinations of the feminine and masculine. They wished boys to be more sensitive to others' feelings and capable of expressing warmth, while girls were encouraged to seek opportunities for learning and self-advancement. All the parents found existing patterns of gender learning difficult to combat. They were reasonably successful at persuading the children to play with nongender-typed toys, but even this proved more difficult than many of them had expected. One mother commented to the researcher:

> If you walk into a toy shop, it's full of war toys for boys and domestic toys for girls, and it sums up society the way it is. This is the way children are being socialized: it's all right for boys to be taught to kill and hurt, and I think it's terrible, it makes me feel sick. I try not to go into toy shops, I feel so angry.

Practically all the children in fact possessed, and played with, gender-typed toys, given to them by relatives.

There are now some storybooks available with strong, independent girls as the main characters, but few depict boys in nontraditional roles. A mother of a five-year-old boy told of her son's reaction when she reversed the sexes of the characters in a story she read to him:

> In fact he was a bit upset when I went through a book which has a boy and a girl in very traditional roles, and changed all the he's to she's and she's to he's. When I first started doing that, he was inclined to say "you don't like boys, you only like girls." I had to explain that

Gender-typed toys are ubiquitous, making it difficult to raise children in a truly nonsexist environment. Barbie, one of the most popular and widely recognized "girl" toys, has been influencing children's ideas about what it means to act "female" for fifty years.

that wasn't true at all, it's just that there's not enough written about girls. (Statham, 1986)

Clearly, gender socialization is very powerful, and challenges to it can be upsetting. Once a gender is "assigned," society expects individuals to act like "females" and "males." It is in the practices of everyday life that these expectations are fulfilled and reproduced (Bourdieu, 1990; Lorber, 1994).

Gender Socialization: The Sociological Debate

FREUD'S THEORY

Perhaps the most influential—and controversial—theory of the emergence of gender identity is that of Sigmund Freud. According to Freud, the learning of gender differences in infants and young children is centered on the possession or absence of the penis. "I have a penis" is equivalent to "I am a boy," while "I am a girl" is equivalent to "I lack a penis." Freud is careful to say that it is not just the anatomical distinctions that matter here; the possession or absence of the penis is symbolic of masculinity and femininity.

At around age four or five, the theory goes, a boy feels threatened by the discipline and autonomy his father demands of him, fantasizing that the father wishes to remove his penis. Partly consciously, but mostly on an unconscious level, the boy recognizes the father as a rival for the affections of his mother. In repressing erotic feelings toward the mother and accepting the father as a superior being, the boy identifies with the father and becomes aware of his male identity. The boy gives up his love for his mother out of an unconscious fear of castration by his father. Girls, on the other hand, supposedly suffer from "penis envy" because they do not possess the visible organ that distinguishes boys. The mother becomes devalued in the little girl's eyes, because she is also seen to lack a penis and to be unable to provide one. When the girl identifies with the mother, she takes over the submissive attitude involved in the recognition of being "second best."

Once this phase is over, the child has learned to repress his erotic feelings. The period from about five years old to puberty, according to Freud, is one of latency—sexual activities tend to be suspended until the biological changes involved in puberty reactivate erotic desires in a direct way. The latency period, covering the early and middle years of school, is the time at which same-sex peer groups are most important in the child's life.

Major objections have been raised against Freud's views, particularly by feminists, but also by many other authors (Mitchell, 1975; Coward, 1984). First, Freud seems to identify gender identity too closely with genital awareness; other, more subtle factors are surely involved. Second, the theory seems to depend on the notion that the penis is superior to the vagina, which is thought of as just a lack of the male organ. Yet why shouldn't the female genitals be considered superior to those of the male? Third, Freud treats the father as the primary disciplining agent, whereas in many cultures the mother plays the more significant part in the imposition of discipline. Fourth, Freud believes that gender learning is concentrated at age four or five. Most later authors have emphasized the importance of earlier learning, beginning in infancy.

CHODOROW'S THEORY

While many writers have made use of Freud's approach in studying gender development, they have usually modified it in major respects. An important example is the sociologist Nancy Chodorow (1978, 1988). Chodorow argues that learning to feel male or female derives from the infant's attachment to his parents from an early age. She places much more emphasis than Freud does on the importance of the mother rather than the father. Children tend to become emotionally involved with the mother, since she is easily the most dominant influence in their early lives. At some point this attachment has to be broken in order for the child to achieve a separate sense of self—the child is required to become less closely dependent.

Chodorow argues that the breaking process occurs in a different way for boys and girls. Girls remain closer to the mother—able, for example, to go on hugging and kissing her and imitating what she does. Because there is no sharp break from the mother, the girl, and later the adult woman, develops a sense of self that is more continuous with other people. Her identity is more likely to be merged with or dependent on another's: first her mother, later a man. In Chodorow's view, this tends to produce characteristics of sensitivity and emotional compassion in women.

Boys gain a sense of self via a more radical rejection of their original closeness to the mother, forging their understanding of masculinity from what is not feminine. They learn not to be "sissies" or "mama's boys." As a result, boys are relatively unskilled in relating closely to others; they develop more analytical ways of looking at the world. They take a more active view of their lives, emphasizing achievement, but they have repressed their ability to understand their own feelings and those of others.

To some extent, Chodorow reverses Freud's emphasis. Masculinity, rather than femininity, is defined by a loss, the forfeiting of continued close attachment to the mother. Male identity is formed through separation; thus, men later in life unconsciously feel that their identity is endangered if they become involved in close emotional relationships with others. Women, on the other hand, feel that the absence of a close relation to another person threatens their self-esteem. These patterns are passed on from generation to generation, because of the primary role women play in the early socialization of children. Women express and define themselves mainly in terms of relationships. Men have repressed these needs and adopt a more manipulative stance toward the world.

Chodorow's work has met with various criticisms. Janet Sayers, for example, has suggested that Chodorow does not explain the struggle of women, particularly in current times, to become autonomous, independent beings (Sayers, 1986). Women (and men), she points out, are more contradictory in their psychological makeup than Chodorow's theory suggests. Femininity may conceal feelings of aggressiveness or assertiveness, which are revealed only obliquely or in certain contexts (Brennan, 1988). Chodorow has also been criticized for her narrow conception of the family, one based on a white, middle-class model. What happens, for example, in one-parent households or, as in many Chicano communities, families where children are cared for by more than one adult (Segura and Pierce, 1993)?

These criticisms don't undermine Chodorow's ideas, which remain important. They teach us a good deal about the nature of femininity, and they help us to understand the origins of what has been called "male inexpressiveness"—the difficulty men have in revealing their feelings to others (Balswick, 1983).

GILLIGAN'S THEORY

Carol Gilligan (1982) has further developed Chodorow's analysis. Her work concentrates on the images adult women and men have of themselves and their attainments. Women, she agrees with Chodorow, define themselves in terms of personal relationships and judge their achievements by reference to the ability to care for others. Women's place in the lives of men is traditionally that of caretaker and helpmate. But the qualities developed in these tasks are frequently devalued by men, who see their own emphasis on individual achievement as the only form of "success." Concern with relationships on the part of women appears to them as a weakness rather than as the strength that in fact it is.

Gilligan carried out intensive interviews with about two hundred American women and men of varying ages and social backgrounds. She asked all of the interviewees a range of questions concerning their moral outlook and conceptions of self. Consistent differences emerged between the views of the women and the men. For instance, the interviewees were asked: "What does it mean to say something is morally right or wrong?" Whereas the men tended to respond to this question by mentioning abstract ideals of duty, justice, and individual freedom, the women persistently raised the theme of helping others. Thus a female college student answered the question in the following way:

> "It [morality] has to do with responsibilities and obligations and values, mainly values. . . . In my life situation I relate morality with interpersonal relationships that have to do with respect for the other person and myself." The interviewer then asked: "Why respect other people?" receiving the answer, "Because they have a consciousness or feelings that can be hurt, an awareness that can be hurt." (Gilligan, 1982)

The women were more tentative in their moral judgments than the men, seeing possible contradictions between following a strict moral code and avoiding harming others. Gilligan suggests that this outlook reflects the traditional situation of women, anchored in caring relationships, rather than the "outward-looking" attitudes of men. Women have in the past deferred to the judgments of men, while being aware that they have qualities that most men lack. Their views of themselves are based on successfully fulfilling the needs of others, rather than on pride in individual achievement (Gilligan, 1982).

Socialization Through the Life Course

The various transitions through which individuals pass during their lives seem at first sight to be biologically fixed—from childhood to adulthood and eventually to death. But the stages of the human **life course** are social as well as biological in nature. They are influenced by cultural differences and also by the material circumstances of people's lives in given types of society. For example, in the modern West, death is usually thought of in relation to old age, because most people enjoy a life span of seventy years or more. In traditional societies of the past, however, more people died in younger age groups than survived to old age.

Childhood

To people living in modern societies, childhood is a clear and distinct stage of life. Children are distinct from babies or toddlers; childhood intervenes between infancy and the teen

This *Madonna and Child*, painted in the thirteenth century by Duccio da Buoninsegna, depicts the infant Jesus with a mature face. Until recently, children in Western society were viewed as little adults.

Japanese and American Teenagers

Studies comparing socialization in varying cultural settings show some interesting contrasts. For example, the idea of the teen years as an extended period of transition between childhood and adulthood emerged in America before it did in Japan. In fact, the Japanese term, *cheenayja,* is an adaptation of the American *teenager.* In premodern Japan, the movement from childhood to adulthood occurred in an instant, because it happened as part of an age-grade system (one that included girls). A child would become an adult when he participated in a special rite. Japanese boys became adults at some point between ages eleven and sixteen, depending on their social rank. The parallel ceremony at which girls were recognized as women was the *kami* age, the age at which they began to wear their hair up rather than down.

Just as in most other nonmodern societies, including those of medieval Europe, young people in Japan knew who they would be and what they would be doing when they became adults. The teenage years weren't a time to experiment. Japanese children were schooled to follow closely the ways of their parents, to whom they owed strict obedience; family norms emphasizing the duties of children toward their parents were very strong.

Such norms have endured to the present day, but they have also come under strain with the high pace of industrial development in contemporary Japan. So are Japanese teenagers now just like American ones? Merry White, a sociologist at Boston University, attempted to answer this question. White interviewed one hundred teens in each culture over a period of three years, trying to gain an in-depth view of their attitudes toward sexuality, school, friendship, and parents (White, 1993). She found big differences between the Japanese and American teenagers, but also came up with unexpected conclusions about both. In neither culture are most teenagers the rebels she expected to find. Instead, she found a

years. Yet the concept of childhood, like so many other aspects of social life today, has only come into being over the past two or three centuries. In earlier societies, the young moved directly from a lengthy infancy into working roles within the community. The French historian Philippe Ariès has argued that "childhood," conceived of as a separate phase of development, did not exist in medieval times (Ariès, 1965). In the paintings of medieval Europe, children are portrayed as little adults, with mature faces and the same style of dress as their elders. Children took part in the same work and play activities as adults, rather than in the childhood games we now take for granted.

Right up to the twentieth century, in the United States and most other Western countries, children were put to work at what now seems a very early age. There are countries in the world today, in fact, where young children are engaged in full-time work, sometimes in physically demanding circumstances (for example, in coal mines). The ideas that children have distinctive rights and that the use of child labor is morally repugnant are quite recent developments.

Because of the long period of childhood that we recognize today, societies now are in some respects more child centered than traditional ones. But a child-centered society, it must be emphasized, is not one in which all children experience love and care from parents or other adults. The physical and sexual abuse of children is a commonplace feature of family life in present-day society, although the full extent of such abuse has only recently come to light. Child abuse has clear connections with what seems to us today like the frequent mistreatment of children in premodern Europe.

It seems possible that as a result of changes currently occurring in modern societies, the separate character of child-

fairly high degree of conformity to wider cultural ideas and an expressed respect for parents in both countries.

What the adults say of their teenage offspring in Japan and the United States is much the same: "Why don't you listen more to what I say?" "When I was your age . . ." The Japanese and American teens also echo each other in some ways: "Do you like me?" "What should I aim for in my life?" "We're cool, but they aren't." Pop music, films, and videos figure large in the experience of both—as does at least a surface sexual knowledgeability, since from an early age in both cultures sexual information, including warnings about sexual disease, is widespread.

The Japanese teenagers, however, come out well ahead of the Americans in terms of school achievements: 95 percent of Japanese teenagers reach a level in academic tests met by only the top 5 percent of young Americans. And while both express respect for parents, the Japanese teenagers remain much closer to theirs than do most of the American teenagers.

The Japanese teenagers are certainly interested in sex but placed it at the bottom of a list of priorities White presented them with; the Americans put it at the top. Teenagers in Japan are nonetheless sexually very active, probably even more so than their American counterparts. Two-thirds of Japanese girls by age fifteen are sexually active. White reports that they are, by Western standards, amazingly forthcoming about their sexual fantasies and practices; nearly 90 percent of the Japanese girls reported that they masturbate twice or more a week.

The Japanese separate clearly three areas of sexuality that are more mixed up for the American teenagers: physical passion, socially approved pairing or marriage, and romantic fantasies. "Love marriages," in which two people establish a

relationship on the basis of emotional and sexual attraction, are now common in Japan. However, they are often the result of an initial introduction of suitable partners arranged by parents, followed by falling in love prior to marriage. Even the most sexually experienced young person in Japan may continue to prefer to have a mature adult arrange an appropriate marriage.

Japanese teenagers often stress that love should grow in marriage, rather than being the basis of choosing a partner in the first place. The sexual activity of young girls tends to involve several older boys and not be bound up with dating. White quotes as typical of young, unmarried Japanese women a respondent who was in her early twenties when interviewed. She first had sexual intercourse at fifteen—like three-quarters of her friends—and since had accumulated many "sex friends." These were not *boifurends* (boyfriends), a relationship that implies emotional attachment. She said, "I do it [have sex] because it is fun. However, marriage is a totally different story, you know. Marriage should be more realistic and practical" (White, 1993).

hood is diminishing once more. Some observers have suggested that children now grow up so fast that this is in fact the case. They point out that even small children may watch the same television programs as adults, thereby becoming much more familiar early on with the adult world than did preceding generations.

The Teenager

The idea of the "teenager," so familiar to us today, also didn't exist until recently. The biological changes involved in puberty (the point at which a person becomes capable of adult sexual activity and reproduction) are universal. Yet in many cultures, these do not produce the degree of turmoil and uncertainty often found among young people in modern soci-

eties. In cultures that foster age-grades, for example, with distinct ceremonials that signal a person's transition to adulthood, the process of psychosexual development generally seems easier to negotiate. Adolescents in such societies have less to "unlearn" since the pace of change is slower. There is a time when children in Western societies are required to be children no longer: to put away their toys and break with childish pursuits. In traditional cultures, where children are already working alongside adults, this process of unlearning is normally much less jarring.

In Western societies, teenagers are betwixt and between: They often try to follow adult ways, but they are treated in law as children. They may wish to go to work, but they are constrained to stay in school. Teenagers in the West live in between childhood and adulthood, growing up in a society subject to continuous change.

Before the twentieth century, young children in many Western countries were put to work at an early age. Some, like the coal mining boys above, were made to do dangerous or physically demanding work.

Young Adulthood

Young adulthood seems increasingly to be a specific stage in personal and sexual development in modern societies (Goldscheider and Waite, 1991). Particularly among more affluent groups, people in their early twenties are taking the time to travel and explore sexual, political, and religious affiliations. The importance of this postponement of the responsibilities of full adulthood is likely to grow, given the extended period of education many people now undergo.

Mature Adulthood

Most young adults in the West today can look forward to a life stretching right through to old age. In premodern times, few could anticipate such a future with much confidence. Death through sickness or injury was much more frequent among all age groups than it is today, and women in particular were at great risk because of the high rate of mortality in childbirth.

On the other hand, some of the strains we experience now were less pronounced in previous times. People usually maintained a closer connection with their parents and other kin than in today's more mobile populations, and the routines of work they followed were the same as those of their forebears. In current times, major uncertainties must be resolved in marriage, family life, and other social contexts. We have to "make" our own lives more than people did in the past. The creation of sexual and marital ties, for instance, now depends on individual initiative and selection, rather than being fixed by parents. This represents greater freedom for the individual, but the responsibility can also impose difficulties.

Keeping a forward-looking outlook in middle age has taken on a particular importance in modern societies. Most people do

In traditional societies, older people are accorded a great deal of respect and play a major role in the community. The Tatas of Togo delegate an elder to greet a new chief.

not expect to be doing the same thing all their lives, as was the case for the majority in traditional cultures. Individuals who have spent their lives in one career may find the level they have reached in middle age unsatisfying and further opportunities blocked. Women who have spent their early adulthood raising a family and whose children have left home may feel themselves to be without any social value. The phenomenon of a "midlife crisis" is very real for many middle-aged people. A person may feel she has thrown away the opportunities that life had to offer, or she will never attain goals cherished since childhood. Yet growing older need not lead to resignation or bleak despair; a release from childhood dreams can be liberating.

Old Age

In traditional societies, older people were normally accorded a great deal of respect. Among cultures that included age-grades, the elders usually had a major—often the final—say over matters of importance to the community. Within families, the authority of both men and women mostly increased with age. In industrialized societies, by contrast, older people tend to lack authority within both the family and the wider social community. Having retired from the labor force, they may be poorer than ever before in their lives. At the same time, there has been a great increase in the proportion of the population over age sixty-five. In 1900, only one in thirty people in the United States was over sixty-five; the proportion today is one in eight and will likely rise to one in five by the year 2030 (U.S. Bureau of the Census, 1996a). The same trend is found in all the industrially advanced countries.

Transition to the age-grade of elder in a traditional culture often marked the pinnacle of the status an individual could achieve. In modern societies, retirement tends to bring the opposite consequences. No longer living with their children and often having retired from paid work, older people may find it difficult to make the final period of their life rewarding. It used to be thought that those who successfully cope with old age do so by turning to their inner resources, becoming less interested in the material rewards that social life has to offer. Although this may often be true, it seems likely that in a society in which many are physically healthy in old age, an outward-looking view will become more and more prevalent. Those in retirement might find renewal in what has been called the "third age," in which a new phase of education begins (see also Chapter 12 on lifelong learning).

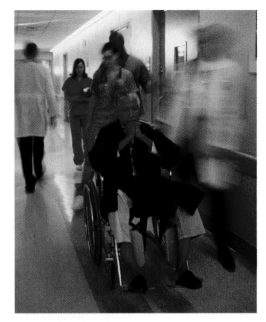

In modern industrial societies, many elderly people face social alienation.

Study Outline

www.wwnorton.com/giddens5

Culture, Society, and Child Socialization

- *Socialization* is the process whereby, through contact with other human beings, the helpless infant gradually becomes a self-aware, knowledgeable human being, skilled in the ways of the given culture and environment.

Theories of Child Development

- According to G. H. Mead, the child achieves an understanding of being a separate agent by seeing how others behave toward him or her in social contexts. At a later stage, entering into organized games, learning the rules of play, the child comes to understand "the *generalized other*"—general values and cultural rules.
- Jean Piaget distinguishes several main stages in the development of the child's capability to make sense of the world. Each stage involves the acquisition of new cognitive skills and depends on the successful completion of the preceding one. According to Piaget these stages of cognitive development are universal features of socialization.

Agents of Socialization

- *Agents of socialization* are structured groups or contexts within which significant processes of socialization occur. In all cultures, the family is the principal socializing agency of the child during infancy. Other influences include *peer groups,* schools, and the *mass media.*
- Through the process of socialization and interaction with others, individuals learn about *social roles*—socially defined expectations that a person in a given social position will follow. One result of this process is the development of a *social identity,* the characteristics that other people attribute to an individual. If social identities mark ways in which individuals are the same as others, *self-identity* sets us apart as distinct individuals. The concept of self-identity, which draws on symbolic interactionism, refers to the process of self-development through which we formulate a unique sense of ourselves and our relationship to the world around us.
- The development of mass communications has enlarged the range of socializing agencies. The spread of mass printed media was later accompanied by the use of electronic communication. TV exerts a particularly powerful influence, reaching people of all ages at regular intervals every day.
- *Gender socialization* begins virtually as soon as an infant is born. Even parents who believe they treat children equally tend to produce different responses to boys and girls. These differences are reinforced by many other cultural influences.

Socialization Through the Life Cycle

• Socialization continues throughout the life cycle. At each distinct phase of life there are transitions to be made or crises to be overcome. This includes facing death as the termination of physical existence.

Key Concepts

age-grade (p. 92)
agents of socialization (p. 91)
cognition (p. 90)
concrete operational stage (p. 91)
egocentric (p. 91)
formal operational stage (p. 91)
gender role (p. 97)
gender socialization (p. 97)
generalized other (p. 90)
identity (p. 96)
life course (p. 101)
mass media (p. 93)
peer group (p. 92)
preoperational stage (p. 91)
self-consciousness (p. 90)
self-identity (personal identity) (p. 97)
sensorimotor stage (p. 90)
social identity (p. 96)
social reproduction (p. 88)
social role (p. 96)
social self (p. 90)
socialization (p. 88)

Review Questions

1. What are the main agents of socialization in contemporary society?
   a. Family, schools, the political system, the economic system, and the urban system
   b. Family, schools, peer groups, the mass media, and work
   c. Movies, videos, computers, and the Internet
   d. Newspapers, magazines, radio, and television

2. When does socialization end?
   a. At the beginning of adulthood
   b. During the midlife crisis
   c. On retirement
   d. Socialization never ends because people are in a process of constant interaction.

3. What is the difference between the "I" and the "me"?
   a. The "I" is the unsocialized infant; the "me" is the social self.
   b. The "I" is the id; the "me" is the ego.
   c. The "I" is the private inner self; the "me" is the social self that others see.
   d. The "I" is the inner self who wants, wants, wants; the "me" is the inner self who works out what "I" actually needs.

4. What part do peer groups play in the gender socialization of children?
   a. None.
   b. A significant role. They help children judge the significance of ongoing changes to their bodies—for example, whether the first signs of puberty are treated as a matter of pride or embarrassment.
   c. A marginal role. Peer groups only interpret what parents and media are telling children.
   d. A dominating role. Only peer groups determine how children understand the significance of gender.

5. According to George Herbert Mead's theory of child development, what is the importance of playing organized games at the age of eight or nine?
   a. Children can have fun at an early age and then focus on succeeding at school and work later in life.
   b. Children begin to understand the overall values and morality according to which social life is conducted.
   c. Children learn to be competitive and see others as rivals.
   d. Children learn how to use a computer keyboard, an important skill throughout one's life.

6. In traditional versus modern societies, what is the most important difference regarding how the elderly are generally viewed?
   a. In traditional societies, elders had little authority in the family and community; in modern societies, elders have a great deal of authority.
   b. In traditional societies, elders had a great deal of authority in the family and community; in modern societies, elders have very little authority.
   c. In traditional societies, the concept of "elder" did not exist; in modern societies, people aspire to the age-grade "elder."
   d. In traditional societies, elders were put to death; in modern societies, elders are put in "old-age" homes.

7. The learning of male or female roles takes place through a process called
   a. genderization.
   b. gender socialization.
   c. sexualization.
   d. sex role learning.

8. Groups or social contexts in which significant processes or socialization occur are called:
   a. context operations.
   b. concrete operations.
   c. sensorimotors.
   d. agents of socialization.

9. Jean Piaget's theory of child development is based on:
   a. the stages of cognitive development.
   b. the emergence of a sense of self, of self-awareness.
   c. the importance of sociobiology.
   d. all of the above.
10. Children learn the ways of their elders, thereby perpetuating the values, norms, and social practices of their culture. This process is known as:
    a. evolution.
    b. social interaction.
    c. socialization.
    d. natural selection.

Thinking Sociologically Exercises

1. Concisely review how an individual becomes a social person according to each of the three leading theorists discussed in this chapter: G. H. Mead, Jean Piaget, and Sigmund Freud. Which of these three theories seems most appropriate and correct to you? Explain why.
2. Using alcoholic beverages is one of many things we do as a result of socialization. Suggest how the family, peers, schools, and mass media help to establish the desire to consume alcoholic drinks. Of the preceding, which force is the most persuasive? Explain.

Data Exercises

www.wwnorton.com/giddens5
Keyword: Data4

In the data exercise for this chapter, you will once again use the General Social Survey data to explore the topic of socialization. Specifically, you will learn more about what behaviors Americans value and believe are important for a child to learn.

The Study of Daily Life

Familiarize yourself with the study of everyday life.

Nonverbal Communication

Know the various forms of nonverbal communication.

Social Rules and Talk

Learn the research process of ethnomethodology, the study of our conversations and how we make sense of each other.

Face, Body, and Speech in Interaction

Recognize the different contexts of our social life and how they are used to convey or hide meaning. Also learn how our social actions are organized in time and space.

Interaction in Time and Space

Understand that interaction is situated, that it occurs in a particular place and for a particular length of time. See that the way we organize our social actions is not unique by learning how other cultures organize their social lives.

Linking Microsociology and Macrosociology

See how face-to-face interactions and broader features of society are closely related.

CHAPTER FIVE

SOCIAL INTERACTION AND EVERYDAY LIFE

eric Schmitz is a personal trainer and fitness director at the Santa Barbara Athletic Club, an upscale health club. He has been employed at the gym since he graduated from the University of Wisconsin–Madison with a degree in Exercise Physiology in 1987.

Schmitz knows hundreds of people who work out at the gym. Some of them he has worked with as fitness director as they were getting to know the machines in their early months there. He has met many others while teaching classes in spinning—a group cycling class. Others he came to know through casual contact, since many of the same people work out at the same time every week.

The personal space is limited within a gym environment, due to the proximity of the exercise equipment. For example, in the weight training circuit at SBAC, one section contains a number of Cybex machines near to one another. Members must work out in close proximity to one another, and their bodies constantly crisscross as they move through their workouts.

It is almost impossible for Schmitz to walk anywhere in this physical space without potentially making eye contact with someone he has at least met. He will greet certain of these patrons the first time he sees them in the day, but afterward it is usually understood that they will go about their own business without acknowledging one another in the way they did earlier.

When passersby quickly glance at each other and then look away again, they demonstrate what Erving Goffman (1967, 1971) calls the **civil inattention** we require of each other in many situations. Civil inattention is not the same as merely ignoring another person. Each individual

Walking along a crowded city street, one engages in civil inattention. Though the people in the photo above can hear the phone conversations these men are having, they make no indication of their awareness.

indicates recognition of the other person's presence but avoids any gesture that might be taken as too intrusive. Can you think of examples of civil inattention in your own life? Perhaps when you are walking down the hall of a dormitory, or trying to decide where to sit in the cafeteria, or simply walking across campus? Civil inattention to others is something we engage in more or less unconsciously, but it is of fundamental importance to the existence of social life, which must proceed efficiently and, sometimes among total strangers, without fear. When civil inattention occurs among passing strangers, an individual implies to another person that she has no reason to suspect his intentions, be hostile to him, or in any other way specifically avoid him.

The best way to see the importance of this is by thinking of examples where it doesn't apply. When a person stares fixedly at another, allowing her face openly to express a particular emotion, it is normally with a lover, family member, or close friend. Strangers or chance acquaintances, whether encountered on the street, at work, or at a party, virtually never hold the gaze of another in this way. To do so may be taken as an indication of hostile intent. It is only where two groups are strongly antagonistic to one another that strangers might indulge in such a practice. Thus, whites in the United States have been known in the past to give a "hate stare" to blacks walking past.

Even friends in close conversation need to be careful about how they look at one another. Each individual demonstrates attention and involvement in the conversation by regularly looking at the eyes of the other, but not staring into them. To look too intently might be taken as a sign of mistrust about, or at least failure to understand, what the other is saying. Yet if each party does not engage the eyes of the other at all, he is likely to be thought evasive, shifty, or otherwise odd.

The Study of Daily Life

Why should we concern ourselves with such seemingly trivial aspects of social behavior? Passing someone on the street or exchanging a few words with a friend seem minor and uninteresting activities, things we do countless times a day without giving them any thought. In fact, the study of such apparently insignificant forms of **social interaction** is of major importance in sociology—and, far from being uninteresting, is one of the most absorbing of all areas of sociological investigation. There are three reasons for this.

First, our day-to-day routines, with their almost constant interactions with others, give structure and form to what we do; we can learn a great deal about ourselves as social beings, and about social life itself, from studying them. Our lives are organized around the repetition of similar patterns of behavior from day to day, week to week, month to month, and year to year. Think of what you did yesterday, for example, and the day before that. If they were both weekdays, in all probability you got up at about the same time each day (an important routine in itself). You may have gone off to class fairly early in the morning, making a journey from home to school or college that you make virtually every weekday. You perhaps met some friends for lunch, returning to classes or private study in the afternoon. Later, you retraced your steps back home, possibly going out later in the evening with other friends.

Of course, the routines we follow from day to day are not identical, and our patterns of activity on weekends usually contrast with those on weekdays. And if we make a major change in our life, like leaving college to take up a job, alterations in our daily routines are usually necessary; but then we establish a new and fairly regular set of habits again.

Second, the study of everyday life reveals to us how humans can act creatively to shape reality. Although social behavior is guided to some extent by forces such as roles, norms, and shared expectations, individuals perceive reality differently according to their backgrounds, interests, and motivations. Because individuals are capable of creative action, they continuously shape reality through the decisions and actions they take. In other words, reality is not fixed or static—it is created through human interactions. This notion of the social construction of reality lies at the heart of the symbolic interactionist perspective introduced in Chapter 1.

Third, studying social interaction in everyday life sheds light on larger social systems and institutions. All large-scale social systems, in fact, depend on the patterns of social interaction we engage in daily. This is easy to demonstrate. Consider again the case of two strangers passing on the street. Such an event may seem to have little direct relevance to large-scale, more permanent forms of social organization. But when we take into account many such interactions, they are no longer irrelevant. In modern societies, most people live in towns and cities and constantly interact with others whom they do not know personally. Civil inattention is one among other mechanisms that give city life, with its bustling crowds and fleeting, impersonal contacts, the character it has.

In this chapter, we will first learn about the nonverbal cues (facial expressions and bodily gestures) all of us use when interacting with each other. We will then move on to analyze everyday speech—how we use language to communicate to others the meanings we wish to get across. Finally, we will focus on the ways in which our lives are structured by daily routines, paying particular attention to how we coordinate our actions across space and time.

Nonverbal Communication

Social interaction requires numerous forms of **nonverbal communication**—the exchange of information and meaning through facial expressions, gestures, and movements of the body. Nonverbal communication is sometimes referred to as "body language," but this is misleading, because we characteristically use such nonverbal cues to eliminate or expand on what is said with words.

"Face," Gestures, and Emotion

One major aspect of nonverbal communication is the facial expression of emotion. Paul Ekman and his colleagues have developed what they call the Facial Action Coding System (FACS) for describing movements of the facial muscles that give rise to particular expressions (Ekman and Friesen, 1978). By this means, they have tried to inject some precision into an area notoriously open to inconsistent or contradictory interpretations—for there is little agreement about how emotions are to be identified and classified. Charles Darwin, the originator of evolutionary theory, claimed that basic modes of emotional expression are the same in all human beings. Although some have disputed the claim, Ekman's research among people from widely different cultural backgrounds seems to confirm Darwin's view. Ekman and W. V. Friesen carried out a

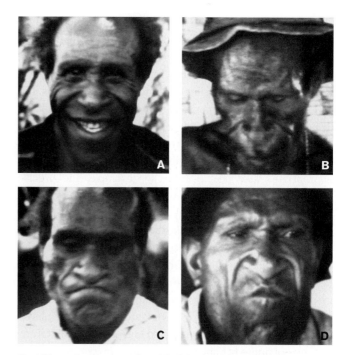

Paul Ekman's photographs of facial expressions from a tribesman in an isolated community in New Guinea helped to test the idea that basic modes of emotional expression are the same among all people. Here the instructions were to show how your face would look if you were a person in a story and (A) your friend had come and you were happy; (B) your child had died; (C) you were angry and about to fight; and (D) you saw a dead pig that had been lying there a long time.

study of an isolated community in New Guinea, whose members had previously had virtually no contact with outsiders. When they were shown pictures of facial expressions conveying six emotions (happiness, sadness, anger, disgust, fear, surprise), the New Guineans were able to identify these emotions.

According to Ekman, the results of his own and similar studies of different peoples support the view that the facial expression of emotion and its interpretation are innate in human beings. He acknowledges that his evidence does not conclusively demonstrate this, and it may be that widely shared cultural learning experiences are involved; however, his conclusions are supported by other types of research. I. Eibl-Eibesfeldt studied six children born deaf and blind to see how far their facial expressions were the same as those of sighted and hearing individuals in particular emotional situations (1972). He found that the children smiled when engaged in obviously pleasurable activities, raised their eyebrows in surprise when sniffing at an object with an unaccustomed smell, and frowned when repeatedly offered a disliked object. Since the children could not have seen other people behaving in these ways, it seems that these responses must be innately determined.

Using the FACS, Ekman and Friesen identified a number of the discrete facial muscle actions in newborn infants that are also found in adult expressions of emotion. Infants seem, for example, to produce facial expressions similar to the adult expression of disgust (pursing the lips and frowning) in response to sour tastes. But although the facial expression of emotion seems to be partly innate, individual and cultural factors influence what exact form facial movements take and the contexts in which they are deemed appropriate. How people smile, for example, the precise movement of the lips and other facial muscles, and how fleeting the smile is all vary among cultures.

There are no gestures or bodily postures that have been shown to characterize all, or even most, cultures. In some societies, for instance, people nod when they mean no, the opposite of Anglo-American practice. Gestures Americans tend to use a great deal, such as pointing, seem not to exist among certain peoples (Bull, 1983). Similarly, a straightened forefinger placed in the center of the cheek and rotated is used in parts of Italy as a gesture of praise but appears to be unknown elsewhere.

Like facial expressions, gestures and bodily posture are continually used to fill out utterances, as well as to convey meanings when nothing is actually said. All three can be used to joke, show irony, or show skepticism. The nonverbal impressions that we convey inadvertently often indicate that what we say is not quite what we really mean. Blushing is perhaps the most obvious example, but innumerable other subtle indicators can be picked up by other people. Genuine facial expressions tend to evaporate after four or five seconds. A smile that lasts longer could indicate deceit. An expression of surprise that lasts too long may indicate deliberate sarcasm—to show that the individual is not in fact surprised after all.

Gender and Nonverbal Communication

Is there a gender dimension to everyday social interaction? There are reasons to believe there is. Because interactions are shaped by the larger social context, it is not surprising that both verbal and nonverbal communication may be perceived and expressed differently by men and women. Understandings of gender and gender roles are greatly influenced by social factors and are related broadly to issues of power and status in society. These dynamics are evident even in standard interactions in daily life. Take as an example one of the most common nonverbal expressions—eye contact. Individuals use eye contact in a wide variety of ways, often to catch someone's attention or to begin a social interaction. In societies where men on the whole dominate women in both public and private life, men may feel freer than women to make eye contact with strangers.

A particular form of eye contact—staring—illustrates the contrasts in meaning between men and women of identical forms of nonverbal communication. A man who stares at a woman can be seen as acting in a "natural" or "innocent" way; if the woman is uncomfortable, she can evade the gaze by looking away or choosing not to sustain the interaction. On the other hand, a woman who stares at a man is often regarded as behaving in a suggestive or sexually leading manner. Taken individually such cases may seem inconsequential; when viewed collectively they help reinforce patterns of gender inequality.

Social Rules and Talk

Although we routinely use nonverbal cues in our own behavior and in making sense of the behavior of others, much of our interaction is done through talk—casual verbal exchange—carried on in informal conversations with others. Sociologists have always accepted that language is fundamental to social life. Recently, however, an approach has been developed that is specifically concerned with how people use language in the ordinary contexts of everyday life.

Ethnomethodology is the study of the "ethnomethods"—the folk, or lay, methods—people use to *make sense* of what others do, and particularly of what they say. We all apply these methods, normally without having to give any conscious attention to them. Often we can only make sense of what is said in conversation if we know the social context, which does not appear in the words themselves. Take the following conversation (Heritage, 1985):

> **A:** *I have a fourteen-year-old son.*
>
> **B:** *Well, that's all right.*
>
> **A:** *I also have a dog.*
>
> **B:** *Oh, I'm sorry.*

What do you think is happening here? What is the relation between the speakers? What if you were told that this is a conversation between a prospective tenant and a landlord? The conversation then becomes sensible: Some landlords accept children but don't permit their tenants to keep pets. Yet if we don't know the social context, the responses of individual B seem to bear no relation to the statements of A. *Part* of the sense is in the words, and *part* is in the way in which the meaning emerges from the social context.

Shared Understandings

The most inconsequential forms of daily talk presume complicated, shared knowledge brought into play by those speaking. In fact, our small talk is so complex that it has so far proved impossible to program even the most sophisticated computers to converse with human beings. The words used in ordinary talk do not always have precise meanings, and we "fix" what we want to say through the unstated assumptions that back it up. If Maria asks Tom: "What did you do yesterday?" the words in the question themselves suggest no obvious answer. A day is a long time, and it would be logical for Tom to answer: "Well, at 7:16, I woke up. At 7:18, I got out of bed, went to the bathroom and started to brush my teeth. At 7:19, I turned on the shower. . . ." We understand the type of response the question calls for by knowing Maria, what sort of activities she and Tom consider relevant, and what Tom usually does on a particular day of the week, among other things.

Garfinkel's Experiments

The "background expectancies" with which we organize ordinary conversations were highlighted by some experiments Harold Garfinkel undertook with student volunteers. The students were asked to engage a friend or relative in conversation and to insist that casual remarks or general comments be actively pursued to make their meaning precise. If someone said, "Have a nice day," the student was to respond, "Nice in what sense, exactly?" "Which part of the day do you mean?" and so forth. One of the exchanges that resulted ran as follows. S is the friend, E the student volunteer (Garfinkel, 1963):

S: *How are you?*

E: *How am I in regard to what? My health, my finances, my school work, my peace of mind, my . . .*

S: *(red in the face and suddenly out of control): Look! I was just trying to be polite. Frankly, I don't give a damn how you are.*

Why do people get so upset when apparently minor conventions of talk are not followed? The answer is that the stability and meaningfulness of our daily social lives depend on the sharing of unstated cultural assumptions about what is said and why. If we weren't able to take these for granted, meaningful communication would be impossible. Any question or contribution to a conversation would have to be followed by a massive "search procedure" of the sort Garfinkel's subjects were told to initiate, and interaction would simply break down. What seem at first sight to be unimportant conventions of talk,

therefore, turn out to be fundamental to the very fabric of social life, which is why their breach is so serious.

Note that in everyday life, people on occasion deliberately feign ignorance of unstated knowledge. This may be done to rebuff the others, poke fun at them, cause embarrassment, or call attention to a double meaning in what was said. Consider, for example, this classic exchange between parent and teenager:

P: *Where are you going?*

T: *Out.*

P: *What are you going to do?*

T: *Nothing.*

The responses of the teenager are effectively the opposite of those of the volunteers in Garfinkel's experiments. Rather than pursuing inquiries where this is not normally done, the teenager declines to provide appropriate answers at all—essentially saying, "Mind your own business!"

The first question might elicit a different response from another person in another context:

A: *Where are you going?*

B: *I'm going quietly round the bend.*

B deliberately misreads A's question in order to convey ironically worry or frustration. Comedy and joking thrive on such deliberate misunderstandings of the unstated assumptions involved in talk. There is nothing threatening about this so long as the parties concerned recognize that the intent is to provoke laughter.

"Interactional Vandalism"

We have already seen that conversations are one of the main ways in which our daily lives are maintained in a stable and coherent manner. We feel most comfortable when the tacit conventions of small talk are adhered to; when they are breached, we can feel threatened, confused, and insecure. In most everyday talk, conversants are carefully attuned to the cues they get from others—such as changes in intonation, slight pauses, or gestures—in order to facilitate conversation smoothly. By being mutually aware, conversants "cooperate" in opening and closing interactions, and in taking turns to speak. Interactions in which one party is conversationally "uncooperative," however, can give rise to tensions.

Garfinkel's students created tense situations by intentionally undermining conversational rules as part of a sociological experiment. But what about situations in the real world in

Interactional Vandalism: A Sociologist's Fieldnote

[The author of this selection, Mitchell Duneier, coauthored this textbook. Duneier describes the behavior and lives of poor and sometimes homeless black men who work or beg in New York's Greenwich Village.]

It is well known that streets and sidewalks are places where women are disadvantaged by public harassment. While the things we are witnessing are a case of the larger public harassments that occur between some people working the street and pedestrians of both genders, perhaps for women it is a problem in distinct ways. Keith is attempting to control the woman *as a woman*, knowing that even privileged women occupy vulnerable positions in public space. Like most males (black and white), he has been taught that to be a male is to possess this power, and he feels entitled to control her. I asked after his awareness of the dog's owner as a woman.

"So, you know the dog's name," I said after they left.

"Yeah."

"Do you know the woman's name?"

"No. I'd rather have the dog than her. You know why? Dog don't want nothing but a little attention. Give him some food. Take the fucker out for a walk. Let him watch TV with you, and it's cool. But she wants room and board, clothing, makeup, hairdos, fabulous dinners, and rent, plus they want a salary for giving you some pussy once in a while.". . .

Out on Sixth Avenue one day, I ask Mudrick to tell me a little about his relationship to women on the street. Since most women ignore him, he says, he talks to all of them. That way he might get to have conversations with some of them.

Three white women in their twenties approach, and I am given a demonstration of his method. "Hi, ladies. How you-all feeling, ladies? You-all look very nice, you know. Have a nice day."

I have seen Mudrick engage in such behavior over and over again, but there is no doubt in my mind that this demon-

stration has been for me, a way of responding to the question I had just asked.

"Let me ask you a question, Mudrick. When you do that, explain to me the pleasure you get out of it."

"I get a good kick out of it."

"Explain to me the kick you get out of it."

"It make me feel good and I try to make them happy, the things I say to them, you understand? The things I say, they can't accept. They gotta deal with it."

"What do you mean, 'They gotta deal with it?'"

"They *have* to deal with it. I say sweet things to a woman. Make her feel good. Like, You look nice. You look very nice. I'd like to be with you someday if I can. Try to make you happy. Some womens treated so wrong they scared to talk to the right man. Men treat women *so* wrong. Women don't give a fuck about men. Now they go to women. They gets a woman to be their man. They turn into be a lesbian. Because they scared to mess with a man."

A woman walks by without acknowledging him, and Mudrick tells me that she must be a lesbian. He claims that the women he addresses never feel harassed, because he gives them respect, and he can tell from their smiles that they *like* the attention.

A white woman wearing sunglasses approaches with her friend.

"Hey, you, with the shades on. You look very nice."

"Thank you," she says.

"Your friend look nice, too."

"Thank you."

He tells me that the women never respond by turning away or looking angry.

"What's the worst things that women will do when you say that to them?"

"They can't do anything. Because, the words I say, they don't have any choice."

SOURCE: Reprinted from Mitchell Duneier, *Sidewalk* (New York: Farrar, Straus and Giroux, 1999), pp. 193–95, 210.

Questions

- In what ways do Mudrick and Keith take advantage of social convention and rules of politeness to interact with women?
- Why do you think these homeless men try to talk to women on the street, even though their remarks don't result in dates or even long conversations? What do they get out of it?
- Why are Mudrick's and Keith's questions and compliments to women a form of interactional vandalism?
- Why is the behavior of these men seen as different from the catcalls of construction workers or fraternity brothers?

which people "make trouble" through their conversational practices? One study investigated verbal interchanges between pedestrians and street people in New York City to understand why such interactions are often seen as problematic by passersby. The researchers used a technique called **conversation analysis** to compare a selection of street interchanges with samples of everyday talk. Conversation analysis is a methodology that examines all facets of a conversation for meaning—from the smallest filler words (such as "um" and "ah") to the precise timing of interchanges (including pauses, interruptions, and overlaps).

The study looked at interactions between black men—many of whom were homeless, alcoholic, or drug addicted—and white women who passed by them on the street. The men would often try to initiate conversations with passing women by calling out to them, paying them compliments, or asking them questions. But something "goes wrong" in these conversations, because the women rarely respond as they would in a normal interaction. Even though the men's comments are rarely hostile in tone, the women tend to quicken their step and stare fixedly ahead. The following shows attempts by Mudrick, a black man in his late fifties, to engage women in conversation (Duneier and Molotch, 1999):

[Mudrick] begins this interaction as a white woman who looks about 25 approaches at a steady pace:
1. **Mudrick:** *I love you baby.*
She crosses her arms and quickens her walk, ignoring the comment.
2. **Mudrick:** *Marry me.*
Next, it is two white women, also probably in their mid-twenties:
3. **Mudrick:** *Hi girls, you all look very nice today. You have some money? Buy some books.*
They ignore him. Next, it is a young black woman.
4. **Mudrick:** *Hey pretty. Hey pretty.*
She keeps walking without acknowledging him.
5. **Mudrick:** *'Scuse me. 'Scuse me. I know you hear me.*
Then he addresses a white woman in her thirties.
6. **Mudrick:** *I'm watching you. You look nice, you know.*
She ignores him.

Negotiating smooth "openings" and "closings" to conversations is a fundamental requirement for urban civility. These crucial aspects of conversation were highly problematic between the men and women. Where the women resisted the men's attempts at opening conversations, the men ignored the women's resistance and persisted. Similarly, if the men succeeded in opening a conversation, they often refused to respond to cues from the women to close the conversation once it had gotten under way (Duneier and Molotch, 1999):

1. **Mudrick:** *Hey pretty.*
2. **Woman:** *Hi how you doin'.*
3. **Mudrick:** *You alright?*
4. **Mudrick:** *You look very nice you know. I like how you have your hair pinned.*
5. **Mudrick:** *You married?*
6. **Woman:** *Yeah.*
7. **Mudrick:** *Huh?*
8. **Woman:** *Yeah.*
9. **Mudrick:** *Where the rings at?*
10. **Woman:** *I have it home.*
11. **Mudrick:** *Y' have it home?*
12. **Woman:** *Yeah.*
13. **Mudrick:** *Can I get your name?*
14. **Mudrick:** *My name is Mudrick, what's yours?*
She does not answer and walks on.

In this instance, Mudrick made nine out of the fourteen utterances in the interaction to initiate the conversation and to elicit further responses from the woman. From the transcript alone, it is quite evident that the woman is not interested in talking, but when conversation analysis is applied to the tape recording, her reluctance becomes even clearer. The woman delays all of her responses—even when she does give them, while Mudrick replies immediately, his comments sometimes overlapping hers. Timing in conversations is a very precise indicator; delaying a response by even a fraction of a second is adequate in most everyday interactions to signal the desire to change the course of a conversation. By betraying these tacit rules of sociability, Mudrick was practicing conversation in a way that was "technically rude." The woman, in return, was also "technically rude" in ignoring Mudrick's repeated attempts to engage her in talk. It is the "technically rude" nature of these street interchanges that make them problematic for passersby to handle. When standard cues for opening and closing conversations are not adhered to, individuals feel a sense of profound and inexplicable insecurity.

The term **interactional vandalism** describes cases like these in which a subordinate person breaks the tacit rules of everyday interaction that are of value to the more powerful. The men on the street often do conform to everyday forms of speech in their interactions with one another, local shopkeepers, the police, relatives, and acquaintances. But when they choose to, they subvert the tacit conventions for everyday talk in a way that leaves passersby disoriented. Even more than physical assaults or vulgar verbal abuse, interactional vandalism leaves victims unable to articulate what has happened.

This study of interactional vandalism provides another example of the two-way links between micro-level interactions and forces that operate on the macro level. To the men on the street, the white women who ignore their attempts at conversation appear distant, cold, and bereft of sympathy—legitimate "targets" for such interactions. The women, meanwhile, may often take the men's behavior as proof that they are indeed dangerous and best avoided. Interactional vandalism is closely tied up with overarching class, gender, and racial structures. The fear and anxiety generated in such mundane interactions help to constitute the outside statuses and forces that, in turn, influence the interactions themselves. Interactional vandalism is part of a self-reinforcing system of mutual suspicion and incivility.

Response Cries

Some kinds of utterances are not talk but consist of muttered exclamations, or what Goffman has called **response cries** (Goffman, 1981). Consider Lucy, who exclaims, "Oops!" after knocking over a glass of water. "Oops!" seems to be merely an uninteresting reflex response to a mishap, rather like blinking your eye when a person moves a hand sharply toward your face. It is not a reflex, however, as shown by the fact that people do not usually make the exclamation when alone. "Oops!" is normally directed toward others present. The exclamation demonstrates to witnesses that the lapse is only minor and momentary, not something that should cast doubt on Lucy's command of her actions.

"Oops!" is used only in situations of minor failure, rather than in major accidents or calamities—which also demonstrates that the exclamation is part of our controlled management of the details of social life. Moreover, the word may be used by someone observing Lucy, rather than by Lucy herself, or it may be used to sound a warning to another. "Oops!" is normally a curt sound, but the "oo" may be prolonged in some situations. Thus, someone might extend the sound to cover a critical moment in performing a task. For instance, a parent may utter an extended "Oops!" or "Oopsadaisy!" when playfully tossing a child in the air. The sound covers the brief phase when the child may feel a loss of control, reassuring him and probably at the same time developing his understanding of response cries.

This may all sound very contrived and exaggerated. Why bother to analyze such an inconsequential utterance in this detail? Surely we don't pay as much attention to what we say as this example suggests? Of course we don't—on a conscious level. The crucial point, however, is that we take for granted an immensely complicated, continuous control of our appearance and actions. In situations of interaction, we are never expected just to be present on the scene. Others expect, as we expect of them, that we will display what Goffman calls "controlled alertness." A fundamental part of being human is continually demonstrating to others our competence in the routines of daily life.

Face, Body, and Speech in Interaction

Let us summarize at this point what we have learned so far. Everyday interaction depends on subtle relationships between what we convey with our faces and bodies and what we express in words. We use the facial expressions and bodily gestures of other people to fill in what they communicate verbally and to check if they are sincere in what they say. Mostly without realizing it, each of us keeps a tight and continuous control over facial expression, bodily posture, and movement in the course of our daily interaction with others.

Face, bodily management, and speech, then, are used to convey certain meanings and to hide others. We also organize our activities in the *contexts* of social life to achieve the same ends, as we shall now see.

Encounters

In many social situations, we engage in what Goffman calls **unfocused interaction** with others. Unfocused interaction takes place whenever individuals exhibit mutual awareness of one another's presence. This is usually the case anywhere large numbers of people are assembled together, as on a busy street, in a theater crowd, or at a party. When people are in the presence of others, even if they do not directly talk to them, they continually communicate nonverbally through their posture and facial and physical gestures.

Focused interaction occurs when individuals directly attend to what others say or do. Except when someone is standing alone, say at a party, all interaction involves both focused and unfocused exchanges. Goffman calls an instance of focused interaction an **encounter**, and much of our day-to-day life consists of encounters with other people—family, friends, colleagues—frequently occurring against the background of unfocused interaction with others present on the scene. Small talk, seminar discussions, games, and routine face-to-face contacts (with ticket clerks, waiters, shop assistants, and so forth) are all examples of encounters.

Encounters always need "openings," which indicate that civil inattention is being discarded. When strangers meet and begin to talk at a party, the moment of ceasing civil inattention is always risky, since misunderstandings can easily occur about the nature of the encounter being established (Goffman, 1971). Hence, the making of eye contact may first be ambiguous and tentative. A person can then act as though he had made no direct move if the overture is not accepted. In focused interaction, each person communicates as much by facial expression and gesture as by the words actually exchanged. Goffman distinguishes between the expressions individuals "give" and those they "give off." The first are the words and facial expressions people use to produce certain impressions on others. The second are the clues that others may spot to check their sincerity or truthfulness. For instance, a restaurant owner listens with a polite smile to the statements of customers about how much they enjoyed their meals. At the same time, he is noting how pleased they seemed to be while eating the food, whether a lot was left over, and the tone of voice they use to express their satisfaction.

Impression Management

Goffman and other writers on social interaction often use notions from the theater in their analyses. The concept of social role, for example, originated in a theatrical setting. **Roles** are socially defined expectations that a person in a given **status** (or **social position**) follows. To be a teacher is to hold a specific position; the teacher's role consists of acting in specified ways toward her pupils. Goffman sees social life as though played out by actors on a stage—or on many stages, because how we act depends on the roles we are playing at a particular time. People are sensitive to how they are seen by others and use many forms of **impression management** to compel others to react to them in the ways they wish. Although we may sometimes do this in a calculated way, usually it is among the things we do without conscious attention. When Philip attends a business meeting, he wears a suit and tie and is on his

best behavior; that evening, when relaxing with friends at a football game, he wears jeans and a sweatshirt and tells a lot of jokes. This is impression management.

As we just noted above, the social roles that we adopt are highly dependent on our social status. A person's social status can be different depending on the social context. For instance, as a "student" you have a certain status and are expected to act a certain way when you are around your professors. As a "son" or "daughter" you have a different status from a student, and society (especially your parents) has different expectations for you. Likewise, as a "friend" you have an entirely different position in the social order, and the roles you adopt would change accordingly. Obviously, a person has many statuses at the same time. Sociologists refer to the group of statuses that you occupy as a **status set**.

Sociologists also like to distinguish between ascribed status and achieved status. An **ascribed status** is one that you are "assigned" based on biological factors such as race, sex, or age. Thus your ascribed statuses could be "white," "female," and "teenager." An **achieved status** is one that is earned through an individual's own effort. Your achieved statuses could be "high school graduate," "athlete," or "employee." While we may like to believe that it is our achieved statuses that are most important, society may not agree. In any society, some statuses have priority over all other statuses and generally determine a person's overall position in society. Sociologists refer to this as a **master status** (Hughes, 1945; Becker, 1963). The most common master statuses are those based on gender and race. Sociologists have shown that in an encounter, one of the first things that people notice about one another is gender and race (Omi and Winant, 1994). As we shall see shortly, both race and gender strongly shape our social interactions.

FRONT AND BACK REGIONS

Much of social life, Goffman suggested, can be divided into front regions and back regions. **Front regions** are social occasions or encounters in which individuals act out formal roles; they are "onstage performances." Teamwork is often involved in creating front-region performances. Two prominent politicians in the same party may put on an elaborate show of unity and friendship before the television cameras, even though each privately detests the other. A wife and husband may take care to conceal their quarrels from their children, preserving a front of harmony, only to fight bitterly once the children are safely tucked in bed.

The **back regions** are where people assemble the props and prepare themselves for interaction in the more formal settings. Back regions resemble the backstage of a theater or the off-camera activities of filmmaking. When they are safely behind the scenes, people can relax and give vent to feelings

"Hmmm... what shall I wear today...?"

This glimpse of former Democratic presidential hopeful Howard Dean moments before addressing a crowd provides a metaphorical depiction of front and back regions. Backstage, or in the back region, Dean composes himself with the support of an assistant. When he takes the stage, or begins his front-region performance, he will need to appear confident, knowledgeable, and enthusiastic.

and styles of behavior they keep in check when on front stage. Back regions permit

> profanity, open sexual remarks, elaborate griping . . . rough informal dress, "sloppy" sitting and standing posture, use of dialect or substandard speech, mumbling and shouting, playful aggressiveness and "kidding," inconsiderateness for the other in minor but potentially symbolic acts, minor self-involvement such as humming, whistling, chewing, nibbling, belching and flatulence. (Goffman, 1973)

Thus, a waitress may be the soul of quiet courtesy when serving a customer but become loud and aggressive once behind the swing doors of the kitchen. Probably few people would continue to patronize restaurants if they could see all that goes on in the kitchens.

ADOPTING ROLES: INTIMATE EXAMINATIONS

For an example of collaboration in impression management that also borrows from the theater, let's look at one particular study in some detail. James Henslin and Mae Biggs studied a specific, highly delicate type of encounter: a woman's visit to a gynecologist (Henslin and Biggs, 1971, 1997). At the time of the study, most pelvic examinations were carried out by male doctors, and hence the experience was (and sometimes still is) fraught with potential ambiguities and embarrassment for both parties. Men and women in the West are socialized to think of the genitals as the most private part of the body, and

seeing, and particularly touching, the genitals of another person is ordinarily associated with intimate sexual encounters. Some women feel so worried by the prospect of a pelvic examination that they refuse to visit the doctor, male or female, even when they suspect there is a strong medical reason to do so.

Henslin and Biggs analyzed material collected by Biggs, a trained nurse, from a large number of gynecological examinations. They interpreted what they found as having several typical stages. Adopting a dramaturgical metaphor, they suggested that each phase can be treated as a distinct scene, in which the parts the actors play alter as the episode unfolds. In the prologue, the woman enters the waiting room preparing to assume the role of patient and temporarily discarding her outside identity. Called into the consulting room, she adopts the "patient" role, and the first scene opens. The doctor assumes a businesslike, professional manner and treats the patient as a proper and competent person, maintaining eye contact and listening politely to what she has to say. If he decides an examination is called for, he tells her so and leaves the room; scene one is over.

As he leaves, the nurse comes in. She is an important stagehand in the main scene shortly to begin. She soothes any worries that the patient might have, acting as both a confidante—knowing some of the "things women have to put up with"—and a collaborator in what is to follow. Crucial to the next scene, the nurse helps alter the patient from a person to a "nonperson" for the vital scene—which features a body, part of which is to be scrutinized, rather than a complete human being. In Henslin and Biggs's study, the nurse not only supervises the patient's undressing, but takes over aspects that normally the patient would control. Thus, she takes the patient's clothes and folds them. Most women wish their underwear to be out of sight when the doctor returns, and the nurse makes sure that this is so. She guides the patient to the examining table and covers most of her body with a sheet before the physician returns.

The central scene now opens, with the nurse as well as the doctor taking part. The presence of the nurse helps ensure that the interaction between the doctor and the patient is free of sexual overtones and also provides a legal witness should the physician be charged with unprofessional conduct. The examination proceeds as though the personality of the patient were absent; the sheet across her separates the genital area from the rest of her body, and her position does not allow her to watch the examination itself. Save for any specific medical queries, the doctor ignores her, sitting on a low stool, out of her line of vision. The patient collaborates in becoming a temporary nonperson, not initiating conversation and keeping any movements to a minimum.

In the interval between this and the final scene, the nurse again plays the role of stagehand, helping the patient to become a full person once more. After the doctor has left the room, the two may again engage in conversation, the patient expressing relief that the examination is over. Having dressed and re-groomed herself, the patient is ready to face the concluding scene. The doctor reenters and, in discussing the results of the examination, again treats the patient as a complete and responsible person. Resuming his polite, professional manner, he conveys that his reactions to her are in no way altered by the intimate contact with her body. The epilogue is played out when she leaves the physician's office, taking up again her identity in the outside world. The patient and the doctor have thus collaborated in such a way as to manage the interaction and the impression each participant forms of the other.

Personal Space

There are cultural differences in the definition of **personal space**. In Western culture, people usually maintain a distance of at least three feet when engaged in focused interaction with others; when standing side by side, they may stand closer together. In the Middle East, people often stand closer to each other than is thought acceptable in the West. Westerners visiting that part of the world are likely to find themselves disconcerted by this unexpected physical proximity.

Edward T. Hall, who has worked extensively on nonverbal communication, distinguishes four zones of personal space. Intimate distance, of up to one and a half feet, is reserved for very few social contacts. Only those involved in relationships in which regular bodily touching is permitted, such as lovers or parents and children, operate within this zone of private space. Personal distance, from one and a half to four feet, is the normal spacing for encounters with friends and close acquaintances. Some intimacy of contact is permitted, but this tends to be strictly limited. Social distance, from four to twelve feet, is the zone usually maintained in formal settings such as interviews. The fourth zone is that of public distance, beyond twelve feet, preserved by those who are performing to an audience.

In ordinary interaction, the most fraught zones are those of intimate and personal distance. If these zones are invaded, people try to recapture their space. We may stare at the intruder as if to say, "Move away!" or elbow him aside. When people are forced into proximity closer than they deem desirable, they might create a kind of physical boundary: A reader at a crowded library desk might physically demarcate a private space by stacking books around its edges (Hall, 1969, 1973).

Interaction in Time and Space

Understanding how activities are distributed in time and space is fundamental to analyzing encounters, and also to understanding social life in general. All interaction is situated—it occurs in a particular place and has a specific duration in time. Our actions over the course of a day tend to be "zoned" in time as well as in space. Thus, for example, most people spend a zone—say, from 9:00 A.M. to 5:00 P.M.—of their daily time working. Their weekly time is also zoned: They are likely to work on weekdays and spend weekends at home, altering the pattern of their activities on the weekend days. As we move through the temporal zones of the day, we are also often moving across space as well: To get to work, we may take a bus from one area of a city to another or perhaps commute in from the suburbs. When we analyze the contexts of social interaction, therefore, it is often useful to look at people's movements across **time-space**.

The concept of **regionalization** will help us understand how social life is zoned in time-space. Take the example of a private house. A modern house is regionalized into rooms, hallways, and floors if there is more than one story. These spaces are not just physically separate areas, but are zoned in time as well. The living rooms and kitchen are used most in the daylight hours, the bedrooms at night. The interaction that occurs in these regions is bound by both spatial and temporal divisions. Some areas of the house form back regions, with "performances" taking place in the others. At times, the whole house can become a back region. Once again, this idea is beautifully captured by Goffman:

> On a Sunday morning, a whole household can use the wall around its domestic establishment to conceal a relaxing slovenliness in dress and civil endeavor, extending to all rooms the informality that is usually restricted to kitchen and bedrooms. So, too, in American middle-class neighborhoods, on afternoons the line between children's playground and home may be defined as backstage by mothers, who pass along it wearing jeans, loafers, and a minimum of make-up. . . . And, of course, a region that is thoroughly established as a front region for the regular performance of a particular routine often functions as a back region before and after each performance, for at these times the permanent fixtures may undergo repairs, restoration, and rearrangement, or the performers may hold dress rehearsals. To see this we need only glance into a restaurant, or store, or home, a few minutes before these establishments are opened to us for the day. (Goffman, 1973)

Clock Time

In modern societies, the zoning of our activities is strongly influenced by **clock time**. Without clocks and the precise timing of activities, and thereby their coordination across space, industrialized societies could not exist (Mumford, 1973). The measuring of time by clocks is today standardized across the globe, making possible the complex international transport systems and communications we now depend on. World standard time was first introduced in 1884 at a conference of nations held in Washington. The globe was then partitioned into twenty-four time zones, each one hour apart, and an exact beginning of the universal day was fixed.

Fourteenth-century monasteries were the first organizations to try to schedule the activities of their inmates precisely across the day and week. Today, there is virtually no group or organization that does not do so—the greater the number of people and resources involved, the more precise the scheduling must be. Eviatar Zerubavel demonstrated this in his study of the temporal structure of a large modern hospital (1979, 1982). A hospital must operate on a twenty-four-hour basis, and coordinating the staff and resources is a highly complex matter. For instance, the nurses work for one time period in ward A, another time period in ward B, and so on, and are also called on to alternate between day- and night-shift work. Nurses, doctors, and other staff, plus the resources they need, must be integrated together both in time and in space.

Social Life and the Ordering of Space and Time

The Internet is another example of how closely forms of social life are bound up with our control of space and time. The Internet makes it possible for us to interact with people we never see or meet, in any corner of the world. Such technological change "rearranges" space—we can interact with anyone without moving from our chair. It also alters our experience of time, because communication on the electronic highway is almost immediate. Until about fifty years ago, most communication across space required a duration of time. If you sent a letter to someone abroad, there was a time gap while the letter was carried, by ship, train, truck, or plane, to the person to whom it was written.

People still write letters by hand today, of course, but instantaneous communication has become basic to our social world. Our lives would be almost unimaginable without it. We are so used to being able to switch on the TV and watch the news or make a phone call or send an e-mail message to a friend in another state that it is hard for us to imagine what life would be like otherwise.

Everyday Life in Cultural and Historical Perspective

Some of the mechanisms of social interaction analyzed by Goffman, Garfinkel, and others seem to be universal. But much of Goffman's discussion of civil inattention and other kinds of interaction primarily concerns societies in which contact with strangers is commonplace. What about very small traditional societies, where there are no strangers and few settings in which more than a handful of people are together at any one time?

To see some of the contrasts between social interaction in modern and traditional societies, let's take as an example one of the least developed cultures in terms of technology remaining in the world: the !Kung (sometimes known as the Bushmen), who live in the Kalahari Desert area of Botswana and Namibia, in southern Africa (Lee, 1968, 1969; the exclamation mark refers to a click sound one makes before pronouncing the name). Although their way of life is changing because of outside influences, their traditional patterns of social life are still evident.

The !Kung live in groups of some thirty or forty people, in temporary settlements near water holes. Food is scarce in their environment, and they must walk far and wide to find it. Such roaming takes up most of the average day. Women and

International Tourism

Have you ever had a face-to-face conversation with someone from another country? Or connected to an overseas Web site? Have you ever traveled to another part of the world? If you answered yes to any of these questions, you have witnessed the effects of globalization on social interaction. Americans, of course, have always interacted with people from foreign lands if for no other reason than America itself is an ethnically and culturally diverse nation. At the same time, globalization—a relatively recent phenomenon—has changed both the frequency and the nature of interactions between people of different nations. The historical sociologist Charles Tilly, in fact, defines globalization in terms of these changes. According to Tilly, "globalization means an increase in the geographic range of locally consequential social interactions" (1995). In other words, with globalization a greater proportion of our interactions come to involve, directly or indirectly, people from other countries.

What are the characteristics of social interactions that take place between individuals of different nations? Important contributions to the study of this problem have been made by those working in the area of the sociology of tourism. Sociologists of tourism note that globalization has

greatly expanded the possibilities for international travel, both by encouraging an interest in other countries and by facilitating the movement of tourists across international borders. As a result, more than 45 million foreign tourists visited the United States in 1994—a significant increase from previous decades. These visitors pumped more than $60 billion into the U.S. economy (OECD, 1996). Americans are also traveling the world in record numbers.

children often stay back in the camp, but equally often the whole group spends the day walking. Members of the community will sometimes fan out over an area of up to a hundred square miles in the course of a day, returning to the camp at night to eat and sleep. The men may be alone or in groups of two or three for much of the day. There is one period of the year, however, when the routines of their daily activities change: the winter rainy season, when water is abundant and food much easier to come by. The everyday life of the !Kung during this period is centered around ritual and ceremonial activities, the preparation for and enactment of which is very time consuming.

The members of most !Kung groups never see anyone they don't know reasonably well. Until contacts with the outside became more common in recent years, they had no word for "stranger." While the !Kung, particularly the males, may spend long periods of the day out of contact with others, in

the community itself there is little opportunity for privacy. Families sleep in flimsy, open dwellings, with virtually all activities open to public view. No one has studied the !Kung with Goffman's observations on everyday life in mind, but it is easy to see that some aspects of his work have limited application to !Kung social life. There are few opportunities, for example, to create front and back regions. The closing off of different gatherings and encounters by the walls of rooms, separate buildings, and the various neighborhoods of cities common in modern societies are remote from the activities of the !Kung.

The Compulsion of Proximity

In modern societies, in complete contrast to the !Kung—as will be explored in the chapters that follow—we are constantly interacting with others whom we may never see or

High levels of international tourism, of course, translate into an increase in the number of face-to-face interactions between people of different countries. According to the British sociologist John Urry (1990), many of these interactions are shaped by the "tourist gaze," the expectation on the part of the tourist that he or she will have "exotic" experiences while traveling abroad. "Exotic" experiences are those that violate our everyday expectations about how social interaction and interaction with the physical environment are supposed to proceed. Americans traveling in England, for example, may delight in the fact that the British drive on the left-hand side of the road. Such behavior is disconcerting to American drivers. Our rules of the road are so ingrained that we experience systematic violations of those rules as strange, weird, and exotic. Yet, as tourists, we take pleasure in this strangeness. In a sense, it is what we have paid money to see—along with Big Ben and the Tower of London. Imagine how disappointed you would be if you traveled to a different country only to find that it was almost exactly the same as the city or town in which you grew up.

Yet most tourists do not want their experiences to be *too* exotic. One of the most popular destinations for young Americans in Paris, for example, is a McDonald's restaurant. Some come to see if there is any truth to the line from the movie *Pulp Fiction* that because the French use the metric system, McDonald's "quarter pounder with cheese" hamburgers are called "Royales with cheese" (it is true, by the way). But many others come for the comfort of eating familiar food in a familiar setting. The contradictory demands for the exotic and the familiar are at the heart of the tourist gaze.

The tourist gaze may put strains on face-to-face interactions between tourists and locals. Locals who are part of the tourist industry may appreciate overseas travelers for the economic benefits they bring to the places they visit. Other locals may resent tourists for their demanding attitudes or for the overdevelopment that often occurs in popular tourist destinations. Tourists may interrogate locals about aspects of their everyday lives, such as their food, work, and recreational habits; they may do this either to enhance their understanding of other cultures or to judge negatively those who are different from themselves.

As tourism increases with the march of globalization, sociologists will have to watch carefully to see what dominant patterns of interaction emerge between tourists and locals, and to determine, among other things, whether these interactions tend to be friendly or antagonistic.

meet. Almost all of our everyday transactions, such as buying groceries or making a bank deposit, bring us into contact—but *indirect* contact—with people who may live thousands of miles away. The banking system, for example, is international. Any money you deposit is a small part of the financial investments the bank makes worldwide.

Some people are concerned that the rapid advances in communications technology such as e-mail, the Internet, and e-commerce will only increase this tendency toward indirect interactions. Our society is becoming "devoiced," some claim, as the capabilities of technology grow ever greater. According to this view, as the pace of life accelerates, people are increasingly isolating themselves; we now interact more with our televisions and computers than with our neighbors or members of the community.

Now that e-mail, instant messages, electronic discussion groups, and chat rooms have become facts of life for many people in industrialized countries, what is the nature of these interactions, and what new complexities are emerging from them? In a 1997 study of office workers, almost half of the respondents said that the Internet had replaced the need for face-to-face communication. A third of them admitted to using e-mail deliberately in order to avoid the need for face-to-face communication. Others reported that the use of abusive or offensive e-mails within the workplace had resulted in the complete breakdown of some office relations. Online communication seems to allow more room for misinterpretation, confusion, and abuse than more traditional forms of communication.

The problem lies in the nature of human communication. We think of it as a product of the mind, but it's done by bodies: faces move, voices intone, bodies sway, hands gesture. . . . On the Internet, the mind is present but the body is gone. Recipients get few clues to the personality and mood of the person, can only guess why messages are sent, what they mean, what responses to make. Trust is virtually out the window. It's a risky business. (Locke, 2000)

Many Internet enthusiasts disagree. They argue that, far from being impersonal, online communication has many inherent advantages that cannot be claimed by more traditional forms of interaction such as the telephone and face-to-face meetings. The human voice, for example, may be far superior in terms of expressing emotion and subtleties of meaning, but it can also convey information about the speaker's age, gender, ethnicity, or social position—information that could be used to the speaker's disadvantage. Electronic communication, it is noted, masks all these identifying markers and ensures that attention focuses strictly on the content of the message. This can be a great advantage for women or other traditionally disadvantaged groups whose opinions are sometimes devalued in other settings (Pascoe, 2000). Electronic interaction is often presented as liberating and empowering, since people can create their own online identities and speak more freely than they would elsewhere.

Who is right in this debate? How far can electronic communication substitute for face-to-face interaction? There is little question that new media forms are revolutionizing the way people communicate, but even at times when it is more expedient to interact indirectly, humans still value direct contact—possibly even more highly than before. People in business, for instance, continue to attend meetings, sometimes flying halfway around the world to do so, when it would seem much simpler and more effective to transact business through a conference call or video link. Family members could arrange "virtual" reunions or holiday gatherings using electronic real-time communications, but we all recognize that they would lack the warmth and intimacy of face-to-face celebrations.

An explanation for this phenomenon comes from Deidre Boden and Harvey Molotch, who have studied what they call the **compulsion of proximity**: the need of individuals to meet with one another in situations of *copresence*, or face-to-face interaction. People put themselves out to attend meetings, Boden and Molotch suggest, because situations of copresence, for reasons documented by Goffman in his studies of interaction, supply much richer information about how other people think and feel, and about their sincerity, than any form of electronic communication. Only by actually being in the presence of people who make decisions affecting us in important ways do we feel able to learn what is going on and confident that we can impress them with our own views and our own sincerity. "Copresence," Boden and Molotch say, "affects access to the body part that 'never lies,' the eyes—the 'windows on the soul.' Eye contact itself signals a degree of inti-macy and trust; copresent interactants continuously monitor the subtle movements of this most subtle body part" (1994).

The Social Construction of Reality: The Sociological Debate

Within sociology, multiple theoretical frameworks are used to explain social reality. These theories differ in their explanations of social phenomena, yet they share the assumption that social reality exists independently of people's talking about it or living in it.

Not all sociologists share this assumption. The theoretical approach called **social constructionism** believes that what individuals and society perceive and understand as reality is itself a creation of the social interaction of individuals and groups. Trying to "explain" social reality, then, would be to overlook and to reify (regard as a given truth) the processes through which such reality is constructed. Therefore, social constructionists argue that sociologists need to document and analyze these processes and not simply the concept of social reality they give rise to.

In their 1966 classic, *The Social Construction of Reality*, the sociologists Peter Berger and Thomas Luckmann examine commonsense knowledge—those things that individuals take for granted as real. They emphasize that these "obvious" facts of social reality may differ among people from different cultures, and even among different people within the same culture. The task becomes an analysis of the *processes* by which individuals come to perceive what is "real" to them as real (Berger and Luckmann, 1966).

Social constructionists apply the ideas of Berger and Luckmann to the investigation of social phenomena, to illuminate the ways in which members of society come to know and simultaneously create what is real. While social constructionists have examined such diverse topics as medicine and medical treatment, gender relations, and emotions, much of their work has focused on social problems, crime, and delinquency.

The work of Aaron Cicourel provides an example of social constructionist research in the area of juvenile delinquency. Within most of sociology, data regarding rates and cases of juvenile delinquency are taken as given (i.e., real), and theories are created to explain the patterns observed in the data. For example, arrest and court data indicate that juveniles from single-parent families are more likely to commit delinquent acts than are juveniles from two-parent homes, thus sociologists develop explanations for this observed relationship: Perhaps children from single-parent homes have less supervision, or perhaps they lack appropriate role models.

By contrast, Cicourel observed the *processes* involved in the arrest and classification of juveniles suspected of delinquency; that is, he observed the creation of the "official" delinquency data. He discovered that police procedures in the handling of juveniles rely on commonsense understandings of what juvenile delinquents are "really like."

For example, when juveniles from lower-class families were arrested, police were more likely to view their offenses as results of poor supervision or a lack of proper role models, and would retain the juveniles in custody. Juveniles from upper-class homes, however, were more likely to be released to their parents' care, where police and parents believed the juvenile could receive proper discipline. Thus, the practices of police serve to formally assign the label of "juvenile delinquent" more often to juveniles from lower-class homes than to those from upper-class homes—even when the youths committed similar offenses. This assignment produces the very data which in turn confirm the relationships held by the commonsense views; for example, that juveniles from poor families are more likely to engage in delinquency. Cicourel's study shows that through interacting with other people in society, we transform our commonsense notions of reality into independent, "objective" proof of their own validity (Cicourel, 1968).

Social constructionism is not without its critics. The sociologists Steve Woolgar and Dorothy Pawluch argue that social constructionists aim to show the subjective creation of social reality, yet in doing so selectively view certain features as objective and others as constructed. For example, in analyses examining which juveniles become labeled as delinquent, social constructionists often argue that the initial behaviors reported for the juveniles are identical; therefore, any differences between those juveniles labeled delinquent and those avoiding such a label must be due to the construction of the label "delinquent." Critics argue that social constructionism inconsistently presents the initial behaviors as objective, while arguing that the labeling process is subjective (Woolgar and Pawluch, 1985).

Other sociologists have criticized social constructionism for its unwillingness to accept broader social forces as powerful influences on observable social outcomes. For example, some critics have argued that while reality may be a constructed perpetuation of commonsense beliefs, these beliefs themselves may be caused by existing social factors such as capitalism or patriarchy.

Ultimately, social constructionism offers a theoretical approach to understanding social reality that radically differs from most other sociological approaches. Rather than assuming that social reality objectively exists, social constructionists work to document and analyze the processes through which social reality is constructed, such that the construction then serves to confirm its own status as social reality.

Linking Microsociology and Macrosociology

As we saw in Chapter 1, *microsociology*, the study of everyday behavior in situations of face-to-face interaction, and *macrosociology*, the study of the broader features of society like class or gender hierarchies, are closely connected. We will now turn to examine social encounters on a crowded city sidewalk to illustrate this point.

Women and Men in Public

Take, for example, a situation that may seem "micro" on its face: A woman walking down the street is verbally harassed by a group of men. In her study, *Passing By: Gender and Public Harassment*, Carol Brooks Gardner found that in various settings, most famously, the edges of construction sites, these types of unwanted interaction occur as something women frequently experience as abusive.

Although the harassment of a single woman might be analyzed in microsociological terms by looking at a single interaction, it is not fruitful to view it that simply. Such harassment is typical of street talk involving men and women who are strangers (Gardner, 1995). And these kinds of interactions cannot simply be understood without also looking at the larger background of gender hierarchy in the United States. In this way we can see how micro- and macroanalysis are connected. For example, Gardner linked the harassment of women by men to the larger system of gender inequality, represented by male privilege in public spaces, women's physical vulnerability, and the omnipresent threat of rape.

Without making this link between micro- and macrosociology, we can have only a limited understanding of these interactions. It might seem as though these types of interactions are isolated instances or that they could be eliminated by teaching people good manners. Understanding the link between micro and macro helps us see that in order to attack the problem at its root cause, one would need to focus on eliminating the forms of gender inequality that give rise to such interactions.

Blacks and Whites in Public

Have you ever crossed to the other side of the street when you felt threatened by someone behind you or someone coming

Immediate assumptions based on race, gender, economic status, and style of dress, among other signs and behavioral cues, affect the way strangers behave toward each other. Elijah Anderson's study of social interaction between strangers on urban streets showed a strong connection between such micro-level interactions and the creation of social order.

toward you? One sociologist who tried to understand simple interactions of this kind is Elijah Anderson.

Anderson began by describing social interaction on the streets of two adjacent urban neighborhoods. His book *Streetwise: Race, Class, and Change in an Urban Community* (1990) found that studying everyday life sheds light on how social order is created by the individual building blocks of infinite micro-level interactions. He was particularly interested in understanding interactions when at least one party was viewed as threatening. Anderson showed that the ways many blacks and whites interact on the streets of a northern city had a great deal to do with the structure of racial stereotypes, which is itself linked to the economic structure of society. In this way, he showed the link between micro interactions and the larger macro structures of society.

Anderson began by recalling Erving Goffman's description of how social roles and statuses come into existence in partic-

ular contexts or locations: "When an individual enters the presence of others, they commonly seek to acquire information about him or bring into play information already possessed.... Information about the individual helps to define the situation, enabling others to know in advance what he will expect of them and they may expect of him."

Following Goffman's lead, Anderson asked, what types of behavioral cues and signs make up the vocabulary of public interaction? He concluded that

> skin color, gender, age, companions, clothing, jewelry, and the objects people carry help identify them, so that assumptions are formed and communication can occur. Movements (quick or slow, false or sincere, comprehensible or incomprehensible) further refine this public communication. Factors like time of day or an activity that "explains" a person's presence can also affect in what way and how quickly the image of "stranger" is neutralized. If a stranger cannot pass inspection and be assessed as "safe," the image of predator may arise, and fellow pedestrians may try to maintain a distance consistent with that image. (Anderson, 1990)

Anderson showed that the people most likely to pass inspection are those who do not fall into commonly accepted stereotypes of dangerous persons: "children readily pass inspection, while women and white men do so more slowly, black women, black men, and black male teenagers most slowly of all." In showing that interactional tensions derive from outside statuses such as race, class, and gender, Anderson shows that we cannot develop a full understanding of the situation by looking at the micro interactions themselves. This is how he makes the link between micro interactions and macro processes.

Anderson argues that people are "streetwise" when they develop skills such as "the art of avoidance" to deal with their felt vulnerability toward violence and crime. According to Anderson, whites who are not streetwise do not recognize the difference between different kinds of black men (e.g., middle-class youths vs. gang members). They may also not know how to alter the number of paces to walk behind a "suspicious" person or how to bypass "bad blocks" at various times of day.

Study Outline

www.wwnorton.com/giddens5

Social Interaction

- Many apparently trivial aspects of our day-to-day behavior turn out on close examination to be both complex and important aspects of *social interaction*. An example is the gaze—looking at other people. In most interactions, eye contact is fairly fleeting. To stare at another person could be taken as a sign of hostility—or on some occasions, of love. The study of social interaction is a fundamental area in sociology, illuminating many aspects of social life.

Nonverbal Communication

- Many different expressions are conveyed by the human face. It is widely held that basic aspects of the facial expressions of emotion are innate. Cross-cultural studies demonstrate quite close similarities between members of different cultures both in facial expression and in the interpretation of emotions registered on the human face.

Ethnomethodology

- The study of ordinary talk and conversation has come to be called *ethnomethodology*, a term first coined by Harold Garfinkel. Ethnomethodology is the analysis of the ways in which we actively—although usually in a taken-for-granted way—make sense of what others mean by what they say and do.

Face, Body, and Speech in Interaction

- *Unfocused interaction* is the mutual awareness individuals have of one another in large gatherings when not directly in conversation together. *Focused interaction*, which can be divided up into distinct *encounters*, or episodes of interaction, is when two or more individuals are directly attending to what the other or others are saying and doing.
- Social interaction can often be illuminatingly studied by applying the dramaturgical model—studying social interaction as if those involved were actors on a stage, having a set and props. As in the theater, in the various contexts of social life there tend to be clear distinctions between *front regions* (the stage itself) and *back regions*, where the actors prepare themselves for the performance and relax afterward.

Interaction in Time and Space

- All social interaction is situated in time and space. We can analyze how our daily lives are "zoned" in both time and space combined by looking at how activities occur during definite durations and at the same time involve spatial movement.
- Some mechanisms of social interaction may be universal, but many are not. The !Kung of southern Africa, for example, live in small mobile bands, where there is little privacy and thus little opportunity to create front and back regions.

Indirect Interaction

- Modern societies are characterized largely by indirect interpersonal transactions (such as making bank deposits), which lack any copresence. This leads to what has been called the *compulsion of proximity*, the tendency to want to meet in person whenever possible, perhaps because this makes it easier to gather information about how others think and feel, and to accomplish *impression management*.

Key Concepts

Review Questions

1. What is the difference between achieved status and ascribed status?
   a. There is no difference between achieved and ascribed status.
   b. Achieved status is a social standing that others accord to us on the basis of attributes we can change, whereas ascribed status is a social standing others accord to us on the basis of attributes we cannot change.
   c. Achieved status has to do with gender and ethnicity, whereas ascribed status has to do with social class.
   d. Achieved status is equivalent to economic status, whereas ascribed status is equivalent to cultural and political status.

2. What is the study of nonverbal communication?
   a. The study of the way people use tone of voice and pronunciation to convey the exact meaning of their words.
   b. The study of the use of dress, makeup, and jewelry to convey personal identity.
   c. The study of facial expressions, gestures, and body movements.
   d. The study of human interaction with such regular features of everyday life as pets and computers, which can communicate, but not verbally.

3. Ethnomethodology studies
   a. conversations in a café.
   b. casual greetings.
   c. response cries.
   d. all of the above.

4. Human beings have a "compulsion to proximity," or the need to
   a. use whatever electronic means are available to communicate.
   b. meet up with one another in situations of copresence.
   c. experience sexual intimacy.
   d. perceive themselves as discrete social units.

5. Which of the following is an example of impression management?
   a. A professor relaxes in the office after teaching.
   b. A physician listens to a patient before prescribing medicine.
   c. A candidate dresses appropriately for a job interview.
   d. A mother shops at a local grocery store.

6. If a waiter says, "Enjoy your meal" and you reply, "Enjoy in what sense, exactly?" then you have utilized one of
   a. Ekman's experiments in facial muscle analysis.
   b. Garfinkel's experiments in ethnomethodology.
   c. Goffman's experiments in conversational analysis.
   d. Goffman's experiments in social interactions.

7. According to Erving Goffman, if individuals at a large party exhibit mutual awareness of one another's presence, it is called
   a. mutual attraction.
   b. focused interaction.
   c. unfocused interaction.
   d. an encounter.

8. Men may feel more freedom than women in making eye contact with strangers in societies where
   a. women dominate men in both public and private life.
   b. men dominate women in both public and private life.
   c. women have the same status as men in both public and private life.
   d. there are more men than women.

9. In a study by Ekman and Friesen, when members of an isolated New Guinea community were shown pictures of facial expressions conveying six emotions, they were able to identify
   a. none of the six emotions.
   b. all of the six emotions.
   c. only half of the six emotions.
   d. one emotion, happiness.

10. Which of the following concepts lies at the heart of the symbolic interactionist perspective?
    a. Inequality
    b. Division of labor
    c. Social construction of reality
    d. Social mobility and social stratification

Thinking Sociologically Exercises

1. Identify the important elements to the dramaturgical perspective. This chapter shows how the theory might be applied in the ministrations of the nurse to his/her patient. Apply the theory similarly to account for a plumber's visit to a client's home. Are there any similarities? Explain.

2. Smoking cigarettes is a pervasive habit found in many parts of the world and a habit that could be explained by both microsociological and macrosociological forces. Give an example of each that would be relevant to explain the proliferation of smoking. How might your suggested micro- and macro-level analyses be linked?

Data Exercises

www.wwnorton.com/giddens5
Keyword: Data5

- This chapter highlights the structures and processes of everyday social interactions that have a significant influence on us, but are often overlooked. It is particularly difficult to accept the idea that social factors like class, race, and gender may affect our interactions with and perceptions of the world. The data exercise for this chapter focuses on how race shapes our understanding of reality.

Social Groups

Learn the variety and characteristics of groups, as well as the affect of groups on an individual's behavior.

Networks

Understand the importance of social networks and the advantages they confer on some people.

Organizations

Know how to define an organization and understand how they developed over the last two centuries.

Theories of Organizations

Learn Max Weber's theory of organizations and view of bureaucracy. Understand the importance of the physical setting of organizations and Michel Foucault's theory about surveillance.

Beyond Bureaucracy?

Familiarize yourself with some of the alternatives to bureaucracy that have developed in other societies or in recent times. Think about the influence of technology on how organizations operate.

Organizations That Span the World

See how organizations have become truly global in scale.

How Do Groups and Organizations Affect Your Life?

CHAPTER SIX

GROUPS, NETWORKS, AND ORGANIZATIONS

O n March 27, 1997, thirty-nine members of a religious group known as "Heaven's Gate" committed mass suicide in their rented mansion in an upscale suburb of San Diego, California. The twenty-one men and eighteen women ranged in age from twenty-six to seventy-two years old. Most were in their forties and fifties. They were, for the most part, educated and intelligent. They ran a successful Web site design company called, appropriately, "The Higher Source." So passionately were they committed to their group's beliefs that none questioned the decision to die.

Their suicide—committed by ingesting massive overdoses of sleeping pills mixed in applesauce—was intended to free group members of their human bodies, or "vehicles." This was viewed as a necessary step in ascending to the "next level," which they believed was waiting for them in the form of a spacecraft concealed by the Hale-Bopp comet then brightly streaking through the sky. Each purple-shrouded body sported brand-new Nike running shoes and exactly five dollars in quarters to see him or her through the journey.

The group's beliefs would strike most people as a bizarre fusion of Christianity, New Age religion, and science fiction. Members were devotees of such TV series as *Star Trek* and *The X-Files*. The group's leader, Marshall Herff Applewhite (who called himself "Do" for the syllable used to denote the first tone of the musical scale), claimed that extraterrestrials from the "Kingdom of Heaven" were monitoring their "garden Earth" in hopes of offering humanity a chance to move to a "higher evolutionary level." "Do" claimed to be allied with a heavenly partner, "Ti" (Bonnie

Lou Nettles, the group's cofounder), who had died twelve years earlier (Heaven's Gate, 1997).

In preparation for their extraterrestrial hereafter, group members followed a strict set of rules. They banned the consumption of drugs and alcohol, terminated all personal attachments outside the group, rejected all material possessions, wore cropped hair and practiced celibacy (many males, following "Do's" lead, were castrated). But the appearance of the Hale-Bopp comet in the spring of 1997 signaled the end of this preparatory stage and the promise of a "boarding pass" to salvation.

Heaven's Gate used the Internet as a recruitment tool as well as a means of earning income for the group. On their Web site, Applewhite called himself the "Present Representative," drawing parallels between himself and Jesus and promising eternal life for those who joined him:

> As was promised—the keys to Heaven's Gate are here again in Ti and Do (the UFO two) as they were in Jesus and His Father 2000 years ago.
>
> Whether Hale-Bopp has a "companion" or not is irrelevant from our perspective. However, its arrival is joyously very significant to us at "Heaven's Gate." The joy is that our Older Member in the Evolutionary Level Above Human (the "Kingdom of Heaven") has made it clear to us that Hale-Bopp's approach is the "marker" we've been waiting for—the time for the arrival of the spacecraft from the Level Above Human to take us home to "Their World"—in the literal Heavens. Our 22 years of classroom here on planet Earth is finally coming to conclusion. . . . We are happily prepared to leave "this world" and go with Ti's crew (Heaven's Gate, 1997).

Heaven's Gate may strike you as an extreme case of how groups exercise influence over their members, who are sometimes willing to conform to group expectations even at the cost of their lives. This behavior is distressing in part because obedience to group dictates and the sacrifice of personal freedom go against the grain of our individualistic culture. However, we all conform, at least to some degree, to groups. From small groups of friends to large organizations such as colleges and universities, we are all subject to the constraints and demands of group life. Indeed, through groups, we enjoy human culture, and to different degrees according to our backgrounds, we also benefit from freedoms and opportunities to pursue our chosen goals in life.

In this chapter you will learn about different kinds of groups and their role in shaping your experiences. For example, you will learn how group size affects your behavior in groups and about the nature of leadership. Special attention is given to sociological research into individual conformity to group norms, helping you understand how such ordinary, intelligent persons as those in the Heaven's Gate group could willingly follow their leader to their deaths. We will also examine the role played by organizations in American society, the major theories of modern organizations, and the ways in which organizations are changing in the modern world. The increased impact of technology on organizations and the prominence of the Internet in our group life is also explored. Finally, the chapter concludes with a consideration of the rising role of global organizations in the world today.

Social Groups

Nearly everything of importance in our lives occurs through some type of social group. You and your roommate make up a social group, as do the members of your introductory sociology class. A **social group** is a collection of people who share a common identity and regularly interact with one another on the basis of shared expectations concerning behavior. People who belong to the same social group identify with each other, expect each other to conform to certain ways of thinking and acting, and recognize the boundaries that separate them from other groups or people. In our need to congregate and belong, we have created a rich and varied group life that gives us our norms, practices, and values—our whole way of life.

Groups: Variety and Characteristics

We may sometimes feel that we are alone, yet we seldom find ourselves far away from one kind of group or another. Every day nearly all of us move through various social situations, such as one involving an intimate two-person group or one within a large bureaucratic organization. We hang out with groups of friends, study with classmates, play team sports, and go online to find new friends or people who share our interests. Like people nearly everywhere, we are organizational addicts (Aldrich and Marsden, 1988).

However, just because people find themselves in each other's company does not make them a social group. People milling around in crowds, waiting for a bus, or strolling on a beach are said to make up a social aggregate. A **social aggregate** is a simple collection of people who happen to be together in a particular place but do not significantly interact or identify with each other. The people waiting together at a bus station, for example, may be conscious of one another's presence, but they are unlikely to think of themselves as a "we"—the group waiting for the next bus to Poughkeepsie or Des Moines. By the same token, people may comprise a **social category**, people sharing a common characteristic (such as gender or occupation) without necessarily interacting or identifying with one another. The sense of belonging to a common social group is missing.

IN-GROUPS AND OUT-GROUPS

The "sense of belonging" that characterizes social groups is sometimes strengthened by groups' scorning the members of other groups (Sartre, 1965, orig. 1948). Creating a sense of belonging in this way is especially true of racist groups, which promote their identity as "superior" by hating "inferior" groups. Jews, Catholics, African Americans and other people of color, immigrants, and gay people are typically the targets of such hatred. This sense of group identity created through scorn is dramatically illustrated by the rantings on the former Web page of a racist skinhead group that called itself Combat 18: "We are the last of our warrior race, and it is our duty to fight for our people. The Jew will do everything to discredit us, but we hold that burning flame in our hearts that drove our ancestors to conquer whole continents" (Combat 18, 1998).

Such proud, disdainful language illustrates the sociological distinction between in-groups and out-groups. **In-groups** are groups toward which one feels particular loyalty and respect—the groups that "we" belong to. **Out-groups**, on the other hand, are groups toward which one feels antagonism and contempt—"*those* people." Most people occasionally use in-group–out-group imagery to trumpet what they believe to be their group's strengths vis-à-vis some other group's presumed weaknesses. For example, members of a fraternity or a sorority may bolster their feelings of superiority—in academics, sports, or campus image—by ridiculing the members of a different house. Similarly, an ethnic group may prefer its sons and daughters to marry only within the group, a church often holds up its "truths" as the only ones, and immigrants—always outsiders upon arriving in a new country—are sometimes accused of ruining the country for "real Americans."

PRIMARY AND SECONDARY GROUPS

Group life differs greatly in how intensely group members experience it. Beginning with the family—the first group to which most of us belong—many of the groups that shape our personalities and lives are those in which we experience strong emotional ties. This experience is common not only for families, but also for groups of friends, including gangs or other peer groups, all of which are known as **primary groups**. Primary groups are usually small groups characterized by face-to-face interaction,

intimacy, and a strong, enduring sense of commitment. In this type of group, there is also often an experience of unity, a merging of the self with the group into one personal "we." Individuals in these groups are also more likely to enjoy relationships for their own sake. Friends may ask you to take advantage of their offer of good theater seats or help writing a paper, but they will be hurt if they feel that that is all you want from them. The sociologist Charles Horton Cooley (1864–1929) termed such groups "primary" because he believed that they were the basic form of association, exerting a long-lasting influence on the development of our social selves (Cooley, 1964, orig. 1902).

In contrast, **secondary groups** are large and impersonal and often involve fleeting relationships. Secondary groups seldom involve intense emotional ties, powerful commitments to the group itself, or an experience of unity. We seldom feel we can "be ourselves" in a secondary group; rather, we are often playing a particular role, such as employee or student. While Cooley argued that people belong to primary groups mainly because such groups are inherently fulfilling, people join secondary groups to achieve some specific goal: to earn a living, get a college degree, or compete in sports. Examples of secondary groups include business organizations, schools, work groups, athletic clubs, and governmental bodies. Secondary groups may of course become primary groups for some of their members. For example, when students taking a course begin to socialize after class, they create bonds of friendship that constitute a primary group.

For most of human history, nearly all interactions took place within primary groups. This pattern began to change with the emergence of larger, agrarian societies, which included such secondary groups as those based on governmental roles or occupation. Today most of our waking hours are spent within secondary groups, although primary groups remain a basic part of our lives.

Some early sociologists, such as Cooley, worried about a loss of intimacy as more and more interactions revolved around large impersonal organizations. However, what Cooley saw as the growing impersonality and anonymity of modern life may also offer an increasing tolerance of individual differences. Primary groups, which often enforce strict conformity to group standards (Simmel, 1955; Durkheim, 1964, orig. 1893), can be suffocating. Impersonal secondary groups are more likely than primary groups to be concerned with accomplishing a task, rather than with enforcing conformity to group standards of behavior.

REFERENCE GROUPS

We often judge ourselves by how we think we appear to others, which Cooley termed the "looking-glass self." Groups as well as individuals provide the standards by which we make self-evaluations. Robert K. Merton elaborated on Cooley's concept by discussing reference groups as measures by which we evaluate ourselves (Merton, 1968, orig. 1938). A **reference group** is a group that provides a standard for judging one's own attitudes or behaviors (see also Hyman and Singer, 1968). The family is typically one of the more crucial reference groups in our lives, as are peer groups and coworkers. All these groups provide points of reference for standards or comparisons. However, you do not have to belong to a group for it to be your reference group. For example, regardless of his or her station in life, a person may identify with the wealth and power of Fortune 500 corporate executives, admire the contribution of Nobel Prize–winning scientists, or be captivated by the glitter of the lives of Hollywood stars. Although most of us seldom interact socially with such reference groups as these, we may take pride in identifying with them, glorify their accomplishments, and even imitate the ways of those people who do belong to them. This is why it is critical for children—minority children in particular, whose groups are often represented stereotypically in the media—to be exposed to reference groups that will shape their lives for the better.

The group to which you compare yourself may not necessarily make you feel better about yourself. An early major study of reference groups (Stouffer et al., 1949; see also Merton and Rossi, 1968, orig. 1949) found that morale among American soldiers was not affected so much by the harshness of their experiences as by how they fared in comparison with other groups of soldiers. If soldiers felt they were "relatively deprived" in comparison with other soldiers, their morale would suffer, even if their actual living circumstances were not so bad.

Reference groups may be primary, such as the family, or secondary, such as a group of soldiers. They may even be fictional. One of the chief functions of advertising, for example, is to create a set of imaginary reference groups that will influence consumers' buying habits. For example, when lean female models with flawless complexions are shown in ads for cosmetics, the message to women is simple: "If you want to look as though you are part of an in-group of highly attractive, eternally youthful women, buy this product." In reality, of course, the models used in the ads seldom have the unblemished features depicted; instead, the ideal features are constructed through artful lighting, photographic techniques, and computer enhancement. Similarly, the happy-go-lucky, physically perfect young men and women seen sailing or playing volleyball or hang gliding on beer commercials have little to do with the reality of most of our lives—or, indeed, with the actual lives of the actors in these commercials. The message, however, is otherwise: "Drink this beer, and you will be viewed by others as a member of the carefree in-group depicted in this ad."

The Effects of Size

Another significant way in which groups differ has to do with their size. Sociological interest in group size can be traced to the German sociologist Georg Simmel (1858–1918), who studied and theorized about the impact of small groups on people's behavior. Since Simmel's time, small-group researchers have conducted a number of laboratory experiments to examine the effects of size on both the quality of interaction in the group and the effectiveness of the group in accomplishing certain tasks. (Homans, 1950; Bales, 1953, 1970; Hare, Borgatta, and Bales, 1965; Mills, 1967).

DYADS

The simplest group, which Simmel (1955) called a **dyad**, consists of two persons. Simmel reasoned that dyads, which involve both intimacy and conflict, are likely to be simultaneously intense and unstable. To survive, they require the full attention and cooperation of both parties. If one person withdraws from the dyad, it vanishes. Dyads are typically the source of our most elementary social bonds, often constituting the group in which we are most likely to share our deepest secrets. But dyads can be very fragile. That is why, Simmel believed, a variety of cultural and legal supports for marriage are found in societies where marriage is regarded as an important source of social stability.

TRIADS

Adding a third person changes the group relationship. Simmel used the term **triad** to describe a group consisting of three persons. Triads are apt to be more stable than dyads, since the presence of a third person relieves some of the pressure on the other two members to always get along and ener-

Advertising creates a set of imaginary reference groups meant to influence consumers' buying habits by presenting unlikely—often impossible—ideals to which consumers aspire.

gize the relationship. In a triad, one person can temporarily withdraw attention from the relationship without necessarily threatening it. In addition, if two of the members have a disagreement, the third can play the role of mediator, as when you try to patch up a falling-out between two of your friends.

On the other hand, however, alliances (sometimes termed "coalitions") may form between two members of a triad, enabling them to gang up on the third and thereby destabilize the group. Alliances are most likely to form when no one member is clearly dominant and when all three members are competing for the same thing—for example, when three friends are given a pair of tickets to a concert and have to decide which two will get to go. The hit TV series *Survivor* provided many examples of alliance formation, as the program's characters forged special relationships with each other to avoid being eliminated in the weekly group vote.

In forming an alliance, a member is most likely to choose the weaker of the two other members as a partner, if there is one. In what has been termed "revolutionary coalitions," the two weaker members form an alliance to overthrow the stronger one (Caplow, 1956, 1959, 1969).

LARGER GROUPS

Going from a dyad to a triad illustrates an important sociological principle first identified by Simmel: As groups increase in size, their intensity decreases, while their stability increases. There are, of course, exceptions to this principle, but in many cases, it is likely to apply. Increasing the size of a group tends to decrease its intensity of interaction, simply because a larger number of potential smaller group relationships exist as outlets for individuals who are not getting along with other members of the group. In a dyad, only a single relationship, that between two people, is possible; however, in a triad, three different two-person relationships can occur. Adding a fourth person leads to six possible combinations of two-person relationships, and this does not count the subgroups of more than two that could form. In a ten-person group, the number of possible two-person relationships explodes to forty-five! When one relationship doesn't work out to your liking, you can easily move on to another, as you probably often do at large parties.

At the same time, larger groups tend to be more stable than smaller ones because the withdrawal of some members does not threaten the group's survival. A marriage or love relationship falls apart if one person leaves, whereas an athletic team or drama club routinely survives—though it may sometimes temporarily suffer from—the loss of its graduating seniors.

Larger groups also tend to be more exclusive, since it is easier for their members to limit their social relationships to the group itself and avoid relationships with nonmembers. This sense of being part of an in group or clique is sometimes found in fraterni-

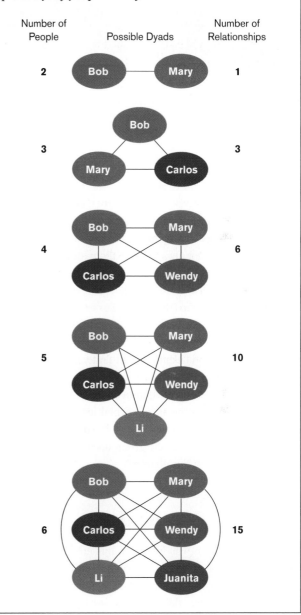

FIGURE 6.1

The larger the number of people, the greater the possible number of relationships. Note that this diagram illustrates only dyads; if triads and more complex coalitions were to be included, the numbers would be still greater (four people yield ten possibilities). Even a small, ten-person group can produce forty-five possible dyads!

Number of People | Possible Dyads | Number of Relationships

2 — Bob, Mary — 1

3 — Bob, Mary, Carlos — 3

4 — Bob, Mary, Carlos, Wendy — 6

5 — Bob, Mary, Carlos, Wendy, Li — 10

6 — Bob, Mary, Carlos, Wendy, Li, Juanita — 15

ties, sororities, and other campus organizations. Cliquishness is especially likely to occur when the group consists of members who are similar to each other in such social characteristics as age, gender, class, race, or ethnicity. Persons from rich families, for example, may be reluctant to fraternize with working-class

Members of a large, exclusive group such as a fraternity or sorority develop a sense of being part of an in-group or clique. They may choose to limit their social relationships to the group itself.

groups, men may prefer to go to the basketball court with other men, and students who belong to a particular ethnic group (for example, African Americans, Latinos, or Asian Americans) may seek out each other's company in the dormitory or cafeteria. Even so, groups do not always foster the restriction of relationships with outsiders. A group with a socially diverse membership is likely instead to foster a high degree of interaction with people outside the group (Blau, 1977). For example, if your social group or club is made up of members from different social classes or ethnic groups, it is more likely that you will come to appreciate such social differences from firsthand experience and seek them out in other aspects of your life.

Beyond a certain size, perhaps a dozen people, groups tend to develop a formal structure. Formal leadership roles may arise, such as president or secretary, and official rules may be developed to govern what the group does. We discuss formal organizations later in this chapter.

Types of Leadership

A **leader** is a person who is able to influence the behavior of other members of a group. All groups tend to have leaders, even if the leader is not formally recognized as such. Some leaders are especially effective in motivating the members of their groups or organizations, inspiring them to achievements that might not ordinarily be accomplished. Such **transformational leaders** go beyond the merely routine, instilling in the members of their group a sense of mission or higher purpose and thereby changing the nature of the group itself (Burns, 1978; Kanter, 1983). These are the leaders who are seen as "leaving their stamp" on their organizations. They can also be a

vital inspiration for social change in the world. For example, Nelson Mandela, the South African leader who spent twenty-seven years in prison after having been convicted of treason against the white-dominated South African society, nonetheless managed to build his African National Congress (ANC) political party into a multiracial force for change. Mandela's transformational leadership was so strong that despite his long imprisonment, as soon as he was freed he assumed leadership of the ANC. After Mandela successfully led the ANC in overthrowing South Africa's system of *apartheid*, or racial segregation, he was elected president—leader—of the entire country.

Most leaders are not as visionary as Mandela, however. Leaders who simply "get the job done" are termed **transactional leaders**. These are leaders concerned with accomplishing the group's tasks, getting group members to do their jobs, and making certain that the group achieves its goals. Transactional leadership is routine leadership. For example, the teacher who simply gets through the lesson plan each day—rather than making the classroom a place where students explore new ways of thinking and behaving—is exercising transactional leadership.

Conformity

Not so long ago, the only part of the body that American teenage girls were likely to pierce was the ears—one hole per ear, enough to hold a single pair of earrings. For the vast majority of boys piercing was not an option at all. Today, earrings are common for many males—from teenage boys to male professional athletes, and a growing number of college students now proudly sport multiple earrings, navel rings, and even studs in their tongues. Pressures to conform to the latest styles are especially strong among teenagers and young adults, among whom the need for group acceptance is often acute.

While wearing navel rings or the latest style of jeans may seem relatively harmless, conformity to group pressure can lead to extremely destructive behavior. This might include drug abuse, murder, or, as we saw in the case of Heaven's Gate, even mass suicide. For this reason, sociologists and social psychologists have long sought to understand why most people tend to go along with others and under what circumstances they do not.

GOING ALONG WITH THE GROUP: ASCH'S RESEARCH

Some of the earliest studies of conformity to group pressures were conducted by psychologist Solomon Asch about fifty years ago (1952). In one of his classic experiments, Asch asked individual subjects to decide which of three lines of different

FIGURE 6.2

In the Asch task, participants were shown a standard line (left) and then three comparison lines. Their task was simply to say which of the three lines matched the standard. When confederates gave false answers first, three-quarters of participants conformed by giving the wrong answer.

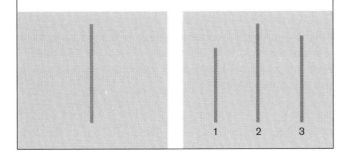

length most closely matched the length of a fourth line. The differences were obvious; subjects had no difficulty in making the correct match. Asch then arranged a version of the experiment in which the subjects were asked to make the matches in a group setting, with each person calling out the answer one at a time.

In this version of the experiment, all but one of the subjects were actually Asch's secret accomplices, and these accomplices all practiced a deception on that one subject. Each accomplice picked two lines that were clearly unequal in length as matches. The unwitting subject, one of the last to call out an answer, felt enormous group pressure to make the same error. Amazingly, one-third of these subjects gave the same wrong answer as the others in the group at least half of the times the experiment was conducted. They sometimes stammered and fidgeted when doing so, but they nonetheless yielded to the unspoken pressure to conform to the group's decision. Asch's experiments clearly showed that many people are willing to discount their own perceptions rather than buck a group consensus.

OBEDIENCE TO AUTHORITY: MILGRAM'S RESEARCH

Another classic study of conformity was Stanley Milgram's research (1963). Milgram's work was intended to shed some light on what had happened in Nazi Germany during World War II. How could ordinary German citizens have gone along with—even participated in—the mass extermination of millions of Jews, Romanies (also known as Gypsies), homosexuals, intellectuals, and others who were judged to be inferior or undesirable by the Nazis?

Obedience is a kind of conformity. Milgram sought to find its limits, and his study produced a chilling answer. Milgram wanted to see how far a person would go when ordered by a scientist to give another person increasingly powerful electric shocks. He did so by setting up an experiment that he told the subjects was about memorizing pairs of words. In reality, it was about obedience to authority.

The male subjects who volunteered for the study were supposedly randomly divided into "teachers" and "learners." In fact, the learners were actually Milgram's employees. The teacher was told to read pairs of words from a list that the learner was to memorize. Whenever the learner made a mistake, the teacher was to give him an electric shock by flipping a switch on a fake but official-looking machine. The control board on the machine indicated shock levels ranging from "15 volts—slight shock" to "450 volts—danger, severe shock." For each mistake, the voltage of the shock was to be increased, until it eventually reached the highest level. In reality, the learner, who was usually carefully concealed from the teacher by a screen, never received any electric shocks. Milgram's study would not be permitted today, since its deception of subjects and potential for doing psychological harm would violate current university ethics standards.

As the experiment progressed, the learner began to scream out in pain for the teacher to stop delivering shocks. (His screams, increasingly louder as the voltage rose, had actually been prerecorded on a tape.) However, Milgram's assistant, who was administering the experiment, exercised his authority as a scientist and ordered the teacher to continue administering shocks if the teacher tried to quit. The assistant would say such things as, "the experiment requires that you continue," even when the learner could be heard protesting—even when he shrieked about his "bad heart."

The teacher was confronted with a major moral decision: Should he obey the scientist and go along with the experiment, even if it meant injuring another human being? Much to Milgram's surprise, over half the subjects in the study kept on administering electric shocks. They continued even until the maximum voltage was reached and the learner's screams had subsided into an eerie silence as he presumably died of a heart attack. How could ordinary people so easily conform to orders that would turn them into possible accomplices to murder?

The answer, Milgram found, was deceptively simple: Ordinary people will conform to orders given by someone in a position of power or authority, even if those orders have horrible consequences. From this, we can learn something about Nazi atrocities during World War II, which were Milgram's original concern, and about the Heaven's Gate group. Many ordinary Germans, who participated in the mass execution of Jews in Nazi concentration camps, did so on the grounds that they were "just following orders." Although "Do's" followers in the

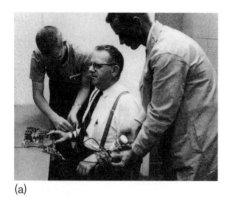

(a)

(b)

(c)

(a) The Milgram experiment required participants to "shock" the confederate learner (seated). The research participant (left) helped apply the electrodes that would be used to shock the learner. (b) An obedient participant shocks the learner in the "touch" condition. Fewer than one-third obeyed the experimenter in this condition. (c) After the experiment, all of the participants were introduced to the confederate learner so they could see he was not actually harmed.

Heaven's Gate group claimed they were seeking a higher spiritual plane, they, too, were obeying their leader's orders ("Do" once compared the obedience of a disciple to that of a good dog). None of this is to say that Milgram's subjects were either Nazis or cult followers. Yet Milgram's research has sobering implications for anyone who thinks that only "others" will always knuckle under to authority, but "not me" (Zimbardo, Ebbesen, and Maslach, 1977).

GROUPTHINK AND GROUP PRESSURES TO CONFORM: JANIS'S RESEARCH

Common sense tells us that "two minds are better than one." But sociological research has found that pressures to "go along with the crowd" sometime result in worse decisions, rather than creative new solutions to problems. You have probably had the experience of being in a group struggling with a difficult decision and feeling uneasy at voicing your opposition to an emerging consensus. Irving L. Janis (1972, 1989; Janis and Mann, 1977) called this phenomenon **groupthink**, a process by which the members of a group ignore ways of thinking and plans of action that go against the group consensus. Not only does groupthink frequently embarrass potential dissenters into conforming, but it can also produce a shift in perceptions so that alternative possibilities are ruled out without being seriously considered. Groupthink may facilitate reaching a quick consensus, but the consensus may also be ill chosen. It may even be downright stupid.

Janis engaged in historical research to see if groupthink had characterized U.S. foreign policy decisions. He examined several critical decisions, including that behind the infamous Bay of Pigs invasion of Cuba in 1961. John F. Kennedy, then the newly elected president, inherited a plan from the previous administration to help Cuban exiles liberate Cuba from the Communist government of Fidel Castro. The plan called for U.S. supplies and air cover to assist an invasion by an ill-prepared army of exiles at Cuba's Bay of Pigs. Although a number of Kennedy's top advisers were certain that the plan was fatally flawed, they refrained from bucking the emerging consensus to carry it out. As it happened, the invasion was a disaster. The army of exiles, after parachuting into a swamp nowhere near their intended drop zone, was immediately defeated, and Kennedy suffered a great deal of public embarrassment.

Kennedy's advisers were people of strong will and independent judgment who had been educated at elite universities. How could they have failed to adequately voice their concerns about the proposed invasion? Janis identified a number of possible reasons. For one, Kennedy's advisers were hesitant to disagree with the president lest they lose his favor. They also did not want to diminish group harmony in a crisis situation where teamwork was all important. In addition, given the intense time pressure to act, they had little opportunity to consult outside experts who might have offered radically different perspectives. All these circumstances contributed to a single-minded pursuit of the president's initial ideas, rather than an effort to generate effective alternatives.

Although groupthink does not always shape decision making, it sometimes plays a major role. To avoid groupthink, the group must ensure the full and open expression of all opinions, even strong dissent.

Networks

"Who you know is often as important as what you know." This adage expresses the value of having "good connections." Sociologists refer to such connections as **networks**—all the direct and indirect connections that link a person or a group with other people or groups. Your personal networks thus include people you know directly (such as your friends) as well as people you know indirectly (such as your friends' friends). Personal networks often include people of similar race, class, ethnicity, and other types of social background, although there are exceptions. For example, if you subscribe to an online mailing list, you are part of a network that consists of all the people on the list, who may be of different racial or ethnic backgrounds and genders. Because groups and organizations, such as sororities or religious groups, can also be networked—for example, all the chapters of Gamma Phi Beta or Hillel that the national organization comprises—belonging to such groups can greatly extend your reach and influence.

Social groups are an important source for acquiring networks; but not all networks are social groups. Many networks lack the shared expectations and common sense of identity that are the hallmark of social groups. For example, you are not likely to share a sense of identity with the subscribers to an online mailing list, nor will you probably even know the neighbors of most of your coworkers at the office, even though they would form part of your social network.

Networks serve us in many ways. Sociologist Mark Granovetter (1973) demonstrated that there can be enormous strength in weak ties, particularly among higher socioeconomic groups. Granovetter showed that upper-level professional and managerial employees are likely to hear about new jobs through connections such as distant relatives or remote acquaintances. Such weak ties can be of great benefit because relatives or acquaintances tend to have very different sets of connections than one's closer friends, whose social contacts are likely to be similar to one's own. Among lower socioeconomic groups, Granovetter argued, weak ties are not necessarily bridges to other networks and so do not really widen one's opportunities (see also Marsden and Lin, 1982; Wellman, Carrington, and Hall, 1988; Knoke, 1990). After graduation from college, you may rely on good grades and a strong résumé to find a job. But it may prove beneficial if it happens that your second cousin went to school with a top person in the organization where you are seeking work.

Most people rely on their personal networks to gain advantages, but not everyone has equal access to powerful networks. Some sociologists argue, for example, that women's business and political networks are weaker than men's, so that women's power in these spheres is reduced (Brass, 1985). The Bohemian Grove is a case in point. This is an annual summer political gathering that has been held on the Russian River, seventy miles north of San Francisco, since 1879. Its all-male membership includes Republican political leaders, the heads of major corporations, businessmen, and entertainers.

The highly exclusive weekend includes horseback riding, meetings, entertainment, "lakeside talks," informal discussion groups—and some serious deal making. In 1999, the "Bohemians" included former president George Bush, then Texas governor (and later president) George W. Bush, former secretary of state Henry Kissinger, retired general Colin Powell (later secretary of state), and former Speaker of the House Newt Gingrich (Domhoff, 1974; Bohan, 1999).

In general, sociologists have found that when women look for work, their job market networks comprise fewer ties than do men's, meaning that women know fewer people in fewer occupations (Marsden, 1987; Moore, 1990). Meager networks tend to channel women into female-typical jobs, which usually offer less pay and fewer opportunities for advancement (Ross and Reskin, 1992; Drentea, 1998). Still, as more and more women move up into higher-level positions, the resulting networks can foster further advancement. One study found that women are more likely to be hired or promoted into job levels that already have a high proportion of women (Cohen, Broschak, and Haveman, 1998).

Networks confer more than economic advantage. You are likely to rely on your networks for a broad range of contacts, from obtaining access to your congressperson or senator to finding a date for Saturday night. Similarly, when you visit another country to study a foreign language or see the Olympics, for example, your friends, school, or religious organization may steer you to their overseas connections, who can then help you find your way around in the unfamiliar environment. When you graduate from school, your alumni group can further extend your network of social support.

The Internet as Social Network

The advantages and potential reach of networks are evident in an increasingly productive means of networking, all but unknown ten years ago: the Internet. Internet use has exploded in recent years. Until the early 1990s, when the World Wide Web was developed, there were few Internet users outside of university and scientific communities. By 2002, however, an estimated 182.13 million Americans used the Internet (Cyberatlas, 2003). With such rapid communication and global reach, it is now possible to radically extend one's personal networks. The Internet is especially useful for networking with like-minded people on specific issues, such as politics, business, hobbies, or romance (Southwick, 1996; Wellman et al., 1996). It also enables people who might otherwise lack contact with others to become part of global networks. For example, shut-ins can join chat rooms to share common interests, and people in small rural communities can now engage in "distance learning" through courses that are offered on the Web.

The Internet fosters the creation of new relationships, often without the emotional and social baggage or constraints that go along with face-to-face encounters. While this might contribute to fleeting, impersonal relationships, it can also create opportunities for the expression of intimate feelings or discussion of topics that might be suppressed in ordinary face-to-face encounters. For example, chat rooms offer support for lesbians and gay men who can't find acceptance in their local communities. Similarly, some Web sites for teenagers provide answers to important questions on health and sexuality that teens may be shy about asking their parents. Internet communication is also effective in strengthening the bonds between friends and acquaintances who would otherwise seldom see each other (Wellman et al., 1996).

In the absence of the usual physical and social cues, such as skin color or residential address, people can get together electronically on the basis of shared interests rather than similar social characteristics. Such factors as social position, wealth, race, ethnicity, gender, and physical disability are less likely to cloud the social interaction (Coate, 1994; Jones, 1995; Kollock and Smith, 1996). The Internet thus enables people to communicate first and then decide if the relationship is worth continuing in person. As a consequence, Internet-based social networks may be socially broader based than other networks (Wellman, 1994). Whether this strengthens social diversity—or downgrades its importance—is a matter of debate.

The Internet can also enable people to join new organizations they otherwise might not have access to, for instance, professional groups or such religious groups as Heaven's Gate. Of course, there may be a downside to these opportunities, too, as seen in the case of the suicidal outcome of the Heaven's Gate group. A similar problem is posed by the Internet presence of hate groups. These groups promote the scapegoating of minority groups in the hate literature that they transmit, and they encourage hate crimes. Some evidence indicates that hate groups concentrate on the Internet, where potential members and lone wolfs attracted to racist notions but not fully committed to the hate movement can take part in it without exposing their identities (Intelligence Report, 2001).

Another problem is that not everyone has equal access to the Internet. Lower-income groups, which disproportionately include minorities, are especially disadvantaged in developing networks online, as are the elderly. Still, within the span of a few years, Internet use has become much more widespread among all groups (Nielson Media Research, 2001b, 2001c). In the words of one recent study that tracked Internet use among different socioeconomic groups, "The Internet was, at first, an elitist country club reserved only for individuals with select financial abilities and technical skills. . . . Now, nearly every socioeconomic group is aggressively adopting the Web" (Nielsen Media Research, 2001b).

Americans are by far the greatest Internet users in the world, although the rest of the world is rapidly coming on line. Besides in North America, Internet use is highest in Europe and East Asia, where the wealthiest countries are found. Some sociologists think that the Internet will eventually strengthen global ties, perhaps at the expense of local ones. Being able to connect with anyone in the world who shares similar interests may mean that one's own community becomes less important:

> On-line relationships may be more stimulating than suburban neighborhoods and alienated offices. Even more than before, on the information highway each person is at the center of a unique personal community and work group. . . . Virtual communities are accelerating the ways in which people operate at the centers of partial, personal communities, switching rapidly and frequently between groups of ties. (Wellman et al., 1996)

The Internet may eventually lead to global communities based on shared interests, having the effect of diminishing local communities made up of families, neighbors, and friends. If this happens, will the ties that have bound people to locality throughout human history slowly disappear?

Organizations

People frequently band together to pursue activities that they could not otherwise readily accomplish by themselves. A principal means for accomplishing such cooperative actions is the **organization**, a group with an identifiable membership that engages in concerted collective actions to achieve a common purpose (Aldrich and Marsden, 1988). An organization can be a small primary group, but it is more likely to be a larger, secondary one: Universities, religious bodies, and business corporations are all examples of organizations. Such organizations are a central feature of all societies, and their study is a core concern of sociology today.

Organizations tend to be highly formal in modern industrial and postindustrial societies. A **formal organization** is rationally designed to achieve its objectives, often by means of explicit rules, regulations, and procedures. The modern bureaucratic organization, discussed later in this chapter, is a prime example of a formal organization. As Max Weber (1979, orig. 1921) first recognized three quarters of a century ago, there has been a long-term trend in Europe and North America toward formal organizations. This rise of formality in organizations is in part the result of the fact that formality is often a re-

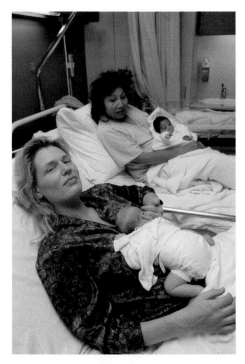

Modern hospitals are complex organizations with impersonal structures and procedures—but they are designed for a very personal outcome.

quirement for legal standing. For a college or university to be legally accredited, for example, it must satisfy explicit written standards governing everything from grading policy to faculty performance to fire safety. Today, formal organizations are the dominant form of organization throughout the entire world.

Most social systems in the traditional world developed over lengthy periods as a result of custom and habit. Organizations, on the other hand, are mostly designed—established with definite aims in view and housed in buildings or physical settings specifically constructed to help realize those aims. The edifices in which hospitals, colleges, or business firms carry on their activities are mostly custom built.

In traditional societies, most people lived in small group settings. In a society such as traditional China, it was rare for members of a local village community ever to meet a national government official. National government edicts barely affected their lives.

In current times, organizations play a much more important part in our everyday lives than was ever true previously. Besides delivering us into this world, they also mark our progress through it and see us out of it when we die. Even before we are born, our mothers, and probably our fathers too, are involved in birthing classes, pregnancy checkups, and so forth, carried out within hospitals and other medical organizations. Every child born today is registered by government organizations, which collect information on us from birth to

death. Most people today die in a hospital—not at home, as was once the case—and each death must be formally registered with the government too.

It is easy to see why organizations are so important to us today. In the premodern world, families, close relatives, and neighbors provided for most needs—food, the instruction of children, work, and leisure-time activities. In modern times, the mass of the population is much more *interdependent* than was ever the case before. Many of our requirements are supplied by people we never meet and who indeed might live many thousands of miles away. A substantial amount of coordination of activities and resources—which organizations provide—is needed in such circumstances.

The tremendous influence organizations have come to exert over our lives cannot be seen as wholly beneficial. Organizations often have the effect of taking things out of our own hands and putting them under the control of officials or experts over whom we have little influence. For instance, we are all *required* to do certain things the government tells us to do—pay taxes, abide by laws, go off to fight wars—or face punishment. As sources of social power, organizations can thus subject the individual to dictates she may be powerless to resist.

Theories of Organizations

Max Weber developed the first systematic interpretation of the rise of modern organizations. Organizations, he argued, are ways of coordinating the activities of human beings, or the goods they produce, in a stable way across space and time. Weber emphasized that the development of organizations depends on the control of information, and he stressed the central importance of writing in this process: An organization needs written rules for its functioning and files in which its "memory" is stored. Weber saw organizations as strongly hierarchical, with power tending to be concentrated at the top. Was Weber right? If he was, it matters a great deal to us all. For Weber detected a clash as well as a connection between modern organizations and democracy that he believed had far-reaching consequences for social life.

Bureaucracy

All large-scale organizations, according to Weber, tend to be bureaucratic in nature. The word *bureaucracy* was coined by Monsieur de Gournay in 1745, who added the word *bureau*, meaning both an office and a writing table, to *cracy*, a term derived from the Greek verb meaning "to rule." **Bureaucracy** is thus the rule of officials. The term was first applied only to government officials, but it gradually was extended to refer to large organizations in general.

From the beginning the concept was used in a disparaging way. De Gournay spoke of the developing power of officials as "an illness called bureaumania." The French novelist Honoré de Balzac saw bureaucracy as "the giant power wielded by pygmies." This sort of view has persisted into current times: Bureaucracy is frequently associated with red tape, inefficiency, and wastefulness. Other writers, however, have seen bureaucracy in a different light—as a model of carefulness, precision, and effective administration. Bureaucracy, they argue, is in fact the most efficient form of organization human beings have devised, because in bureaucracies all tasks are regulated by strict rules of procedure.

Weber's account of bureaucracy steers a way between these two extremes. A limited number of bureaucratic organizations, he pointed out, existed in the traditional civilizations. For example, a bureaucratic officialdom in imperial China was responsible for the overall affairs of government. But it is only in modern times that bureaucracies have developed fully.

According to Weber, the expansion of bureaucracy is inevitable in modern societies; bureaucratic authority is the only way of coping with the administrative requirements of large-scale social systems. However, Weber also believed bureaucracy exhibits a number of major failings, as we will see, which have important implications for the nature of modern social life.

In order to study the origins and nature of the expansion of bureaucratic organizations, Weber constructed an ideal type of bureaucracy. (*Ideal* here refers not to what is most desirable, but to a pure form of bureaucratic organization. An **ideal type** is an abstract description constructed by accentuating certain features of real cases so as to pinpoint their most essential characteristics.) Weber listed several characteristics of the ideal type of bureaucracy (1979):

1. **There is a clear-cut hierarchy of authority**, such that tasks in the organization are distributed as "official duties." A bureaucracy looks like a pyramid, with the positions of highest authority at the top. There is a chain of command stretching from top to bottom, thus making coordinated decision making possible. Each higher office controls and supervises the one below it in the hierarchy.

2. **Written rules govern the conduct of officials at all levels of the organization.** This does not mean that bureaucratic duties are just a matter of routine. The higher the office, the more the rules tend to encompass a wide variety of cases and demand flexibility in their interpretation.

3. **Officials are full time and salaried.** Each job in the hierarchy has a definite and fixed salary attached to it. Individuals are expected to make a career within the organization. Promotion is possible on the basis of capability, seniority, or a mixture of the two.

4. **There is a separation between the tasks of an official within the organization and his life outside.** The home life of the official is distinct from his activities in the workplace and is also physically separated from it.

5. **No members of the organization own the material resources with which they operate.** The development of bureaucracy, according to Weber, separates workers from the control of their means of production. In traditional communities, farmers and craft workers usually had control over their processes of production and owned the tools they used. In bureaucracies, officials do not own the offices they work in, the desks they sit at, or the office machinery they use.

Weber believed that the more an organization approaches the ideal type of bureaucracy, the more effective it will be in pursuing the objectives for which it was established. He often likened bureaucracies to sophisticated machines operating according to rational principles (see Chapter 1). Yet he recognized that bureaucracy could be inefficient and accepted that many bureaucratic jobs are dull, offering little opportunity for the exercise of creative capabilities. While Weber feared that the rationalization of society could have negative consequences, he concluded that bureaucratic routine and the authority of officialdom over our lives are prices we pay for the technical effectiveness of bureaucratic organizations. Since Weber's time, the rationalization of society has become more widespread. Critics of this development who share Weber's initial concerns have questioned whether the efficiency of rational organizations comes at a price greater than Weber could have imagined. The most prominent of these critiques is known as "the McDonaldization of society," discussed later in this chapter.

FORMAL AND INFORMAL RELATIONS WITHIN BUREAUCRACIES

Weber's analysis of bureaucracy gave prime place to **formal relations** within organizations, the relations between people as stated in the rules of the organization. Weber had little to say about the informal connections and small-group relations that may exist in all organizations. But in bureaucracies, informal ways of doing things often allow for a flexibility that couldn't otherwise be achieved.

In a classic study, Peter Blau (1963) looked at **informal relations** in a government agency whose task was to investigate possible income-tax violations. Agents who came across problems they were unsure how to deal with were supposed to discuss them with their immediate supervisor; the rules of procedure stated that they should not consult colleagues working at the same level as themselves. Most officials were wary of approaching their supervisors, however, because they felt this might suggest a lack of competence on their part and reduce their promotion chances. Hence, they usually consulted one another, violating the official rules. This not only helped to provide concrete advice; it also reduced the anxieties involved in working alone. A cohesive set of loyalties of a primary group kind developed among those working at the same level. The problems these workers faced, Blau concludes, were probably coped with much more effectively as a result. The group was able to develop informal procedures allowing for more initiative and responsibility than was provided for by the formal rules of the organization.

Informal networks tend to develop at all levels of organizations. At the very top, personal ties and connections may be more important than the formal situations in which decisions are supposed to be made. For example, meetings of boards of directors and shareholders supposedly determine the policies of business corporations. In practice, a few members of the board often really run the corporation, making their decisions informally and expecting the board to approve them. Informal networks of this sort can also stretch across different corporations. Business leaders from different firms frequently consult one another in an informal way and may belong to the same clubs and leisure-time associations.

John Meyer and Brian Rowan (1977) argue that formal rules and procedures in organizations are usually quite distant from the practices actually adopted by the organizations' members. Formal rules, in their view, are often "myths" that people profess to follow but that have little substance in reality. They serve to legitimate—to justify—ways in which tasks are carried out, even while these ways may diverge greatly from how things are "supposed to be done" according to the rules.

Formal procedures, Meyer and Rowan point out, often have a ceremonial or ritual character. People will make a show of conforming to them in order to get on with their real work using other, more informal procedures. For example, rules governing ward procedure in a hospital help justify how nurses act toward patients in caring for them. Thus a nurse will faithfully fill in a patient's chart that hangs at the end of the bed but will check the patient's progress by means of other, informal criteria—how well the person is looking and whether he or she seems alert and lively. Rigorously keeping up the charts impresses the patients and keeps the doctors happy, but is not always essential to the nurse's assessments.

Deciding how far informal procedures generally help or hinder the effectiveness of organizations is not a simple matter. Systems that resemble Weber's ideal type tend to give rise to a forest of unofficial ways of doing things. This is partly because the flexibility that is lacking ends up being achieved by unofficial tinkering with formal rules. For those in dull jobs, informal procedures often also help to create a more satisfying work environment. Informal connections between officials in higher positions may be effective in ways that aid the organization as a whole. On the other hand, these officials may be more concerned about advancing or protecting their own interests than furthering those of the overall organization.

THE DYSFUNCTIONS OF BUREAUCRACY

Robert Merton, a functionalist scholar, examined Weber's bureaucratic ideal type and concluded that several elements inherent in bureaucracy could lead to harmful consequences for the smooth functioning of the bureaucracy itself (1957). He referred to these as "dysfunctions of bureaucracy." First, Merton noted that bureaucrats are trained to rely strictly on written rules and procedures. They are not encouraged to be flexible, to use their own judgment in making decisions, or to seek creative solutions; bureaucracy is about managing cases according to a set of objective criteria. Merton feared that this rigidity could lead to *bureaucratic ritualism*, a situation in which the rules are upheld at any cost, even in cases where another solution might be a better one for the organization as a whole.

A second concern of Merton's is that adherence to the bureaucratic rules could eventually take precedence over the underlying organizational goals. Because so much emphasis is placed on the correct procedure, it is possible to lose sight of the big picture. A bureaucrat responsible for processing insurance claims, for example, might refuse to compensate a policyholder for legitimate damages, citing the absence of a form or a form being completed incorrectly. In other words, processing the claim correctly could come to take precedence over the needs of the client who has suffered a loss.

Merton foresaw the possibility of tension between the public and bureaucracy in such cases. This concern was not entirely misplaced. Most of us interact with large bureaucracies on a regular basis—from insurance companies to local government to the IRS. Not infrequently we encounter situations in which public servants and bureaucrats seem to be unconcerned with our needs. One of the major weaknesses of bureaucracy is the difficulty it has in addressing cases that need special treatment and consideration.

The *Columbia* Shuttle Disaster: A Sociological Perspective

The tragic disintegration of the Space Shuttle *Columbia* on February 1, 2003 set me on an unexpected and remarkable eight-month journey in public sociology. In the hours after the accident, I was deluged with calls from the press. I had studied the causes of the 1986 *Challenger* disaster and written the book, *The Challenger Launch Decision: Risky Technology, Culture, and Deviance at NASA* (1996). I was defined as an expert the press could consult to give them bearings on this latest accident. Viewing this as both a teaching opportunity and professional responsibility, I tried to respond to everyone.

What I was teaching were the theoretical explanation and key concepts of the book, linking them to data about *Challenger* and *Columbia* as the changing press questions dictated. Because the investigation went on for months, these conversations became an ongoing exchange where the press brought me new information and I gave a sociological interpretation. I noticed that the concepts of the book—the normalization of deviance, institutional failure, organization culture, structure,

missed signals—began appearing in print early in the investigation and continued, whether I was quoted or not.

The book also led to my association with the *Columbia* Accident Investigation Board. Two weeks after the accident, the publicity director at Chicago sent a copy of *The Challenger Launch Decision* to retired Admiral Harold Gehman, who headed the Board's investigation. [***]

The new centrality of sociological ideas and the connection with the *Challenger* accident were not lost on the media. In press conferences, Admiral Gehman stressed the importance of the social causes and used the book's central concepts. When he announced that I would testify before the Board in Houston, the field's leading journal, *Aviation Week and Space Technology,* headlined "*Columbia* Board Probes the Shuttle Program's Sociology," while the *New York Times* ran "Echoes of *Challenger.*" Unaware of the extent of the book's influence on the Board's thinking, however, I arrived in Houston in late April anxious about the public grilling to come.

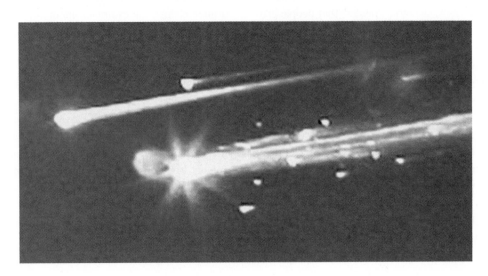

But subsequent events showed me the Board was receptive to sociological analysis. I met separately with the Group 2 investigators assigned the decision making and organization chapters to discuss their data and analysis, then gave the Board a pre-testimony briefing, which turned into a three-hour conversation. My testimony covered the social causes of the *Challenger* accident, compared it to the *Columbia* incident, and identified systemic institutional failures common to both. The book's theory and concepts traveled farther as my testimony—like that of other witnesses—was shown live on NASA TV and videostreamed into television, radio, and press centers and the Internet.

[***]

So the Board's report gave equal weight to social causes of the accident—not only because the Admiral believed in the potential of sociology, but also because I, a sociologist, became part of this large team of Board and staff, working under deadline. Information and ideas flew fast and freely between people and chapters. Their extraordinary investigative effort, data, analysis, and insights were integrated into my chapter; sociological connections and concepts became integrated into theirs. [***]

The Admiral kept the press informed of report changes, so prior to report publication, the *New York Times* announced the equal weight the report would give to technical and social causes, identifying me as the source of the Board's approach and author of Chapter 8. Upon the August 26 [2003] release, the language of sociology became commonplace in the press. The theory of the book traveled one more place that week. An [Associated Press] wire story, "NASA Finally Looks to Sociologist," revealed that NASA had invited me to headquarters to talk with top officials, who had shifted from denial to acknowledge that the systemic institutional failures that led to *Challenger* also caused *Columbia*.

Never did I foresee the extent of my involvement or the impact that I ultimately had. [***] The theory and concepts that explained *Challenger* were an analogical fit with the *Co-*

lumbia data and made sense of what happened for journalists and the Board. Analogy was the mechanism that enabled the theory and concepts of the book to travel. My book and university affiliation gave me the opportunity to engage in ongoing dialogic teaching—akin to daily grassroots activism—but with two tribunals of power with authoritative voice. Together, the press and the Board were a "polished machinery of dissemination," as Burawoy calls powerful advocacy groups, translating the ideas of the book into grist for critical public dialogue.

SOURCE: Diane Vaughan, "How Theory Travels: A Most Public Public Sociology," *Public Sociology in Action*, ASA Footnotes, Nov/Dec. 2003.

DIANE VAUGHAN *teaches sociology at Boston College. Her other books are* Uncoupling: Turning Points in Intimate Relationships, *and* Controlling Unlawful Organizational Behavior. *Currently, she is writing about the uses of analogy in sociology and doing fieldwork on air traffic control.*

Organizations as Mechanistic and Organic Systems

Can bureaucratic procedures be applied effectively to all types of work? Some scholars have suggested that bureaucracy makes logical sense for carrying out routine tasks but that it can be problematic in contexts where the demands of work change unpredictably. In their research on innovation and change in electronics companies, Tom Burns and G. M. Stalker found that bureaucracies are of limited effectiveness in industries where flexibility and being on the cutting edge are prime concerns (Burns and Stalker, 1994; orig. 1966).

Burns and Stalker distinguished between two types of organizations: *mechanistic* and *organic*. Mechanistic organizations are bureaucratic systems in which there is a hierarchical chain of command, with communication flowing vertically through clear channels. Each employee is responsible for a discrete task; once the task is completed, responsibility passes onto the next employee. Work within such a system is anonymous, with people at the top and those at the bottom rarely in communication with one another.

Organic organizations, by contrast, are characterized by a looser structure in which the overall goals of the organization take precedence over narrowly defined responsibilities. Communication flows and directives are more diffuse, moving along many trajectories, not simply vertical ones. Everyone involved in the organization is seen as possessing legitimate knowledge and input that can be drawn on in solving problems; decisions are not the exclusive domain of people at the top.

According to Burns and Stalker, organic organizations are much better equipped to handle the changing demands of an innovative market, such as telecommunications, computer software, or biotechnology. The more fluid internal structure means that they can respond more quickly and appropriately to shifts in the market and can come up with solutions more creatively and rapidly. Mechanistic organizations are better suited to more traditional, stable forms of production that are less susceptible to swings in the market. Although their study was first published more than thirty years ago, it is highly relevant to present-day discussions of organizational change. Burns and Stalker foreshadowed many of the issues that have taken center stage in recent debates over globalization, flexible specialization, and debureaucratization.

The Physical Setting of Organizations

Most modern organizations function in specially designed physical settings. A building that houses a particular organization possesses specific features relevant to the organization's activities, but it also shares important architectural characteristics with buildings of other organizations. The architecture of a hospital, for instance, differs in some respects from that of a business firm or a school. The hospital's separate wards, consulting rooms, operating rooms, and offices give the overall building a definite layout, whereas a school may consist of classrooms, laboratories, and a gymnasium. Yet there is a general resemblance: Both are likely to contain hallways with doors leading off and to use standard decoration and furnishings throughout. Apart from the differing dress of the people moving through the corridors, the buildings in which modern organizations are usually housed have a definite sameness to them. And they often look similar from the outside as well as within their interiors. It would not be unusual to ask, on driving past a building, "Is that a school?" and receive the response, "No, it's a hospital." Although major internal modifications will be required, it can happen that a school takes over buildings that once housed a hospital.

MICHEL FOUCAULT'S THEORY OF ORGANIZATIONS: THE CONTROL OF TIME AND SPACE

Michel Foucault showed that the architecture of an organization is directly involved with its social makeup and system of authority (Foucault, 1971, 1979). By studying the physical characteristics of organizations, we can shed new light on the problems Weber analyzed. The offices Weber discussed abstractly are also architectural settings—rooms, separated by corridors. The buildings of large firms are sometimes actually constructed physically as a hierarchy, in which the more elevated one's position in the hierarchy of authority, the nearer to the top of the building one's office is; the phrase "the top floor" is sometimes used to mean those who hold ultimate power in the organization.

In many other ways, the geography of an organization will affect its functioning, especially in cases where systems rely heavily on informal relationships. Physical proximity makes forming primary groups easier, whereas physical distance can polarize groups, resulting in a "them" and "us" attitude between departments.

SURVEILLANCE IN ORGANIZATIONS

The arrangement of rooms, hallways, and open spaces in an organization's buildings can provide basic clues to how its system of authority operates. In some organizations, groups of people work collectively in open settings. Because of the dull, repetitive nature of certain kinds of industrial work, such as

Workers on an assembly line build the circuit board and other computer devices that will become an electronic gambling machine for a Las Vegas casino. This arrangement allows for a high level of what Foucault calls *surveillance*.

assembly-line production, regular supervision is needed to ensure that workers sustain the pace of labor. The same is often true of routine work carried out by telephone operators who respond to calls for information, who sit together where their activities are visible to their supervisors. Foucault laid great emphasis on how visibility, or lack of it, in the architectural settings of modern organizations influences and expresses patterns of authority. Their level of visibility determines how easily subordinates can be subject to what Foucault calls **surveillance**, the supervision of activities in organizations. In modern organizations, everyone, even in relatively high positions of authority, is subject to surveillance; but the lowlier a person is, the more his or her behavior tends to be closely scrutinized.

Surveillance takes two forms. One is the direct supervision of the work of subordinates by superiors. Consider the example of a school classroom. Pupils sit at tables or desks, usually arranged in rows, all in view of the teacher. Children are supposed to look alert or otherwise be absorbed in their work. Of course, how far this actually happens in practice depends on the abilities of the teacher and the inclinations of the children to conform to what is expected of them.

The second type of surveillance is more subtle but equally important. It consists of keeping files, records, and case histories about people's work lives. Weber saw the importance of written records (nowadays often computerized) in modern organizations but did not fully explore how they can be used to regulate behavior. Employee records usually provide complete work histories, registering personal details and often giving character evaluations. Such records are used to monitor employees' behavior and assess recommendations for promotion. In many business firms, individuals at each level in the organization prepare annual reports on the performance of those in the levels just below them. School records and college transcripts are also used to monitor individuals' performance as they move through the organization. Records are kept on file for academic staff, too.

Organizations cannot operate effectively if employees' work is haphazard. In business firms, as Weber pointed out, people are expected to work regular hours. Activities must be consistently coordinated in time and space, something promoted both by the physical settings of organizations and by the precise scheduling of detailed timetables. **Timetables** regularize activities across time and space—in Foucault's words, they "efficiently distribute bodies" around the organization. Timetables are a condition of organizational discipline, because they slot the activities of large numbers of people together. If a university did not strictly observe a lecture timetable, for example, it would soon collapse into complete chaos. A timetable makes possible the intensive use of time and space: Each can be packed with many people and many activities.

UNDER SURVEILLANCE! THE PRISON

Foucault paid a great deal of attention to organizations, like prisons, in which individuals are physically separated for long periods from the outside world. In such organizations, people are incarcerated—kept hidden away—from the external social environment. A prison illustrates in clear detail the nature of surveillance because it seeks to maximize control over inmates' behavior. Foucault asks, "Is it surprising that prisons resemble factories, schools, barracks, hospitals, which all resemble prisons?" (1979).

According to Foucault, the modern prison has its origins in the Panopticon, an organization planned by the philosopher and social thinker Jeremy Bentham in the nineteenth century. "Panopticon" was the name Bentham gave to an ideal prison he designed, which he tried on various occasions to sell to the British government. The design was never fully implemented, but some of its main principles were incorporated into prisons built in the nineteenth century in the United States, Britain, and Europe. The Panopticon was circular in shape, with the cells built around the outside edge. In the center was an inspection tower. Two windows were placed in every cell, one facing

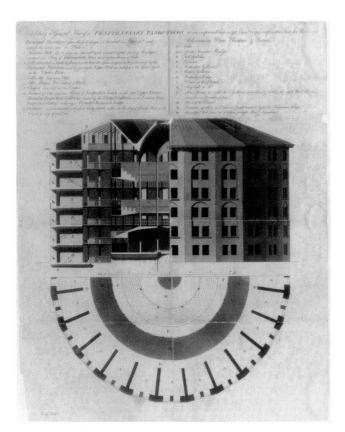

Elevation, cross-section, and plan of Jeremy Bentham's Panopticon, drawn in 1790.

the inspection tower and the other facing outside. The aim of the design was to make prisoners visible to guards at all times. The windows in the tower itself were equipped with venetian blinds, so that while the prison staff could keep the prisoners under constant observation, they themselves could be invisible.

THE LIMITS OF SURVEILLANCE

Foucault was right about prisons. Even today, most prisons look remarkably like the Panopticon. He was also right about the central role of surveillance in modern societies, an issue that has become even more important now because of the growing impact of information and communications technologies. We live in what some have called the **surveillance society** (Lyon, 1994)—a society in which information about our lives is gathered by all types of organizations.

But Weber's and Foucault's argument that the most effective way to run an organization is to maximize surveillance—to have clear and consistent divisions of authority—is a mistake, at least if we apply it to business firms, which don't (as prisons do) exert total control over people's lives in closed settings. Prisons are not a good model for organizations as a whole. Direct supervision may work tolerably well when the

people involved, as in prisons, are basically hostile to those in authority over them and do not want to be where they are. But in organizations where managers desire others to cooperate with them in reaching common goals, the situation is different. Too much direct supervision alienates employees, who feel they are denied any opportunities for involvement in the work they do (Sabel, 1982; Grint, 1991).

This is one main reason why organizations founded on the sorts of principles formulated by Weber and Foucault, such as large factories involving assembly-line production and rigid authority hierarchies, eventually ran into great difficulties. Workers weren't inclined to devote themselves to their work in such settings; continuous supervision was in fact *required* to get them to work reasonably hard at all, but it promoted resentment and antagonism (for further discussion, see Chapter 14).

People are also likely to resist high levels of surveillance in the second sense mentioned by Foucault, the collection of written information about them. That was in effect one of the main reasons why the Soviet-style communist societies broke down. In these societies, people were spied on regularly either by the secret police or by others in the pay of the secret police—even relatives and neighbors. The government also kept detailed information on its citizenry in order to clamp down on possible opposition to their rule. The result was a form of society that was politically authoritarian and, toward the end, economically inefficient. The whole society did indeed come almost to resemble a gigantic prison, with all the discontents, conflicts, and modes of opposition prisons generate—and from which, in the end, the population broke free.

Bureaucracy and Democracy

Even in democracies like the United States, government organizations hold enormous amounts of information about us, from records of our dates of birth, schools attended, and jobs held to data on income used for tax collecting and information used for issuing drivers' licenses and allocating Social Security numbers. Since we don't have access to the files of most government agencies, such surveillance activities can infringe on the principle of democracy.

The diminishing of democracy with the advance of modern forms of organization was something that worried Weber a great deal (see also Chapter 13). What especially disturbed him was the prospect of rule by faceless bureaucrats. How can democracy be anything other than a meaningless slogan in the face of the increasing power bureaucratic organizations are wielding over us? After all, Weber reasoned, bureaucracies are necessarily specialized and hierarchical. Those near the bottom of the organization inevitably find themselves reduced to carrying out mundane tasks and have no power over what they do; power passes to those at the top. Weber's student Robert Michels (1967) invented a phrase that has since become famous, to refer to this loss of power: In large-scale organizations, and more generally a society dominated by organizations, he argued, there is an **iron law of oligarchy**. **Oligarchy** means rule by the few. According to Michels, the flow of power toward the top is simply an inevitable part of an increasingly bureaucratized world—hence the term *iron law*.

Was Michels right? It surely is correct to say that large-scale organizations involve the centralizing of power. Yet there is good reason to suppose that the "iron law of oligarchy" is not quite as hard and fast as Michels claimed. The connections between oligarchy and bureaucratic centralization are more ambiguous than he supposed.

We should recognize first of all that unequal power is not just a function of size. In modest-sized groups there can be very marked differences of power. In a small business, for instance, where the activities of employees are directly visible to the directors, much tighter control might be exerted than in offices in larger organizations. As organizations expand in size, power relationships often in fact become looser. Those at the middle and lower levels may have little influence over general policies forged at the top. On the other hand, because of the specialization and expertise involved in bureaucracy, people at the top also lose control over many administrative decisions, which are handled by those lower down.

In many modern organizations power is also quite often openly delegated downward from superiors to subordinates. In many large companies, corporate heads are so busy coordinating different departments, coping with crises, and analyzing budget and forecast figures that they have little time for original thinking. They hand over consideration of policy issues to others below them, whose task is to develop proposals about them. Many corporate leaders frankly admit that for the most part they simply accept the conclusions given to them.

Gender and Organizations

Until some two decades ago, organizational studies did not devote very much attention to the question of gender. Weber's theory of bureaucracy and many of the influential responses to Weber that came in subsequent years were written by men and presumed a model of organizations that placed men squarely at the center. The rise of feminist scholarship in the 1970s, however, led to examinations of gender relations in all the main institutions in society, including organizations and bureaucracy. Feminist sociologists not only focused on the imbalance of gender roles within organizations, they also explored the ways in which modern organizations themselves had developed in a specifically gendered way.

Feminists have argued that the emergence of the modern organization and the bureaucratic career depended on a particular gender configuration. They point to two main ways in which gender is embedded in the very structure of modern organizations. First, bureaucracies are characterized by occupational gender segregation. As women began to enter the labor market in greater numbers, they tended to be segregated into categories of occupations that were low paying and involved routine work. These positions were subordinate to those occupied by men and did not provide opportunities for women to be promoted. Women were used as a source of cheap, reliable labor but were not granted the same opportunities as men to build careers.

Second, the idea of a bureaucratic career was in fact a *male* career in which women played a crucial supporting role. In the workplace, women performed the routine tasks—as clerks, secretaries, and office managers—thereby freeing up men to advance their careers. Men could concentrate on obtaining promotions or landing big accounts because the female support staff handled much of the busywork. In the domestic sphere, women also supported the bureaucratic career by caring for the home, the children, and the man's day-to-day well-being. Women serviced the needs of the male bureaucrat by allowing him to work long hours, travel, and focus solely on his work without concern about personal or domestic issues.

As a result of these two tendencies, early feminist writers argued, modern organizations have developed as male-dominated preserves in which women are excluded from power, denied opportunities to advance their careers, and victimized on the basis of their gender through sexual harassment and discrimination.

Although most early feminist analysis focused on a common set of concerns—unequal pay, discrimination, and the male hold on power—there was no consensus about the best approach to take in working for women's equality. Two of the leading feminist works on women and organizations exemplified the split between liberal and radical feminist perspectives.

One was Rosabeth Moss Kanter's *Men and Women of the Corporation* (1977), one of the earliest examinations of women in bureaucratic settings. Kanter investigated the position of women in corporations and analyzed the ways in which they were excluded from gaining power. She focused on "male homosociability"—the way in which men successfully kept power within a closed circle and allowed access only to those who were part of the same in-group. Women and ethnic minorities were effectively denied opportunities for advancement and were shut out of the social networks and personal relationships that were crucial for promotions.

Although Kanter was critical of these gender imbalances within modern corporations, she was not entirely pessimistic about the future. In her eyes, the problem was one of *power*, not gender. Women were in a disadvantaged position, not because they were women per se, but because they did not wield sufficient power within organizations. As greater numbers of women came to assume powerful roles, according to Kanter, the imbalances would be swept away. Her analysis can be described as a liberal feminist approach because she is primarily concerned with equality of opportunity and ensuring that women are permitted to attain positions comparable with those of men.

The radical feminist approach was presented by Kathy Ferguson in *The Feminist Case against Bureaucracy* (1984), which differs greatly from that of Kanter. Ferguson did not see the gender imbalance within organizations as something that could be resolved with the promotion of more women to positions of power. In Ferguson's view, modern organizations were fundamentally tainted by male values and patterns of domination. Women would always be relegated to subordinate roles within such structures, she argued. The only true solution was for women to build their own organizations on principles very different from those designed by and for men. Women, she argued, have the capacity to organize in a way that is more democratic, participatory, and cooperative than men, who are prone to authoritarian tactics, inflexible procedures, and an insensitive management style.

WOMEN IN MANAGEMENT

As women have entered professional occupations in greater numbers in recent decades, the debate over gender and organizations has taken new turns. Many scholars now see an opportunity to assess the impact of women leaders and managers on the organizations in which they work. Was Kanter correct when she predicted that gender imbalances would diminish as more women entered powerful positions? One of the most hotly contested questions today is whether women managers are making a difference in their organizations by introducing a "female" style of management into contexts that have long been dominated by male culture, values, and behavior.

Organizations of all types are confronted with the need to become more flexible, efficient, and competitive in today's global economy. This challenge is affecting organizations at all levels, from production processes and shop-floor relations to the use of technology and management practices. In recent years, many leadership qualities commonly associated with women have been held up as essential assets for organizations attempting to become more flexible in their operations. Rather than relying on top-down, rigid management styles, organizations are encouraged to adopt policies that ensure employee commitment, collective enthusiasm for organizational goals, shared responsibility, and a focus on people. Communication, consensus, and teamwork are cited by management theorists as key approaches that will distinguish successful organizations in the new global age. These so-called soft management skills are ones traditionally associated with women.

Some writers claim that this shift toward a more "female" management style can already be felt. Women are attaining unprecedented influence at the top levels of power, they argue, and are doing so according to their own rules rather than adopting typically male management techniques (Rosener, 1997). As the success of women's leadership is increasingly felt throughout the organizational world, some predict that a new way of thinking about management will emerge in which men will also adopt many of the techniques long favored by women, such as delegating responsibility, sharing information and resources, and collective goal setting.

Others do not subscribe to the view that women are successfully exercising a distinctly "female" brand of management. In *Managing Like a Man* (1998), Judy Wajcman takes issue with this approach on a number of grounds. First, she argues that the number of women who actually make it to the top levels of power is extremely limited. It is true, she says, that women are making substantial progress within the ranks of middle management, but despite their greater numbers in middle management, women are still largely prevented from accessing power at the highest levels. One out of thirteen senior executives (executive vice president or higher) are women. This is a dramatic increase from one in forty in 1995 (Epstein, 2003). However, many of these positions held by women are "staff" positions or otherwise distanced from direct influence on profit margins. In Fortune 500 companies 90 percent of executive positions with direct influence on profit and loss were held by men (Epstein, 2003). Men continue to receive higher levels of pay for equivalent work and are employed in a broader spectrum of roles than women, who tend to be clustered in fields such as human resources and marketing.

When women do reach top management positions, they tend to manage like men. Although great advances have been made in the past two decades in the areas of equal employment, sexual harassment policies, and overall consciousness about gender issues, Wajcman argues that organizational culture and management style remain overwhelmingly male. In her study of 324 senior-level managers in multinational corporations, she found that management techniques are dominated much more by the overall organizational culture than they are by the gender or personal style of individual managers. In order for women to get access to power and maintain their influence, they must adapt to the prevailing managerial style, which emphasizes aggressive leadership, tough tactics, and top-down decision making.

Wajcman argues forcefully that organizations are thoroughly gendered, in ways both obvious and subtle. The day-to-day organizational culture—including the way in which people

As women climb the corporate ladder, will they change the methods as well as the face of management or will they learn to "manage like men"?

talk to each other—is dominated by quick, competitive interactions. Despite a drop in overt sexual harassment—no longer tolerated in most organizations—more subtle sexualized relations remain prominent in the workplace and usually work to the disadvantage of women. Social networks and informal ties are the crucial elements behind job promotions and advancement, but these continue to be run in the style of an "old boys" network. Many women find this realm alienating or uncomfortable, as one of Wajcman's respondents explained:

> You've got to be one of the boys. . . . I don't mind going down to the pub with the boys. . . . I don't get offended by the jokes . . . . [T]hat's how you get to the top . . . you start to see the breaks or where something's not going quite right and you make use of it . . . I personally don't like playing that game. It's not worth the hassle. (1998)

There is also reason to believe that it is difficult for women to break into traditional mentoring patterns in organizations. The model of mentoring has traditionally been the older man who takes on a young protégé in whom he sees traces of himself at a younger age. The mentor would work behind the scenes to advance the young employee's interests and to facilitate his future career moves. This dynamic is less easy to replicate between older male bosses and younger female employees, and there are not enough women in senior positions to serve as mentors to younger women. Among Wajcman's respondents, women were more likely than men to cite a lack of career guidance as a major barrier in their advancement.

Wajcman is skeptical about claims that a new age of flexible, decentralized organizations is upon us. Her findings reveal that traditional forms of authoritarian management are still firmly present. In her view, certain surface attributes of organizations may have been transformed, but the gendered nature of organizations—and the overwhelmingly dominant power of men within them—has not been challenged.

Beyond Bureaucracy?

For quite a long while in the development of Western societies, Weber's model, closely mirrored by that of Foucault, held good. In government, hospital administration, universities, and business organizations, bureaucracy seemed to be dominant. Even though, as Peter Blau showed, informal social groups always develop in bureaucratic settings and are in fact effective, it seemed as though the future might be just what Weber had anticipated: constantly increasing bureaucratization.

Bureaucracies still exist aplenty in the West, but Weber's idea that a clear hierarchy of authority, with power and knowledge concentrated at the top, is the only way to run a large organization is starting to look archaic. Numerous organizations are overhauling themselves to become less, rather than more, hierarchical.

Almost four decades ago, Burns and Stalker concluded that traditional bureaucratic structures can stifle innovation and creativity in cutting-edge industries (1994); in today's electronic economy, few would dispute the importance of these findings. Departing from rigid vertical command structures, many organizations are turning to "horizontal," collaborative models in order to become more flexible and responsive to fluctuating markets. In this section we shall examine some of the main forces behind these shifts, including globalization and the growth of information technology, and consider some of the ways in which late modern organizations are reinventing themselves in the light of the changing circumstances.

Organizational Change: The Japanese Model

Many of the changes that can now be witnessed in organizations around the world were first pioneered in Japanese companies some decades ago. Although the Japanese economy has suffered recession in recent years, it was phenomenally successful during the 1980s. This economic success was often attributed to the distinctive characteristics of large Japanese corporations—which differed substantially from most business firms in the West (Vogel, 1979). As we shall see, many of the unique organizational characteristics of Japanese corporations have been adapted and modified in other countries in recent years.

Japanese companies, especially in the 1980s and 1990s, diverged from the characteristics that Weber associated with bureaucracy in several ways:

1. **Bottom-Up Decision Making.** The big Japanese corporations do not form a pyramid of authority as Weber portrayed it, with each level being responsible only to the one above. Rather, workers low down in the organization are consulted about policies being considered by management, and even the top executives regularly meet with them.

2. **Less Specialization.** In Japanese organizations, employees specialize much less than their counterparts in the West. Take the case of Sugao, as described by William Ouchi (1982). Sugao is a university graduate who has just joined the Mitsubeni Bank in Tokyo. He will enter the firm in a management-training position, spending his first year learning generally how the various departments of the bank operate. He will then work in a local branch for a while as a teller and will subsequently be brought back to the bank's headquarters to learn commercial banking. Then he will move out to yet another branch dealing with loans. From there he is likely to return to headquarters to work in the personnel department. Ten years will have elapsed by this time, and Sugao will have reached the position of section chief.

   By the time Sugao reaches the peak of his career, some thirty years after beginning as a trainee, he will have mastered all the important tasks. In contrast, a typical American bank-management trainee of the same age will almost certainly specialize in one area of banking early on and stay in that specialty for the remainder of her working life.

3. **Job Security.** The large corporations in Japan are committed to the long-term employment of those they hire; the employee is guaranteed a job. Pay and responsibility are geared to seniority—how many years a worker has been with the firm—rather than to a competitive struggle for promotion. This still remains a value, although it has weakened in recent years.

4. **Group Orientation.** At all levels of the corporation, people are involved in small cooperative "teams," or work groups. The groups, rather than individual members, are evaluated in terms of their performance. Unlike their Western counterparts, the *organization charts* of Japanese companies—maps of the authority system—show only groups, not individual positions. This is important because it contradicts the supposed *iron law of oligarchy.*

5. **Merging of Work and Private Lives.** In Weber's depiction of bureaucracy, there is a clear division between the work of people within the organization and their activities outside. This is in fact true of most Western corporations, in which the relation between firm and employee is an economic one. Japanese corporations, by contrast, provide for many of their employees' needs, expecting in return a high level of loyalty to the firm. Japanese employees, from workers on the shop floor to top executives, often wear company uniforms. They may assemble to sing the "company song" each morning, and they regularly take part in leisure activities organized by the corporation on weekends. (A few Western corporations, like IBM and Apple, now also have company songs.) Workers receive material benefits from the company over and above their salaries. The electrical firm Hitachi, for example, studied by Ronald Dore (1980), provided housing for all unmarried workers and nearly half of its married male employees. Company loans were available for the education of children and to help with the cost of weddings and funerals.

Studies of Japanese-run plants in the United States and Britain indicate that bottom-up decision making does work outside Japan. Workers seem to respond positively to the greater level of involvement these plants provide (White and Trevor, 1983). It seems reasonable to conclude, therefore, that the Japanese model does carry some lessons relevant to the Weberian conception of bureaucracy. Organizations that closely resemble Weber's ideal type are probably much less effective than they appear on paper, because they do not permit lower-level employees to develop a sense of control over, and involvement in, their work tasks.

Drawing on the example of Japanese corporations, Ouchi (1979, 1982) has argued that there are clear limits to the effectiveness of bureaucratic hierarchy, as emphasized by Weber. Overly bureaucratized organizations lead to internal failures of functioning because of their rigid, inflexible, and uninvolving nature. Forms of authority Ouchi calls *clans*—groups having close personal connections with one another—are more efficient than bureaucratic types of organization. The work groups in Japanese firms are one example, but clan-type systems often develop informally within Western organizations as well.

The Transformation of Management

Most of the components of the Japanese model described above come down to issues of management. While it is impossible to ignore specific production-level practices developed by the Japanese, a large part of the Japanese approach focused on management-worker relations and ensured that employees at all levels felt a personal attachment to the company. The emphasis on teamwork, consensus-building approaches, and broad-based employee participation were in stark contrast to traditional Western forms of management that were more hierarchical and authoritarian.

In the 1980s, many Western organizations began to introduce new management techniques in order to boost productivity and competitiveness. Two popular branches of management theory—*human resource management* and the *corporate culture* approach—indicated that the Japanese model had not gone unnoticed in the West. **Human resource management** is a style of management that regards a company's work-force as vital to its economic competitiveness: If the employees are not completely dedicated to the firm and its product, the firm will never be a leader in its field. In order to generate employee enthusiasm and commitment, the entire organizational culture must be retooled so that workers feel they have an investment in the workplace and in the work process. According to human resource management theory, human resources issues should not be the exclusive domain of designated personnel officers, but should instead be a top priority for all members of company management.

The second management trend—creating a distinctive **corporate culture**—is closely related to human resources management. In order to promote loyalty to the company and pride in its work, the company's management works with employees to build an organizational culture involving rituals, events, or traditions unique to that company alone. These cultural activities are designed to draw all members of the firm—from the most senior managers to the newest employee—together so that they make common cause with each other and strengthen group solidarity. Company picnics, "casual Fridays" (days on which employees can dress down), and company-sponsored community service projects are examples of techniques for building a corporate culture.

In recent years a number of Western companies have been founded according to the management principles described above. Rather than constructing themselves according to a traditional bureaucratic model, companies like the Saturn car company in the United States have organized themselves along these new managerial lines. At Saturn, for example, employees at all levels have the opportunity to spend time at positions in other areas of the company in order to gain a better sense of the operation of the firm as a whole. Shop-floor workers spend time with the marketing team, sharing insights into the way the vehicles are made. Sales staff rotate through the servicing department to become more aware of common maintenance problems that might concern prospective buyers. Representatives from both sales and the shop floor are involved in product design teams in order to discuss shortcomings that the management may not have been aware of in earlier models. A corporate culture focused on friendly and knowledgeable customer service unifies company employees and enhances the sense of company pride.

Technology and Modern Organizations

The development of **information technology**—computers and electronic communication media such as the Internet—is another factor currently influencing organizational structures (Zuboff, 1988; Kanter, 1991). Anyone who draws money out of a bank or buys an airline ticket depends on a computer-based communications system. Since data can be processed instantaneously in any part of the world linked to such a system, there is no need for physical proximity between those involved. As a result, the introduction of new technology has allowed many companies to "reengineer" their organizational structure. The impact of these changes, while beneficial to organizational efficiency, can have both positive and negative consequences for the individuals within the organization.

For example, a particular company found the sales of some of its products falling and was faced with the need to reduce costs. The traditional route in such circumstances would be to lay off staff. But instead, the firm set up those who might have been laid off as independent consultants and established a computerized support network called Xanadu to provide basic office services to each of them working out of their homes. The company then "bought back" a substantial proportion of these former employees' working time for a number of years, but also left them free to use other time to work for different clients. The idea was that the new system would provide the corporation with access to the skills possessed by their former employees, but at a cheaper rate since it no longer needed to provide office space or company benefits (pension, life insurance, etc.). The former employees, in their turn, had the opportunity to build up their own businesses. Initially, at least, the scheme seems to have worked well for both parties. In such a scheme, though, the burden is placed on the former employees since they have to match the loss of company benefits with their ability to attract new business clients.

This is just one example of how large organizations have become more decentralized as the more routine tasks disappear, reinforcing the tendency toward smaller, more flexible types of enterprises (Burris, 1998). Another example of this process is the rise of "telecommuting." A good deal of office work, for instance, can be carried out at home by "telecommuters" who use the Internet and other mobile technologies, such as cell phones, to do their work at home or somewhere other than their employer's primary office. According to the International Telework Association and Council (ITAC), in

The Computerization of the Workplace

For businesses competing in the global economy, investment in information technology—computer and communications equipment—is a necessity. Firms in the financial sector rely heavily on computers to engage in transactions in international financial markets; manufacturing firms depend on communications equipment to coordinate global production processes; and the customers of consumer services firms demand twenty-four-hour-a-day access to their accounts by telephone or the Internet. In short, information technology has become part of the basic infrastructure of business. In the service sector alone, businesses spent approximately $750 billion on information technology hardware between 1980 and 1990 (National Research Council, 1994). This investment was a doubling of the amount spent per worker on technology and enabled firms to process vastly more transactions than they could in the past. Yet the investment in high-tech hardware did not pay off in terms of increased worker productivity until the late 1990s.

Although some of these technologies have made workers' lives easier, there is reason to worry that the new high-tech workplace may erode workers' power and rights. First, business reliance on information technology may undermine coalitions among workers. There is great demand today for employees with high-tech skills, whereas those who finish high school or college with few such skills find themselves eli-

gible only for a limited number of positions. Increasingly, there are coming to be two "classes" of employees in firms: a privileged class with high-tech skills and another class relegated to lower-status work. But when employees negotiate with management over such issues as wages, hours, and benefits, employee unity is essential for securing concessions. Will high-tech workers side with lower-skilled employees in workplace disputes, or will they be more likely to side with management? The status of worker rights and benefits in the next century may well hinge on the answer to this question.

2001 28 million Americans telecommuted, which is approximately one fifth of the population of adult workers in the United States (Davis and Polonko, 2001). Of these, 21 percent worked at home, while the rest are about equally divided between working at special telework centers, satellite offices, or working while traveling (ITAC, 2004). Telecommuters in the United States are typically males from the Northeast and West who have college degrees and work in professional or managerial positions (Davis and Polonko, 2001). To reduce costs and increase productivity, several large firms in the United States and elsewhere have set up information networks connecting employees who work from home with the main office. For instance, in 2001 AT&T reported saving $65 million annually in increased productivity and $25 million an-

nually in lower real estate costs (ITAC, 2004). With the advent of high-speed Internet access, telecommuting has become even more efficient: ITAC estimated that upgrading the Internet service used by telecommuters to broadband could save employers as much as $5,000 per worker (Pratt, 2003). One rationale for why telecommuting increases productivity is that it eliminates time spent by workers commuting to and from the office, permitting greater concentration of energy on work-related tasks. Hartig et al. (2003) found that telecommuters actually spend more time on paid work when working at home than their counterparts do while working in the office. However, there are repercussions from these new work arrangements. First, the employees lose the human side of work; computer terminals are not an attractive substitute for

Second, in part because new communications technologies allow the branch offices and production facilities of multinational firms to communicate easily with each other, a higher proportion of manufactured goods is coming to be produced on a transnational basis—a situation that may make individual workers more easily replaceable. The former U.S. Secretary of Labor Robert Reich provides the following example of a global production process: "Precision ice-hockey equipment is designed in Sweden, financed in Canada, and assembled in Cleveland and Denmark for distribution in North America and Europe, respectively, out of alloys whose molecular structure was researched and patented in Delaware and fabricated in Japan. An advertising campaign is conceived in Britain; film footage is shot in Canada, dubbed in Britain, and edited in New York" (Reich, 1991). Although high-tech, high-skilled workers will be needed to carry out many aspects of the production process, these skills may no longer give workers the same bargaining power vis-à-vis management that skilled craftsmanship carried with it in previous eras. Because the manufacturing process has now been broken down into many small components, and because each of these components is carried out at a different production facility, the number of skills that any one worker must have is more limited than was the case in previous eras, making it easier for companies to replace contentious workers. Communications technologies thus arguably further the process that the Marxist scholar Harry Braverman called "the deskilling of labor."

Third, the nature of workplace surveillance is likely to change substantially as information technology becomes even more important for business. Employers have always watched their employees closely, monitoring performance, seeking to improve efficiency, checking to make sure they do not steal.

But as a greater proportion of work comes to be done by computer, the capacity of managers to scrutinize the behavior of their employees increases. Computerized performance evaluations, scrutiny of employee e-mail, and enhanced management access to personal employee information—such an Orwellian scenario becomes more likely as the role of information technology in the workplace expands.

Do you think these dangers are real, or is the impact of information technology on organizations essentially benign for employees? What steps, if any, do you think can be taken to counter these trends?

face-to-face interaction with colleagues and friends at work. In addition, female telecommuters face more stress resulting from greater housework and child-care responsibilities (Olson and Primps, 1984; Olson, 1989). Nearly 59 percent of telecommuters say that they work longer hours because they are working at home, though employers view this increased productivity as a primary benefit of telecommuting (ITAC, 2004). On the other hand, management cannot easily monitor the activities of employees not under direct supervision (Kling, 1996). While this may create problems for employers, it allows employees greater flexibility in managing their non-work roles, thus contributing to increased worker satisfaction (Davis and Polonko, 2001). According to surveys by *Computer World* magazine, in the information technology field, workers

perceive telecommuting as significant in determining the desirability of working for a particular company (*Computer World*, 2002). Telecommuting also creates new possibilities for older and disabled workers to remain independent, productive, and socially connected (Bourma et al., 2004).

The growth of telecommuting is affecting profound changes in many social realms. It is restructuring business management practices and authority hierarchies within businesses (Spinks and Wood, 1996) as well as contributing to new trends in housing and residential development that prioritize spatial and technological requirements for telework in homes, which are built at increasing distances from city centers (Hartig et al., 2003). Finally, some have argued that telecommuting is contributing to a shift in the distribution of income

Workplace Design

In the early nineteen-sixties, Jane Jacobs lived on Hudson Street, in Greenwich Village, near the intersection of Eighth Avenue and Bleecker Street. It was then, as now, a charming district of nineteenth-century tenements and town houses, bars and shops, laid out over an irregular grid, and Jacobs loved the neighborhood. In her 1961 masterpiece, "The Death and Life of Great American Cities," she rhapsodized about [the Village]. . . . It was, she said, an urban ballet.

The miracle of Hudson Street, according to Jacobs, was created by the particular configuration of the streets and buildings of the neighborhood. Jacobs argued that when a neighborhood is oriented toward the street, when sidewalks are used for socializing and play and commerce, the users of that street are transformed by the resulting stimulation: they form relationships and casual contacts they would never have otherwise. The West Village, she pointed out, was blessed with a mixture of houses and apartments and shops and offices and industry, which meant that there were always people "outdoors on different schedules and . . . in the place for different purposes." It had short blocks, and short blocks create the greatest variety in foot traffic. It had lots of old buildings, and old buildings have the low rents that permit individualized and creative uses. And, most of all, it had people, cheek by jowl, from every conceivable walk of life. Sparsely populated suburbs may look appealing, she said, but without an active sidewalk life, without the frequent, serendipitous interactions of many different people, "there is no public acquaintanceship,

no foundation of public trust, no cross-connections with the necessary people—and no practice or ease in applying the most ordinary techniques of city public life at lowly levels." . . .

The parallels between neighborhoods and offices are striking. There was a time, for instance, when companies put their most valued employees in palatial offices, with potted plants in the corner, and secretaries out front, guarding access. Those offices were suburbs—gated communities, in fact—and many companies came to realize that if their best employees were isolated in suburbs they would be deprived of public acquaintanceship, the foundations of public trust, and cross-connections with the necessary people. In the eighties and early nineties, the fashion in corporate America was to follow what designers called "universal planning"—rows of identical cubicles, which resembled nothing so much as a Levittown. Today, universal planning has fallen out of favor, for the same reason that the postwar suburbs like Levittown did: to thrive, an office space must have a diversity of uses—it must have the workplace equivalent of houses and apartments and shops and industry. . . .

The task of the office, then, is to invite a particular kind of social interatction—the casual, nonthreatening encounter that makes it easy for relative strangers to talk to each other. Offices need the sort of social milieu that Jane Jacobs found on the sidewalks of the West Village. "It is possible in a city street neighborhood to know all kinds of people without unwelcome entanglements, without boredom, necessity for excuses, explanations, fears of giving offense, embarrassments respecting impositions or commitments, and all such paraphernalia of obligations which can accompany less limited relationships," Jacobs wrote. If you substitute "office" for "city street neighborhood," that sentence becomes the perfect statement of what the modern employer wants from the workplace. . . .

The point of the new offices is to compel us to behave and socialize in ways that we otherwise would not—to overcome our initial inclination to be office suburbanites. But, in all the studies of the new workplaces, the reservations that employees have about a more social environment tend to diminish once they try it. Human behavior, after all, is shaped by context, but how it is shaped—and whether we'll be happy with the result—we can understand only with experience. Jane Jacobs knew the virtues of the West Village because she lived there. What she couldn't know was that her ideas about com-

munity would ultimately make more sense in the workplace. From time to time, social critics have bemoaned the falling rates of community participation in American life, but they have made the same mistake. The reason Americans are content to bowl alone (or, for that matter, not bowl at all) is that, increasingly, they receive all the social support they need—all the serendipitous interactions that serve to make them happy and productive—from nine to five.

SOURCE: Reprinted from Malcolm Gladwell, "Designs for Working," *New Yorker*, December 11, 2000.

Questions

- Why would it be in a company's interest to direct employees away from individual work and toward group interaction?
- This article describes a model for a white-collar office. Would the same kind of interaction and cooperative work be a productive model for blue-collar or unskilled labor also?
- Gladwell describes the old-fashioned office as a form of suburbia. Does the analogy hold? Why or why not?

toward the technologically literate while affecting marital and family relationships and altering demands for child care (Raines and Leathers, 2001).

The experiences of telecommuters are reminders that negative consequences can result from the implementation of information technology to reorder organizations. While computerization has resulted in a reduction in hierarchy, it has created a two-tiered occupational structure composed of technical "experts" and less-skilled production or clerical workers. In these restructured organizations, jobs are redefined based more on technical skill than rank or position. For "expert" professionals, traditional bureaucratic constraints are relaxed to allow for creativity and flexibility, but other workers have limited autonomy (Burris, 1993). Although professionals benefit more from this expanded autonomy, computerization makes production and service workers more visible and vulnerable to supervision (Zuboff, 1988; Wellman et al., 1996). For instance, computerization allows organizations to carefully monitor employees' work patterns to the point that they can count the number of seconds per phone call or keystrokes per minute, which in turn can lead to higher levels of stress for employees.

Granted, the computerization of the workplace does have some positive effects. It has made some mundane tasks associated with clerical jobs more interesting and flexible. It can also promote social networking (Wellman et al., 1996). For example, office computers can be used for recreation; private exchanges with other workers, friends, or family members; and work-related interaction. In some workplaces, computer-mediated communication can promote a more democratic type of workplace interaction. And, as in the case of telecommuting, computerization can contribute to greater flexibility for workers to manage both their personal and professional lives. But in the large majority of workplaces, computerization benefits the professionals who possess the knowledge and expertise about how to gain from it. It has not brought commensurate improvements in the career opportunities or salaries of the average worker (Kling, 1996). As Foucault thought, in the new computerized workplace, knowledge and information are important sources of power and a means of controlling people.

Organizations as Networks

Traditionally, identifying the boundaries of organizations has been fairly straightforward. Organizations were generally located in defined physical spaces, such as an office building, a suite of rooms, or, in the case of a hospital or university, a whole campus. The mission or tasks an organization aimed to fulfill were also usually clear cut. A central feature of bureaucracies, for example, was adherence to a defined set of responsibilities and procedures for carrying them out. Weber's view of bureaucracy was that of a self-contained unit that intersected with outside entities at limited and designated points.

We have already seen how the physical boundaries of organizations are being broken down by the capacity of new information technology to transcend countries and time zones. But the same process is also affecting the work that organizations do and the way in which it is coordinated. Many organizations no longer operate as independent units, as they once did. A growing number are finding that their operations run more effectively when they are linked into a web of complex relationships with other organizations and companies. No longer is there a clear dividing line between the organization and outside groups. Globalization, information technology, and trends in occupational patterns mean that organizational boundaries are more open and fluid than they once were.

In *The Rise of the Network Society* (1996), Manuel Castells argues that the "network enterprise" is the organizational form best suited to a global, informational economy. By this he means that it is increasingly impossible for organizations— be they large corporations or small businesses—to survive if they are not part of a network. What enables the process of networking to occur is the growth of information technology: Organizations around the world are able to locate each other, enter readily into contact, and coordinate joint activities through an electronic medium. Castells cites several examples of organizational networking and emphasizes that they have originated in diverse cultural and institutional contexts. According to Castells, however, they all represent "different dimensions of a fundamental process"—the disintegration of the traditional, rational bureaucracy.

An example of organizations as networks can be seen in the powerful strategic alliances formed between top companies. Increasingly the large corporation is less and less a big business and more an "enterprise web"—a central organization that links smaller firms together. IBM, for example, used to be a highly self-sufficient corporation, wary of partnerships with others. Yet in the 1980s and early 1990s, IBM joined with dozens of U.S.-based companies and more than eighty foreign-based firms to share strategic planning and cope with production problems.

Recent high-profile mergers among media and telecommunications companies have shown that even large and profitable corporations feel pressure to keep ahead of the rapidly changing market. The intentions of AOL, the popular online provider, and Time-Warner, the television and print media giant, in their merger proposals were to produce the world's largest corporation and link together the Internet and traditional media products. At a time when technological innovation is essential to remain competitive, it is difficult for even the leading firms to remain on top without drawing on the skills and resources of others. And as the financial difficulties of the AOL–TimeWarner merger show, technological innovation by itself cannot guarantee success.

Decentralization is another process that contributes to organizations functioning as networks. When change becomes both more profound and more rapid, highly centralized Weberian-style bureaucracies are too cumbersome and too entrenched in their established ways to cope. Stanley Davis argues that as business firms, and other organizations too, increasingly come to be networks, they go through a process of *decentralization* where power and responsibility are devolved downward throughout the organization, rather than remaining concentrated at the top levels (1988).

Networked organizations offer at least two advantages over more formal, bureaucratic ones: They can foster the flow of information, and they can enhance creativity. As you've already learned, bureaucratic hierarchy can impede the flow of information: One must go through the proper channels, fill out the right forms, and often avoid displeasing people in higher positions. These bureaucratic processes not only impede the sharing of information but also stifle creative problem solving. In networked organizations, by contrast, when a problem arises, instead of writing a memo to your boss and waiting for a reply before you act, you can simply pick up the phone or dash off an e-mail to the person who is responsible for working out a solution. As a result, members of networked organizations learn more easily from one another than do bureaucrats. It is therefore easier to solve routine problems and to foster more innovative solutions to all types of problems (Hamel, 1991; Powell and Brantley, 1992; Powell, Koput, and Smith-Doerr, 1996).

The "McDonaldization" of Society?

Not everyone agrees that our society and its organizations are moving away from the Weberian view of rigid, orderly bureaucracies. Some critics point out that a number of high-profile cases—such as the Saturn car corporation or Benetton—are seized on by the media and commentators, who in turn pronounce the birth of a trend that does not in fact exist. The idea that we are witnessing a process of debureaucratization, they argue, is overstated.

In a contribution to the debate over debureaucratization, George Ritzer (1993) has developed a vivid metaphor to express his view of the transformations taking place in industrialized societies. He argues that although some tendencies toward debureaucratization have indeed emerged, on the whole what we are witnessing is the "McDonaldization" of society. According to Ritzer, McDonaldization is "the process by which the principles of the fast-food restaurants are coming to dominate more and more sectors of American society as well as the rest of the world." Ritzer uses the four guiding principles for McDonald's restaurants—efficiency, calculability, uniformity, and control through automation—to show that our society is becoming ever *more* rationalized with time.

If you have ever visited McDonald's restaurants in two different cities or countries, you will have noticed that there are very few differences between them. The interior decoration may vary slightly and the language spoken will most likely differ from country to country, but the layout, the menu, the procedure for ordering, the staff uniforms, the tables, the packaging, and the "service with a smile" are virtually identical. The McDonald's experience is designed to be the same whether you are in Bogota or Beijing. No matter where they are located, visitors to McDonald's know that they can expect quick service with a minimum of fuss and a standardized product that is reassuringly consistent. The McDonald's system is deliberately constructed to maximize efficiency and minimize human responsibility and involvement in the process. Except for certain key tasks such as taking orders and pushing the start and stop buttons on cooking equipment, the restaurants' functions are highly automated and largely run themselves.

Ritzer argues that society as a whole is moving toward this highly standardized and regulated model for getting things done. Many aspects of our daily lives, for example, now involve interactions with automated systems and computers instead of human beings. E-mail and voice mail are replacing letters and phone calls, e-commerce is threatening to overtake trips to the stores, bank machines are outnumbering bank tellers, and prepackaged meals provide a quicker option than cooking. If you have recently tried to call a large organization, such as an airline, you will know that it is almost impossible to speak to a human being. Automated Touch-Tone information services are designed to answer your requests; only in certain cases will you be connected to a live employee of the company. Computerized systems of all sorts are playing an ever greater role in our daily lives. Ritzer, like Weber before him, is fearful of the harmful effects of rationalization on the human spirit and creativity. He argues that McDonaldization is making social life more homogeneous, more rigid, and less personal.

Organizations That Span the World

For the first time in history, organizations have become truly global in scale. Information technologies have rendered national borders less meaningful, since they can no longer contain key economic, cultural, and environmental activities. As a consequence, international organizations are expected to continue to grow in number and importance, providing a measure of predictability and stability in a world where nations are no longer the all-powerful actors they once were (Union of International Associations, 1996).

Sociologists therefore study international organizations to understand better how it is possible to create institutions that span national borders and what their effects will be. Some sociologists even argue that global organizations will push the world's countries to become more and more alike (Thomas et al., 1987; Scott and Meyer, 1994; McNeely, 1995).

International organizations are not new, however. For example, organizations concerned with managing trade across borders have existed for centuries. The Hanseatic League, a business alliance among German merchants and cities, was one such organization, dominating trade in the North and Baltic Seas from the middle of the thirteenth century to the middle of the seventeenth century. But it was not until the creation of the short-lived League of Nations in 1919 that truly global organizations, with elaborate bureaucracies and member nations around the world, were formed. The United Nations, created in 1945, is perhaps the most prominent modern example of a global organization.

Sociologists divide international organizations into two principal types: *International governmental organizations* are composed of national governments, while *international nongovernmental organizations* comprise private organizations. We will consider each of these separately.

International Governmental Organizations

The first type of global organization is the **international governmental organization (IGO)**, a type of international organization established by treaties between governments for purposes of conducting business between the nations making up its membership. Such organizations emerge for reasons of national security (both the League of Nations and the United Nations were created after highly destructive world wars), the regulation of trade (for example, by the World Trade Organization), social welfare or human rights, or, increasingly, environmental protection.

Some of the most powerful IGOs today were created to unify national economies into large and powerful trading blocks. One of the most advanced IGOs is the European Union (EU), whose rules now govern twenty-five countries, mostly in Western Europe. The EU was formed to create a single European economy, in which businesses could operate freely across borders in search of markets and labor and workers could move freely in search of jobs without having to go through customs or show passports at border crossings. EU members have common economic policies, and twelve of them even share a single currency (the euro). Thirteen additional countries, mostly of Eastern Europe and representing 168 million people, have applied for membership, ten of which joined the EU in 2004 (Europa, 2004). Not all Europeans welcome this development, however, since it means that member countries must surrender most of their economic decision making to the EU as a whole.

At the beginning of the twentieth century, there were only about three dozen IGOs in the world, although data for that time are sketchy. By 1981, when consistent reporting criteria were adopted, there were 1,039; by 1996, there were 1,830 (Union of International Associations, 1996). Today it is estimated that there are as many as 6,415 international governmental organizations (Union of International Organizations, 2003).

International Nongovernmental Organizations

The second type of global organization is the **international nongovernmental organization (INGO)**. International organizations are established by agreements between the individuals or private organizations making up their membership. Examples include the International Planned Parenthood Federation, the International Sociological Association, the International Council of Women, and the environmental group Greenpeace. Like the number of IGOs, the number of INGOs has increased explosively in recent years—from fewer than two hundred near the beginning of the twentieth century to about 15,000 in the mid-1990s, (Union of International Associations, 1996). There are an estimated 43,958 international nongovernmental organizations today (Union of International Organizations, 2003).

In general, INGOs are primarily concerned with promoting the global interests of their members, largely through influencing the UN, other IGOs, or individual governments. They also engage in research and education and spread information by means of international conferences, meetings, and journals. INGOs have succeeded in shaping the policies of powerful nations.

One prominent (and highly successful) example of an INGO is the International Campaign to Ban Landmines. The campaign, along with its founder Jody Williams, was awarded

Jody Williams, founder of the International Campaign to Ban Landmines, was awarded the Nobel Peace Prize in 1997 for her work and its eventual success in effecting the end of landmine use by a majority of the world's countries.

the Nobel Peace Prize in 1997 for its success in getting a majority of the world's countries to agree to a treaty banning the devastating use of land mines. The Nobel Prize committee commended the campaign for changing "a vision to a feasible reality," adding that "this work has grown into a convincing example of an effective policy for peace that could prove decisive in the international effort for disarmament" (ICBL, 2001).

The International Campaign to Ban Landmines is affiliated with over a thousand other INGOs in some sixty countries. Together they have focused public attention on the dangers posed to civilians of the more than 100 million antipersonnel mines that are a deadly legacy of former wars fought in Europe, Asia, and Africa. These mines are unlike other weapons. They can remain active for decades after a war, terrorizing and trapping whole populations. In Cambodia, for example, fertile croplands have been mined, threatening with starvation farmers who are not willing to risk a misstep that could reduce them or their families to a shower of scraps. The campaign's efforts resulted in a treaty banning the use, production, stockpiling, and transfer of antipersonnel land mines. The treaty, which became international law in March 1999, has been ratified by 141 countries. Nine other countries are in the process of ratifying the agreement (ICBL, 2003).

Although they are far more numerous than IGOs and have achieved some successes, INGOs have far less power, since legal power (including enforcement) ultimately lies with governments. In the effort to ban land mines, for instance, al-

though most of the major powers in the world signed the treaty, the United States, citing security concerns in Korea, refused, as did Russia. Some INGOs, like Amnesty International and Greenpeace, have nonetheless achieved considerable influence.

How Do Groups and Organizations Affect Your Life?

Social Capital: The Ties That Bind

One of the principal reasons people join organizations is to gain connections and increase their influence. The time and energy invested in an organization can bring welcome returns. Parents who belong to the PTA, for example, are more likely to be able to influence school policy than those who do not belong. The members know whom to call, what to say, and how to exert pressure on school officials.

Sociologists call these fruits of organizational membership **social capital**, the social knowledge and connections that enable people to accomplish their goals and extend their influence (Loury, 1987; Coleman, 1988, 1990; Putnam, 1993, 1995, 2000). Social capital includes useful social networks, a sense of mutual obligation and trustworthiness, an understanding of the norms that govern effective behavior, and in general, other social resources that enable people to act effectively. For example, college students often become active in the student government or the campus newspaper partly because they hope to learn social skills and make connections that will pay off when they graduate. They may, for example, get to interact with professors and administrators, who then will go to bat for them when they are looking for a job or applying to graduate school.

Differences in social capital mirror larger social inequalities. In general, for example, men have more capital than women, whites more than nonwhites, the wealthy more than the poor. The Bohemian Grove you read about earlier, an important source of social capital for those who are invited to attend, is limited to wealthy, mainly white males. Attendance gives these men access to powerful social, political, and business resources, helping to extend their wealth and influence. Differences in social capital can also be found among countries. According to the World Bank (2001), countries with high levels of social capital, where businesspeople can effectively develop the "networks of trust" that foster healthy economies, are more likely to experience economic growth. An example is the rapid growth experienced by many East Asian economies in the 1980s, a growth some sociologists have argued was fueled by strong business networks.

Robert Putnam, a political scientist who has completed an extensive study of social capital in the United States, distinguishes two types of social capital: *bridging social capital*, which is outward looking and inclusive, and *bonding social capital*, which is inward looking and exclusive. Bridging social capital unifies people across social cleavages. The capacity to unify people can be seen in such examples as the civil rights movement, which brought blacks and whites together in the struggle for racial equality, and interfaith religious organizations. Bonding social capital reinforces exclusive identities and homogeneous groups; it can be found in ethnic fraternal organizations, church-based women's reading groups, and fashionable country clubs (Putnam, 2000).

People who actively belong to organizations are more likely to feel "connected"; they feel engaged, able to somehow "make a difference." From the standpoint of the larger society, social capital, the bridging form in particular, provides people with a feeling that they are part of a wider community, and one that includes people who are different from themselves. Democracy flourishes when social capital is strong. Indeed, cross-national survey evidence suggests that levels of civic engagement in the United States are among the highest in the world (Putnam, 1993, 2000). But there is equally strong evidence that during the past quarter century, the ties of political involvement, club membership, and other forms of social and civic engagement that bind Americans to one another have significantly eroded. Could it be that democracy is eroding as a result?

Such declines in organizational membership, neighborliness, and trust in general have been paralleled by a decline in democratic participation. Voter turnout has dropped by 25 percent since the 1960s. In recent presidential elections, for example, the winning candidate (George H. W. Bush in 1988, Bill Clinton in 1992 and 1996 and George W. Bush in 2000) received roughly only a quarter of the votes of all those who were eligible to cast a ballot. About half of the eligible voters did not bother to go to the polls. Similarly, attendance at public meetings concerning education or civic affairs has dropped sharply since the 1970s, and three out of four Americans today tell pollsters that they either "never" trust the government or do so only "sometimes" (Putnam, 1995).

Even the recent increase in membership in organizations such as the Sierra Club, the National Organization for Women (NOW), and the American Association of Retired Persons (AARP, with 35 million members) is deceiving: The vast majority of these organizations' members simply pay their annual dues and receive a newsletter. Very few members actively participate, failing to develop the social capital Putnam regards as an important underpinning of democracy. Many of the most popular organizations today, such as twelve-step programs or weight loss groups, emphasize personal growth and health rather than collective goals to benefit society as a whole.

There are undoubtedly many reasons for these declines. For one, women, who were traditionally active in voluntary organizations, are more likely to hold a job than ever before. For another, people are increasingly disillusioned with government and less likely to think that their vote counts. Furthermore, the flight to the suburbs increases commuting time, using up time and energy that might have been available for civic activities. But the principal source of declining civic participation, according to Putnam is simple: television. The many hours Americans spend at home alone watching TV has replaced social engagement in the community.

Conclusion

You know better now how the groups and organizations you belong to exert an enormous influence over your life. They help to determine whom you know, and in many ways who you are. The primary groups of your earliest years were crucial in shaping your sense of self—a sense that changes very slowly thereafter. Throughout your life, groups are a wellspring of the norms and values that enable and enrich social life. At the same time, groups are also a source of nonconformist behavior: The rebel as much as the upright citizen is shaped by group membership.

Although groups remain central in our lives, group affiliation in the United States is rapidly changing. As you have seen in this chapter, conventional groups appear to be losing ground in our daily life. For example, today's college students are less likely to join civic groups and organizations—or even vote—than were their parents, a decline that may well signal a lower commitment to their communities. Some sociologists worry that this signals a weakening of society itself, which could bring about social instability.

As you have also seen, the global economy and information technology are redefining group life in ways that are now beginning to be felt. For instance, your parents are likely to spend much of their careers in a relative handful of long-lasting, bureaucratic organizations; you are much more likely to be part of a larger number of networked, "flexible" ones. Many of your group affiliations will be created through the Internet or through other forms of communication that today can barely be envisioned. It will become increasingly easy to connect with like-minded people anywhere on the planet, creating geographically dispersed groups that span the planet—and whose members may never meet each other face-to-face.

How will these trends affect the quality of your social relationships? For nearly all of human history, most people interacted exclusively with others who were close at hand. The industrial revolution, which facilitated the rise of large, impersonal bureaucracies where people knew one another poorly if at all, changed social interaction. Today, the information revolution is once again changing human interaction. Tomorrow's groups and organizations could provide a renewed sense of communication and social intimacy—or they could spell further isolation and social distance.

Study Outline

www.wwnorton.com/giddens5

Social Groups

- *Social groups*, collections of people who share a sense of common identity and regularly interact with one another on the basis of shared expectations, shape nearly every experience in our lives. Among the types of social groups are *in-groups* and *out-groups, primary groups* and *secondary groups*.
- *Reference groups* provide standards by which we judge ourselves in terms of how we think we appear to others, what sociologist Charles Horton Cooley termed the "looking-glass self."
- Group size is an important factor in group dynamics. Although their intensity may diminish, larger groups tend to be more stable than smaller groups of two (*dyads*) or three (*triads*). Groups of more than a dozen or so people usually develop a formal structure.
- *Leaders* are able to influence the behavior of the other members of a group. The most common form of leadership is *transactional*, that is, routine leadership concerned with getting the job done. Less common is *transformational leadership*, which is concerned with changing the very nature of the group itself.
- Research indicates that people are highly conformist to group pressure. Many people will do what others tell them to do, even when the consequences could involve injury to others, as demonstrated by Stanley Milgram.
- *Networks* constitute a broad source of relationships, direct and indirect, including connections that may be extremely important in business and politics. Women, people of color, and lower-income people typically have less access to the most influential economic and political networks than do white males in American society.

Organizations

- All modern organizations are in some degree bureaucratic in nature. Bureaucracy is characterized by a clearly defined hierarchy of authority; written rules governing the conduct of officials (who work full time for a salary); and a separation between the tasks of the official within the organization and life outside it. Members of the organization do not own the material resources with which they operate. Max Weber argued that modern bureaucracy is a highly effective means of organizing large numbers of people, ensuring that decisions are made according to general criteria.
- Informal networks tend to develop at all levels both within and between organizations. The study of these informal ties is as important as the more formal characteristics on which Weber concentrated his attention.
- The physical settings of organizations strongly influence their social features. The architecture of modern organizations is closely connected to surveillance as a means of securing obedience to those in authority. *Surveillance* refers to the supervision of people's activities, as well as to the keeping of files and records about them.

Theories of Organizations

- The work of Weber and Michels identifies a tension between bureaucracy and democracy. On the one hand, long-term processes of the centralization of decision making are associated with the development of modern societies. On the other hand, one of the main features of the past two centuries has been expanding pressures toward democracy. The trends conflict, with neither one in a position of dominance.

Gender and Organizations

- Modern organizations have evolved as gendered institutions. Women have traditionally been segregated into certain occupational categories that support the ability of men to advance their careers. In recent years, women have been entering professional and managerial positions in greater numbers, but some believe that women have to adopt a traditionally male management style in order to succeed at top levels.

Alternatives to Bureaucracy

- Large organizations have started to restructure themselves over recent years to become less bureaucratic and more flexible. Many Western firms have adopted aspects of Japanese management systems: more consultation of lower-level workers by managerial executives; pay and responsibility linked to seniority; and groups, rather than individuals, evaluated for their performance.

- New information technology is changing the way in which organizations work. Many tasks can now be completed electronically, a fact that allows organizations to transcend time and space. The physical boundaries of organizations are being eroded by the capabilities of new technology. Many organizations now work as loose networks, rather than as self-contained independent units.

Global Organizations

- Two important forms of global organization are *international governmental organizations (IGOs)* and *international nongovernmental organizations (INGOs)*. Both play an increasingly important role in the world today, and IGOs—particularly the United Nations—may become key organizational actors as the pace of globalization increases.

Social Capital

- *Social capital* refers to the knowledge and connections that enable people to cooperate with one another for mutual benefit and extend their influence. Some social scientists have argued that social capital has declined in the United States during the last quarter century, a process they worry indicates a decline in Americans' commitment to civic engagement.

Key Concepts

bureaucracy (p. 142)
corporate culture (p. 153)
dyad (p. 134)
formal organization (p. 140)
formal relations (p. 142)
groupthink (p. 138)
human resource management (p. 153)
ideal type (p. 142)
in-group (p. 133)
informal relations (p. 143)
information technology (p. 153)
international governmental organization (IGO) (p. 160)
international nongovernmental organization (INGO) (p. 160)
iron law of oligarchy (p. 149)
leader (p. 136)
network (p. 139)
oligarchy (p. 149)
organization (p. 140)
out-group (p. 133)
primary group (p. 133)
reference group (p. 134)
secondary group (p. 133)
social aggregate (p. 132)

social capital (p. 161)
social category (p. 133)
social group (p. 132)
surveillance (p. 147)
surveillance society (p. 148)
timetable (p. 147)
transactional leader (p. 136)
transformational leader (p. 136)
triad (p. 134)

Review Questions

1. The term for the social knowledge and connections that enable people to accomplish their goals and extend their influence is
   a. cultural capital.
   b. political capital.
   c. social capital.
   d. economic capital.

2. Which kind of group provides standards by which we judge ourselves?
   a. In-group
   b. Primary group
   c. Out-group
   d. Reference group

3. What is the derivation of the word *bureaucracy*?
   a. It was coined in 1910 by Max Weber: "bureau" means "writing table," and "cracy" is derived from the Greek verb "to know."
   b. It was coined in 1745 by Monsieur de Gournay: "bureau" means both office and writing table, and "cracy" is derived from the Greek verb "to rule."
   c. It was coined in 1859 by Karl Marx: "bureau" means house, and "cracy" is derived from the Greek verb "to control."
   d. It was coined in 1810 by Madame de Blancmange: "bureau" means officer, and "cracy" is derived from the Greek verb "to exhibit signs of madness."

4. Which of the following scholars is concerned with the influence of cultural contexts on organizational forms?
   a. Henry Mintzberg
   b. Stuart Clegg
   c. George Ritzer
   d. Peter Blau

5. What is the difference between the way a new employee would be trained in (1) a Western corporation and the way he or she would be trained in (2) a Japanese corporation?
   a. In (1) employees are expected to acquire all relevant training themselves by investing in their own educations, whereas in (2) employees are expected to learn most of the skills relevant to their job through in-house training.
   b. In (1) the employee would spend up to a decade alternating between different branches and divisions and the head office, whereas in (2) the employee would specialize in the affairs of one department in one place from the very beginning.

c. In (1) employees are expected to learn most of the skills relevant to their job through in-house training, whereas in (2) employees are expected to acquire all relevant training themselves by investing in their own educations.

d. In (1) the employee would specialize in the affairs of one department in one place from the very beginning, whereas in (2) the employee would spend up to a decade alternating between different branches and divisions and the head office.

6. Transformational leaders are concerned with
a. changing the very nature of a group.
b. getting the job done.
c. the well-being of group members.
d. all of the above.

7. What is "bottom-up" decision making?
a. The American system of letting the stock price and quarterly earnings dictate a firm's business strategy.
b. A euphemism for paying attention to employees.
c. The Japanese system of running large organizations with greater levels of participation from rank and file employees.
d. A euphemism for the point at which the stock price has fallen so far that the directors have—metaphorically—put their heads between their knees.

8. Which of the following is *not* a characteristic of a primary group?
a. members interacting on a face-to-face basis
b. intimacy
c. members interacting to achieve a specific goal
d. a strong sense of bonding and commitment

9. International governmental organizations (IGOs) emerge for reasons of
a. national security.
b. the regulation of trade.
c. social welfare of human rights.
d. all of the above.

10. How do liberal feminists (early feminists) differ from radical feminists in their study of organizations?
a. Liberal feminists and radical feminists do not differ in their study of organizations.
b. Liberal feminists focus on unequal pay, discrimination, and the male hold on power.

c. Radical feminists argue that women "serviced" the needs of the male bureaucrat by allowing him to work long hours, travel, and focus solely on his work without concern about personal or domestic issues.

d. Liberal feminists maintain that to eliminate inequality in organizations women need to establish their own organizations on principles very different from those of men.

Thinking Sociologically Exercises

1. According to George Simmel, what are the primary differences between dyads and triads? Explain, according to his theory, how the addition of a child would alter the relationship between a husband and wife. Does the theory fit this situation?

2. The advent of computers and the computerization of the workplace may change our organizations and relationships with coworkers. Explain how you see modern organizations changing with the adaptation of newer information technologies.

Data Exercises

www.wwnorton.com/giddens5
Keyword: Data6

- After reading this chapter you can understand how important group memberships are to personal and social development. However, when individuals get involved in groups society can also benefit, as the discussion of social capital and civic engagement demonstrates. In the data exercise for Chapter 6 you will explore some of the current debate about this important issue.

The Study of Deviant Behavior

Learn how we define deviance and how it is closely related to social power and social class. See the ways in which conformity is encouraged. Familiarize yourself with some traditional explanations for deviance and their limitations as theories.

Society and Crime: Sociological Theories

Know the leading sociological theories of crime and how each is useful in understanding deviance.

Crime and Crime Statistics

Recognize the helpfulness and limitations of crime statistics. Learn some important differences between men and women related to crime. Familiarize yourself with some of the varieties of crime. Think about the best solutions to reduce crime.

Victims and Perpetrators of Crime

Understand that some individuals or groups are more likely to commit or be the victims of crime.

Crime-Reduction Strategies

Consider the ways in which individuals and governments can address crime.

CHAPTER SEVEN

CONFORMITY, DEVIANCE, AND CRIME

Willie was a street vendor who lived and worked on a street in New York City. He earned money by taking magazines out of recycled trash and reselling them to passersby. Willie lived on a corner for about six years, ever since he was released from serving a prison sentence for committing a robbery. During the early 1990s, he was one of approximately 600,000 people released from prison every year—about 1,600 per day (Mauer, 2004).

In 2002, the number of prisoners held in federal, state, and county facilities exceeded 2 million people. One and a half million Americans were detained in prisons and jails for drug offenses, a threefold increase since 1980. This extreme focus on drug offenses has led the United States to become the world leader in this regard, surpassing Russia. The U.S. rate of incarceration is five to eight times higher than Canada and the countries of Western Europe (Garland, 2002).

This dramatic increase in incarceration has had a major impact on the African American and Latino populations in particular. According to Marc Mauer, a leading student of incarceration, "In 1997, the state-wide population of Maryland, Illinois, North Carolina, South Carolina, and Louisiana was two thirds or more white, but prison growth since 1985 was 80% non-white. . . . In New York, where the state's adult minority population is less than 31.7%, nine out of ten new prisoners are from an ethnic or racial minority" (Mauer, 2004).

The impact of the criminal justice system is clear in the lives of people like Willie. While they are in prison, they are not part of the labor force, and thus a large amount of joblessness is not

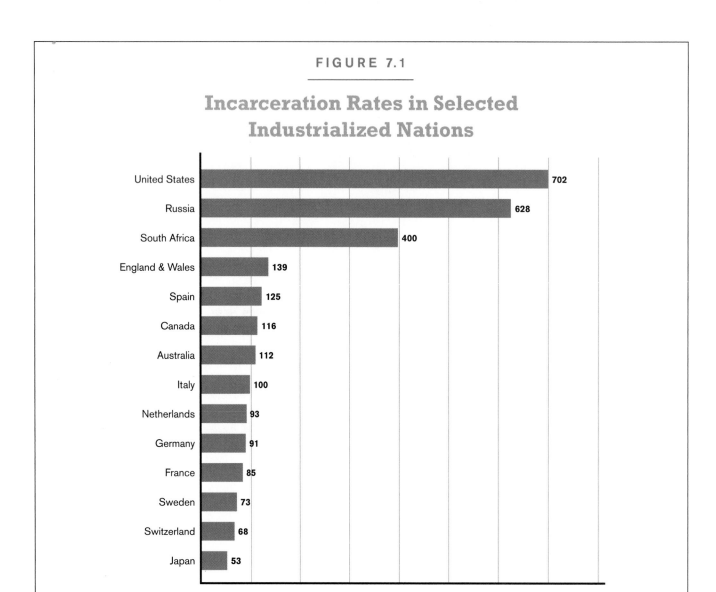

FIGURE 7.1

Incarceration Rates in Selected Industrialized Nations

United States — 702
Russia — 628
South Africa — 400
England & Wales — 139
Spain — 125
Canada — 116
Australia — 112
Italy — 100
Netherlands — 93
Germany — 91
France — 85
Sweden — 73
Switzerland — 68
Japan — 53

Incarceration rate (number of people in prision per 100,000 population)

SOURCE: Marc Mauer, "Comparative Rates of Incarceration: An Examination of Causes and Trends," The Sentencing Project, 2003, www.sentencingproject.org/pdfs/pub9036.pdf.

reflected in the rates of unemployment reported by the government. At the same time, incarceration also increases the long-term chances of unemployment for men like Willie once they are released from prison (Western and Beckett, 1999).

Although the United States has imprisoned over 2 million people at the state and local level over the past few years, it has failed to make adequate preparations for their release (Gonnerman, 2004). From prison, Willie went directly to the streets. He had nowhere to work and nowhere else to go. People he knew from prison were already living on this corner and he heard he could find them there.

Willie is a man who many people would define as a deviant. We all know who deviants are, or so we tend to think. Deviants are those individuals who refuse to live by the rules that the majority of us follow. Sometimes they're violent criminals, drug addicts, or down-and-outs, who don't fit in with what most people would define as normal standards of acceptability. These are the cases that seem easy to identify. Yet things are not quite as they appear—a lesson sociology often teaches us, for it encourages us to look beyond the obvious. The notion of the deviant, as we shall see, is actually not an easy one to define.

We have learned in previous chapters that social life is governed by rules or norms. Our activities would collapse into chaos if we didn't stick to rules that define some kinds of behavior as proper in particular contexts and others as inappropriate. As we learned earlier in talking about the concept of culture, **norms** are definite principles or rules people are expected to observe; they represent the "dos" and "don'ts" of society. Orderly behavior on the highway, for example, would be impossible if drivers didn't observe the rule of driving on the right. No deviants here, you might think, except perhaps for the drunken or reckless driver. If you did think this, you would be incorrect. When we drive, most of us are not merely deviants but criminals. For most drivers regularly drive at well above the legal speed limits—assuming there isn't a police car in sight. In such cases, breaking the law is normal behavior!

We are all rule breakers as well as conformists. We are all also rule creators. Most American drivers may break the law on the freeways, but in fact they've evolved informal rules that are superimposed on the legal rules. When the legal speed limit on the highway is 65 mph, most drivers don't go above 75 or so, and they drive slower when driving through urban areas.

In most European countries, the legal speed limits are higher than in the United States—between 65 and 70 mph, depending on the country. Drivers there break the law most of the time just as they do in the United States, but their informal rules about proper driving produce higher speeds than in America. People regularly drive at 80–90 mph. Conventional rules about what is and isn't reckless driving also vary. Americans who drive in the south of Italy, for example, where drivers break other traffic rules as well, are apt to find the experience a hair-raising one.

When we begin the study of deviant behavior, we must consider which rules people are observing and which they are breaking. Nobody breaks *all* rules, just as no one conforms to all rules. Even an individual who might seem wholly outside the pale of respectable society, such as Willie, is likely to be following many rules of the groups and societies of which he is a member.

For example, when Willie would get enough money for a meal, he would go to a small Chinese restaurant around the corner from where he lived. There he would sit and eat his egg rolls, chow mein, and egg drop soup with the same manners as other diners. In this restaurant, he hardly appears as a deviant. When Willie is out on the street, he follows the rules of the other street vendors who subsisted on the street. In the world of street vendors, he appears as a conformist most of the time. Indeed, some "deviant" groups such as the homeless have strict codes of social behavior for those who live among them. Those who deviate from these informal codes of behavior may be ostracized or expelled from the group and be forced to go elsewhere (Duneier, 1999). Thus, even "deviants" are conformists at times.

Willie's life is an example of what happens to large numbers of people with drug convictions who spend time in the American criminal justice system. Because prisons and jails make little accommodation for people after release, many former prisoners are unable to find homes or jobs in the formal econ-

omy. Working on the street is hardly a long-term solution for men like Willie, and after six years of "staying clean" on Sixth Avenue he was rearrested for another drug offense. This is very common: Almost two thirds of all reentering prisoners are likely to be rearrested within three years (Mauer, 2004).

The Study of Deviant Behavior

The study of deviant behavior is one of the most intriguing yet complex areas of sociology. It teaches us that none of us is quite as normal as we might like to think. It also helps us see that people whose behavior might appear incomprehensible or alien can be seen as rational beings when we understand why they act as they do.

The study of deviance, like other fields of sociology, directs our attention to social *power*, as well as the influence of social class—the divisions between rich and poor. When we look at deviance from or conformity to social rules or norms, we always have to bear in mind the question, *Whose* rules? As we shall see, social norms are strongly influenced by divisions of power and class.

What Is Deviance?

Deviance may be defined as nonconformity to a given set of norms that are accepted by a significant number of people in a community or society. No society, as has already been stressed, can be divided up in a simple way between those who deviate from norms and those who conform to them. Most of us on some occasions transgress generally accepted rules of behavior.

The scope of the concept of deviance is very broad, as some examples will illustrate. Kevin Mitnick has been described as the "world's most celebrated computer hacker." It is probably fair to say that the thirty-six-year-old Californian is revered and despised in equal measure. To the world's estimated 100,000 computer hackers, Mitnick is a pioneering genius whose five-year imprisonment in a U.S. penitentiary was unjust and unwarranted—concrete proof of how misunderstood computer hacking has become with the spread of information technology. To U.S. authorities and high-tech corporations—such as Sun Microsystems, Motorola, and Nokia—Mitnick is one of the world's most dangerous men. He was captured by the FBI in 1995 and later convicted of downloading source codes and stealing software allegedly worth millions of dollars from these and other companies. As a condition of his release

Computer hacker Kevin Mitnick was arrested in 1995 and later convicted of stealing millions of dollars worth of software from a number of technology companies. His release in 2000 was conditioned upon the understanding that he would refrain from using computers or speaking publicly about technology issues.

from prison in January 2000, Mitnick was forbidden to use computers or to speak publicly about technology issues.

Over the past decade or so, hackers have been gradually transformed from a little-noticed population of computer enthusiasts to a much-maligned group of deviants who are believed to threaten the very stability of the information age. The distributed denial of service (DDoS) attacks on prominent e-commerce Web sites that occurred in February 2000 provoked a type of "hacker hysteria" in the media, the corporate world, and among international law-enforcement bodies. Some of the Internet's most heavily trafficked sites—such as Yahoo!, eBay, and Amazon.com—came to a standstill for hours as their servers were bombarded with millions of phony requests for information from computers around the world. Before anyone involved in the online raids was apprehended, fingers were pointed at computer hackers—portrayed as a shadowy population of socially maladjusted young people (mostly male) who avoid contact with human beings by creating alternative lives for themselves behind anonymous online user names.

Yet, according to Mitnick and others in the hacker community, such pathological depictions could not be further from the truth. "Hacker is a term of honor and respect," claimed Mitnick in an article written shortly after his release from prison. "It is a term that describes a skill, not an activity, in the same way that doctor describes a skill. It was used for decades to describe talented computer enthusiasts, people whose skill at using computers to solve technical problems and puzzles was—and is—respected and admired by others possessing similar technical skills" (Mitnick, 2000). Hackers are quick to point out that most of their activities are not criminal. Rather, they are primarily interested in exploring the edges of computer technology, trying to uncover loopholes and to discover how far it is possible to penetrate into other computer systems. Once flaws have been discovered, the "hacker ethic" demands that the information be shared publicly. Many hackers have even served as consultants for large corporations and government agencies, helping them to defend their systems against outside intrusion.

As another example, we might take the career of Ted Bundy. Bundy's way of life, on the face of things, conformed to the norms of behavior of a good citizen. He led what seemed not only a normal life, but a most worthy one. For example, he played an active role in the Samaritans, an association that organizes a twenty-four-hour phone-in service for people who are distressed or suicidal. Yet Bundy also carried out a series of horrific murders. Before sentencing him to death, the judge at his trial praised Bundy for his abilities (he had prepared his own defense) but finished by noting what a waste he had made of his life. Bundy's career shows that a person can seem entirely normal while secretly engaging in acts of extreme deviance.

Deviance does not refer only to individual behavior; it concerns the activities of groups as well. An illustration is the Heaven's Gate cult (discussed earlier, in Chapter 6), a religious group whose beliefs and ways of life were different from those of the majority of Americans. The cult was established in the early 1970s when Marshall Herff Applewhite made his way around the West and Midwest of the United States preaching his beliefs, ultimately advertising on the Internet his belief that civilization was doomed and that the only way people could be saved was to kill themselves so their souls could be rescued by a U.F.O. On March 26, 1997, thirty-nine members of the cult followed his advice in a mass suicide at a wealthy estate in Rancho Santa Fe, California.

The Heaven's Gate cult represents an example of a **deviant subculture**. They were able to survive fairly easily within the wider society, supporting themselves by running a Web site business and recruiting new members by sending e-mail messages to people they thought might be interested in their beliefs. They had plenty of money and lived together in an expensive home in a wealthy California suburb. Their position diverges from that of another deviant subculture that we discussed in the introduction to this chapter: the homeless.

Defining Deviance:
The Sociological Debate

Many people take it for granted that a well-structured society is designed to prevent deviant behavior from occurring. But Émile Durkheim argued otherwise. He believed that deviance has an important part to play in a well-ordered society. Why did Durkheim think this? He said that by defining what is deviant, we become aware of what is not deviant and thereby become aware of the standards we share as members of a society. It is not necessarily the case, then, that we should aim to completely eliminate deviance. It is more likely that society needs to keep it within acceptable limits.

Seventy years after Durkheim's work appeared, the sociologist Kai Erikson published *Wayward Puritans*, a study of deviance in seventeenth-century New England. Erikson sought "to test [Durkheim's] notion that the number of deviant offenders a community can afford to recognize is likely to remain stable over time." His research led him to conclude that

> a community's capacity for handling deviance, let us say, can be roughly estimated by counting its prison cells and hospital beds, its policemen and psychiatrists, its courts and clinics. . . . The agencies of control often seem to define their job as that of keeping deviance within bounds rather than obliterating it altogether. (Erikson, 1966)

Erikson advanced the hypothesis that societies need their quotas of deviance and that they function in such a way as to keep them intact.

What does a society do when the amount of deviant behavior gets out of hand? In a controversial 1993 article, "Defining Deviance Down," the former New York senator Daniel Patrick Moynihan argued that the levels of deviance in American society have increased beyond the point that it can afford to recognize. As a result, we have been "redefining deviance so as to exempt much conduct previously stigmatized," and also quietly raising the "normal" level so that behavior seen as abnormal by an earlier standard is no longer considered to be so.

How has American society gone about this? One example that Moynihan gives is the deinstitutionalization movement within the mental health profession that began in the 1950s. Instead of being forced into institutions, the mentally ill were treated with tranquilizers and released. As a result, the number of psychiatric patients in New York dropped from 93,000 in 1955 to 11,000 by 1992.

What happened to all of those psychiatric patients? Many of them are the homeless who today are sleeping in doorways. In "defining deviance down," people sleeping on the street are defined not as insane, but as persons lacking affordable hous-

ing. At the same time, the "normal" acceptable level of crime has risen. Moynihan points out that after the St. Valentine's Day massacre in 1929, in which seven gangsters were murdered, the nation was outraged. Today, violent gang murders are so common that there is hardly a reaction. Moynihan also sees the underreporting of crime as another form of "normalizing" it. As he concludes, "We are getting used to a lot of behavior that is not good for us."

Norms and Sanctions

We most often follow social norms because, as a result of socialization, we are used to doing so. Individuals become committed to social norms through interactions with people who obey the law. Through these interactions, we learn self-control. The more numerous these interactions, the fewer opportunities there are to deviate from conventional norms. And, over time, the longer that we interact in ways that are conventional, the more we have at stake in continuing to act in that way (Gottfredson and Hirschi, 1990).

All social norms are accompanied by sanctions that promote conformity and protect against nonconformity. A **sanction** is any reaction from others to the behavior of an individual or group that is meant to ensure that the person or group complies with a given norm. Sanctions may be positive (the offering of rewards for conformity) or negative (punishment for behavior that does not conform). They can also be formal or informal. Formal sanctions are applied by a specific body of people or an agency to ensure that a particular set of norms is followed. Informal sanctions are less organized and more spontaneous reactions to nonconformity, such as when a student is teasingly accused by friends of working too hard or being a "nerd" if he decides to spend an evening studying rather than going to a party.

The main types of formal sanctions in modern societies are those represented by the courts and prisons. The police, of course, are the agency charged with bringing offenders to trial and possible imprisonment. **Laws** are norms defined by governments as principles that their citizens must follow; sanctions are used against people who do not conform to them. Where there are laws, there are also **crimes**, since crime can most simply be defined as any type of behavior that breaks a law.

It is important to recognize, however, that the law is only a guide to the kind of norms that exist in a society. Oftentimes, subcultures invent their own dos and don'ts. For example, the street people that Willie lives among have created their own norms for determining where each of them can set up the magazines that he sells on the sidewalk. Other homeless vendors don't set up in Willie's spot on the sidewalk because that

Burning Man

Stopped at the gas station for directions to the Burning Man Festival. Grizzled, portly Nevadan local growls: "If ya have to ask, you *don't belong* there!" [***]

Burning Man is an art gig by tradition. Over the longer term it's evolved into something else; maybe something like a physical version of the Internet. The art here is like fan art. It's very throwaway, very appropriative, very cut-and-paste. The camp is like a giant swap meet where no one sells stuff, but people trade postures, clip art, and attitude. People come here in clumps: performance people, drumming enthusiasts, site-specific sculptors, sailplane people, ravers, journalists, cops. [***]

I went to Burning Man. I took my kids. It's not scary, it's not pagan, it's not devilish or satanic. There's no public orgies, nobody gets branded or hit with whips. Hell, it's less pagan than the Shriners. It's just big happy crowds of harmless arty people expressing themselves and breaking a few pointless shibboleths that only serve to ulcerate young people anyway. There ought to be Burning Man festivals held downtown once a year in every major city in America. It would be good for us. We need it. In fact, until we can just relax every once in a while and learn how to do this properly, we're probably never gonna get well.

SOURCE: Bruce Sterling, "Greetings from Burning Man!" *Wired* 4.11 (November 1996). Bruce Sterling's article introduced Burning Man to the wider world, as he described his first trip to the Temporary Autonomous Zone. Since this article was written, attendance has ballooned to over 30,000 people in 2004.

I'm a Burner. I think we should have that straight from the outset.

I wasn't always a Burner. For several years after my first trip to Burning Man, I maintained a more or less objective viewpoint. Even when I went to the playa weeks before the event and helped construct various stages, roads and towers, I was half uncertain whether the event would survive its periodic attacks by the various governments that regulate its existence. There were times when I wasn't even sure it should survive.

Now I'm convinced the event should and will survive, although it may evolve. Actually, my theory is that the event must evolve or it will collapse under the weight of monotony.

This is a theory that won't be tested under any scientific rigor, but my belief is that this is the year that Burning Man grew up. It reached and probably slightly surpassed 30,000 attendees, the number that has often been bandied about by organizers as the end of population increase, the organizational endpoint of this party on the Black Rock Desert. If that's true, then this year was the first true representation of what the Burning Man Festival will be until the fire's put out. But I get ahead of myself. [***]

Burning Man is a counterculture, anticonsumerism art event that happens up near Gerlach every Labor Day weekend. It attracts artists and people who like art. It doesn't generally attract the kind of artists who make paintings you'd hang on a wall in a museum. It attracts the kind of artists who

build fanciful, thought-provoking and inspirational artifacts of steel and gas and light and wood. Especially wood.

Because wood burns.

The festival used to culminate with the burning of a large wood-and-neon man. Hence the name. [***]

The event has been going since 1986, when founder Larry Harvey burned an effigy on Baker Beach in San Francisco. When the event got too large and attracted too much official attention, it moved to the Black Rock Desert playa, about 120 miles north of Reno, in 1990. In years past, local governments castigated event organizers for allowing too much freedom, too much nudity, too many drugs, too few rules. [***]

Back in the day, local businesses accepted the participants' money, but behind their backs they'd often call participants hippies, druggies, weirdoes, freaks, pretty much anything except what they were: artists and tourists. But that was when the participants numbered in the thousands. Now the event is a financial windfall, bringing $10 million, according to some estimates, into the local economy every year. [***]

The question of whether Burning Man will be able to attract 30,000 first- and second-timers will remain moot, as long as Larry Harvey and company can keep the themes and the art fresh. [***]

Back in 1995, Harvey told me that his art, the thing that most interested him about Burning Man, was the movement of people, the art and science of how to motivate and control crowds. At the time, I didn't truly understand what he was talking about, but Saturday I think I did. It was beautiful and frightening and a hint of things to come. [***]

I've seen more children and elderly people this year than I've seen in years past. Other people tell me I'm wrong, but if there are not more children, then the children that are here are being brought to more of the performances and are out riding their bikes and playing in community areas without adult supervision.

I think I understand the reason for this. In reaching maturity, Black Rock City became a safer city. I don't have a feeling for whether drug use has increased or decreased this year. I

do feel that users are more discreet. I know drugs are there; I see people on drugs, and I hear people talk about having been on drugs, but nobody offers me cocaine or acid or mushrooms, and the smell of burning herb is infrequent. I've also heard many comments that the police presence has increased this year, but I don't really see evidence of that, either.

Anyway, this is a peaceful city by almost any definition. While bikes are stolen with frequency, apparently often by people who just want to get somewhere fast, who then abandon the bikes, there isn't the kind of violence you'd associate with a rock concert, street festival or classic-car event. [***]

It's difficult to say where Burning Man will go from here. Recent published interviews with Larry Harvey have suggested that he will integrate this Burning Man with the other ones that happen around the world, bringing together a very large community of people who think life should mimic art, instead of the other way round. Maybe he'll be able to institute some political and social change. I wouldn't be surprised.

I don't know; my job won't change, and nearly every year I'll continue to write these essays. It's obvious why I do it—Burning Man is the largest cultural event held in this neck of the woods. More important, though, is why does anybody care to read this stuff? [***]

The reason people want to read about Burning Man is because Burning Man matters.

At least it matters to us Burners. And there are a lot of us.

SOURCE: D. Brian Burghart, "About a Man," *Reno News and Review* (September 4, 2003).

would show "disrespect." This example further illustrates that even members of so-called deviant groups usually live in accordance with some norms. What makes them deviant subcultures is that these norms are at odds with the norms of the mainstream of society.

We shall now turn to the main sociological theories that have been developed to interpret and analyze deviance. In contrast to some areas of sociology, in which a theoretical perspective has emerged over time as preeminent, many theoretical strands remain relevant to the study of deviance. After a brief look at biological and psychological explanations, we shall turn to the four sociological approaches that have been influential within the sociology of deviance: *functionalist theories, interactionist theories, conflict theories*, and *control theories*.

The Biological View of Deviance

Some of the first attempts to explain crime were essentially biological in character. The Italian criminologist Cesare Lombroso, working in the 1870s, believed that criminal types could be identified by the shape of the skull. He accepted that social learning could influence the development of criminal behavior, but he regarded most criminals as biologically degenerate or defective. Lombroso's ideas became thoroughly discredited, but similar views have repeatedly been suggested. Another popular method of trying to demonstrate the influence of heredity on criminal tendencies was to study family trees. But this demonstrates virtually nothing about the influence of heredity, because it is impossible to disentangle inherited and environmental influences.

A later theory distinguished three main types of human physique and claimed that one type was directly associated with delinquency. Muscular, active types (mesomorphs), the theory went, are more likely to become delinquent than those of thin physique (ectomorphs) or more fleshy people (endomorphs) (Sheldon et al., 1949; Glueck and Glueck, 1956). This research has also been widely criticized. Even if there were an overall relationship between body type and delinquency, this would show nothing about the influence of heredity. People of the muscular type may be drawn toward criminal activities because these offer opportunities for the physical display of athleticism. Moreover, nearly all studies in this field have been restricted to delinquents in reform schools, and it may be that the tougher, athletic-looking delinquents are more liable to be sent to such schools than fragile-looking, skinny ones. Although older studies on the biological explanations of crime have been dismissed, more recent research has sought to rekindle the argument. In a study of New Zealand children, researchers sought to prove that childrens' propensity to ag-

gression was linked to biological factors present at a child's birth (Moffitt, 1996).

However, studies such as this only show that some individuals might be inclined toward irritability and aggressiveness, and this could be reflected in crimes of physical assault on others. Yet there is no decisive evidence that any traits of personality are inherited in this way, and even if they were, their connection to criminality would at most be only a distant one. In fact, the New Zealand study did not argue that there is a biological cause to crime, but rather that biological factors, when combined with certain social factors such as one's home environment, could lead to social situations involving crime.

The Psychological View of Deviance

Like biological interpretations, psychological theories of crime associate criminality with particular types of personality. Some have suggested that in a minority of individuals, an amoral, or psychopathic, personality develops. **Psychopaths** are withdrawn, emotionless characters who delight in violence for its own sake.

Individuals with psychopathic traits do sometimes commit violent crimes, but there are major problems with the concept of the psychopath. It isn't at all clear that psychopathic traits are inevitably criminal. Nearly all studies of people said to possess these characteristics have been of convicted prisoners, and their personalities inevitably tend to be presented negatively. If we describe the same traits positively, the personality type sounds quite different, and there seems no reason why people of this sort should be inherently criminal. Should we be looking for psychopathic individuals for a research study, we might place the following ad:

ARE YOU ADVENTUROUS?

Researcher wishes to contact adventurous, carefree people who've led exciting, impulsive lives. If you're the kind of person who'd do almost anything for a dare, call 337-XXXX any time. (Widom and Newman, 1985)

Such people might be explorers, spies, gamblers, or just bored with the routines of day-to-day life. They *might* be prepared to contemplate criminal adventures but could be just as likely to look for challenges in socially respectable ways.

Psychological theories of criminality can at best explain only some aspects of crime. While some criminals may possess personality characteristics distinct from the remainder of the population, it is highly improbable that the majority of criminals do so. There are all kinds of crimes, and it is implausible to suppose that those who commit them share some specific psychological characteristics. Even if we confine ourselves to one category of crime, such as crimes of violence, different circumstances are involved. Some such crimes are carried out by lone individuals, whereas others are the work of organized groups. It is not likely that the psychological makeup of people who are loners will have much in common with the members of a close-knit gang. Even if consistent differences could be linked to forms of criminality, we still couldn't be sure which way the line of causality would run. It might be that becoming involved with criminal groups influences people's outlooks, rather than that the outlooks actually produce criminal behavior in the first place.

Both biological and psychological approaches to criminality presume that deviance is a sign of something "wrong" with the individual, rather than with society. They see crime as caused by factors outside an individual's control, embedded either in the body or the mind. Therefore, if scientific criminology could successfully identify the causes of crime, it would be possible to treat those causes. In this respect, both biological and psychological theories of crime are *positivist* in nature. As we learned in our discussion of Comte in Chapter 1, positivism is the belief that applying scientific methods to the study of the social world can reveal its basic truths. In the case of positivist criminology, this led to the belief that empirical research could pinpoint the causes of crime and in turn make recommendations about how to eradicate it.

Society and Crime: Sociological Theories

Early criminology came under great criticism from later generations of scholars. They argued that any satisfactory account of the nature of crime must be sociological, for what crime is depends on the social institutions of a society. One of the most important emphases of sociological thinking about crime is on the interconnections between conformity and deviance in different social contexts. Modern societies contain many different subcultures, and behavior that conforms to the norms of one particular subculture may be regarded as deviant outside it; for instance, there may be strong pressure on a member of a boys' gang to prove himself by stealing a car. Moreover, there are wide divergences of wealth and power in society that greatly influence opportunities open to different groups. Theft and burglary, not surprisingly, are carried out mainly by people from the poorer segments of the population; embezzling and tax evasion are by definition limited to persons in positions of some affluence.

Functionalist Theories

Functionalist theories see crime and deviance resulting from structural tensions and a lack of moral regulation within society. If the aspirations held by individuals and groups in society do not coincide with available rewards, this disparity between desires and fulfillment will be felt in the deviant motivations of some of its members.

CRIME AND ANOMIE: DURKHEIM AND MERTON

As we saw in Chapter 1, the notion of **anomie** was first introduced by Émile Durkheim, who suggested that in modern societies traditional norms and standards become undermined without being replaced by new ones. Anomie exists when there are no clear standards to guide behavior in a given area of social life. Under such circumstances, Durkheim believed, people feel disoriented and anxious; anomie is therefore one of the social factors influencing dispositions to suicide.

Durkheim saw crime and deviance as social facts; he believed both of them to be inevitable and necessary elements in modern societies. According to Durkheim, people in the modern age are less constrained than they were in traditional societies. Because there is more room for individual choice in the modern world, it is inevitable that there will be some nonconformity. Durkheim recognized that no society would ever be in complete consensus about the norms and values that govern it.

Deviance is also necessary for society, according to Durkheim; it fulfills two important functions. First, deviance has an *adaptive* function. By introducing new ideas and challenges into society, deviance is an innovative force. It brings about change. Second, deviance promotes *boundary maintenance* between "good" and "bad" behaviors in society. A criminal event can provoke a collective response that heightens group solidarity and clarifies social norms. For example, residents of a neighborhood facing a problem with drug dealers might join together in the aftermath of a drug-related shooting and commit themselves to maintaining the area as a drug-free zone.

Durkheim's ideas on crime and deviance were influential in shifting attention from individual explanations to social forces. His notion of anomie was drawn on by the American sociologist Robert K. Merton, who constructed a highly influential theory of deviance that located the source of crime within the very structure of American society (1957).

Merton modified the concept of anomie to refer to the strain put on individuals' behavior when accepted norms conflict with social reality. In American society—and to some degree in other industrial societies—generally held values emphasize material success, and the means of achieving success are supposed to be self-discipline and hard work. Accordingly, it is believed that people who really work hard can succeed no matter what their starting point in life. This idea is not in fact valid, because most of the disadvantaged are given only limited conventional opportunities for advancement, or none at all. Yet those who do not "succeed" find themselves condemned for their apparent inability to make material progress. In this situation, there is great pressure to try to get ahead by any means, legitimate or illegitimate. According to Merton, then, deviance is a by-product of economic inequalities.

Merton identifies five possible reactions to the tensions between socially endorsed values and the limited means of achieving them. *Conformists* accept both generally held values and the conventional means of realizing them, whether or not they meet with success. The majority of the population fall into this category. *Innovators* continue to accept socially approved values but use illegitimate or illegal means to follow them. Criminals who acquire wealth through illegal activities exemplify this type.

Ritualists conform to socially accepted standards although they have lost sight of the values behind these standards. They follow rules for their own sake without a wider end in view, in a compulsive way. A ritualist would be someone who dedicates herself to a boring job, even though it has no career prospects and provides few rewards. *Retreatists* have abandoned the competitive outlook altogether, thus rejecting both the dominant values and the approved means of achieving them. An example would be the members of a self-supporting commune. Finally, *rebels* reject both the existing values and the means but wish actively to substitute new ones and reconstruct the social system. The members of radical political groups fall into this category.

Merton's writings addressed one of the main puzzles in the study of criminology: At a time when society as a whole is becoming more affluent, why do crime rates continue to rise? By emphasizing the contrast between rising aspirations and persistent inequalities, Merton points to a sense of relative deprivation as an important element in deviant behavior.

SUBCULTURAL EXPLANATIONS

Later researchers located deviance in terms of subcultural groups that adopt norms that encourage or reward criminal behavior. Like Merton, Albert Cohen saw the contradictions within American society as the main cause of crime. But while Merton emphasized individual deviant responses to the tension between values and means, Cohen saw the responses occurring collectively through subcultures. In *Delinquent Boys* (1955), Cohen argued that boys in the lower working class who are frustrated with their positions in life often join together in *delinquent subcultures*, such as gangs. These subcultures reject middle-class values and replace them with norms that celebrate defiance, such as delinquency and other acts of nonconformity.

Richard A. Cloward and Lloyd E. Ohlin (1960) agree with Cohen that most delinquent youths emerge from the lower working class. But they argued that such gangs arise in subcultural communities where the chances of achieving success legitimately are slim, such as among deprived ethnic minorities. Their work rightly emphasized connections between conformity and deviance: Lack of opportunity for success in the terms of the wider society is the main differentiating factor between those who engage in criminal behavior and those who do not.

Recent research by sociologists has examined the validity of claims that immediate material deprivation can lead people

Members of a Los Angeles gang show off scars and tattoos. Are these men, like those in Cohen's *Delinquent Boys*, replacing the values of the middle class with norms that express pride in defiance and nonconformity, in this case bullet and knife wounds?

to commit crimes. A survey of homeless youth in Canada, for instance, shows a strong correlation between hunger, lack of shelter, and unemployment, on the one hand, and theft, prostitution, and even violent crime on the other (Hagan and McCarthy, 1992).

Functionalist theories rightly emphasize connections between conformity and deviance in different social contexts. We should be cautious, however, about the idea that people in poorer communities, like Willie, aspire to the same level of success as more affluent people. Most tend to adjust their aspirations to what they see as the reality of their situation. Merton, Cohen, and Cloward and Ohlin can all be criticized for presuming that middle-class values have been accepted through society. It would also be wrong to suppose that a mismatch of aspirations and opportunities is confined to the less privileged. There are pressures toward criminal activity among other groups too, as indicated by the so-called white-collar crimes of embezzlement, fraud, and tax evasion, which we will study later.

Interactionist Theories

Sociologists studying crime and deviance in the interactionist tradition focus on deviance as a socially constructed phenomenon. They reject the idea that there are types of conduct that are inherently "deviant." Rather, interactionists ask how behaviors initially come to be defined as deviant and why certain groups and not others are labeled as deviant.

LEARNED DEVIANCE: DIFFERENTIAL ASSOCIATION

One of the earliest writers to suggest that deviance is learned through interaction with others was Edwin H. Sutherland. In 1949, Sutherland advanced a notion that was to influence much of the later interactionist work: He linked crime to what he called **differential association** (Sutherland, 1949). This idea is very simple. In a society that contains a variety of subcultures, some social environments tend to encourage illegal activities, whereas others do not. Individuals become delinquent through associating with people who are the carriers of criminal norms. For the most part, according to Sutherland, criminal behavior is learned within primary groups, particularly peer groups. This theory contrasts with the view that psychological differences separate criminals from other people; it sees criminal activities as learned in much the same way as law-abiding ones and as directed toward the same needs and values. Thieves try to make money just like people in orthodox jobs, but they choose illegal means of doing so.

Differential association can be used to assess Willie's life. Before Willie went to prison, he lived in Pennsylvania Station with a group of homeless men. From this group, he learned how to target and rob restaurant delivery boys, whom he learned were unlikely to report the crime to the police because many of them were illegal immigrants from Mexico and China. Willie would not have known these facts unless he had learned them from associating with others who were already the carriers of criminal norms.

LABELING THEORY

One of the most important interactionist approaches to the understanding of criminality is called **labeling theory**—although this term itself is a label for a cluster of related ideas rather than a unified view. Labeling theory originally came to be associated with Howard S. Becker's studies of marijuana smokers (1963). In the early 1960s, marijuana use was a marginal activity carried on by subcultures rather than the lifestyle choice—that is, an activity accepted by many in the mainstream of society—it is today (Hathaway, 1997). Becker found that becoming a marijuana smoker depended on one's acceptance into the subculture, close association with experienced users, and one's attitudes toward nonusers. Labeling theorists like Becker interpret deviance not as a set of characteristics of individuals or groups, but as a *process* of interaction between deviants and nondeviants. In other words, it is not the act of marijuana smoking that makes one a deviant, but the way others react to marijuana smoking that makes it deviant. In the view of labeling theorists, we must discover why some people become tagged with a "deviant" label in order to understand the nature of deviance itself.

People who represent the forces of law and order or are able to impose definitions of conventional morality on others do most of the labeling. The labels that create categories of deviance thus express the power structure of society. By and large, the rules in terms of which deviance is defined are framed by the wealthy for the poor, by men for women, by older people for younger people, and by ethnic majorities for minority groups. For example, many children wander into other people's gardens, steal fruit, or play truant. In an affluent neighborhood, these might be regarded by parents, teachers, and police alike as relatively innocent pastimes of childhood. In poor areas, they might be seen as evidence of tendencies toward juvenile delinquency.

Once a child is labeled a delinquent, he is stigmatized as a criminal and is likely to be considered untrustworthy by teachers and prospective employers. He then relapses into further criminal behavior, widening the gulf with orthodox social conventions. Edwin Lemert (1972) called the initial act of transgression **primary deviation.** **Secondary deviation** occurs when the individual comes to accept the label and sees himself as deviant. Other research has shown that how we think of ourselves and how we believe others perceive us influences our propensity for committing crime. One study examining self-appraisals of a random national sample of young men showed that such appraisals are strongly tied to levels of criminality (Matsueda, 1992).

Take, for example, Luke, who smashes a shop window while spending a Saturday night out on the town with his friends. The act may perhaps be called the accidental result of overboisterous behavior, an excusable characteristic of young men. Luke might escape with a reprimand and a small fine. If he is from a "respectable" background, this is a likely result. And the smashing of the window stays at the level of primary deviance if the youth is seen as someone of good character who on this occasion became too rowdy. If, on the other hand, the police and courts hand out a suspended sentence and make Luke report to a social worker, the incident could become the first step on the road to secondary deviance. The process of "learning to be deviant" tends to be reinforced by the very organizations supposedly set up to correct deviant behavior—prisons and social agencies.

Labeling theory is important because it begins from the assumption that no act is intrinsically criminal. Definitions of criminality are established by the powerful through the formulation of laws and their interpretation by police, courts, and correctional institutions. Critics of labeling theory have sometimes argued that certain acts are consistently prohibited across virtually all cultures, such as murder, rape, and robbery. This view is surely incorrect; even within our own culture, killing is not always regarded as murder. In times of war, killing of the enemy is positively approved, and until recently the laws in most U.S. states did not recognize sexual intercourse forced on a woman by her husband as rape.

We can more convincingly criticize labeling theory on other grounds. First, in emphasizing the active process of labeling, labeling theorists neglect the processes that *lead* to acts defined as deviant. For labeling certain activities as deviant is not completely arbitrary; differences in socialization, attitudes, and opportunities influence how far people engage in behavior likely to be labeled deviant. For instance, children from deprived backgrounds are on average more likely to steal from shops than are richer children. It is not the labeling that leads them to steal in the first place so much as the background from which they come.

Second, it is not clear whether labeling actually does have the effect of increasing deviant conduct. Delinquent behavior tends to increase following a conviction, but is this the result of the labeling itself? Other factors, such as increased interaction with other delinquents or learning about new criminal opportunities, may be involved.

Conflict Theory

Conflict theory draws on elements of Marxist thought to argue that deviance is deliberately chosen and often political in nature. Conflict theorists reject the idea that deviance is "determined" by factors such as biology, personality, anomie, social disorganization, or labels. Rather, they argue, individuals actively choose to engage in deviant behavior in response to the inequalities of the capitalist system. Thus, members of countercultural groups regarded as "deviant"—such as supporters of the black power or gay liberation movements—are engaging in distinctly political acts that challenged the social order. Theorists of the **new criminology** framed their analysis of crime and deviance in terms of the structure of society and the preservation of power among the ruling class.

For example, they argued that laws are tools used by the powerful to maintain their own privileged positions. They rejected the idea that laws are neutral and are applied evenly across the population. Instead, they claimed that as inequalities increase between the ruling class and the working class, law becomes an ever more important instrument for the powerful to maintain order. This dynamic can be seen in the workings of the criminal justice system, which had become increasingly oppressive toward working-class "offenders"; or in tax legislation that disproportionately favored the wealthy. This power imbalance is not restricted to the creation of laws, however. The powerful also break laws, scholars argued, but are rarely caught. These crimes on the whole are much more significant than the everyday crime and delinquency that attracts the most attention. But fearful of the implications of pursuing white-collar criminals, law enforcement instead focuses its efforts on less powerful members of society, such as prostitutes, drug users, and petty thieves (Pearce, 1976; Chambliss, 1988).

These studies and others associated with the new criminology were important in widening the debate about crime and deviance to include questions of social justice, power, and politics. They emphasized that crime occurs at all levels of society and must be understood in the context of inequalities and competing interests between social groups.

Control Theory

Control theory posits that crime occurs as a result of an imbalance between impulses toward criminal activity and the social or physical controls that deter it. It is less interested in individuals' motivations for carrying out crimes; rather, it is assumed that people act rationally and that, given the opportunity, everyone would engage in deviant acts. Many types of crime, it is argued, are a result of "situational decisions"—a person sees an opportunity and is motivated to act.

One of the best-known control theorists, Travis Hirschi, has argued that humans are fundamentally selfish beings who make calculated decisions about whether or not to engage in criminal activity by weighing the potential benefits and risks of doing so. In *Causes of Delinquency* (1969), Hirschi claimed that there are four types of bonds that link people to society and law-abiding behavior: attachment, commitment, involvement, and belief. When sufficiently strong, these elements help to maintain social control and conformity by rendering people *unfree* to break rules. If these bonds with society are weak, however, delinquency and deviance may result. Hirschi's approach suggests that delinquents are often individuals whose low levels of self-control are a result of inadequate socialization at home or at school (Gottfredson and Hirschi, 1990).

Some control theorists see the growth of crime as an outcome of the increasing number of opportunities and targets for crime in modern society. As the population grows more affluent and consumerism becomes more central to people's lives, goods such as televisions, video equipment, computers, cars, and designer clothing—favorite targets for thieves—are owned by more and more people. Residential homes are increasingly left empty during the daytime as more and more women take on employment outside the home. Motivated offenders interested in committing crimes can select from a broad range of suitable targets.

Responding to such shifts, many official approaches to crime prevention in recent years have focused on limiting the opportunities for crime to occur. Central to such policies is the idea of *target hardening*—making it more difficult for crimes to take place by intervening directly into potential crime situations. Control theorists argue that rather than changing the criminal, the best policy is to take practical measures to control the criminal's ability to commit crime.

Target hardening techniques and zero tolerance policing have gained favor among politicians in recent years and appear to have been successful in some contexts in curtailing crime. But criticisms of such an approach can also be made. Target hardening and zero tolerance policing do not address the underlying causes of crime but instead are aimed at protecting and defending certain elements of society from its reach. The growing popularity of private security services, car alarms, house alarms, guard dogs, and gated communities has led some people to believe that we are living in an armored society where segments of the population feel compelled to defend themselves against others. This tendency is occurring not only in the United States, as the gap between the wealthiest and the most deprived widens, but is particularly marked in countries such as South Africa, Brazil, and those of the former Soviet Union, where a "fortress mentality" has emerged among the privileged.

There is another unintended consequence of such policies: As popular crime targets are "hardened," patterns of crime may simply shift from one domain to another. Target hardening and zero tolerance approaches run the risk of displacing criminal offenses from better protected areas into more vulnerable ones. Neighborhoods that are poor or lacking in social cohesion may well experience a growth in crime and delinquency as affluent regions increase their defenses.

THE THEORY OF "BROKEN WINDOWS"

Target hardening and zero tolerance policing are based on a theory known as "broken windows" (Wilson and Kelling, 1982). The theory is based on a study by the social psychologist Philip Zimbardo, who abandoned cars without license plates and with their hoods up in two entirely different social settings, the wealthy community of Palo Alto, California, and a poor neighborhood in the Bronx, New York. In both places, both cars were vandalized once passersby, regardless of class or race, sensed that the cars were abandoned and that "no one cared" (Zimbardo, 1969). Extrapolating from this study, the authors of the "broken windows" theory argued that any sign of social disorder in a community, even the appearance of a broken window, encourages more serious crime to flourish. One unrepaired broken window is a sign that no one cares, so breaking more windows—that is, committing more serious crimes—is a rational response by criminals to this situation of social disorder. As a result, minor acts of deviance can lead to a spiral of crime and social decay.

In the late 1980s and 1990s, the "broken windows" theory served as the basis for new policing strategies that aggressively focused on "minor" crimes such as drinking or using drugs in public and traffic violations. Studies have shown that proactive policing directed at maintaining public order can have a positive effect on reducing more serious crimes such as robbery (Sampson and Cohen, 1988). However, one flaw of the "broken windows" theory is that the police are left to identify "social disorder" however they want. Without a systematic definition of disorder, the police are authorized to see almost anything as a sign of disorder and anyone as a threat. In fact, as crime rates fell throughout the 1990s, the number of complaints of police abuse and harassment went up, particularly by young, urban, black men who fit the "profile" of a potential criminal.

Linking Micro- and Macrosociology: The Saints and the Roughnecks

The connections between the processes by which deviant behavior occurs and the larger class structure were noted by William Chambliss in a famous study, "The Saints and the Roughnecks" (Chambliss, 1973). Chambliss studied two groups of delinquents in an American high school, one from upper-middle-class families ("the Saints") and the other from poor families ("the Roughnecks"). Although the Saints were constantly involved in petty crimes such as drinking, vandalism, truancy, and theft, none of their members was ever arrested. The Roughnecks were involved in similar criminal activities, yet they were constantly in trouble with the police. After Chambliss concluded that neither group was more delinquent than the other, he looked to other factors that could explain the different reaction of the police and the broader community to these two groups.

Chambliss found, for example, that the upper-class gang had automobiles and thus were able to remove themselves from the eyes of the community. The lower-class boys, through necessity, congregated in an area where everyone in the community frequently saw them. Chambliss concluded that differences of this sort were indicative of the class structure of American society, which gave certain wealthier groups advantages when it came to being labeled as deviant. For instance, the parents of the Saints saw their sons' crimes as harmless pranks, while the parents of the Roughnecks acquiesced to the police's labeling of their sons' behavior as criminal. The community as a whole also seemed to agree with these different labels.

These boys went on to have lives consistent with this labeling, with the Saints living conventional middle-class lives and the Roughnecks having continual problems with the law. As we saw earlier in the chapter, this outcome is linked to what Lemert called "secondary deviance," because it is thought to result from the inability of a person to carry on as "normal" once he has been labeled as a "deviant."

Chambliss's study is widely cited by sociologists for showing the connection between macrosociological factors such as social class and microsociological phenomena such as how people become labeled as deviant. This study provides an example of how difficult it is to isolate micro- and macro-level factors in the social construction of deviance.

Theoretical Conclusions

The contributions of the sociological theories of crime are twofold. First, these theories correctly emphasize the continuities between criminal and "respectable" behavior. The contexts in which particular types of activity are seen as criminal and punishable by law vary widely. Second, all agree that context is important in criminal activities. Whether someone engages in a criminal act or comes to be regarded as a criminal is influenced fundamentally by social learning and social surroundings.

In spite of its deficiencies, labeling theory is perhaps the most widely used approach to understanding crime and de-

viant behavior. This theory sensitizes us to the ways in which some activities come to be defined as punishable in law and the power relations that form such definitions, as well as to the circumstances in which particular individuals fall foul of the law.

The way in which crime is understood directly affects the policies developed to combat it. For example, if crime is seen as the product of deprivation or social disorganization, policies might be aimed at reducing poverty and strengthening social services. If criminality is seen as voluntaristic, or freely chosen by individuals, attempts to counter it will take a different form. Now let's look directly at the nature of the criminal activities occurring in modern societies, paying particular attention to crime in the United States.

Crime and Crime Statistics

How dangerous *are* our streets compared with yesteryear? Is American society more violent than other societies? You should be able to use the sociological skills you have developed already to answer these questions.

In Chapter 2, for example, we learned something about how to interpret statistics. The statistics of crime are a constant focus of attention on television and in the newspapers. Most TV and newspaper reporting is based on official statistics on crime, collected by the police and published by the government. But many crimes are never reported to the police at all. Some criminologists think that about half of all serious crimes, such as robbery with violence, are not reported. The proportion of less serious crimes, especially small thefts, that don't come to the attention of the police is even higher. Since 1973, the Bureau of the Census has been interviewing households across the country to find out how many members were the victims of particular crimes over the previous six months. This procedure, which is called the National Crime Victimization Survey, has confirmed that the overall rate of crime is higher than the reported crime index. For instance, in 1999, only 37 percent of rapes were reported, 61 percent of robberies, 43 percent of assaults, and 49 percent of burglaries.

Public concern in the United States tends to focus on crimes of violence—murder, assault, and rape—even though only about 10 percent of all crimes are violent (see Figure 7.2). In the United States, the most common victims of murder and other violent crimes (with the exception of rape) are young, poor, African American men living in the larger cities (see Figure 7.3). The rate of murder among black male teenagers is particularly high, over seven times the rate for

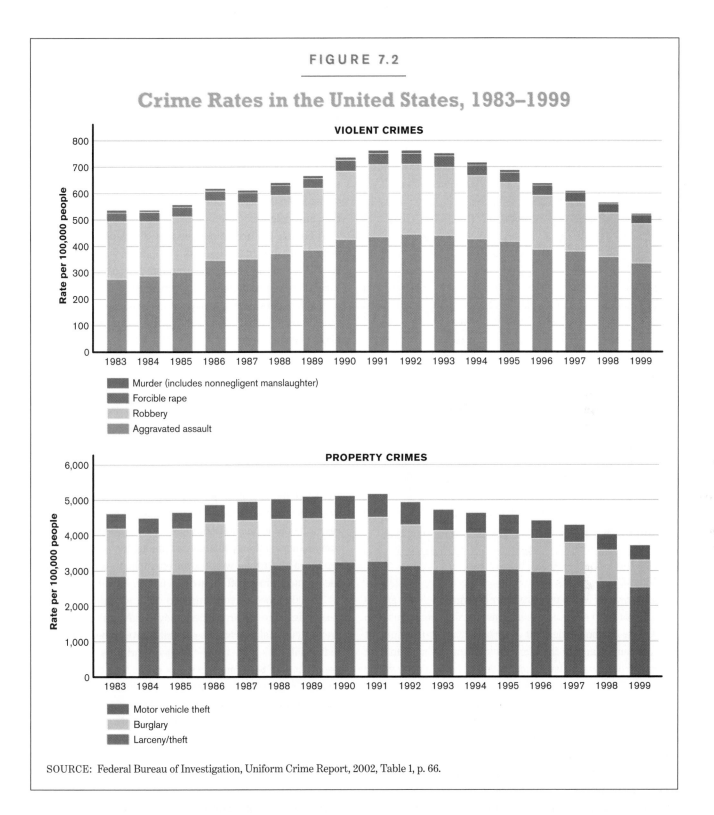

FIGURE 7.2

Crime Rates in the United States, 1983–1999

VIOLENT CRIMES

Rate per 100,000 people

1983 1984 1985 1986 1987 1988 1989 1990 1991 1992 1993 1994 1995 1996 1997 1998 1999

■ Murder (includes nonnegligent manslaughter)
■ Forcible rape
▪ Robbery
■ Aggravated assault

PROPERTY CRIMES

Rate per 100,000 people

1983 1984 1985 1986 1987 1988 1989 1990 1991 1992 1993 1994 1995 1996 1997 1998 1999

■ Motor vehicle theft
▪ Burglary
■ Larceny/theft

SOURCE: Federal Bureau of Investigation, Uniform Crime Report, 2002, Table 1, p. 66.

their white counterparts. In general, whether indexed by police statistics or by the National Crime Victimization Survey, violent crime, burglary, and car theft are more common in cities than in the suburbs surrounding them, and they are more common in the suburbs than in smaller towns (see Table 7.1).

In the 1990s, there was a drop in the overall crime rate throughout the United States to its lowest levels since 1973, when the victimization survey was first used. Rates of violent crime in particular dropped substantially, murders by 31 percent and robberies by 32 percent. There is no one prevailing explanation among sociologists for this decline, although many

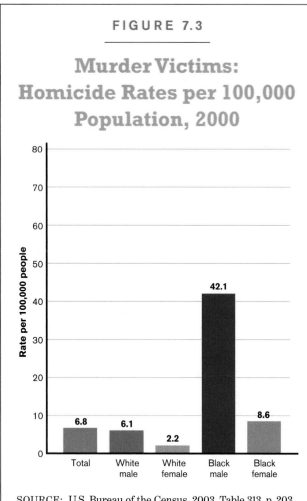

FIGURE 7.3

Murder Victims: Homicide Rates per 100,000 Population, 2000

Rate per 100,000 people

Total	White male	White female	Black male	Black female
6.8	6.1	2.2	42.1	8.6

SOURCE: U.S. Bureau of the Census, 2003, Table 313, p. 203.

of firearms, the general influence of the "frontier tradition," and the subcultures of violence in the large cities. Violence by frontiersmen and vigilantes is an honored part of American history. Some of the first established immigrant areas in the cities developed their own informal modes of neighborhood control, backed by violence or the threat of violence. Similarly, young people in African American and Hispanic communities today have developed subcultures of manliness and honor associated with rituals of violence, and some belong to gangs whose everyday life is one of drug dealing, territory protection, and violence.

A notable feature of most crimes of violence is their mundane character. Most assaults and homicides bear little resemblance to the murderous, random acts of gunmen or the carefully planned homicides given most prominence in the media. Murders generally happen in the context of family and other interpersonal relationships; the victim usually knows his or her murderer.

Victims and Perpetrators of Crime

Are some individuals or groups more likely to commit crimes or to become the victims of crime? Criminologists say yes—research and crime statistics show that crime and victimization are not randomly distributed among the population. Men are more likely than women, for example, to commit crimes; the young are more often involved in crime than older people.

The likelihood of someone becoming a victim of crime is closely linked to the area where they live. Areas suffering from greater material deprivation generally have higher crime rates. Individuals living in inner-city neighborhoods run a much greater risk of becoming victims of crime than do residents of more affluent suburban areas. That ethnic minorities are concentrated disproportionately in inner-city regions appears to be a significant factor in their higher rates of victimization.

Gender and Crime

Like other areas of sociology, criminological studies have traditionally ignored half the population. Feminists have been correct in criticizing criminology for being a male-dominated discipline in which women are largely invisible in both theoretical considerations and empirical studies. Since the 1970s, many important feminist works have drawn attention to the way in which criminal transgressions by women occur in dif-

politicians would like to take credit for it. Aggressive new efforts by local police to stop the use of guns certainly contributed to the decrease in homicides, but other social factors were also at work. Foremost among these is related to the declining market for crack cocaine and the stigmatization of crack among young urban dwellers. Another factor was the booming economy of the 1990s, which provided job opportunities for those who may have been enticed to work in the drug trade (Butterfield, 1998).

One reason often given for the relatively high rates of violent crime in the United States is the widespread availability of handguns and other firearms. This is relevant but does not provide a complete answer. Switzerland has very low rates of violent crime, yet firearms are easily accessible. All Swiss males are members of the citizen army and keep weapons in their homes, including rifles, revolvers, and sometimes other automatic weapons, plus ammunition; nor are gun licenses difficult to obtain.

The most likely explanation for the high level of violent crime in the United States is a combination of the availability

TABLE 7.1

Crime Rates in Metropolitan vs. Rural Areas for 2002

TYPE OF CRIME	METROPOLITAN RATE (PER 100,000 POPULATION)	RURAL RATE
Violent crime	545.6	212.6
Murder	6.2	3.6
Forcible rape	33.8	23.8
Robbery	173.4	16.7
Assault	332.3	168.5
Property crime	3,863.5	1,696.1
Burglary	768.5	558.2
Larceny	2,596.4	1,005.0
Auto theft	498.6	132.8

SOURCE: U.S. Bureau of the Census, 2002, Table 313, p. 203.

women's predominantly domestic role as providing them with the opportunity to commit crimes at home and in the private sphere. Pollak regarded women as naturally deceitful and highly skilled at covering up their crimes. He claimed this was grounded in biology, as women had learned to hide the pain and discomfort of menstruation from men and were also able to fake interest in sexual intercourse in a way that men could not! Pollak also argued that female offenders are treated more leniently because male police officers tend to adopt a "chivalrous" attitude toward them (1950).

Pollak's portrayal of women as conniving and deceptive is based in groundless stereotypes, yet the suggestion that women are treated more leniently by the criminal justice system has prompted much debate and examination. The *chivalry thesis* has been applied in two ways. First, it is possible that police and other officials may regard female offenders as less dangerous than men and let pass activities for which males would be arrested. Second, in sentencing for criminal offenses, women tend to be much less likely to be imprisoned than male offenders. A number of empirical studies have been undertaken to test the chivalry thesis, but the results remain inconclusive. One of the main difficulties is assessing the relative influence of gender compared to other factors such as age, class, and race. For example, it appears that older women offenders tend to be treated less aggressively than their male counterparts. Other studies have shown that black women receive worse treatment than white women at the hands of the police.

ferent contexts from those by men and how women's experiences with the criminal justice system are influenced by certain gendered assumptions about appropriate male and female roles. Feminists have also played a critical role in highlighting the prevalence of violence against women, both at home and in public.

MALE AND FEMALE CRIME RATES

The statistics on gender and crime are startling. For example, of all crimes reported in 2002, an overwhelming 77 percent of arrestees were men (see Table 7.2). There is also an enormous imbalance in the ratio of men to women in prison, not only in the United States but in all the industrialized countries. Women make up only 6 percent of the prison population. There are also contrasts between the types of crimes men and women commit. The offenses of women rarely involve violence and are almost all small scale. Petty thefts like shoplifting and public order offenses such as public drunkenness and prostitution are typical female crimes.

Of course, it may be that the real gender difference in crime rates is less than the official statistics show. In the 1950s, Otto Pollak suggested as much, contending that certain crimes perpetrated by women tend to go unreported. He saw

TABLE 7.2

Percentage of Crimes Committed by Men, 2002

CRIME	PERCENTAGE MALE
Murder	89.2
Rape	98.6
Robbery	89.7
Assault	79.8
Burglary	86.7
Theft	63.0
Auto theft	83.5
Arson	84.8

Note: Data represent arrests (not charges), estimated by the FBI.

SOURCE: Federal Bureau of Investigation, Uniform Crime Report, 2002, Table 42, p. 251.

Another perspective, which has been adopted by feminists, examines how social understandings about "femininity" affect women's experiences in the criminal justice system. It has been argued that women are treated more harshly in cases where they have allegedly deviated from the norms of female sexuality. For example, young girls who are perceived to be sexually promiscuous are more often taken into custody than boys. In such cases, women are seen as doubly deviant—not only have they broken the law, but they have also flouted "appropriately" female behavior. In such cases, they are judged less on the nature of the offense and more on their "deviant" lifestyle choice. Thus, a double standard exists within the criminal justice system: Where male aggression and violence is seen as a natural phenomenon, explanations for female offenses are sought in psychological imbalances (Heidensohn, 1985).

In an effort to make female crime more visible, feminists have conducted a number of detailed investigations on female criminals—from girl gangs to female terrorists to women in prison. Such studies have shown that violence is not exclusively a characteristic of male criminality. Women are much less likely than men to participate in violent crime but are not always inhibited from taking part in violent episodes. Why, then, are female rates of criminality so much lower than those of men?

There is some evidence that female lawbreakers are quite often able to escape coming before the courts because they are able to persuade the police or other authorities to see their actions in a particular light. They invoke what has been called the "gender contract"—the implicit contract between men and women whereby to be a woman is to be erratic and impulsive on the one hand and in need of protection on the other (Worrall, 1990).

Yet differential treatment could hardly account for the vast difference between male and female rates of crime. The reasons are almost certainly the same as those that explain gender differences in other spheres. "Male crimes" remain "male" because of differences in socialization and because men's activities and involvements are still more nondomestic than those of most women.

Ever since the late nineteenth century, criminologists have predicted that gender equality would reduce or eliminate the differences in criminality between men and women, but as yet crime remains a gendered phenomenon. Whether the variations between female and male crime rates will one day disappear we still cannot say with any certainty.

CRIMES AGAINST WOMEN

There are certain categories of crime where men are overwhelmingly the aggressors and women the victims. Domestic violence, sexual harassment, sexual assault, and rape are crimes in which males use their superior social or physical power against women. While each of these has been practiced by women against men, they remain almost exclusively crimes carried out against women. It is estimated that one quarter of women are victims of violence at some point in their lives, but all women face the threat of such crimes either directly or indirectly.

For many years, these offenses were ignored by the criminal justice system; victims had to persevere tirelessly to gain legal recourse against an offender. Even today, the prosecution of crimes against women remains far from straightforward. Yet feminist criminology has done much to raise awareness of crimes against women and to integrate such offenses into mainstream debates on crime. In this section we shall examine the crime of rape, leaving discussions of domestic violence and sexual harassment to other chapters (see Chapters 10 and 15).

The extent of rape is very difficult to assess with any accuracy. Only a small proportion of rapes actually come to the attention of the police and are recorded in the statistics. In 2000, 92,000 cases of rape and 169,000 instances of sexual assault were reported to the police. However, the true number of rapes and sexual assaults in the United States is closer to 750,000.

During the 1990s, there was an increase in the number of reported incidents in which the attacker was known to the victim. Sixty-two percent of sexual assaults are committed by relatives, friends, former partners, or recent acquaintances—so-called date or acquaintance rapes. It is estimated that half of all acquaintance rapes involve someone whom the victim has known for less than twenty-four hours. While the number of acquaintance rapes has risen, reported rapes involving strangers have dropped and account for 34 percent of all attacks.

There are many reasons why a woman might choose not to report sexual violence to the police. The majority of women who are raped either wish to put the incident out of their minds or are unwilling to participate in what can be a humiliating process of medical examination, police interrogation, and courtroom cross-examination. The legal process often takes a long time and can be intimidating. Courtroom procedure is public and the victim must come face to face with the accused. Proof of penetration, the identity of the rapist, and the fact that the act occurred without the woman's consent all have to be forthcoming. A woman may feel that *she* is the one on trial, particularly if her own sexual history is examined publicly, as is often the case.

Over the last few years, women's groups have pressed for change in both legal and public thinking about rape. They have stressed that rape should not be seen as a sexual offense but as a type of violent crime. It is not just a physical attack but an assault on an individual's integrity and dignity. Rape is clearly related to the association of masculinity with power, dominance, and toughness. It is not for the most part the result of overwhelming sexual desire but of the ties between sexuality and feelings of power and superiority. The sexual act itself is less significant than the debasement of the woman (Estrich, 1987). The campaign has had some real results in changing legislation, and rape is today generally recognized in law to be a specific type of criminal violence.

There is sense in which all women are victims of rape. Women who have never been raped often experience anxieties similar to those who have. They may be afraid to go out alone at night, even on crowded streets, and may be almost equally fearful of being on their own in a house or apartment. Emphasizing the close connection between rape and orthodox male sexuality, Susan Brownmiller has argued that rape is part of a system of male intimidation that keeps all women in fear. Those who are not raped are affected by the anxieties thus provoked and by the need to be much more cautious in everyday aspects of life than men have to be (Brownmiller, 1975).

Crimes Against Gays and Lesbians

Feminists have pointed out that understandings of violence are highly gendered and are influenced by common-sense perceptions about risk and responsibility. Because women are generally seen as less able to defend themselves against violent attack, common sense holds that they should modify *their* behavior in order to reduce the risk of becoming a victim of violence. For example, not only should women avoid walking in unsafe neighborhoods alone and at night, but they should be careful not to dress provocatively or to behave in a manner that could be misinterpreted. Women who fail to do so can be accused of "asking for trouble." In a court setting, their behavior can be taken as a mitigating factor in considering the perpetrator's act of violence (Dobash and Dobash, 1992; Richardson and May, 1999).

It has been suggested that a similar common-sense logic applies in the case of violent acts against gay men and lesbians. Victimization studies reveal that homosexuals experience a high incidence of violent crime and harassment. A national survey of over four thousand gay men and women found that in the previous five years, one third of gay men and one quarter of lesbians had been the victim of at least one violent attack. One third had experienced some form of harassment, including threats or vandalism. An overwhelming 75 percent had been verbally abused in public.

Because sexual minorities remain stigmatized and marginalized in many societies, there is a greater tendency for them to be treated as deserving of crime, rather than as innocent victims. Homosexual relationships are still seen as belonging to the private realm, while heterosexuality is the overwhelming norm in public spaces. Lesbians and gay men who deviate from this private–public contract by displaying their homosexual identities in public are often blamed for making themselves vulnerable to crime. There is a sense that introducing homosexuality into the public sphere represents a form of provocation.

This notion forms the basis of the "homosexual panic" legal defense that can be used in the legal system to reduce a charge of murder to that of manslaughter. The accused murderer can claim that an unwanted homosexual advance caused him or her to lose control and to attack the victim. Such a defense was recently used successfully by a young man in the state of Wyoming in the murder trial of university student Matthew Shepard. The accused and two other men severely beat Shepard outside a bar before leaving him tied to a fence in the woods, in near-freezing temperatures. After 18 hours he was found, and he died several days later. In cases like these, homophobic violence is taken as a justifiable response and the essential "personhood," or right to life, of the victim is discounted or denied. Crimes such as the murder of Matthew Shepard have led to calls by many social groups for the adoption of hate crime legislation to protect the human rights of groups who remain stigmatized in society.

Youth and Crime

Popular fear about crime centers on offenses such as theft, burglary, assault, and rape—street crimes that are largely seen as the domain of young working-class males. Media coverage of rising crime rates often focuses on moral breakdown among young people and highlights such issues as vandalism, school truancy, and drug use to illustrate the increasing permissiveness in society. This equation of youth with criminal activity is not a new one, according to some sociologists. Young people are often taken as an indicator of the health and welfare of society itself.

Official statistics about crime rates do reveal high rates of offense among young people. Two fifths of all offenders arrested for criminal offenses in 1999 were under the age of twenty-one. For both males and females, the peak age of offending was eighteen (U.S. Bureau of Justice Statistics, 2000). Yet we must approach assumptions about youth and crime with some caution. Moral panics about youth criminality may not accurately reflect social reality. An isolated event involving young people and crime can be transformed symbolically into a full-blown crisis of childhood, demanding tough law-and-order responses. The high-profile mass murder at Columbine High School is an example of how moral outrage can deflect attention from larger societal issues. Columbine was a watershed event in media portrayals of youth crime, and some have speculated that it led to "copycat" school killings in high schools in Arkansas, Kentucky, California, and elsewhere. Even though the number of murders committed on school grounds has been declining, attention to these mass murders has led many to think that all young children are potential violent threats. Although the perpetrators of the Columbine killings were labeled "monsters" and "animals," less attention was paid to how easily they were able to obtain the weapons they used to commit these murders.

Similar caution can be expressed about the popular view of drug use by teenagers. A survey of more than seven thousand adolescents aged fifteen and sixteen revealed that more than 94 percent drank alcohol, about one third had smoked a cigarette within the previous thirty days, and 42 percent had tried illegal drugs at least once. Trends in drug use have shifted away from hard drugs such as heroin and toward combinations of substances such as amphetamines, alcohol, and the drug ecstasy. Ecstasy in particular has become a "lifestyle" drug associated with the rave and club subcultures, rather than the basis of an expensive, addictive habit. The war on drugs, some have argued, criminalizes large segments of the youth population who are generally law abiding (Muncie, 1999).

What makes one drug a psychological tool and another a national menace? Ecstasy, the chemical compound MDMA (methylenedioxymethamphetamine), gives users a sustained feeling of pleasure by sending waves of the neurotransmitters serotonin and dopamine into the brain. In this regard, it is not dissimilar to antidepressants such as Prozac, which also influence the amount of serotonin that the brain produces. The use of both ecstasy and antidepressants by college students has risen dramatically in recent years, yet one is illegal and the other is a routinely prescribed medical option. Admittedly, the amphetaminelike and mildly hallucinogenic effects of ecstasy are considerably more dramatic and short lived than the effects of Prozac. Long-term ecstasy use may cause brain damage. Nonetheless, MDMA was legal in the United States until 1985; because it has the effect of overcoming emotional inhibitions, some therapists used it on their patients in therapy sessions. More recently, MDMA has been used to treat rape victims in Spain, sufferers from posttraumatic stress disorder in Switzerland, and end-stage cancer patients in the United States.

The divergent ways in which ecstasy and Prozac have been viewed illustrate how "deviant" behavior is socially defined. From the perspective of lawmakers, MDMA became a dangerous drug as it morphed into ecstasy, now associated with youth culture, parties, and hedonism rather than medicine. Media coverage of ecstasy has also often been monolithic. It has become common for teen-oriented television shows such as *Dawson's Creek* to do an ecstasy episode. Invariably, the protagonist taking ecstasy for the first time has a bad reaction and has to be rushed to the hospital. This is easier to portray than the more common experience: Ecstasy users find their early experiences with the drug to be blissful; problems occur over time, as the brain's receptivity to the drug diminishes.

Taking illegal drugs, like other forms of socially deviant behavior, is often defined in racial, class, and cultural terms; different drugs come to be associated with different groups and behaviors. When crack cocaine appeared in the 1980s, it was quickly defined by the media as the drug of choice for black, inner-city kids who listened to hip-hop. Perhaps as a result, jail sentences for crack possession were set at higher levels than sentences for possession of cocaine, which was associated more with white and suburban users. Ecstasy has, until recently, had similar white and middle- or upper-class associations.

Crimes of the Powerful

It is plain enough that there are connections between crime and poverty. But it would be a mistake to suppose that crime is concentrated among the poor. Crimes carried out by people in positions of power and wealth can have farther-reaching consequences than the often petty crimes of the poor.

The term **white-collar crime**, first introduced by Edwin Sutherland (1949), refers to crime typically carried out by people in the more affluent sectors of society. This category of criminal activity includes tax fraud, antitrust violations, illegal sales practices, securities and land fraud, embezzlement, the manufacture or sale of dangerous products, and illegal environmental pollution, as well as straightforward theft. The distribution of white-collar crimes is even harder to measure than that of other types of crime; most do not appear in the official statistics at all.

Efforts made to detect white-collar crime are ordinarily limited, and it is only on rare occasions that those who are caught go to jail. Although the authorities regard white-collar crime in a more tolerant light than crimes of the less privileged, it has been calculated that the amount of money involved in white-collar crime in the United States is forty times greater than the amount involved in crimes against property, such as robberies, burglaries, larceny, forgeries, and car thefts (President's Commission on Organized Crime, 1986). Some forms of white-collar crime, moreover, affect more people than lower-class criminality. An embezzler might rob thousands—or today, via computer fraud, millions—of people.

CORPORATE CRIME

Some criminologists have referred to **corporate crime** to describe the types of offenses that are committed by large corporations in society. Pollution, product mislabeling, and violations of health and safety regulations affect much larger numbers of people than does petty criminality. The increasing power and influence of large corporations and their rapidly growing global reach mean that our lives are touched by them in many ways. Corporations are involved in producing the cars we drive and the food we eat. They also have an enormous impact on the natural environment and financial markets, aspects of life that affect all of us.

Both quantitative and qualitative studies of corporate crime have concluded that a large number of corporations do not adhere to the legal regulations that apply to them (Slapper and Tombs, 1999). Corporate crime is not confined to a few "bad apples" but is instead pervasive and widespread. Studies have revealed six types of violations linked to large corporations: *administrative* (paperwork or noncompliance), *environmental* (pollution, permits violations), *financial* (tax violations, illegal payments), *labor* (working conditions, hiring practices), *manufacturing* (product safety, labeling), and *unfair trade practices* (anticompetition, false advertising).

Sometimes there are obvious victims, as in environmental disasters such as the spill at the Bhopal chemical plant in India and the health dangers posed to women by silicone breast implants. The most famous recent case of white-collar crime with obvious victims was the Enron scandal. Enron grew to become America's seventh largest company in just fifteen years, but the company and its accountants lied about its profits and concealed its debts so they would not appear in the company accounts. The victims include pension holders, employees, and investors. Several executives including Andrew Fastow and Kenneth Lay face fraud and money-laundering charges. Recently those injured in car crashes or relatives of those who were killed have called for the executives of car manufacturers to be brought to trial when the companies have shown negligence. But very often victims of corporate crime do not see themselves as such. This is because in "traditional" crimes the proximity between victim and offender is much closer—it is difficult not to realize that you have been mugged! In the case of corporate crime, greater distances in time and space mean that victims may not realize they have been victimized or may not know how to seek redress for the crime.

The effects of corporate crime are often experienced unevenly within society. Those who are disadvantaged by other types of socioeconomic inequalities tend to suffer disproportionately. For example, safety and health risks in the workplace tend to be concentrated most heavily in low-paying occupations. Many of the risks from health care products and pharmaceuticals have had a greater impact on women than on men, as is the case with contraceptives or fertility treatments with harmful side effects (Slapper and Tombs, 1999).

Violent aspects of corporate crime are less visible than in cases of homicide or assault, but they are just as real—and may on occasion be much more serious in their consequences. For example, flouting regulations concerning the preparation of new drugs, safety in the workplace, or pollution may cause physical harm or death to large numbers of people. Deaths from hazards at work far outnumber murders, although precise statistics about job accidents are difficult to obtain. Of course, we cannot assume that all, or even the majority, of these deaths and injuries are the result of employer negligence in relation to safety factors for which they are legally liable. Nevertheless, there is some basis for supposing that many are due to the neglect of legally binding safety regulations by employers or managers.

Organized Crime

Organized crime refers to forms of activity that have some of the characteristics of orthodox business but that are illegal. Organized crime embraces illegal gambling, drug dealing, 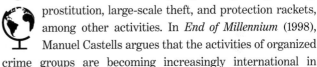 prostitution, large-scale theft, and protection rackets, among other activities. In *End of Millennium* (1998), Manuel Castells argues that the activities of organized crime groups are becoming increasingly international in scope. He notes that the coordination of criminal activities across borders—with the help of new information technologies—is becoming a central feature of the new global economy. Involved in activities ranging from the narcotics trade to counterfeiting to smuggling immigrants and human organs, organized crime groups are now operating in flexible international networks rather than within their own territorial realms.

According to Castells, criminal groups set up strategic alliances with each other. The international narcotics trade, weapons trafficking, the sale of nuclear material, and money laundering have all become linked across borders and crime groups. Criminal organizations tend to base their operations in "low-risk" countries where there are fewer threats to their activities. In recent years, the former Soviet Union has been one of the main points of convergence for international organized crime. The flexible nature of this networked crime makes it relatively easy for crime groups to evade the reach of law enforcement initiatives. If one criminal safe haven becomes more risky, the organizational geometry can shift to form a new pattern.

The international nature of crime has been felt in the United States. Among the newest arrivals are criminals from the former Soviet Union. Some commentators believe that the new Russian mafia is the world's most dangerous organized crime syndicate. Russian criminal networks are deeply involved in money laundering, linking up their activities with Russia's largely unregulated banks. Some think the Russian groups may come to be the world's largest criminal networks. They have their basis in a mafia-riddled Russian state, where underworld protection is now routine for many businesses. The most worrying possibility is that Russia's new mobsters are smuggling nuclear materials on an international scale, materials taken from the old Soviet nuclear arsenal.

Despite numerous campaigns by the government and the police, the narcotics trade is one of the most rapidly expanding international criminal industries, having an annual growth rate of more than 10 percent in the 1980s and early 1990s and an extremely high level of profit. Heroin networks stretch across the Far East, particularly South Asia, and are also located in North Africa, the Middle East, and Latin America. Supply lines also pass through Vancouver and other parts of Canada, from where drugs are commonly supplied to the United States.

Cybercrime

Not only is international organized crime greatly facilitated by recent advances in information technology, it seems certain that the information and telecommunications revolution will change the face of crime in fundamental ways. Advances in technology have provided exciting new opportunities and benefits, but they also heighten vulnerability to crime.

There are indications that **cybercrime** is already on the rise. Internet-based fraud was the fastest growing category of crime in the United States in the late 1990s. From 1999 to 2000, losses from Internet fraud and forgery rose from $12 million to $117 million over the course of one year. The increase has been attributed to the growth in Internet-based crime.

The global reach of telecommunications crime poses particular challenges for law enforcement. Criminal acts perpetrated in one country have the power to affect victims across the globe. This has troubling implications for detecting and prosecuting crimes. It becomes necessary for police from the countries involved to determine the jurisdiction in which the act occurred and to agree on extraditing the offenders and providing the necessary evidence for prosecution. Although police cooperation across national borders may improve with the growth of cybercrime, at present cybercriminals have a great deal of room to maneuver.

At a time when financial, commercial, and production systems in countries around the world are being integrated electronically, rising levels of Internet fraud and unauthorized electronic intrusions such as the DDoS attacks are serving as potent warnings of the vulnerability of existing computer security systems. From the FBI to the Japanese government's new antihacker police force, governments are scrambling to contend with new and elusive forms of cross-national computer activity.

Crime-Reduction Strategies

Despite the misleading picture presented by official statistics, when they are taken together with data from victimization surveys it becomes clear that criminal offenses are assuming a more prominent role in society. Moreover, citizens *perceive* themselves to be at greater risk of falling victim to crime than in times past. Residents of inner-city areas have more reason to be concerned about crime than people living in other settings.

In the face of so many changes and uncertainties in the world around us, we are all engaged in a constant process of risk management. Crime is one of the most obvious risks that confront people in the late modern age. Yet it is not only individuals that have been caught up in risk management: Governments are now faced with societies that seem more dangerous and uncertain than ever before. One of the central tasks of social policy in modern states has been controlling crime and delinquency. But if at one time government sought to guarantee security for its citizens, increasingly policies are aimed at managing insecurity.

Are Prisons the Answer?

"What are we going to do about these kids (monsters) who kill with guns??? Line them up against the wall and get a firing squad and pull, pull, pull. I am volunteering to pull, pull, pull" (anonymous letter received by a judge in Dade County, Florida).

This letter writer isn't alone. Although as measured by police statistics (problematic, as we have seen) rates of violent crime have declined since 1990, many people in the United States have started to view crime as their most serious social concern—more so than unemployment or the state of the economy (Lacayo, 1994). Surveys show that Americans also favor tougher prison sentences for all but relatively minor crimes. The price of imprisonment, however, is enormous: It costs an average of $460,000 to keep a prisoner behind bars for twenty years. Moreover, even if the prison system were expanded, it wouldn't reduce the level of serious crime a great deal. Only about a fifth of all serious crimes result in an arrest—and this is of crimes known to the police, an underestimate of the true rate of crime. And no more than half of arrests for serious crimes result in a conviction. Even so, America's prisons are so overcrowded (see Figure 7.4) that the average convict only serves a third of his sentence. The United States already locks up more people (nearly all men) per capita than any other country.

The United States has by far the most punitive justice system in the world. More than 2 million people are presently in-

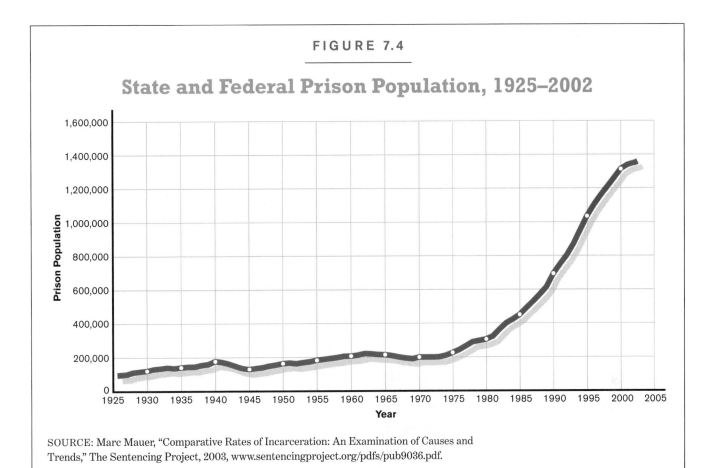

FIGURE 7.4

State and Federal Prison Population, 1925–2002

SOURCE: Marc Mauer, "Comparative Rates of Incarceration: An Examination of Causes and Trends," The Sentencing Project, 2003, www.sentencingproject.org/pdfs/pub9036.pdf.

carcerated in American prisons, with another 4.3 million falling under the jurisdiction of the penal system. Although the United States makes up only 5 percent of the world's overall population, it accounts for 25 percent of the world's prisoners.

The American prison system employs more than 500,000 people and costs $35 billion annually to maintain. It has also become partially privatized, with private companies now able to win government contracts to build and administer prisons to accommodate the growing inmate population. Critics charge that a "prison-industrial complex" has emerged: Large numbers of people—including bureaucrats, politicians, and prison employees—have vested interests in the existence and further expansion of the prison system.

Support for *capital punishment* (the death penalty) is high in the United States. In 1999, 71 percent of adults surveyed said that they believed in capital punishment; 21 percent opposed it. This represents a significant shift from 1965, when 38 percent of those surveyed supported the death penalty and 47 percent were opposed. The number of individuals awaiting execution has climbed steadily since 1977, when the Supreme Court upheld state capital punishment laws. At the end of 2002, 3,557 prisoners were held on death row. All were convicted of murder. Of these, 98.5 percent were men, 54 percent where white,

and 44 percent were black. In 2003, 65 prisoners were executed in 11 states. Sixty-five of these were men, 41 were white and 20 were black (Bureau of Justice Statistics, 2004).

In addition, more than one quarter of African American men are either in prison or under the control of the penal system. Some 57 percent of individuals imprisoned in the United States are serving sentences for nonviolent drug-related crimes.

While we might suppose that imprisoning large numbers of people or stiffening sentences would deter individuals from committing crimes, there is little evidence to support this. In fact, sociological studies have demonstrated that prisons can easily become schools for crime. Instead of preventing people from committing crimes, prisons often actually make them more hardened criminals. The more harsh and oppressive prison conditions are, the more likely inmates are to be brutalized by the experience. Yet if prisons were made into attractive and pleasant places to live, would they have a deterrent effect?

Although prisons do keep some dangerous men (and a tiny minority of dangerous women) off the streets, evidence suggests that we need to find other means to deter crime. Robert Gangi, director of the Correctional Association of New York, says that "building more prisons to address crime is like building more graveyards to address a fatal disease" (quoted

Drug Trafficking

How easy would it have been for you to purchase marijuana in high school? How easy would it be to do so today? Lamentable as it may seem to some, most young people in the United States have relatively easy access to illegal drugs. According to recent congressional testimony given by the director of the Office of National Drug Control Policy, "nine percent of twelve to seventeen year olds are current drug users . . . 49.6 percent of high school seniors reported having tried marijuana at least once . . . [and] in every grade (eighth, tenth and twelfth) 2.1 percent of students have tried heroin" (McCaffrey, 1998).

What factors determine the availability of illegal drugs in your community? The level of police enforcement is important, of course, as is the extent of local demand. But no less important is the existence of networks of traffickers able to transport the drugs from the countries in which they are grown to your hometown. These networks have been able to flourish in part because of globalization.

While the cultivation of marijuana in the United States represents a major illicit industry, almost all of the world's coca plants and opium poppies are grown in the developing world. The U.S. government spends billions of dollars each year to as-

in Molowe, 1994). A sociological interpretation of crime makes clear that there are no quick fixes. The causes of crime, especially crimes of violence, are bound up with structural conditions of American society, including widespread poverty, the condition of the inner cities, and the deteriorating life circumstances of many young men.

The Mark of a Criminal Record

A recent experiment by sociologist Devah Pager (2003) showed the long-term consequences of prison on the lives of felons. Pager had pairs of young black and white men apply for real entry-level job openings throughout the city of Milwaukee. The applicant pairs were matched by appearance, interpersonal style, and, most important, by all job-related characteristics such as education level and prior work experience. In addition to varying the race of the applicant pairs, Pager also had applicants alternate presenting themselves to employers as having criminal records. One member of each of

the applicant pairs would check the box "yes" on the applicant form in answer to the question, "Have you ever been convicted of a crime?" The pair alternated each week which young man would play the role of the ex-offender, in order to make sure that it was the criminal record—not the individual—that made a difference in employment outcomes.

The value of this experimental design is that it allows the sociologist to control for all the individual differences that may lead members of one group to be preferred to members of another. If whites, for example, on average have higher levels of education or more steady work experience than blacks, it's hard to determine whether race influences their employment opportunities or whether these other "skill differences" determine the results. The same problem applies to the question of how individuals with criminal records fare in the job market. Some would argue that a criminal record doesn't hold people back; instead, they might argue, it's the fact that people with criminal records don't work as hard as nonoffenders, or aren't as qualified for many jobs. The experiment allowed Pager to make the applicant pairs identical on all job-relevant

sist developing nations with eradication efforts and also devotes significant resources to stopping the flow of drugs past U.S. borders. In 1995, the federal government spent more than $8.2 billion on the "war on drugs" and between 1981 and 1996 spent a total of $65 billion (Bertram et al., 1996). Despite this massive expenditure, there is little evidence that eradication or interdiction efforts have significantly decreased the supply of illegal drugs in the United States. Why have these efforts failed?

One answer is that the profit is simply too great. Farmers struggling to scratch out a living for themselves in Bolivia or Peru, members of the Colombian drug cartels, and low-level street dealers in the United States all receive substantial monetary rewards for their illegal activities. These rewards create a strong incentive to devise ways around antidrug efforts and to run the risk of getting caught.

Another answer—one discussed at a summit attended by leaders of the eight major industrial powers—is that drug traffickers have been able to take advantage of globalization. First, in their attempts to evade the authorities, traffickers make use of all the communications technologies that are available in a global age. As one commentator put it, drug traffickers "now use sophisticated technology, such as signal interceptors, to plot radar and avoid monitoring . . . [and] they can use faxes, computers and cellular phones to coordinate their activities and make their business run smoothly" (Chepesiuk, 1998). Second, the globalization of the financial sector has helped create

an infrastructure in which large sums of money can be moved around the world electronically in a matter of seconds, making it relatively easy to "launder" drug money (i.e., to make it appear to have come from a legitimate business venture). Third, recent changes in government policy designed to allow the freer flow of persons and legitimate goods across international borders have increased the opportunities for smuggling.

At the same time, globalization may create new opportunities for governments to work together to combat drug trafficking. Indeed, world leaders have called for greater international cooperation in narcotics enforcement, stressing the need for information sharing and coordinated enforcement efforts.

characteristics so that she could know for sure that any differences she saw were the result of discrimination. It tested whether employers respond differently to otherwise equal candidates on the basis of race or criminal record alone.

Pager's study revealed some striking findings. To begin with, whites were much preferred over blacks, and nonoffenders were much preferred over ex-offenders. Whites with a felony conviction were half as likely to be considered by employers as equally qualified non-offenders. For blacks the effects were even larger! Black ex-offenders were only one-third as likely to receive a call back compared to non-offenders. But most surprising was the comparison of these two effects: Blacks with *no criminal history* fared no better than did whites with a felony conviction! Essentially, these results suggest that being a black male in America today is about the same as being a convicted criminal, at least in the eyes of Milwaukee employers. For those who believe that race no longer represents a major barrier to opportunity, these results represent a powerful challenge. Being a black felon is a particularly tough obstacle to overcome.

Situational Crime Prevention

"Situational" crime prevention—such as target hardening and surveillance systems—has been a popular approach to managing the risk of crime. Such techniques are often favored by policy makers because they are relatively simple to introduce alongside existing policing techniques, and they reassure citizens by giving the impression that decisive action against crime is being taken. Yet because such techniques do not engage with the underlying causes of crime—such as social inequalities, unemployment, and poverty—their greatest success lies in protecting certain segments of the population against crime and displacing delinquency into other realms.

One illustration of this dynamic can be seen in the physical *exclusion* of certain categories of people from common spaces in an attempt to reduce crime and the perceived risk of crime. In response to feelings of insecurity among the population at large, public spaces in society—such as libraries, parks, and even street corners—are increasingly being transformed into "security bubbles." Risk-management practices such as police

When a Dissertation Makes a Difference

For Devah Pager, a young sociologist from Honolulu, "kulia i ka nu'u"—"to strive for the summit"—means to do research that can influence policy, a realistic quest for her if the last few years are any indication.

As a graduate student at the University of Wisconsin, she studied the difficulties of former prisoners trying to find work and, in the process, came up with a disturbing finding: it is easier for a white person with a felony conviction to get a job than for a black person whose record is clean.

Ms. Pager's study won the American Sociological Association's award for the best dissertation of the year in August [2003], prompting a *Wall Street Journal* columnist to write about it. Howard Dean repeated her main finding in stump speeches and interviews throughout his glory days as the front-runner.

Then, addressing the overall problem convicted felons have re-entering the job market, President Bush announced in the State of the Union message a $300 million program to provide mentoring and help them get work. Jim Towey, the director of the White House Office of Faith-Based and Community Initiatives, said that Ms. Pager's study was one of the many sources of information that helped shape the administration's four-year plan.

Ms. Pager, 32, is thrilled to see the issue receive national attention. More than half a million inmates will leave penal institutions this year, and "the Administration is finally recognizing that the problems created by our incarceration policies can no longer be ignored," she said. Even if the promised amount is trivial, she said, the gesture is important symbolically.

Conversation with Ms. Pager flows easily. Over a plate of pancakes, she brushes aside a crush of thick loose auburn curls to punctuate less serious points with flashes of the wide, arresting smile her colleagues say is emblematic. She is known for her good nature and charismatic style, but it is her research that has made her one of the most promising young sociologists around.

Initially Ms. Pager's interest was race, stirred by her move from Hawaii to Los Angeles to attend the University of California. "I was struck by the level of separation between racial groups on campus, throughout the city," she said. "Race seemed to define space. Hawaii, by contrast, has the highest rate of intermarriage in the country. Growing up, every other person, it seemed, was *hapa,* or half, the term used to describe someone multiracial or mixed." She added, "When you grow up with that being normal, everything else seems strange—and wrong."

She completed a master's degree at Stanford University and a second master's at the University of Cape Town in South Africa, her father's native country. He is a professor of computer science. Her mother, a pediatrician, was born in Australia, making Ms. Pager something of a *hapa* herself, a

Jewish one. A one-year visiting professorship at the University of Hawaii took Ms. Pager's parents to Honolulu from London before she was born. They never left.

"Hawaii is an amazing place to grow up," Ms. Pager said. "It's got a small-town community feeling, despite the fact that Honolulu is a city of about a million people."

Though her family is "solidly upper middle class," she said, her parents obliged her and her two older brothers to work to pay part of their college expenses. "I resented it initially," she said, "but in fact it ended up being a great way for me to get involved in things I wouldn't have been involved with otherwise."

The interest in released prisoners arose while she was studying for her doctorate in Madison, Wisconsin. She organized a karaoke night for the sociology department ("I'm a diva," she wrote in an e-mail message, playing off the pronunciation of her given name. "I love to sing."), and she volunteered for an organization that provides services and shelter to homeless men. There she met many black men with prison records. "It was a nice break to get out and do some direct service," she said. She spent time with the men, distributed their mail and made herself available "as a resource, to allow them to unload." Those who had served jail time often talked about how it complicated the job search. "That was one of the first things that clued me into what an immutable barrier it was standing in their way," she said.

At about this time Human Rights Watch and the Sentencing Project reported that in seven states felony convictions had permanently disenfranchised one in four African American men. An innovative but difficult research plan began to take shape.

Both of her main advisers, Robert M. Hauser and Erik Olin Wright, tried to dissuade her, gently suggesting how hard it is for graduate students to obtain financial support, manage complicated field work and end up with meaningful results.

"She was undaunted," Mr. Wright said. "Her pluckiness is part of what makes her successful. She knew she could do it."

To isolate the effect of a criminal record on the job search, Ms. Pager sent pairs of young, well-groomed, well-spoken college men with identical resumes to apply for 350 advertised entry-level jobs in Milwaukee. The only difference was that one said he had served an 18-month prison sentence for cocaine possession. Two teams were black, two white.

A telephone survey of the same employers followed. For her black testers, the callback rate was 5 percent if they had a criminal record and 14 percent if they did not. For whites, it was 17 percent with a criminal record and 34 percent without.

"I expected there to be an effect of race, but I did not expect it to swamp the results as it did," Ms. Pager said. "It really was a surprise."

Jeff Manza, a colleague at Northwestern University, where she teaches, said, "Devah's work demonstrates in a new and convincing way the extent to which the 'second chance' that Bush talks about runs headlong into the realities of race and the fear of crime and criminals."

Similarly, Reginald Wilkinson, Ohio's top corrections official and the president of the Association of State Correctional Administrators, was impressed by her findings and methodology. "In my estimation, we can't eliminate the race question when we're talking about re-entry," he said. "I think what Professor Pager has done is raise consciousness about this."

More reserved was James J. Heckman of the University of Chicago, a Nobel laureate in economics. In a telephone interview, he said Ms. Pager's findings were important but not surprising. Mr. Heckman, who has written extensive critiques of similarly designed studies, said that she had created "a very clean study" of the impact of a criminal record on job seekers in general, but that he did not buy the race findings.

"I believe there is serious reason for caution here," he said. "The comparison across the black and white pairs is just not strong because it's not an experimental design and the samples are just too small."

Ms. Pager is replicating her research on a grander scale with one of the field's leading experts, Bruce Western of Princeton University, where she will join the sociology faculty this fall.

The new study is another chance to further document the effects of race and imprisonment, another chance at "kulia i ka nu'u."

SOURCE: Brooke Kroeger, "When a Dissertation Makes a Difference," *New York Times*, March 20, 2004.

monitoring, private security teams, and surveillance systems are aimed at protecting the public against potential risks. In shopping malls, for example, security measures are becoming more prominent as part of a contractual bargain between businesses and consumers. In order to attract and maintain a customer base, businesses must ensure the safety and comfort of their clients. Young people tend to be excluded from such spaces disproportionately because they are perceived as a greater threat to security as males create "locations of trust" for consumers. Young people find that the public spaces open to them are shrinking.

Police forces have also been expanded in response to growing crime. When crime rates are on the rise, there is almost inevitably public clamor for putting more police on the street. Governments eager to appear decisive on crime tend to favor increasing the number and resources of the police in an attempt to deter crime. The popularly held view of policing is that it is the cornerstone of maintaining law and order. But what is the role of the police in actually controlling crime? It is not clear that a greater number of police necessarily translates into lower crime rates. In the United States, official statistics on the violent crime rate and number of police cast doubt on the link between the two (see Figure 7.5). This raises

several puzzling questions. If increased policing does not prevent violent crime, why does the public demand a visible police presence? What role does policing play in our society?

Policing

Some sociologists and criminologists have suggested that visible policing techniques, such as patrolling the streets, are reassuring for the public. Such activities are consistent with the perception that the police are actively engaged in controlling crime, investigating offenses, and supporting the criminal justice system. But sociologists also suggest that we need to reassess the role of policing in the late modern age. Although maintaining law and order, interacting with citizens, and providing services are indeed part of a contemporary policing, they represent only a fraction of what the police actually do. Policing, sociologists argue, is now less about controlling crime and more about detecting and managing risks. Most of all, it is about communicating knowledge about risk to other institutions in society that demand that information (Ericson and Haggerty, 1997).

According to this view police are first and foremost "knowledge workers." By this sociologists mean that the vast

---

FIGURE 7.5

Justice Employment and Crime Rates

Although the number of police steadily increased between 1982 and 2001, the crime rate dropped, increased, and dropped again during this period. Therefore, no causal link can be made between the number of police and the crime rate.

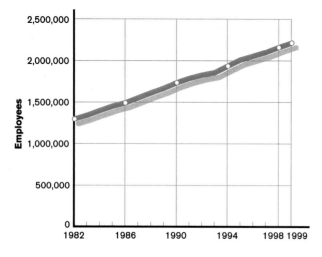
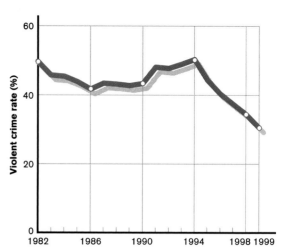

SOURCE: Bureau of Justice Statistics, March 2004, www.ojp.usdoj.gov/bjs/glance/tables/viortrdtab.htm and www.ojp.usdoj.gov/bjs/eande.htm.

---

majority of police time is spent on activities aimed at processing information, drafting reports, or communicating data. The "simple" case of an automobile accident in Ontario, Canada, illustrates this point. A police officer is called to the scene of an automobile accident involving two vehicles. No one has been killed, but there are minor injuries and one of the drivers is drunk. The investigation of the incident takes one hour; the drunk driver is criminally charged with the impaired operation of a motor vehicle causing bodily harm and with operating a motor vehicle with excess alcohol. The driver's license is automatically suspended for twelve hours.

Following this routine investigation, the officer spends three hours writing up sixteen separate reports documenting the incident. It is here that the role of police as brokers of information is clear:

- The *provincial motor registry* requires information about the location of the accident and the vehicles and people involved. This is used for "risk profiling" for use in accident prevention initiatives, traffic management, and resource allocation.
- The *automobile industry* needs to know about the vehicles involved in the accident in order to improve safety standards, to report back to regulatory agencies, and to provide safety information to consumer groups.
- The *insurance companies* involved need information about the accident in order to determine responsibility and make awards in the case. They also require police information in order to develop their own statistical profiles of risk in order to set premiums and compensation levels for clients.
- The *public health system* requires details on the injuries involved and how they occurred. This knowledge is used for statistical profiles and in order to plan emergency service provision.
- The *criminal courts* require police information as material for the prosecution and as proof that the scene was properly investigated and evidence collected.
- The *police administration* itself requires reports on the incident for both internal records and national computer databases.

This example reveals how the police are a key node in a complicated information circuit of institutions that are all in the business of risk management. With the help of new forms of technology, police work is increasingly about "mapping" and predicting risk within the population.

The informational demands of other institutions, such as the insurance industry, now directly shape the way in which the police work. Police must gather and report information in a way that is compatible with the informational needs of outside agencies. Computerized systems and forms now define the way in which police report information. Rather than writing narrative accounts of incidents, police input the facts of a case into standardized forms by checking off boxes and choosing among available options. The information entered into such formats is used to categorize people and events as part of creating risk profiles. But, the closed-ended nature of such reporting formats influences what police observe and investigate, how they understand and interpret an incident, and the approach they take to resolving a problem.

This emphasis on information collection and processing can be alienating and frustrating for police. For many police officers, there is a distinction between real police work—such as investigating crimes—and the "donkey work" of reports and paper trails. Bureaucratic reporting procedures such as these are like a one-way mirror for many police officers who do not see the point of the extensive documentation that is required.

Crime and Community

Preventing crime and reducing fear of crime are both closely related to rebuilding strong communities. As we saw in our earlier discussions of the "broken windows" theory, one of the most significant innovations in criminology in recent years has been the discovery that the decay of day-to-day civility relates directly to criminality. For a long while attention was focused almost exclusively on serious crime—robbery, assault, and other violent crime. More minor crimes and forms of public disorder, however, tend to have a cumulative effect. When asked to describe their problems, residents of troubled neighborhoods mention abandoned cars, graffiti, prostitution, youth gangs, and similar phenomena.

People act on their anxieties about these issues: They leave the areas in question if they can, or they buy heavy locks for their doors and bars for their windows and abandon public places. Unchecked disorderly behavior signals to citizens that the area is unsafe. Fearful citizens stay off the streets, avoid certain neighborhoods, and curtail their normal activities and associations. As they withdraw physically, they also withdraw from roles of mutual support with fellow citizens, thereby relinquishing the social controls that formerly helped to maintain civility within the community.

COMMUNITY POLICING

What should be done to combat this development? One idea that has grown in popularity in recent years is that the police should work closely with citizens to improve local community standards and civil behavior, using education, persuasion, and counseling instead of incarceration.

Community policing implies not only drawing in citizens themselves, but changing the characteristic outlook of police forces. A renewed emphasis on crime prevention rather than law enforcement can go hand in hand with the reintegration of policing with the community. The isolation of the police from those they are supposed to serve often produces a siege mentality, since the police have little regular contact with ordinary citizens.

In order to work, partnerships among government agencies, the criminal justice system, local associations, and community organizations have to be inclusive—all economic and ethnic groups must be involved (Kelling and Coles, 1997). Government and business can act together to help repair urban decay. One model is the creation of business improvement districts providing tax breaks for corporations that participate in strategic planning and offer investment in designated areas. To be successful, such schemes demand a long-term commitment to social objectives.

Emphasizing these strategies does not mean denying the links between unemployment, poverty, and crime. Rather, the struggle against these social problems should be coordinated with community-based approaches to crime prevention. These approaches can in fact contribute directly and indirectly to furthering social justice. Where social order has decayed along with public services, other opportunities, such as new jobs, decline also. Improving the quality of life in a neighborhood can revive them.

SHAMING AS PUNISHMENT

The current emphasis on imprisonment as a means of deterring crime has a potentially crippling effect on the social ties within certain communities. In recent years, **shaming**, a form of punishing criminal and deviant behavior that attempts to maintain the ties of the offender to the community, has grown in popularity as an alternative to incarceration. According to some criminologists, the fear of being shamed within one's community is an important deterrent to crime. As a result, the public's formal disapproval could achieve the same deterrent effect as incarceration, without the high costs of building and maintaining prisons.

The criminologist John Braithwaite (1996) has suggested that shaming practices can take two forms: reintegrative shaming and stigmatizing shaming. Stigmatizing shaming is related to labeling theory, which we discussed earlier in the chapter, by which a criminal is labeled as a threat to society and is treated as an outcast. As a result, the labeling process and society's efforts to marginalize the individual reinforce that person's criminal conduct, perhaps leading to future criminal behavior and higher crime rates. The much different practice of reintegrative shaming works as follows. People central to the criminal's immediate community—such as family members, employers and coworkers, and friends—are brought into court to state their condemnation of the offender's behavior. At the same time, these people must accept responsibility for reintegrating the offender back into the community. The goal is to rebuild the social bonds of the individual to the community as a means of deterring future criminal conduct.

Japan, with one of the lowest crime rates in the world, has been quite successful in implementing this approach. The process is largely based on a voluntary network of over five hundred thousand local crime prevention associations dedicated to facilitating reintegration into the community and on a criminal justice system that is encouraged to be lenient for this purpose. As a result, in Japan only 5 percent of persons convicted for a crime serve time in prison, as compared to 30 percent in the United States. Though reintegrative shaming is not a standard practice in the American criminal justice system, it is a familiar practice in other social institutions such as the family. Think of a child who misbehaves. The parent may express disapproval of the child's behavior and try to make the child feel ashamed of her conduct, but the parent may also reassure the child that she is a loved member of the family.

Could reintegrative shaming succeed in the United States? In spite of the beliefs that these tactics are "soft" on crime, that Americans are too individualistic to participate in community-based policing, and that high-crime areas are less community oriented, community networks have been successful in working with the police in preventing crime. These social bonds could also be fostered to increase the power of shame and reintegrate offenders into local networks of community involvement.

Study Outline

www.wwnorton.com/giddens5

Deviant Behavior

- Deviant behavior refers to actions that transgress commonly held norms. What is regarded as deviant can shift from time to time and place to place; "normal" behavior in one cultural setting may be labeled "deviant" in another.
- *Sanctions*, formal or informal, are applied by society to reinforce social norms. *Laws* are norms defined and enforced by governments; *crimes* are acts that are not permitted by those laws.

Biological and Psychological Theories of Crime and Deviance

- Biological and psychological theories have been developed claiming that crime and other forms of deviance are genetically determined, but these have been largely discredited. Sociologists argue that conformity and deviance intertwine in different social contexts. Divergencies of wealth and power in society strongly influence opportunities open to different groups of individuals and determine what kinds of activities are regarded as criminal. Criminal activities are learned in much the same way as are law-abiding ones and in general are directed toward the same needs and values.

Society and Crime: Sociological Theories

- Functionalist theories see crime and deviance as produced by structural tensions and a lack of moral regulation within society. Durkheim introduced the term *anomie* to refer to a feeling of anxiety and disorientation that comes with the breakdown of traditional life in modern society. Robert Merton extended the concept to include the strain felt by individuals whenever norms conflict with social reality. Subcultural explanations draw attention to groups, such as gangs, that reject mainstream values and replace them with norms celebrating defiance, delinquency, or nonconformity.
- *Interactionist theories* focus on deviance as a socially constructed phenomenon. Sutherland linked crime to *differential association*, the concept that individuals become delinquent through associating with people who are carriers of criminal norms. *Labeling theory*, a strain of interactionist theory that assumes that labeling someone as deviant will reinforce their deviant behavior, is important because it starts from the assumption that no act is intrinsically criminal (or normal). Labeling theorists are interested in how some behaviors come to be defined as deviant and why certain groups, but not others, are labeled as deviant.

- Conflict theories analyze crime and deviance in terms of the structure of society, competing interests between social groups, and the preservation of power among elites.
- *Control theories* posit that crime occurs when there are inadequate social or physical controls to deter it from happening. The growth of crime is linked to the growing number of opportunities and targets for crime in modern societies. The theory of broken windows suggests that there is a direct connection between the appearance of disorder and actual crime.

Gender and Crime

- Rates of criminality are much lower for women than for men, probably because of general socialization differences between men and women, and the greater involvement of men in nondomestic spheres. Unemployment and the "crisis of masculinity" have been linked to male crime rates. In some types of crimes, women are overwhelmingly the victims. Rape is almost certainly much more common than the official statistics reveal. There is a sense in which all women are victims of rape, since they have to take special precautions for their protection and live in fear of rape. Homosexual men and women experience high levels of criminal victimization and harassment, yet they are often seen as "deserving" of crime rather than innocent victims because of their marginalized position in society.

Types of Crime

- Popular fear about crime often focuses on street crimes—such as theft, burglary, and assault—that are largely the domain of young, working-class males. Official statistics reveal high rates of offense among young people, yet we should be wary of moral panics about youth crime. Much deviant behavior among youth, such as antisocial behavior and nonconformity, is not in fact criminal.
- *White-collar crime* and *corporate crime* refer to crimes carried out by those in the more affluent sectors of society. The consequences of such crime can be farther-reaching than the petty crimes of the poor, but there is less attention paid to them by law enforcement. *Organized crime* refers to institutionalized forms of criminal activity, in which many of the characteristics of orthodox organizations appear but the activities engaged in are systematically illegal. *Cybercrime* describes criminal activity that is carried out with the help of information technology, such as electronic money laundering and Internet fraud.

Crime, Deviance, and Social Order

- Prisons have developed partly to protect society and partly with the intention of reforming the criminal. Prisons do not seem to deter crime, and the degree to which they rehabilitate prisoners to face the outside world without relapsing into criminality is dubious. Alternatives to prison, such as community-based punishment, have been suggested.

Key Concepts

anomie (p. 175)
community policing (p. 196)
conflict theory (p. 178)
control theory (p. 178)
corporate crime (p. 186)
crime (p. 171)
cybercrime (p. 188)
deviance (p. 169)
deviant subculture (p. 170)
differential association (p. 177)
labeling theory (p. 177)
law (p. 171)
new criminology (p. 178)
norm (p. 169)
organized crime (p. 187)
primary deviation (p. 177)
psychopath (p. 174)
sanction (p. 171)
secondary deviation (p. 177)
shaming (p. 196)
white-collar crime (p. 186)

Review Questions

1. What is deviance?
   a. A transgression of social norms that are accepted by most people in a community
   b. Breaking the law
   c. The kind of behavior engaged in by members of groups that have been marginalized by society
   d. None of the above
2. What is the theory of differential association?
   a. Individuals become delinquents by associating with those who are different from themselves.
   b. Individuals become delinquents by associating with carriers of criminal norms.
   c. Individuals become delinquents by associating with a range of deviant groups.
   d. Individuals become delinquents by associating with such aspects of aggressive male culture as professional wrestling and hunting clubs.
3. Compared with ordinary crimes against property (robberies, burglaries, larceny, etc.), the amount of money stolen in white-collar crime (tax fraud, insurance fraud, etc.) is:
   a. about the same. Crimes against property cost the nation about as much as white-collar crime.
   b. less. White-collar crimes involve only one quarter of the money involved in crimes against property.
   c. more. White-collar crime involves perhaps forty times as much money as crimes against property.
   d. not really comparable. White-collar crimes such as embezzlement affect very few people.
4. Crime is sociological in nature because
   a. anomie is common in modern societies.
   b. the definition of crime depends on the social context.
   c. criminals are socialized into committing crimes.
   d. criminals tend to be psychopaths.
5. Why did Émile Durkheim think a certain amount of crime was functional for society?
   a. Because it gave a healthy release for male aggression.
   b. Because it highlighted the boundaries of social norms.
   c. Because it kept the police and court system active.
   d. Because the existence of crime makes law-abiding citizens more careful about protecting their property.
6. Why is the crime rate so much higher in the United States than in other industrialized countries?
   a. It isn't.
   b. Crime rates in most of America are close to the average for industrialized countries, but the U.S. average is pulled up by very high crime rates in New York City.
   c. It is caused by a combination of ready access to firearms, the influence of the "frontier tradition," and the violent subculture of American cities.
   d. It comes from the fast pace of American life and our bad diet: the potent concoction of junk food packed with carbohydrates and artificial sweeteners, endless traffic congestion, and violent television shows make Americans more bad tempered and hostile to one another than people in other industrialized countries.
7. What is target hardening?
   a. A technique to make it more difficult for crimes to take place by intervening directly in potential "crime situations"
   b. Any small sign of social disorder that will encourage more serious crime
   c. A form of punishing criminal and deviant behavior that attempts to maintain the ties of the offender to the community
   d. A theory that posits that crime occurs as a result of an imbalance between impulses toward criminal activity and the social or physical controls that deter it
8. Howard S. Becker found a number of reasons to account for a person becoming a marijuana smoker. Which of the following is not a factor mentioned by Becker?
   a. Acceptance into the marijuana subcultures
   b. Close association with experienced users

c. Peer pressure

d. Attitudes toward nonusers

9. What is the attitude toward capital punishment in the United States over the past few decades?

a. More people are in favor of capital punishment.

b. Fewer people are in favor of capital punishment.

c. There has been no change in attitude toward capital punishment during the past few decades.

d. There is no clear trend in people's attitudes toward capital punishment.

10. What is the essence of labeling theory?

a. Deviance is defined through the process of interaction between deviants and nondeviants.

b. Deviance is in the eye of the officeholder.

c. One person's deviance is another's indulgence.

d. Deviants resist the labels they are given by law enforcement authorities.

Thinking Sociologically Exercises

1. Briefly summarize several leading theories explaining crime and deviance presented in this chapter: differential association, anomie, labeling, conflict, and control theories. Which theory appeals to you more than the others? Explain why.

2. Explain how differences in power and social influence can play a significant role in defining and sanctioning deviant behavior.

Data Exercises

www.wwnorton.com/giddens5
Keyword: Data7

- How much do you know about patterns of crime in your community, your state, or in the United States as a whole? What are your sources of information—personal experiences, the experiences of family or friends, or the media? In the data exercise for Chapter 7 you will have a chance to study state-level crime rates and the changes in the rate over time in order to gain a better understanding of what the patterns are like.

PART THREE

STRUCTURES
OF POWER

Power is an ever-present phenomenon in social life. In all human groups, some individuals have more authority or influence than others, while groups themselves have varying degrees of power. Power and inequality tend to be closely linked. The powerful are able to accumulate valued resources, such as property and wealth; possession of such resources is in turn a means of generating more power.

In this part, we look at some of the main systems of power and inequality. Chapter 8 discusses stratification and class structure—the ways in which inequalities are distributed within societies. Chapter 9, on global inequality, builds on this and examines the ways in which inequalities are distributed across societies. Chapter 10 then analyzes the differences and inequalities between men and women and how these inequalities are tied to other forms of inequality based on class and race. Chapter 11, on race and ethnicity, examines the tensions and hostilities often found between people who are physically or culturally different from one another. Chapter 12, on aging, discusses the experience of growing old and analyzes the social problems resulting from this experience. Chapter 13 analyzes the state, political power, and social movements. Governments are specialists in power; they are the source of the directives that influence many of our daily activities. On the other hand, they are also the focus of resistance and rebellion, political action that can lead to far-reaching political and social change.

Systems of Stratification

Learn about social stratification and the importance of social background in an individual's chances for material success.

Classes in Western Societies Today

Know the class differences that exist in U.S. society, what they are influenced by, and how they are defined and determined.

Inequality in the United States: A Growing Gap Between Rich and Poor

Recognize the many ways in which the gap between rich and poor has grown larger.

Social Mobility

Understand the dynamics of social mobility, and think about your own mobility.

Poverty in the United States

Learn about the conditions of poverty in the United States today, competing explanations for why it exists, and means for combating it.

Social Exclusion

Learn the processes by which people become marginalized in a society and the forms that it takes.

Theories of Stratification in Modern Societies

Become acquainted with the most influential theories of stratification—those of Karl Marx, Max Weber, and Erik Olin Wright.

Growing Inequality in the United States

CHAPTER EIGHT

STRATIFICATION, CLASS, AND INEQUALITY

across the street from the campus of New Mexico State University, there is a juice bar and restaurant called Island Juice. The restaurant, which specializes in fruit smoothies and tortilla-wrapped sandwiches ("wraps"), is owned by Richard Rivera, who had the idea for it while attending Chapman University in southern California, where smoothies and wraps became popular in the mid-1990s. As a college student, Rivera never thought he would own a business like Island Juice. Rivera was born in Brooklyn, New York, and grew up in a government-owned housing project. His parents did not attend college and worked most of their lives in a factory. Money was always short in Rivera's family, but his parents saved enough to send him to private Catholic schools, where he excelled in all of his classes and eventually earned a scholarship to Chapman University. He was the first in his family ever to attend college. At Chapman, he studied computer information systems and then later received a master's degree in finance. On receiving his master's degree, he went to work for a number of Fortune 500 companies. Meanwhile, he had the idea for Island Juice and, at the age of twenty-seven, decided to open it in Las Cruces, New Mexico. Between the success of his business and the income from his job, Rivera earns over $200,000 per year. He is living the "American dream."

Is Richard Rivera's story just an isolated incident or does it somehow represent trends in contemporary American society? Will you, like Richard, also make more money than your parents? What about other members of your generation who, unlike you, do not go to college? How much chance does someone from a lowly background have of reaching the top of the economic ladder? For every Richard Rivera in our society, how many people struggle to make ends meet? Why do economic inequalities exist in our society? How unequal are modern societies? What are the reasons for the persistence of poverty in affluent countries like the United States? What social factors will influence your economic position in society? Are your chances any different if you are a woman? How does the globalization of the economy affect your life chances? How about the life chances of others?

These are just a few of the sorts of questions that sociologists ask and try to answer. These questions are the focus of this chapter. The study of social inequalities is one of the most important areas of sociology, because our material resources determine a great deal about our lives.

Sociologists speak of **social stratification** to describe inequalities among individuals and groups within human societies. Often we think of stratification in terms of assets or property, but it can also occur on the basis of other attributes, such as gender, age, religious affiliation, or military rank. The three key aspects of social stratification are class, status, and power (Weber, 1947). Although they frequently overlap, this is not always the case. The "rich and famous" often enjoy high status; their wealth often provides political influence and sometimes direct access to political power. Yet there are exceptions. Drug lords, for example, may be wealthy and powerful, yet they usually enjoy low status. On the other hand, when Mahatma Gandhi died in 1948, his total worldly possessions could be carried in his blanket. Although he chose to live in poverty, he enjoyed the highest status and power in India, having led his country to independence from Britain through nonviolent civil disobedience. In this chapter, we focus on stratification in terms of inequalities based on wealth and income, status, and power. In later chapters, we will look at the ways in which gender (Chapter 10), race and ethnicity (Chapter 11), and age (Chapter 12) all play a role in stratification.

Individuals and groups enjoy unequal access to rewards on the basis of their position within the stratification scheme. Thus, stratification can most simply be defined as **structured inequalities** among different groupings of people. Sociologists believe that these inequalities are built into the system, rather than resulting from individual differences or chance occurrences, such as winning a lottery. It is useful to think of stratification like the geological layering of rock in the earth's surface. Societies can be seen as consisting of "strata" in a hierarchy, with the more favored at the top and the less privileged nearer the bottom.

We can speak of an American system of stratification because individuals' chances for material success are strongly influenced by their social background. We will study stratification and inequality in the United States later in the chapter,

but first we need to analyze the different types of stratification that exist and have existed in the past.

Systems of Stratification

All socially stratified systems share three characteristics:

1. **The rankings apply to social categories of people who share a common characteristic without necessarily interacting or identifying with each other.** Women may be ranked differently from men; wealthy people differently from the poor. This does not mean that individuals from a particular category cannot change their rank; however it does mean that the category continues to exist even if individuals move out of it and into another category.

2. **People's life experiences and opportunities depend heavily on how their social category is ranked.** Being male or female, black or white, upper class or working class makes a big difference in terms of your life chances—often as big a difference as personal effort or good fortune (such as winning a lottery).

3. **The ranks of different social categories tend to change very slowly over time.** In U.S. society, for example, only in the last quarter century have women as a whole begun to achieve equality with men (see Chapter 10). Only in the past quarter century have significant numbers of African Americans begun to obtain economic and political equality with whites—even though slavery was abolished nearly a century and a half ago and discrimination outlawed in the 1950s and 1960s (see Chapter 11).

As you saw in Chapter 3, stratified societies have changed throughout human history. The earliest human societies, which were based on hunting and gathering, had very little social stratification—mainly because there was very little by way of wealth or other resources to be divided up. The development of agriculture produced considerably more wealth and, as a result, a great increase in stratification. Social stratification in agricultural societies increasingly came to resemble a pyramid, with a large number of people at the bottom and a successively smaller number of people as you move toward the top. Today, industrial and postindustrial societies are extremely complex; their stratification is more likely to resemble a teardrop, with large number of people in the middle and lower-middle ranks (the so-called middle class), a slightly smaller number of people at the bottom, and very few people as one moves toward the top.

But before turning to stratification in modern societies, let's first review the three basic systems of stratification: slavery, caste, and class.

Slavery

Slavery is an extreme form of inequality, in which certain people are owned as property by others. The legal conditions of slave ownership have varied considerably among different societies. Sometimes slaves were deprived of almost all rights by law, as was the case on Southern plantations in the United States. In other societies, their position was more akin to that of servants. For example, in the ancient Greek city-state of Athens, some slaves occupied positions of great responsibility. They were excluded from political positions and from the military but were accepted in most other types of occupation. Some were literate and worked as government administrators; many were trained in craft skills. Even so, not all slaves could count on such a good fate. For the less fortunate, their days began and ended in hard labor in the mines.

Throughout history, slaves have often fought back against their subjection; the slave rebellions in the American South before the Civil War are one example. Because of such resistance, systems of slave labor have tended to be unstable. High productivity could only be achieved through constant supervision and brutal punishment. Slave-labor systems eventually broke down, partly because of the struggles they provoked and partly because economic or other incentives motivate people to produce more effectively than does direct compulsion. Slavery is simply not economically efficient. Moreover, from about the eighteenth century on, many people in Europe and America came to see slavery as morally wrong. Today, slavery is illegal in every country of the world, but it still exists in some places. Recent research has documented that people are taken by force and held against their will—from enslaved brick makers in Pakistan to sex slaves in Thailand and domestic slaves in France. Slavery remains a significant human rights violation in the world today (Bales, 1999).

Caste Systems

A **caste system** is a social system in which one's social status is given for life. In **caste societies,** therefore, different social levels are closed, so that all individuals must remain at the social level of their birth throughout life. Everyone's social status is based on personal characteristics—such as perceived race or ethnicity (often based on such physical characteristics as skin color), parental religion, or parental caste—that are accidents of birth and are therefore believed to be unchangeable. A person is born into a caste and remains there for life. In a sense, caste societies can be seen as a special type of class society—in which class position is ascribed at birth, rather than achieved through personal accomplishment. They have typically been found in agricultural societies that have not yet developed industrial capitalist economies, such as rural India or South Africa prior to the end of white rule in 1992.

Prior to modern times, caste systems were found throughout the world. In Europe, for example, Jews were frequently treated as a separate caste, forced to live in restricted neighborhoods and barred from intermarrying (and in some instances even interacting) with non-Jews. The term *ghetto,* for example, is said to derive from the Venetian word for "foundry," the site of one of Europe's first official Jewish ghettos, established by the government of Venice in 1516. The term eventually came to refer to those sections of European towns where Jews were legally compelled to live, long before it was used to describe minority neighborhoods in U.S. cities, with their castelike qualities of racial and ethnic segregation.

In caste systems, intimate contact with members of other castes is strongly discouraged. Such "purity" of a caste is often maintained by rules of **endogamy,** marriage within one's social group as required by custom or law.

CASTE IN INDIA AND SOUTH AFRICA

The few remaining caste systems in the world are being seriously challenged by globalization. The Indian caste system, for example, reflects Hindu religious beliefs and is more than two thousand years old. According to Hindu beliefs, there are four major castes, each roughly associated with broad occupational groupings. The four castes consist of the *Brahmins* (scholars and spiritual leaders) on top, followed by the *Ksyatriyas* (soldiers and rulers), the *Vaisyas* (farmers and merchants), and the *Shudras* (laborers and artisans). Beneath the four castes are those known as the "untouchables" or *Dalits* ("oppressed people"), who—as their name suggests—are to be avoided at all costs. Untouchables are limited to the worst jobs in society such as removing human waste, and they often resort to begging and searching in garbage for their food. In traditional areas of India, some members of higher castes still regard physical contact with untouchables to be so contaminating that mere touching requires cleansing rituals. India made it illegal to discriminate on the basis of caste in 1949, but aspects of the caste system remain in full force today, particularly in rural areas.

As India's modern capitalist economy brings people of different castes together, whether it be in the same workplace, airplane, or restaurant, it is increasingly difficult to maintain

Women from the Dalit caste (formally known as Untouchables) earn a living as sewage scavengers in the slums of Ranchi. They are paid between 30 and 100 rupees per house per month for retrieving human waste from residential dry latrines and emptying the buckets into nearby gutters and streams.

the rigid barriers required to sustain the caste system. As more and more of India becomes touched by globalization, it seems reasonable to assume that its caste system, will weaken still further.

Before its abolition in 1992, the South African caste system, termed *apartheid* (pronounced "a-PART-ide"; Afrikaans for "separateness"), rigidly separated black Africans, Indians, "colored" (people of mixed races), and Asians from whites. In this case, caste was based entirely on race. Whites, who made up only 15 percent of the total population, controlled virtually all of the country's wealth, owned most of the usable land, ran the principal businesses and industries, and had a monopoly on political power, since blacks lacked the right to vote. Blacks—who made up three quarters of the population—were segregated into impoverished *bantustans* ("homelands") and were allowed out only to work for the white minority.

Apartheid, widespread discrimination, and oppression created intense conflict between the white minority and the black, mixed-race, and Asian majority. Decades of often violent struggle against apartheid finally proved successful in the 1990s. The most powerful black organization, the African National Congress (ANC), mobilized an economically devastating global boycott of South African businesses, forcing South Africa's white leaders to dismantle apartheid, which was abolished by popular vote among South African whites in 1992. In 1994, in the country's first ever multiracial elections, the black majority won control of the government, and Nelson Mandela—the black leader of the ANC, who had spent twenty-seven years imprisoned by the white government—was elected president.

CASTE IN THE UNITED STATES

In the South in United States before the Civil War, African Americans were officially members of a lower caste. As in South Africa, their caste was based on their race. Most African Americans were born as slaves and died as slaves. They were forbidden to marry across racial lines and were legally treated as the property of their white "owners." Although the North's victory in the Civil War officially put an end to slavery in 1865, legal segregation of schools, restaurants, and public facilities maintained aspects of the caste system in many southern states for another century. The U.S. Supreme Court, in the landmark *Brown v. Board of Education* decision in 1954, ended legal segregation in public schools, and the Civil Rights Act of 1964 abolished discrimination on the basis of race. The treatment of African Americans as a separate caste is no longer legal in the United States, but it continues nonetheless in the form of discrimination and prejudice: For example, it was not until November 2000 that Alabama voters deleted a part of the state's constitution that prohibited interracial marriages. Studies show that when equally qualified black and white individuals apply for the same job, whites are much more likely than blacks to be hired (Bendick, Jackson, and Reinoso, 1993). Blacks are also more likely than whites to be turned down for bank loans for mortgages, automobile insurance, or small businesses (*Business Journal,* 2000; Hamilton, 2000).

Class

The concept of **class** is most important for analyzing stratification in industrialized societies like the United States. Everyone has heard of class, but most people in everyday talk use the word in a vague way. As employed in sociology, it has some precision.

A social class is a large group of people who occupy a similar economic position in the wider society. The concept of life chances, introduced by Max Weber, is the best way to understand what class means. Your **life chances** are the opportunities you have for achieving economic prosperity. A person from a humble background, for example, has less chance of ending up wealthy than someone from a more prosperous one. And the best chance an individual has of being wealthy is to start off as wealthy in the first place.

America, it is always said, is the land of opportunity. For some, this is so. There are many examples of people who have risen from lowly circumstances to positions of great wealth and power. There are many more cases, however, of people like Richard Rivera who have done better than their parents but not become superrich. And yet there are more cases of people who have not, including a disproportionate share of women and members of minority groups. The idea of life chances is important because it emphasizes that although class is an important influence on what happens in our lives, it is not completely determining. Class divisions affect which neighborhoods we live in, what lifestyles we follow, and even which sexual or marriage partners we choose (Mare, 1991; Massey, 1996). Yet they don't fix people for life in specific social positions, as the older systems of stratification did. A person born into a caste position has no opportunity of escaping from it; the same isn't true of class.

Class systems differ from slavery and castes in four main respects:

1. **Class systems are fluid.** Unlike the other types of strata, classes are not established by legal or religious provisions. The boundaries between classes are never clear cut. There are no formal restrictions on intermarriage between people from different classes.

2. **Class positions are in some part achieved.** An individual's class is not simply assigned at birth, as is the case in the other types of stratification systems. Social mobility—movement upward and downward in the class structure—is more common than in the other types.

3. **Class is economically based.** Classes depend on economic differences between groups of individuals—inequalities in the possession of material resources. In the other types of stratification systems, noneconomic factors (such as race in the former South African caste system) are generally most important.

4. **Class systems are large scale and impersonal.** In the other types of stratification systems, inequalities are expressed primarily in personal relationships of duty or obligation—between slave and master or lower- and higher-caste individuals. Class systems, by contrast, operate mainly through large-scale, impersonal associations. For instance, one major basis of class differences is in inequalities of pay and working conditions.

WILL CASTE GIVE WAY TO CLASS?

There is some evidence that globalization will hasten the end of legally sanctioned caste systems throughout the world. Most official caste systems have already given way to class-based ones in industrial capitalist societies; South Africa, mentioned earlier, is the most prominent recent example (Berger, 1986). Modern industrial production requires that people move about freely, work at whatever jobs they are suited or able to do, and change jobs frequently according to economic conditions. The rigid restrictions found in caste systems interfere with this necessary freedom. Furthermore, as the world increasingly becomes a single economic unit, caste-like relationships will become more and more vulnerable to economic pressures. Nonetheless, elements of caste persist even in postindustrial societies. For example, some Indian immigrants to the United States seek to arrange traditional marriages for their children along caste lines, while the relatively small number of intermarriages between blacks and whites in the United States suggests the strength of caste barriers.

IS INEQUALITY DECLINING IN CLASS-BASED SOCIETIES?

There is some evidence that at least until recently, the class systems in mature capitalist societies became increasingly open to movement between classes, thereby reducing the level of inequality. In 1955, the Nobel Prize–winning economist Simon Kuznets proposed a hypothesis that has since been called the **Kuznets curve:** a formula showing that inequality increases during the early stages of capitalist development, then declines, and eventually stabilizes at a relatively low level (Kuznets, 1955; see Figure 8.1). Studies of European countries, the United States, and Canada suggested that inequality peaked in these places before World War II, declined through the 1950s, and remained roughly the same through the 1970s (Berger, 1986; Nielsen, 1994). Lowered postwar inequality was due in part to economic expansion in industrial societies, which created opportunities for people at the bottom to move up, and because of government health insurance, welfare, and other programs aimed at reducing inequality. However, Kuznets's prediction may well turn out to apply only to industrial societies. As you will see later in this chapter, the emergence of postindustrial society has brought with it an increase in inequality in the United States.

Classes in Western Societies Today

Let us begin our exploration of class differences in modern societies by looking at basic divisions of income, wealth, educational attainment, and occupational status within the population as a whole.

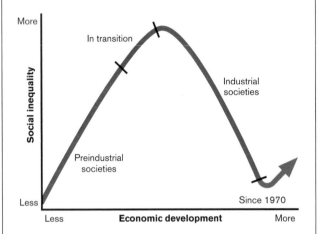
Income

Income refers to wages and salaries earned from paid occupations, plus unearned money from investments. One of the most significant changes occurring in Western countries over the past century has been the rising real income of the majority of the working population. (Real income is income excluding rises owing to inflation, to provide a fixed standard of comparison from year to year.) Blue-collar workers in Western societies now earn three to four times as much in real income as their counterparts at the turn of the century, even if their real income has dropped over the past twenty years. Gains for white-collar, managerial, and professional workers have been higher still. In terms of earnings per person (per capita) and the range of goods and services that can be purchased, the majority of the population today are vastly more affluent than any peoples have previously been in human history. One of the most important reasons for this growth is the increasing productivity—output per worker—that has been

secured through technological development in industry. The volume of goods and services produced per worker has risen more or less continually since the 1900s.

Nevertheless, income distribution is quite unequal. In 2001, the top 5 percent of earners in the United States received 21 percent of total income; the highest 20 percent obtained 47.7 percent; and the bottom 20 percent received only 4.2 percent (see Figure 8.2). Between 1977 and 2001, income inequality has increased dramatically. The average pretax earnings of the bottom 80 percent of people in the United States declined by 11.7 percent (U.S. Bureau of the Census, 2002). During the same period, the richest fifth saw their incomes grow by 16.6 percent before taxes, while the richest 5 percent of the population increased their share of all income by over 40 percent—and the tax burden on these people was lower in 2001 than it had been in 1977. For the top 1 percent of earners, incomes approximately doubled during the same period. And despite the growth of the economy and the creation of millions of new jobs, these trends continued throughout the 1990s, leading some observers to deem the United States a "two-tiered society" (Freeman, 1999).

Wealth

Wealth refers to all assets individuals own: cash, savings and checking accounts, investments in stocks, bonds, real estate properties, and so on. While most people earn their income from their work, the wealthy often derive the bulk of theirs from investments, some of them inherited. Some scholars argue that wealth—not income—is the real indicator of social class.

Wealth is highly concentrated in the United States, with enormous differences according to income, age, and education. The wealthiest 10 percent of families in 2001, for example, had a median net worth of $833,600—105 times as much as the poorest 20 percent of families, whose median net worth was only $7,900 (see Table 8.1). Education also pays off in terms of wealth: The median net worth of college graduates is more than eight times greater than that of high school dropouts. Owning a home makes a great difference, since homes are the principal asset for most families: Homeowners' net worth is $171,700, compared with only $4,800 for renters. Finally, age matters also, at least to some extent: Net worth, like income, increases with age, although it peaks by age seventy-five, after which savings are likely to be used as income and thus depleted.

If one excludes the ownership of cars and homes—which for most people are not really sources of wealth that can be used to pay the bills or used to get richer—the difference in wealth between high-income families and everyone else is even more pronounced. Net financial assets are far lower for minority groups than whites (Oliver and Shapiro, 1995). Be-

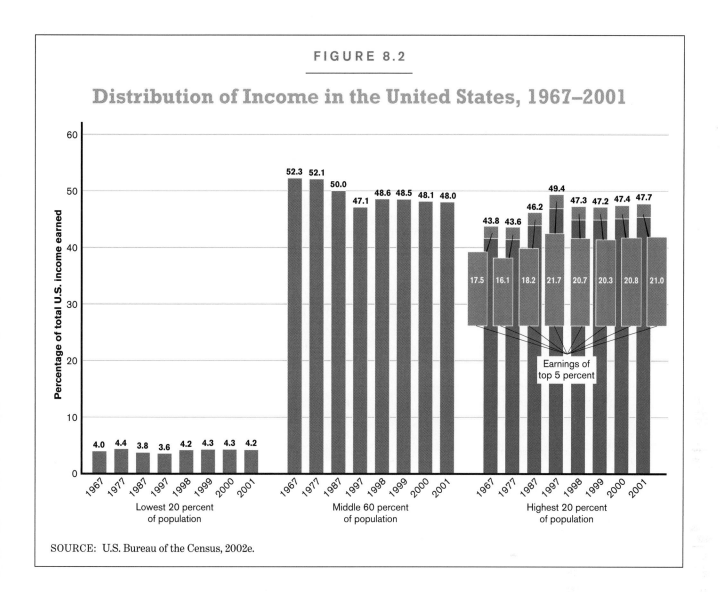

FIGURE 8.2

Distribution of Income in the United States, 1967–2001

Percentage of total U.S. income earned

Lowest 20 percent of population: 1967: 4.0, 1977: 4.4, 1987: 3.8, 1997: 3.6, 1998: 4.2, 1999: 4.3, 2000: 4.3, 2001: 4.2

Middle 60 percent of population: 1967: 52.3, 1977: 52.1, 1987: 50.0, 1997: 47.1, 1998: 48.6, 1999: 48.5, 2000: 48.1, 2001: 48.0

Highest 20 percent of population: 1967: 43.8, 1977: 43.6, 1987: 46.2, 1997: 49.4, 1998: 47.3, 1999: 47.2, 2000: 47.4, 2001: 47.7

Earnings of top 5 percent: 1967: 17.5, 1977: 16.1, 1987: 18.2, 1997: 21.7, 1998: 20.7, 1999: 20.3, 2000: 20.8, 2001: 21.0

SOURCE: U.S. Bureau of the Census, 2002e.

tween 1983 and 2000, the net financial assets of white Americans nearly tripled, from $19,900 to $58,716 (see Table 8.2). African Americans, on average, began to accumulate net financial assets only in the 1990s; by 2000, the median net worth was $6,166. Households of Hispanic origin have only recently begun to realize this important source of wealth; their median financial net worth has grown dramatically from effectively zero in 1998 to surpass African Americans with a median net worth of $6,766 in 2000.

What are some of the reasons for the racial disparity in wealth? Is it simply that blacks have less money with which to purchase assets? To some degree, the answer is yes. The old adage "It takes money to make money" is a fact of life for those who start with little or no wealth. Since whites historically have enjoyed higher incomes and levels of wealth than blacks, whites are able to accrue even more wealth, which they then are able to pass on to their children (Conley, 1999). In fact,

economists estimate that more than half the wealth that one accumulates in a lifetime can be traced to a person's progenitors. But family advantages are not the only factors. Oliver and Shapiro argued that it is easier for whites to obtain assets, even when they have fewer resources than blacks, because discrimination plays a major role in the racial gap in home ownership. Blacks are rejected for mortgages 60 percent more often than whites, even when they have the same qualifications and credit worthiness. When blacks do receive mortgages, the authors found, they pay on average a 0.5 percent higher interest rate, or about $12,000 more over the life of a thirty-year, median fixed-rate mortgage. These issues are particularly important since home ownership is the primary means of the accumulation of wealth for most American families.

In 1998, the wealthiest 1 percent of all Americans accounted for 38 percent of the nation's total net worth; the top 20 percent accounted for 83 percent of net worth. Of the top

TABLE 8.1

Median Family Net Worth, by Percentile of Family Income, Age, and Housing Tenure, 2001

	PERCENTAGE OF ALL U.S. FAMILIES	MEDIAN NET WORTH ($)
All families	100	86,100
Percentile of income		
Less than 20	20	7,900
20–39.9	20	37,200
40–59.9	20	62,500
60–79.9	20	141,500
80–89.9	10	263,100
90–100	10	833,600
Education of head of household		
No high school diploma	16	25,500
High school diploma	31.7	58,100
Some college	18.3	71,600
College degree	34	213,300
Age of head (years)		
Less than 35	22.7	11,600
35–44	22.3	77,600
45–54	20.6	132,000
55–64	13.2	181,500
65–74	10.7	176,300
75 or more	10.4	151,400
Housing status		
Owner	67.7	171,700
Renter or other	32.3	4,800
Percentile of net worth		
Less than 25	25	1,100
25–49.9	25	40,800
50–74.9	25	156,100
75–89.9	15	430,200
90–100	10	1,301,900

SOURCE: U.S. Federal Reserve Board, "Family Net Worth, by Selected Characteristics of Families, 1992, 1995, 1998, and 2001" surveys, December 2003. www.federalreserve.gov/pubs/bulletin/2003/0103lead.pdf.

TABLE 8.2

Median Financial Net Worth ($), 1983–2000: Whites, African Americans, and Latinos

RACE/ETHNICITY	1983	1989	1992	1995	1998	2000
White	19,900	26,900	21,900	19,300	37,600	67,000
African American	0	0	200	200	1,200	6,166
Latino	0	0	0	0	0	6,766

SOURCE: Hartman, 2000; Wolff, 2000; U.S. Census Bureau, 2003.

20 percent, 95 percent were white, 4 percent were Asian, and 1 percent were black (Keister, 2000). At the other end of the scale, in 1998 the bottom 60 percent of Americans accounted for less than 5 percent of the country's total net worth (Wolff, 2000). For this group, accumulating stocks or bonds in hopes of cashing them in someday to pay for their children's college educations is not even a fantasy. In fact, it is more likely that they owe far more than they own. In recent years, many Americans have gone increasingly into debt, using credit cards and refinancing their mortgages to pay for their lifestyles, rather than relying on their earnings. The average amount owed on credit cards increased nearly fivefold between 1970 and 1998, to more than $4,000 (U.S. Federal Reserve Board, 2000). During the following two years, credit card debt increased another 11 percent. Increased debt means less net worth, which for Americans as a whole declined in 2000 for the first time since the government began recording such figures in 1945 (Leonhardt, 2001).

Wealth is highly unequal globally as well. The richest 1 percent of the world population have incomes equivalent to the poorest 57 percent. But even the poorest 10 percent of Americans are better off than two thirds of the world population (*The Guardian*, 2002). We'll come back to this in Chapter 20.

Differences in wealth often take the form of differences in privilege, which in turn affects a person's life chances as much as income does. Members of Congress, high-level military officers at the Pentagon, and White House staff members do not have gargantuan salaries like the chief executive officers of corporations. What they do have, however, are privileges that translate into wealth. Members of Congress and White House staff members enjoy access to limousines and military aircraft, not to mention expense accounts that pay for many of their meals and hotel bills when they travel.

Education

Sociologists also believe that education, or the number of years of schooling a person has completed, is an important dimension of social stratification. The value of a college education has increased significantly in the past twenty years as a result of the increased demand for and wages paid to educated workers in the more computer- and information-based economy (Danziger and Gottschalk, 1995). Education is one of the strongest predictors of one's occupation, income, and wealth later in life. As we will see later in this chapter, how much education one receives is often influenced by the social class of one's parents.

Racial differences in levels of education persist, and this explains in part why racial differences in income and wealth also persist. In 2001, roughly 89 percent of whites and Asian Americans had completed high school, whereas only 79.5 percent of African Americans had a high school degree (Infoplease.com, 2003).

Occupation

Status refers to the prestige that goes along with one's social position. In the United States and other industrialized societies, occupation is an important indicator of one's social standing. Occupational status depends heavily on one's level of educational attainment. In fact, in studies where persons are asked to rate jobs in terms of how "prestigious" they are, the occupations that are ranked most highly are those requiring the most education (Treiman, 1977). These studies use what is called the Standard International Occupational Prestige Scale. Research shows that physicians, college professors, lawyers,

Income Inequality
in the Global Economy

Although many economists, politicians, and businesspeople have sung the praises of globalization, there is reason to approach such claims cautiously. Globalization may well be increasing economic inequality in the world's advanced industrial societies. Although the U.S. economy has been consistently growing since the end of the recession of 1982–1983, the gap between the wages of high-skilled and low-skilled workers has also been increasing. In 1979, college graduates taking entry-level positions earned on average 37 percent more than those without college degrees. By 1993, the differential had grown to 77 percent (*USA Today* magazine, May 1998). And although this growing "wage premium" has encouraged more Americans to go to college—such that nearly 27 percent of the American work force had college degrees in 2002, compared with 18 percent in 1979 (U. S. Census, 2002c; *Business Week,* December 15, 1997)—it has also helped widen the gap between the wealthiest and the poorest workers. As an analyst for the U.S. Department of Labor put it, "it is by now almost a

and dentists are at the top of the scale, while garbage collectors and gas station attendants are at the bottom. About at the middle are jobs such as registered nurse, computer programmer, and insurance sales representative. Interestingly, similar rankings occur regardless of who does the ranking and in what country. Comparisons of status rankings across fifty-five countries show that there is a general agreement as to how high status an occupation is (see Table 8.3).

Class and Lifestyle

In analyzing class location, sociologists have traditionally relied on conventional indicators of class location such as market position, relations to the means of production, and occupation. Some recent authors, however, argue that we should evaluate individuals' class location not only, or even mainly, in terms of economics and employment, but also in relation to cultural fac-

tors such as lifestyle and consumption patterns. According to this approach, our current age is one in which symbols and markers related to *consumption* are playing an ever greater role in daily life. Individual identities are structured to a greater extent around *lifestyle choices*—such as how to dress, what to eat, how to care for one's body, and where to relax—and less around more traditional class indicators such as employment.

The French sociologist Pierre Bourdieu sees class groups as identifiable according to their varying levels of *cultural and economic capital* (1984). Increasingly, individuals distinguish themselves from others not according to economic or occupational factors, but on the basis of cultural tastes and leisure pursuits. They are aided in this process by the proliferation of "need merchants," the growing number of people involved in presenting and representing goods and services—either symbolic or actual—for consumption within the capitalist system. Advertisers, marketers, fashion designers, style consultants, interior designers, personal trainers, therapists, and Web

platitude . . . that wage inequality has increased quite sharply since the late 1970s, for both men and women" (U.S. Dept. of Labor, 1997).

Although few studies have directly implicated globalization as a cause of this growing inequality, there is reason to view it as an indirect causal factor. It is true that whereas countries such as the United States, Canada, and the United Kingdom have witnessed a growth in earnings inequality since the late 1970s, countries like Germany, Japan, and France—which have, presumably, been equally affected by the forces of globalization—have seen either a decline or little change in inequality. At the same time, many of the factors that sociologists see as causes of inequality are clearly linked to globalization. First, in some cases, U.S. companies that manufacture in the United States lowered wages to compete with other U.S. firms that manufacture their products overseas, especially in the developing world. Second, globalization has encouraged immigration to the United States. Immigrants—many of whom are relegated to low-wage work—increase the competition for jobs among those in the low-wage labor pool, lowering wages somewhat in this segment of the labor market. Third, globalization has undermined the strength of U.S. labor unions. A number of studies have shown that when firms that used to do the bulk of their manufacturing in one region begin to spread their manufac-

turing base out across countries and continents, it becomes increasingly difficult for unions to organize workers and negotiate with management. But strong unions decrease earnings inequality through their commitment to raising wages.

Of course, globalization is not the only cause of inequality. Many researchers, for example, blame increasing inequality on the spectacular growth of high-tech industries, which employ mostly well-paid, white-collar workers and offer little in the way of traditional blue-collar employment. Still, it seems safe to conclude that globalization is not without its role in the growing stratification of American society.

page designers, to name but a few, are all involved in influencing cultural tastes and promoting lifestyle choices among an ever widening community of consumers.

In general, it would be difficult to dispute that stratification within classes, as well as between classes, has come to depend not only on occupational differences but also on differences in consumption and lifestyle. This is borne out by looking at trends in society as a whole. The rapid expansion of the service economy and the entertainment and leisure industry, for example, reflects an increasing emphasis on consumption within industrialized countries. Modern societies have become consumer societies, geared to the acquisition of material goods. In some respects a consumer society is a "mass society," where class differences are to a degree overridden; thus, people from different class backgrounds may all watch similar television programs or shop for clothing in the same mall stores. Yet class differences can also become *intensified* through variations in lifestyle and "taste" (Bourdieu, 1984).

While bearing these shifts in mind, however, it is impossible to ignore the critical role played by economic factors in the reproduction of social inequalities. For the most part, individuals experiencing extreme social and material deprivations are not doing so as part of a lifestyle choice. Rather, their circumstances are constrained by factors relating to the economic and occupational structure (Crompton, 1998).

A Picture of the U.S. Class Structure

Although money clearly cannot buy everything, one's class position can make an enormous difference in terms of lifestyle. Most sociologists identify social classes in terms of wealth and income, noting how social class makes a difference in terms of consumption, education, health, and access to political power.

TABLE 8.3

Occupational Prestige in the United States and Around the World

OCCUPATION	UNITED STATES	AVERAGE OF 55 COUNTRIES	OCCUPATION	UNITED STATES	AVERAGE OF 55 COUNTRIES
Supreme Court judge	85	82	Professional athlete	51	48
College president	82	86	Social worker	50	56
Physician	82	78	Electrician	49	44
College professor	78	78	Secretary	46	53
Lawyer	75	73	Real estate agent	44	49
Dentist	74	70	Farmer	44	47
Architect	71	72	Carpenter	43	37
Psychologist	71	66	Plumber	41	34
Airline pilot	70	66	Mail carrier	40	33
Electrical engineer	69	65	Jazz musician	37	38
Biologist	68	69	Bricklayer	36	34
Clergy	67	60	Barber	36	30
Sociologist	65	67	Truck driver	31	33
Accountant	65	55	Factory worker	29	29
Banker	63	67	Store sales clerk	27	34
High school teacher	63	64	Bartender	25	23
Registered nurse	62	54	Lives on public aid	25	16
Pharmacist	61	64	Cab driver	22	28
Veterinarian	60	61	Gas station attendant	22	25
Classical musician	59	56	Janitor	22	21
Police officer	59	40	Waiter or waitress	20	23
Actor or actress	55	52	Garbage collector	13	13
Athletic coach	53	50	Street sweeper	11	13
Journalist	52	55	Shoe shiner	9	12

SOURCE: Treiman, 1997.

The purpose of the following discussion is to describe broad class differences in the United States. Bear in mind that there are no sharply defined boundaries between the classes.

THE UPPER CLASS

The **upper class** consists of the very wealthiest Americans—those households earning more than $145,099 or approximately 5 percent of all American households (U.S. Bureau of the Census, 2002a). Most Americans in the upper class are wealthy but not superrich. They are likely to own a large suburban home as well as a town house or a vacation home, to drive expensive automobiles, to fly first class to vacations abroad, to educate their children in private schools and colleges, and to have their desires attended to by a staff of servants. Their wealth stems in large part from their substantial investments, from stocks and bonds to real estate. They are politically influential at the national, state, and local levels. The upper class does include the superwealthy as well—the heads of major corporations, people who have made large amounts of money through investments or real estate, those fortunate enough to have inherited great wealth from their parents, a few highly successful celebrities and professional athletes, and a handful of others.

At the very top of this group are the superrich, people who have accumulated vast fortunes permitting them to enjoy a lifestyle unimaginable to most Americans. The superrich are highly self-conscious of their unique and privileged social class position; some give generously to such worthy causes as the fine arts, hospitals, and charities. Their homes are often lavish and sometimes filled with collections of fine art. Their common class identity is strengthened by such things as being listed in the social register or having attended the same exclusive private secondary schools (to which they also send their children). They sit on the same corporate boards of directors and belong to the same private clubs. They contribute large sums of money to their favorite politicians and are likely to be on a first-name basis with members of Congress and perhaps even with the president (Domhoff, 1998).

The turn of this century saw extraordinary opportunities for the accumulation of such wealth. Globalization is one reason. Those entrepreneurs who are able to invest globally often prosper, both by selling products to foreign consumers, and by making profits cheaply by using low-wage labor in developing countries. The information revolution is another reason for the accumulation of wealth. Before the dot-com bubble finally burst in 2001, young entrepreneurs with startup high-tech companies such as Yahoo! or eBay made legendary fortunes. As a consequence, the number of superrich Americans has exploded in recent years. At the end of World War II, there were only thirteen thousand people worth a million dollars or more in the United States. In 2004, there were nearly 5 *million* millionaires in the United States, along with 277 *billionaires* (*Forbes,* 2004). The four hundred richest Americans are worth more than a *trillion* dollars—equal to almost one tenth the gross domestic product of the United States and only slightly less than the gross domestic product of China (Sklair, 1999).

Unlike "old-money" families such as the Rockefellers or the Vanderbilts, who accumulated their wealth in earlier generations and thus are viewed as a sort of American aristocracy, this "new wealth" often consists of upstart entrepreneurs such as Microsoft's Bill Gates, whose net worth—estimated by *Forbes* at $46.6 billion in 2004—makes him the wealthiest individual in the world (*Forbes,* 2004).

THE MIDDLE CLASS

When Americans are asked to identify their social class, the large majority claim to be middle class. The reason is partly the American cultural belief that the United States is relatively free of class distinctions. Few people want to be identified as being too rich or too poor. Most Americans seem to think that others are not very different from their immediate

Jerry Yang, cofounder of Yahoo! was part of the explosion of wealth associated with the dot-com information revolution.

family, friends, and coworkers (Vanneman and Cannon, 1987; Simpson, Stark, and Jackson, 1988; Kelley and Evans, 1995). Many blue-collar workers, for example, prefer to think of themselves as middle class rather than working class (although sociologists would classify blue-collar workers as working class). Since people rarely interact with others outside of their social class, they tend to see themselves as like "most other people," who they then regard as being "middle class" (Kelley and Evans, 1995).

The **middle class** is a catchall for a diverse group of occupations, lifestyles, and people who earn stable and sometimes substantial incomes at primarily white-collar jobs. It grew throughout much of the first three quarters of the twentieth century, then shrank during most of the last quarter century. During the late 1990s, however, economic growth halted this decline. Whether this trend will continue will depend on whether or not the economy expands or contracts during the next several years. Currently, the middle class includes slightly more than half of all American households. While the middle class was once largely white, today it is increasingly diverse, both racially and culturally, including African Americans, Asian Americans, and Latinos.

The American middle class can be subdivided into two groups: the upper middle class and the lower middle class.

The Upper Middle Class The *upper middle class* consists of relatively high-income professionals (doctors and lawyers, engineers and professors), mid-level corporate managers, people who own or manage small businesses and retail shops, and even some large-farm owners. Household incomes in this group range from about $83,500 to perhaps $154,498. It includes approximately 15 percent of all American households (U.S. Bureau of the Census, 2002a). Its members are likely to be college educated, and many hold advanced degrees. Their children almost always receive a college education as well. Their jobs have historically been relatively secure, as well as likely to provide them with retirement programs and health benefits. They own comfortable homes, often in the suburbs or in trendy downtown neighborhoods. They drive the more expensive late-model cars or sport utility vehicles. They have some savings and investments. They are likely to be active in local politics and civic organizations.

The Lower Middle Class The *lower middle class* in the United States consists of trained office workers (for example, secretaries and bookkeepers), elementary and high school teachers, nurses, salespeople, police officers, firefighters, and others who provide skilled services. Often members of this group enjoy relatively high status; it is their relatively low income that determines their class position. Household incomes in this group, which includes about 40 percent of American households, range from about $33,314 to $83,499 (U.S. Bureau of the Census, 2002a). They may own a modest house, although many live in rental units. Their automobiles may be late models, but they are not the more expensive varieties. Almost all have a high school education, and some have college degrees. They want their children to have a college education, although this will usually have to be paid for with the help of work-study programs and student loans. They are less likely to be politically active beyond exercising their right to vote.

THE WORKING CLASS

The **working class,** which makes up about 20 percent of all American households, includes primarily blue-collar and pink-collar laborers. Household incomes in this group range from perhaps $17,970 to $33,300 (U.S. Bureau of the Census, 2002a), and at least two people in each household will usually have to work to make ends meet. Family income is just enough to pay the rent or the mortgage, to put food on the table, and perhaps to save for a summer vacation. The working class includes factory workers, mechanics, secretaries, office workers, sales clerks, restaurant and hotel workers, and others who earn a modest weekly paycheck at a job that involves little control over the size of their income or working conditions. As you will see later in this chapter, many blue-collar jobs in the United States are threatened by economic globalization, and so members of the working class today are likely to feel insecure about their own and their family's future.

The working class is racially and ethnically diverse. While older members of the working class may own a home that was bought a number of years ago, younger members are likely to rent. The home or apartment is likely to be in a lower-income suburb or a city neighborhood. The household car, a lower-priced model, is unlikely to be new. Children who graduate from high school are unlikely to go to college and will attempt to get a job immediately instead. Most members of the working class are not likely to be politically active even in their own community, although they may vote in some elections.

THE LOWER CLASS

The **lower class,** which makes up roughly 15 percent of American households, includes those who work part time or not at all; household income is typically lower than $17,000 (U.S. Bureau of the Census, 2002a). Most lower-class individuals are found in cities, although some live in rural areas and earn a little money as farmers or part-time workers. Some manage to find employment in semiskilled or unskilled manufacturing or service jobs, ranging from making clothing in sweatshops to cleaning houses. Their jobs, when they can find them, are dead-end jobs, since years of work are unlikely to lead to promotion or substantially higher income. Their work is probably part time and highly unstable, without benefits such as medical insurance, disability, or social security. Even if they are fortunate enough to find a full-time job, there are no guarantees that it will be around next month or even next week. Many people in the lower class live in poverty. Very few own their own homes. Most of the lower class rent, and some are homeless. If they own a car at all, it is likely to be a used car. A higher percentage of the lower class is nonwhite than is true of other social classes. Its members do not participate in politics, and they seldom vote.

THE "UNDERCLASS"

In the lower class, some sociologists have recently identified a group they call the **underclass** because they are "beneath" the class system in that they lack access to the world of work and mainstream patterns of behavior. Located in the highest-poverty neighborhoods of the inner city, the underclass is sometimes called the "new urban poor."

The underclass includes many African Americans, who have been trapped for more than one generation in a cycle of poverty from which there is little possibility of escape (Wacquant, 1993, 1996; Wacquant and Wilson, 1993; Wilson, 1996). These are the poorest of the poor. Their numbers have grown rapidly over the past quarter century and today include unskilled and unemployed men, young single mothers and their children on welfare, teenagers from welfare-dependent families, and many of the homeless. They live in poor neighborhoods troubled by drugs, teenage gangs, drive-by shootings, and high levels of violence. They are the truly disadvantaged, people with extremely difficult lives who have little realistic hope of ever making it out of poverty.

The emergence of an underclass of the new urban poor has been attributed to social forces that have come together during the past quarter century (Sawhill, 1989; Wacquant, 1993, 1996; Wilson, 1996). First, economic globalization has led to unemployment among workers lacking education and skills, since many unskilled and semiskilled jobs have moved to low-wage countries. The threat of such job loss, in turn, has depressed wages in the remaining unskilled jobs. Since African Americans and recent immigrants from Latin America (and to some extent Asia) provide much of the unskilled labor in the United States, they are particularly disadvantaged in today's labor market. Furthermore, racial discrimination has made it especially difficult for minority groups to compete for the dwindling supply of unskilled jobs.

Second, government programs that once provided assistance for the poor were cut back sharply during the 1980s under the Reagan and elder Bush administrations, so that the poor were left with few resources to use to get ahead. These problems were compounded during the Clinton administration, whose welfare reforms severely restricted the length of time people could remain on welfare. This approach reduced the number of people on welfare, and the growing economy of the 1990s provided low-wage jobs for many welfare recipients. A sustained economic slowdown, however, could swell the ranks of the new urban poor, by leaving a growing number of people both jobless and without welfare benefits.

More recently, some sociologists have argued that members of the underclass perpetuate their own inequality because the difficult conditions they face have made them "ill suited to the requirements of the formally rational sector of the economy" (Wacquant, 2002). Although these scholars see the sources of such behavior in the social structure, they believe the culture of the underclass has taken on a life of its own, serving as both cause and effect. Such claims have generated considerable controversy, inspiring a number of studies that have taken issues with these claims. Those who stand on the other side argue that although urban poverty is an immobile stratum, it is not simply a "defeated" and disconnected class, as theorists of the underclass believe. Thus, studies of fast-food workers and homeless street vendors have argued that the separations between the urban poor and the rest of society are not as great as scholars of the underclass believe (Newman, 2000; Duneier, 1999).

Inequality in the United States: A Growing Gap Between Rich and Poor

The United States prides itself on being a nation of equals. Indeed, except for the Great Depression of the 1930s, inequality declined throughout much of the twentieth century, reaching its lowest levels during the 1960s and early 1970s. But during the past quarter century inequality has started to increase once again. The rich have gotten much, much richer. Middle-class incomes have stagnated. The poor have grown in number and are poorer than they have been since the 1960s. Currently, the gap between rich and poor in the United States is the largest since the Census Bureau started measuring it in 1947 (U.S. Bureau of the Census, 2000b) and the largest in the industrial world (see Figure 8.3). One statistical analysis of income and poverty among industrial nations found that the United States had the most unequal distribution of household income among all twenty-one industrial countries studied (Sweden had the most equal) (Smeeding, 2000).

In 1999, the richest 20 percent of all U.S. households accounted for over half of all income generated in the United States (see Figure 8.2). Moreover, their share has steadily increased. Table 8.4 divides American households into five equal-sized groups, based on household income in 1999. It also looks at the richest 5 percent of all households. The table compares the average after-tax income of each group in 1999 with the income each group would have had if its share of total income had remained the same as it was in 1974—that is, if inequality had not increased during the twenty-five year period. Four out of the five groups were worse off in 1999 than they would have been had inequality not increased; the range was between $2,200 and $6,000 poorer. The top fifth, on the other hand, was roughly $17,300 richer; the top 5 percent, about $61,300 richer.

Corporate Executives versus Their Workers

The earnings gap between top corporate officials and average working Americans has ballooned in recent years. According to *BusinessWeek* magazine's annual Executive Pay Scoreboard, the average pay of the chief executive officers (CEOs) at 362 of the largest U.S. companies rose from $10.6 million in 1998 to $13.1 million in 2000—a 24 percent increase. The top

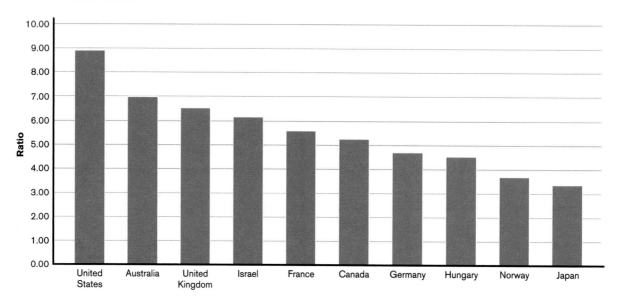

FIGURE 8.3

Income Inequality in Selected Industrialized Countries: Ratio of Richest 20 Percent to Poorest 20 Percent for 1999

In the 1990s, the richest fifth of all Americans were on average nine times richer than the poorest fifth, one of the highest ratios in the industrialized world. In Japan, at the other extreme, the ratio was about 3.4 to 1.

SOURCE: World Bank, *World Development Indicators,* 2000, Table 2.8.

TABLE 8.4

How Has an Increase in Income Inequality Affected American Households?

INCOME CATEGORY	ACTUAL 1999 MEAN INCOME ($)	1999 INCOME IF INEQUALITY HAD NOT CHANGED FROM 1974 ($)	DIFFERENCE: HOW MUCH POORER OR RICHER ($)
Lowest fifth	9,940	12,148	−2,208
Second fifth	24,436	29,103	−4,668
Middle fifth	40,879	46,914	−6,035
Fourth fifth	63,555	67,664	−4,109
Highest fifth	135,401	118,133	+17,268
Top 5 percent	235,392	174,080	+61,311

SOURCE: Calculations based on U.S. Bureau of the Census, 2000j.

earner was John Reed, CEO of the financial conglomerate Citicorp Group, who took home $293 million, mostly in stocks in his company (*BusinessWeek,* 2001). According to *Forbes* magazine (2001c) the eight hundred CEOs of the largest U.S. firms took home $6 billion that year in total pay.

The average U.S. factory worker averaged $13.74 an hour in 2000, earning $28,574 for the entire year, assuming he or she labored for fifty-two weeks a year, forty hours a week (U.S. Bureau of Labor Statistics, 2001a). In other words, the average CEO earned about 458 times as much as the average factory worker in 2000. Moreover, the gap has grown sharply: Average worker pay (not adjusting for inflation) increased by roughly one third between 1990 and 2000, whereas the average CEO pay increased sixfold.

The difference between executive and worker compensation is even more pronounced if one takes into account that U.S. firms today rely increasingly on workers in low-income countries. To take one example, *Forbes* reported that Millard Drexler earned $173 million in 1999 as CEO of Gap. Inc., America's largest clothing retailer (*Forbes,* 2001c). Virtually all of the thousand or so factories that make Gap clothing are in low-wage countries, where it can be estimated that workers average perhaps $800 a year (roughly $3 a day). The Gap's "wage gap" between Drexler's pay and that of the average Gap worker is 216,250 to 1!

Demonstrators protest the Gap for exploiting low-wage workers in the Third World.

Minorities versus White Americans

There are substantial differences in income based on race and ethnicity, since minorities in the United States are more likely to hold the lowest-paying jobs. Black and Latino household income, for example, averages about two thirds that of whites (see Figure 8.4). For blacks, this is a slight improvement over previous years, as a growing number of blacks have gone to college and moved into middle-class occupations. For Latinos, however, the situation has worsened, as recent immigrants from rural areas in Mexico and Central America find themselves working at low-wage jobs (U.S. Bureau of the Census, 2001a).

Oliver and Shapiro (1995) found that the "wealth gap" between blacks and whites is even greater than the income gap. While blacks on average earned two thirds that of whites, their net worth was only a tenth as much. Moreover, these differences increased between 1967 and 1988. More recent data show that the wealth gap has decreased only slightly: In 2000, whites had a median net worth of $58,716, compared with $6,166 for blacks and $6,766 for Hispanics (U.S. Bureau of the Census, 2003). Oliver and Shapiro also found that when blacks attained educational or occupational levels comparable to whites, the wealth gap still did not disappear. For example, the net worth of college-educated blacks was only $17,000 in 1988, compared with nearly $75,000 for whites.

Oliver and Shapiro (1995) argue that blacks have encountered numerous barriers to acquiring wealth throughout American history, beginning with slavery and continuing to the present day. After the Civil War ended slavery in 1865, legal discrimination (such as mandatory segregation in the South or separate schools) tied the vast majority of blacks to the lowest rungs of the economic ladder, until racial discrimination was made illegal by the Civil Rights Act of 1964. Nonetheless, discrimination has remained, and although some blacks have moved into middle-class occupations, many have remained poor or in low-wage jobs where the opportunities for accumulating wealth are nonexistent. Among those who successfully started businesses, many found there were racial barriers to breaking into the more profitable white markets. In effect, many blacks have suffered from a vicious cycle that prevents them from accumulating wealth. Less wealth means less social and cultural capital: fewer dollars to invest in schooling for one's children, a business, or

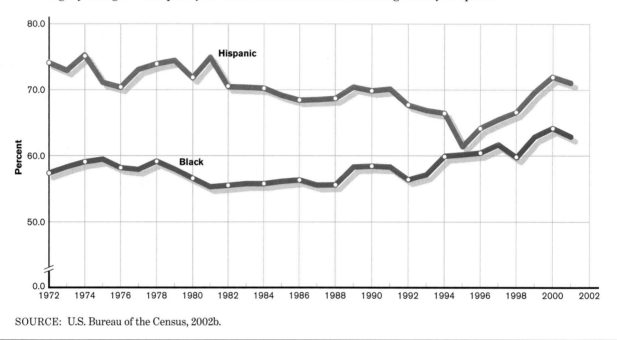

FIGURE 8.4

Black and Hispanic Income Compared to Whites'

During the past decade and a half, blacks have seen their income improve slightly relative to whites. By 2001, blacks were averaging 62.9 percent of whites' income ($39,248 for blacks, versus $62,444 for whites)— up from 57.6 percent of white income in 1972. Latinos, on the other hand, were worse off relative to whites than they had been 24 years earlier. In 2001, Latinos were averaging 71.1 percent of white income, compared with 74.4 percent of white income in 1972. Overall, the relative position of both blacks and Latinos improved slightly during the latter part of the 1990s due to the sustained economic growth of that period.

SOURCE: U.S. Bureau of the Census, 2002b.

the stock market—investments that in the long run would create greater wealth for future investments.

Single-Parent Families versus Married-Couple Families

Single-parent families are especially likely to have low incomes. Those headed by men earned only 69 percent as much as all married families in 2001, while those headed by women earned only 49 percent as much as all married families. Race and ethnicity also play a significant role: Black married-couple families earned 75 percent as much as white married-couple families, while Latino married-couple families earned only 57 percent as much. Finally, nonwhite families headed by single women are by far the worst off: Black female-headed families earned only about 36 percent as much as white

married-couple families while Latino female-headed families earned 41 percent as much as white married-couple families (U.S. Bureau of the Census, 2002).

Social Mobility

In studying stratification and inequality, we must consider not only the differences between economic positions but also what happens to the individuals who occupy them. **Social mobility** refers to the movement of individuals and groups between different class positions as a result of changes in occupation, wealth, or income.

There are two ways of studying social mobility. First, we can look at people's own careers—how far they move up or down the socioeconomic scale in the course of their working lives. This is called **intragenerational mobility**. Alternatively, we can analyze where children are on the scale compared with their parents or grandparents. Mobility across the generations is called **intergenerational mobility**.

Another important distinction sociologists make is between structural mobility and exchange mobility. If there were such a thing as a society with complete equality of opportunity—where each person had the same chance of getting on in life as everyone else—there would be a great deal of downward as well as upward mobility. This is what is meant by **exchange mobility**: There is an exchange of positions, such that more talented people in each generation move up the economic hierarchy, while the less talented move down.

In practice, there is no society that even approaches full equality of opportunity, and most mobility, whether intra- or intergenerational, is **structural mobility**, upward mobility made possible by an expansion of better-paid occupations at the expense of more poorly paid ones. Most mobility in the United States since World War II has depended on continually increasing prosperity. Levels of downward mobility, therefore, have been historically low.

Intergenerational Mobility

Much of the research on intergenerational mobility has been at least implicitly motivated by the **industrialism hypothesis,** which says that societies become more open to movement between classes as they become more technologically advanced (Kerr et al., 1960). The hypothesis says that as societies become more industrial, workers increasingly get jobs because of *achievement,* or skill, rather than because of **ascription,** which refers to placement in a particular social status based on characteristics such as family of origin, race, and gender.

Some evidence supports the industrialism hypothesis. A review of mobility patterns in thirty-five countries finds a gradual increase in openness over time within all of the countries (Ganzeboom, Luijkx, and Treiman, 1989). However, much research contradicts the industrialism hypothesis. The earliest study of comparative mobility, by Pitirim Sorokin (1927), analyzed a wide range of societies, from traditional Rome and China to the United States. Sorokin concluded that opportunities for rapid ascent in the United States were more limited than American folklore suggested. The techniques he used to gather his data, however, were relatively primitive. Another classical study of social mobility was carried out by Seymour Lipset and Reinhard Bendix (1959). Their research—drawing on data from Britain, France, West Germany, Sweden, Switzerland, Japan, Denmark, Italy, and the United States—concentrated on the mobility of men from blue-collar to white-collar work. Contrary to the re-

searchers' expectations, they also found no evidence that the United States was more open to social mobility than the European societies. They concluded that all of the countries were experiencing an expansion of white-collar jobs. This led to increased structural mobility, and an "upward surge of mobility." More recently, Robert Erikson and John Goldthorpe (1992) compared twelve European and three non-European industrialized nations. They found that most countries had similar patterns of intergenerational mobility. However, they also discovered significant variations: Sweden, for example, was found to be considerably more open to social mobility than the other Western countries. In contrast to the industrialism hypothesis, societies did not tend to get more open to movement between classes over time.

There are also big differences within societies—for example, differences in mobility between racial and ethnic groups (Featherman and Hauser, 1978). The obvious comparison in the United States is between African Americans and whites. The black middle class is much smaller than the white middle class relative to the proportions of blacks and whites in the population as a whole. Someone born in a black inner-city ghetto has only a fraction of the chance of a person from a white background of obtaining a white-collar or professional job.

Research on intergenerational mobility has tended to find that children of parents who had low-status or high-status occupations are likely to work at occupations with similar status. Children of parents with middle-status occupations, such as crafts or service, tend to be relatively more mobile (Featherman and Hauser, 1978; Grusky and Hauser, 1984).

Intragenerational Mobility

Relatively less research has focused on intragenerational mobility. The work that has been done finds that earnings, status, and satisfaction increase most dramatically when workers are in their twenties, with more subtle increases later on (Spilerman, 1977). Workers tend to be promoted twice: first by the time they are thirty-four and then again between their mid-thirties and early fifties (Rosenbaum, 1979; DiPrete and Soule, 1988; Lashbrook, 1996).

This pattern is slightly different for women than for men. Women are more likely to continue changing jobs after the early part of their careers than are men (DiPrete and Nonnemaker, 1997). In addition, women workers have recently been affected by two historical trends: a decline in occupational gender segregation and increased labor force participation. This means that women are more likely now than they were in the 1950s to hold the same jobs as men (Goldin, 1990). And many more women are working today than was the case in the 1950s (Siegel, 1993; Quinn and Burkhauser, 1994).

Defending Workers at Berkeley

After four years of steady service as a food service worker at the University of California at Berkeley, Sam makes twelve dollars and seven cents an hour. Approaching his fiftieth birthday, Sam is barely able to make ends meet. He does not own a home. "No, of course not. I stay in a little studio apartment, and I have great grandchildren. It's not easy. By the time I pay my rent and buy my food and put gas in my car, I'm already waiting for the next paycheck two days after maybe I've gotten the [last] paycheck. [***] Every now and then I get to go to a movie or something to just kind of break up the boredom, but it's not very often that I do anything different than go to work and come home. . . . It's not easy. It's not easy at all."

The standard of living that Sam's salary permits him is a far cry from the one he had anticipated when he started working as a young man, thirty years ago. Back then, Sam had what he considered to be a good job at Ford down in Milpitas [California]. That was when "you came to work and did your job. You automatically got put on [steady employment] and had benefits . . . you had medical, dental and all of that. You had a paycheck every week and you didn't have to worry about getting paid all of your money, which is a bad problem here [at Cal]. You got your vacation without any hassle." Sam

worked happily at Ford until 1983 when the plant closed. Before he got laid off, Sam had been making thirteen dollars and thirty-nine cents an hour, not at all an unreasonable salary given the Bay Area cost of living at that time. He never imagined that twenty years later his hourly wage would be lower, even without adjusting for inflation. [***]

Sam's story is not unique. Behind the stately façade of America's most prestigious public university, custodians, food service workers, groundskeepers, and clerical workers toil under conditions that betray the very principles which we want our university to embody. And yet, students, professors, and administrators know surprisingly little about the sacrifices made and injuries suffered by those who clean their classrooms and dormitories, cook their meals, maintain the grounds, and record their grades.

As sociology graduate students at the University of California at Berkeley, we usually focus our scholarly attention on "the world out there," far beyond Sproul Plaza and Sather Gate. In our capacity as graduate student instructors, we encourage our students to explore the causes of poverty, the repercussions of inequality, and the often invisible power dynamics in our society. Rarely do we, as scholars and teachers

in the making, explore the social ills that exist right here in our cherished halls of learning.

[***]

Many workers, like most students and professors, also came to U.C. Berkeley with high expectations about contributing to a world-class educational institution. What we discovered, however, is that their expectations were quickly crushed once they got on the job. Not wanting to complain, they tell cautiously at first, but passionately once they get going about finding themselves on the brink of poverty and routinely facing dangerous and degrading employment practices. [***]

Workers' experiences at U.C. Berkeley can only be understood against the backdrop of the widespread corporatization of American universities. This transformation of the university reflects the rise over the last three decades of a free market fundamentalism which posits that unregulated capitalism is the best system, both morally and practically, for organizing all spheres of society. [***]

As we became aware of the increasing corporatization of the university, we formed a graduate student research collective and worked with the guidance of author and journalist Barbara Ehrenreich. Our collective built on a confluence of movements. We were inspired by the student initiatives for economic justice springing up around the country, especially the movement for a living wage at Harvard Univeristy. We were also emboldened by calls to sociologists, voiced by prominent members of our faculty, to conduct Public Sociology—sociological research that seeks to open up public dialogue about the pressing issues of our time. We thus decided to use the tools available to us as budding social scientists to study and report on the working conditions and everyday experiences of University workers.

[***]

Three troubling themes emerged from these interviews. First, wages have not kept up with the rising costs of living; many workers cannot afford the basic necessities of life—reasonable housing, childcare, and transportation. Second, the conditions of work are unacceptably dangerous. Once injured, workers are treated as if they are disposable and do not receive the physical and emotional care they deserve. Finally, many workers [***] report routinely being treated with disrespect by their supervisors. The lack of standardized procedures leaves workers subject to the luck of the draw: some supervisors are fair; others make unreasonable demands and take advantage of their power.

Organized around these three main themes of wages, health and safety, and dignity and respect, this report tells a story about the university that is seldom told, presented

through the voices of those who are seldom heard. With the publication and dissemination of this report, we hope to accomplish three concrete objectives:

Education: to educate students, faculty, parents and alumni about the wages and working conditions of the U.C. Berkeley workforce.

Mobilization: in coalition with campus unions and other student groups, to mobilize the collective energies of the campus community to send an unequivocal message to university administrators that it is unacceptable for members of our community to work for less than a living wage, to be endangered by their work, or to be accorded less than the dignity and respect any other member of the university community would expect and deserve.

Change: to call on the university administration to take ten steps—outlined in the conclusion of this report—that will improve the wages and working conditions of university employees.

[***]

SOURCE: Gretchen Purser, Amy Schalet, and Ofer Sharone, *Berkeley's Betrayal: Wages and Working Conditions at Cal.* (Berkeley, CA: University Labor Research Project, 2004). To view the entire report, visit www.berkeleysbetrayal.org.

GRETCHEN PURSER *is a Ph.D. candidate in sociology at the University of California at Berkeley. Her research focuses on the contingent labor market and urban poverty in the United States.* AMY SCHALET *is a postdoctoral fellow at the Center for Reproductive Health Research and Policy at the University of California at San Francisco. She has written and taught on the American welfare state in comparative perspective. She is currently preparing her book on adolescent sexuality and parental panic in the United States and the Netherlands for publication with Chicago University Press.* OFER SHARONE *is a Ph.D. candidate in sociology at the University of California at Berkeley. He specializes in the sociology of work and researches overwork and unemployment in the United States and Israel.*

Opportunities for Mobility: Who Gets Ahead?

Why is it more difficult for someone from the "new urban poor" to become an upper-class professional? Many people in modern societies believe it is possible for anyone to reach the top through hard work and persistence. Why should it be difficult to do so? Sociologists have sought to answer these questions by trying to understand which social factors are most influential in determining an individual's status or position in society.

In a classic study of social mobility in the United States, the sociologists Peter Blau and Otis Dudley Duncan surveyed over twenty thousand men in order to assess intergenerational mobility (1967). Blau and Duncan concluded that while there has been a great deal of **vertical mobility,** or movement along the socioeconomic scale, nearly all of it was between occupational positions quite close to one another. Long-range mobility, that is from working class to upper-middle class, was rare. Why? Blau and Duncan sought to answer this question by assessing the impact of social background in determining ultimate social status. They concluded that the key factor behind status was educational attainment. But a child's education is influenced by its family's social status; this, in turn, affects the child's social position later in life. The sociologists William Sewell and Robert Hauser later confirmed Blau and Duncan's conclusions (1980). They added to the argument by claiming that the connection between family background and educational attainment occurs because parents, teachers, and friends influence the educational and career aspirations of the child and that these aspirations then become an important part of the status attainment process throughout the child's life. Sewell and Hauser sought to prove that social status was influenced by a pattern of related social influences going back to one's birth: Family background affects the child's aspirations, which in turn affect the child's educational attainment, which in turn affects the adult's later occupational prestige, and so on and so on.

The French sociologist Pierre Bourdieu has also been a major figure in examining the importance of family background to social status, but his emphasis is on the cultural advantages that parents can provide to their children (1984, 1988). Bourdieu argues that among the factors responsible for social status the most important is the transmission of cultural capital. Those who own economic capital often manage to pass much of it on to their children. The same is true, Bourdieu argues, of the cultural advantages that coming from a "good home" confers. These advantages stem partly from having greater economic capital, which succeeding generations inherit, thus perpetuating inequalities. As we have seen, wealthier families are able to afford to send their children to better schools, an economic advantage that benefits the children's social status as adults. In addition to this material advantage, parents from the upper and middle classes are mostly highly educated themselves and tend to be more involved in their children's education—reading to them, helping with homework, purchasing books and learning materials, and encouraging their progress. Bourdieu notes that working-class parents are concerned about their children's education, but they lack the economic and cultural capital to make a difference. Bourdieu's study of French society confirmed his theory. He found that a majority of office professionals with high levels of educational attainment and income were from families of the "dominant class" in France. Likewise, office clerical workers often originated from the working classes.

The socioeconomic order in the United States is similar. Those who already hold positions of wealth and power have many chances to perpetuate their advantages and to pass them on to their offspring. They can make sure their children have the best available education, and this will often lead them into the best jobs. Most of those who reach the top had a head start; they came from professional or affluent backgrounds. Studies of people who have become wealthy show that hardly anyone begins with nothing. The large majority of people who have "made money" did so on the basis of inheriting or being given at least a modest amount initially—which they then used to make more. In American society, it's better to start at the top than at the bottom (Jaher, 1973; Rubinstein, 1986; Duncan et al., 1998).

Your Own Mobility Chances

Sometime in the next four years, you will graduate from college and be faced with the prospect of starting a new career. Do you have any idea what you will do? If you are like most of your classmates, you have no idea. Perhaps you are a person like Richard Rivera, who has a passion for something like fruit smoothies and will make a go of something that is interesting to you. Or perhaps you will go to work for someone else and become interested in something you have never heard of, working your way up the hierarchy of an organization in a formal career. What implications might be drawn from mobility studies about the career opportunities you are faced with, as someone searching for a good job? Managerial and professional jobs may continue to expand relative to lower-level positions. Those who have done well in the educational system and earned a college degree are most likely to fill these openings and make a high income. Indeed, 60 percent of Americans in the top fifth of income earners graduated from college, whereas in the bottom fifth, just 6 percent hold a college degree (Cox and Alm, 1999). Educational attainment seems to be the key variable for upward mobility in the United States. Even for someone like Richard Rivera, who sells juice for a living, a college education provided him with training in entrepreneurship, accounting, and computer applications (Hout, 1988).

Research indicates, however, that the impact of education on your mobility chances has decreased somewhat (Hout, 1988; Hout and Lucas, 1996). Because you are a college student, chances are that one or both of your parents are college educated and middle class or above. Even if you earn a good income, you might not enjoy upward mobility. Additionally, as a result of global economic competition, not nearly enough well-paid positions are open for all who wish to enter them, and some of you are bound to find that your careers do not match your expectations. Even if a higher proportion of jobs are created at managerial and professional levels than existed before, the overall number of jobs available in the future may not keep pace with the number of people with college degrees seeking work. One reason for this is the growing number of women entering the work force. Another is the increasing use of information technology in production processes. Because computerized machinery can now handle tasks—even of a highly complicated kind—that once only humans could do, it is possible that many jobs will be eliminated in future years.

If you are a woman, although your chances of entering a good career are improving, you face certain obstacles to your progress. Male managers and employers still discriminate against female applicants, compared with males seeking the same positions. They do so at least partly because of their belief that women are not really interested in careers and are likely to leave the workforce to begin families. This latter factor substantially affects opportunities for women, who are often forced to choose between a career and having children. Men are rarely willing to share equal responsibility for domestic work and child care.

Downward Mobility

Although downward mobility is less common than upward mobility, about 20 percent of men in the United States are downwardly mobile intergenerationally, although most of this movement is short range. A person with **short-range downward mobility** moves from one job to another that is similar—for example, from a routine office job to semiskilled blue-collar work. Downward intragenerational mobility, also a common occurrence, is often associated with psychological problems and anxieties. Some people are simply unable to sustain the lifestyle into which they were born. But another source of downward mobility among individuals arises through no fault of their own. During the late 1980s and early 1990s, corporate

America was flooded with instances in which middle-aged men lost their jobs because of company mergers or takeovers. These executives either had difficulty finding new jobs or could only find jobs that paid less than their previous jobs.

Many of the intragenerational downwardly mobile are women. It is still common for women to abandon promising careers on the birth of a child. After spending some years raising children, such women often return to the paid work force at a level lower than when they left—for instance, in poorly paid, part-time work. (This situation is changing, although not as fast as might be hoped.)

Downward mobility is particularly common today among divorced or separated women with children. As an illustration, we might take the life of Sandra Bolton, described by John Schwarz and Thomas Volgy in their book *The Forgotten Americans* (1992). Sandra's fate belies the idea that people who work hard and follow the rules will be able to prosper. Sandra's husband had regularly assaulted her during the six years of their marriage, and child welfare officials considered him a threat to their two children. She divorced her husband after the Child Protective Services told her that the state would take her children if she didn't leave him.

Sandra receives no maintenance from her ex-husband, who, two weeks before the divorce was finalized, piled their furniture and valuables into a truck and drove away, not to be seen again. Whereas while married she sustained a moderately comfortable, middle-class way of life, Sandra now lives a hand-to-mouth existence. She tried to remain in college, supporting herself and her children by doing various menial jobs, but was unable to earn enough money to keep up.

A neighbor looked after her children while she took a full-time job as a secretary at a medical center. Taking courses at night and during the summers, she eventually completed a college degree. Although she applied at many places, she was not able to find a position paying more than her secretarial job. She took on a second job, as a checkout person in a supermarket, in the evenings just to make ends meet. "You try to do the responsible thing," she said, "and you're penalized, because the system we have right now doesn't provide you with a way to make it. I mean, I work so hard. There's only so much a person can do" (Schwarz and Volgy, 1992). As a result of her divorce, Sandra sank from a life of some comfort to living in poverty. She is not alone.

Gender and Social Mobility

Although so much research into social mobility has focused on men, in recent years more attention has begun to be paid to patterns of mobility among women. At a time when girls

The Information Revolution and Inequality

What impact will the information revolution have on social inequality?

The answer in part depends on how well the American educational system responds to the challenge of preparing students for a high-technology world. A good education can pay off in the digital society. Although Bill Gates may be the world's richest college dropout (Gates left Harvard to found Microsoft), he is clearly the exception to the rule.

Recall what has happened to blue-collar factory work—the kinds of jobs that made possible a middle-class lifestyle throughout much of this century. As you have seen in this chapter, thanks to the information revolution, U.S. businesses today can relocate their manufacturing operations around the globe with the click of a mouse, filling out orders on their suppliers' Web pages almost as easily as consumers buy books on Amazon.com. Beginning in the late 1970s, U.S. firms began to take advantage of modern information technology to downsize, moving their production to low-wage countries. The re-

sult: stagnant or declining wages for much of the American working class. Inequality has increased for people whose skills limit them to blue-collar work.

College graduates today earn more than they did a decade ago—the higher the degree, the greater the gains. High school dropouts, on the other hand, earn less (Hout, 1997). One U.S. Census Bureau study (2002e) found that in 2001, men with a professional degree had a median income of $81,602, three times as much as men with only a high school diploma ($28,343). The U.S. Bureau of Labor Statistics (2001b) predicts that between 1998 and 2008 the four fastest-growing occupations will all be directly related to the digital society. Jobs for computer engineers, computer support specialists, and computer systems analysts will more than double, while jobs for database administrators will increase approximately 80 percent. These are all jobs in which education pays a large dividend.

How well are students today being educated for tomorrow's digital world? A recent U.S. Department of Education

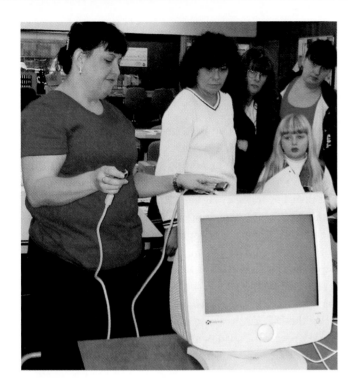

with science and technology training. The program would provide elementary school children and their families with help in buying computers, connecting to the Internet, and learning skills required to use them (Carnevale, 2000). A growing number of American colleges and universities, as well as some private companies, are beginning to provide "virtual high schools" over the Internet, offering college prep and advanced placement courses to students in inner-city schools that traditionally lack such offerings (Carr, 1999; Carr and Young, 1999). The state of Maine recently approved a program to provide every seventh- and eighth-grade student with a laptop computer to be used throughout high school. Maine, which currently ranks thirty-seventh in the nation in per capita income, hopes that a high-tech future will reverse its economic fortunes (*Ellsworth American,* 2001; Goldberg, 2001).

It is still too early to give a final grade to American schools. The digital revolution is fairly recent, and schools and teachers are only beginning to catch up with it. It remains to be seen whether the new information technology ultimately reinforces existing social inequalities—or is used to overcome them.

study (NCES, 2000) gives mixed grades to public schools. The report, *Teachers' Tools for the 21st Century,* surveyed public school teachers in 1999, asking them about the technology that was available in their classrooms and how well prepared they were to use it. The good news was that virtually all of the teachers reported that their schools had computers connected to the Internet. Nearly all had at least one computer in their classroom, and two thirds of the classrooms were hooked up to the Internet as well. The bad news was that only half of the teachers used computers or the Internet to teach their students. Perhaps this was because only a third reported feeling prepared to use computers and the Internet in their classrooms.

Current patterns of computer use in public schools reinforce existing social stratification. For example, teachers in white middle-class schools were much more likely to use computers for Internet research than teachers in schools with large numbers of poor minority students. They were also less likely to report that outdated, unreliable computers were a barrier to their classroom instruction (NCES, 2000). Poor inner-city schools, which often lack basic instructional materials such as textbooks, much less computers, are especially ill equipped to prepare their students.

There are some promising signs that the digital revolution may yet reach a broad cross section of American students. For example, Brown University, in conjunction with MCI World-Com, recently announced a small program to finance twenty college-community partnerships to help provide low-income children in inner-city schools and on Indian tribal reservations

Questions

- Describe how the advent of computers and the information technology industry could affect the kind of jobs available in the United States. How could the American occupational makeup change? How has it changed already?
- Can the use of computers in schools close the digital divide? Why or why not?
- How might the rise in high-tech jobs and the end of blue-collar jobs affect American society and lifestyle? Will society be increasingly stratified? How might it become more egalitarian?

are outperforming boys in school and females are outnumbering males in higher education, it is tempting to conclude that long-standing gender inequalities in society may be relaxing their hold. Has the occupational structure become more open to women, or are their mobility chances still guided largely by family and social background?

One study traced the lives of nine thousand people born during the same week in 1970. In the most recent survey of the respondents, at age twenty-six, it was found that for both men and women family background and class of origin remain powerful influences. The study concluded that the young people who were coping best with the transition to adulthood were those who had obtained a better education, postponed children and marriage, and had fathers in professional occupations. Individuals who had come from disadvantaged backgrounds had a greater tendency to remain there.

The study found that, on the whole, women today are experiencing much greater opportunity than did their counterparts in the previous generation. Middle-class women have benefited the most. They were just as likely as their male peers to go to college and to move into well-paid jobs on graduation. This trend toward greater equality was also reflected in women's heightened confidence and sense of self-esteem, compared with a similar cohort of women born just twelve years earlier.

Poverty in the United States

At the bottom of the class system in the United States are the millions of people who exist in conditions of poverty. Many do not maintain a proper diet and live in miserable conditions; their average life expectancy is lower than that of the majority of the population. In addition, the number of individuals and families who have become homeless has greatly increased over the past twenty years.

In defining poverty, a distinction is usually made between absolute and relative poverty. **Absolute poverty** means that a person or family simply can't get enough to eat. People living in absolute poverty are undernourished and, in situations of famine, may actually starve to death. Absolute poverty is common in the poorer developing countries.

In the industrial countries, **relative poverty** is essentially a measure of inequality. It means being poor as compared with the standards of living of the majority. It is reasonable to call a person poor in the United States if he lacks the basic re-

sources needed to maintain a decent standard of housing and healthy living conditions.

Measuring Poverty

When President Lyndon B. Johnson began his War on Poverty in 1964, around 36 million Americans lived in poverty. Within a decade, the number had dropped sharply, to around 23 million (see Figure 8.5 for changes in poverty rates since 1959). But then, beginning in the early 1970s, poverty again began to climb, peaking in 1993 at 39 million people. Since that time, the number of poor has dropped by 4.4 million people, and in 2002, it stood at 34.6 million people, roughly 12 percent of the population (U.S. Bureau of the Census, 2003a). Yet even this level of poverty greatly exceeds that of most other industrial and postindustrial nations. In the mid-1990s, for example, when the U.S. poverty rate was around 14 percent, France's was 10 percent, Canada's and Germany's 7 percent (Smeeding, Rainwater, and Burtless, 2000).

What does it mean to be poor in the world's richest nation? The U.S. government calculates the **poverty line** as an income equal to three times the cost of a nutritionally adequate diet—a strict no-frills budget that assumes a nutritionally adequate diet could be purchased in 1999 for only $3.86 per day for each member, along with about $7.72 on all other items (including rent and utilities, clothing, medical expenses, and transportation). For a family of four persons in 2002, that works out to an annual cash income of $18,244 (U.S. Bureau of the Census, 2003b).

How realistic is this formula? Some critics believe it *over*-estimates the amount of poverty. They point out that the current standard fails to take into account noncash forms of income available to the poor, such as food stamps, Medicare, Medicaid, and public housing subsidies, as well as cash obtained from work at odd jobs that is concealed from the government. For example, one study looked at the poorest tenth of all families with children, comparing government survey data on their reported income with comparable data on their reported expenditures (Mayer and Jencks, 1994). It found that these families actually spent twice as much, on average, as the income they reported to the government.

Other critics argue that the government's formula greatly *under*estimates the amount of poverty. They argue that to label a three-person family as "nonpoor" in 1999 because it earned more than $12,680 (less than $35 a day) is simply unrealistic. Some scholars point out that such figures are based on an assumption from a half century ago that an "average" family spends a third of its income on food, even though more recent studies show that the actual figure is closer to one sixth, and that as much as three quarters of a poor family's income

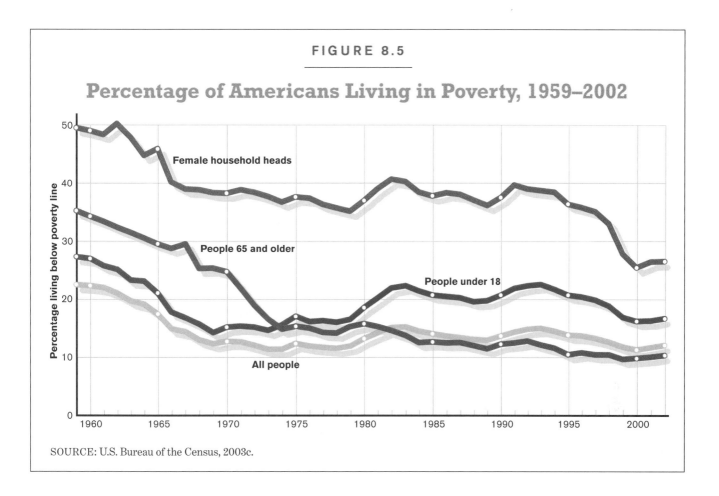

FIGURE 8.5

Percentage of Americans Living in Poverty, 1959–2002

Percentage living below poverty line

Female household heads

People 65 and older

People under 18

All people

1960 1965 1970 1975 1980 1985 1990 1995 2000

SOURCE: U.S. Bureau of the Census, 2003c.

may go to rent alone (Schwarz and Volgy, 1992; Stone, 1993; Joint Center for Housing Studies, 1994; Dolbeare, 1995). By this reasoning, food expenditures should be multiplied by at least 6, rather than 3, to yield the poverty level. Patricia Ruggles (1990, 1992), an adviser to the University of Wisconsin's Institute for Research on Poverty, estimates that this formula would effectively double the official number of Americans living in poverty. That would mean that in 2000, over 62 million people were living in poverty, or 22.6 percent—almost a quarter—of the population, instead of the official Census Bureau estimate for that year of 31.1 million people, or only 11.3 percent of the population.

The official U.S. poverty rate is the highest among the major industrial and postindustrial nations, more than three times that of such European countries as Sweden or Norway (Smeeding, Rainwater, and Burtless, 2000). The largest concentrations of poverty in the United States are found in the South and the Southwest, in central cities, and in rural areas. Among the poor, 12.7 million Americans (or 4.6 percent of the country) live in extreme poverty: Their incomes are only *half* of the official poverty level, meaning that they live at near-starvation levels (U.S. Bureau of the Census, 2000e, 2000f).

Who Are the Poor?

What do you think about poverty? Most Americans of all social classes think of the poor as people who are unemployed or on welfare. Americans also tend to display more negative attitudes toward welfare provisions and benefits than people in other Western countries. Surveys repeatedly show that the majority of Americans regard the poor as being responsible for their own poverty and are antagonistic to those who live on "government handouts." For example, a Gallup poll found that 55 percent of the public believed that lack of effort by the poor was the principal reason for poverty. Nearly two-thirds believed that government assistance programs reduced incentives to work. These views, however, are out of line with the realities of poverty. The poor are as diverse as other groups.

WORKING POOR

Many Americans are the **working poor,** that is, people who work but whose earnings are not high enough to lift them above poverty. The 2003 U.S. minimum wage, $5.15 an hour, results in a yearly income of $10,300, if the person is working full time. This is only about three quarters of the poverty-level income of $14,494 for a single parent supporting two children (U.S. Bureau of the Census, 2003b). About one third of those officially living in poverty are actually working. In 1999, the working poor included 2.5 million Americans who worked full time and another 9.1 million working part time. Most poor people, contrary to popular belief, don't receive welfare payments, because they earn too much to qualify for welfare.

Katherine Newman spent two years documenting the lives of three hundred low-wage workers and job seekers at fast-food restaurants in Harlem, a predominantly African American section of New York City. Her award-winning book *No Shame in My Game* found that the people interviewed were hard workers who valued their jobs, despite the low status associated with "slinging burgers." Moreover, Newman found that the working poor had to overcome enormous obstacles simply to survive: They typically lacked adequate educations, and some attended school while working; they had no health insurance to cover medical costs; and many were supporting families on poverty-level wages (Newman, 2000).

POVERTY, RACE, AND ETHNICITY

Poverty rates are much higher among most minority groups, even though more than two thirds of the poor are white. As Table 8.5 shows, blacks and Latinos continue to earn around two thirds of what whites earn in the United States, while experiencing three times the poverty rate whites experience. This is because they often work at the lowest-paying jobs and because of racial discrimination. Asian Americans have the highest income of any group, but their poverty rate is almost one and a half times that of whites, reflecting the recent influx of relatively poor immigrant groups.

Latinos have somewhat higher incomes than blacks, although their poverty rate is comparable. Nonetheless, the number of blacks living in poverty has declined considerably in recent years. In 1959, 55.1 percent of blacks were living in poverty; by 2002 that figure had dropped to 23.9 percent. The recent high point for black poverty came during the recession of 1992, when 33.4 percent of the black population was poor. Since that time, the number of blacks in poverty has fallen by 2.5 million. This is mainly because the economic expansion of the 1990s created new job opportunities. A similar pattern is seen for Latinos: Poverty grew steadily between 1972 and 1994, peaking at 30.7 percent of the Latino population. By 1999, however, the poverty rate for Latinos had fallen to 22.8 percent (U.S. Bureau of the Census, 2000g).

THE FEMINIZATION OF POVERTY

Much of the growth in poverty is associated with the **feminization of poverty,** an increase in the proportion of the poor who are female. Growing rates of divorce, separation, and single-parent families have placed women at particular disadvantage, since it is extremely difficult for unskilled or semiskilled, low-income, poorly educated women to raise children by themselves while they also hold down a job that could raise them out of poverty. As a result, in 2002 over a quarter (26.5 percent) of all single-parent families headed by women

---

TABLE 8.5

Median Income and Poverty Rates for Households in 2002, by Race and Ethnicity

	WHITE	ASIAN AMERICAN	LATINO	BLACK	TOTAL U.S.
Median income($)*	46,305	53,635	33,565	29,470	42,816
Percentage of median income of whites	100	116	72	64	92
Poverty rate (%)**	8	10.1	21.8	24.1	12.1

*2001 data

**2002 data

SOURCE: U.S. Bureau of the Census, 2002b, 2003a.

---

were poor, compared to only 5.3 percent of married couples with children (U.S. Bureau of the Census, 2003c).

Households headed by single parents are much more likely to live in poverty than those headed by married couples, and the incidence of poverty is far higher if the single parent is a woman. The feminization of poverty is particularly acute among families headed by Latino women (see Table 8.6). Although the rate declined by nearly 5 percent in four years, 41.4 percent of all female-headed Latino families lived in poverty in 2002. An almost identical percentage (41.3 percent) of female-headed African American families also live in poverty; both considerably higher than that of white female-headed families (26.2 percent) (U.S. Bureau of the Census, 2003d).

A single woman attempting to raise children alone is caught in a vicious cycle of hardship and poverty. If she does succeed in finding a job, she must find someone to take care of her children, since she cannot afford to hire a baby-sitter or pay for day care. From her standpoint, she will take in more money if she accepts welfare payments from the government and tries to find illegal part-time jobs that pay cash not reported to the government rather than find a regular full-time job paying minimum wage. Even though welfare will not get her out of poverty, if she finds a regular job she will lose her welfare altogether. As a result, she and her family may even be worse off economically.

CHILDREN IN POVERTY

Given the high rates of poverty among families headed by single women, it follows that children are the principal victims of poverty in the United States. Child poverty rates (defined as poverty among people under eighteen) in the United States are by far the highest in the industrial world. Nonetheless, the child poverty rate has varied considerably over the last forty years, declining when the economy expands or the government increases spending on antipoverty programs and rising when the economy slows and government antipoverty spending falls. The child poverty rate declined from 27.3 percent of all children in 1959 to 14.4 percent in 1973—a period associated with both economic growth and the War on Poverty declared by the Johnson administration (1963–1969). During the late 1970s and 1980s, as economic growth slowed and cutbacks were made in government antipoverty programs, child poverty grew, exceeding 20 percent during much of the period. The economic expansion of the 1990s saw a drop in child poverty rates, and in 2002 the rate had fallen to 16.3 percent, a twenty-year low (U.S. Bureau of the Census, 2003e).

The statistics are significantly higher for racial minorities and children of single mothers. In 2002, those in poverty included 8.9 percent of white children, 28.2 percent of Latino children, 32.1 percent of black children, and 56.4 percent of

---

TABLE 8.6

Families with Children: Percentage in Poverty, by Race and Ethnicity, Marital Status, and Sex of Head of Household, 2002

	MARRIED COUPLE	MALE HEAD	FEMALE HEAD
White	4.1	10.4	26.2
Black	8.5	26.5	41.3
Latino	17.7	23.6	41.4
Asian	5.9	19	21.2

SOURCE: U.S. Bureau of the Census, 2003d.

---

children who lived with single mothers (U.S. Bureau of the Census, 2003f).

Child poverty is not due only to the state of the national economy, or government spending on antipoverty programs. As the above statistics show, child poverty is most severe among children who live with single mothers. During the past forty years, the number of single-parent families headed by women more than doubled, contributing to the increase in child poverty.

Explaining Poverty: The Sociological Debate

Explanations of poverty can be grouped under two main headings: theories that see poor individuals as responsible for their own poverty and theories that view poverty as produced and reproduced by structural forces in society. These competing approaches are sometimes described as "blame the victim" and "blame the system" theories, respectively. We shall briefly examine each in turn.

There is a long history of attitudes that hold the poor responsible for their own disadvantaged positions. Early efforts to address the effects of poverty, such as the poorhouses of the nineteenth century, were grounded in a belief that poverty was the result of an inadequacy or pathology of individuals.

The poor were seen as those who were unable—due to lack of skills, moral or physical weakness, absence of motivation, or below-average ability—to succeed in society. Social standing was taken as a reflection of a person's talent and effort; those who deserved to succeed did so, while others less capable were doomed to fail. The existence of winners and losers was regarded as a fact of life.

Such outlooks have enjoyed a renaissance, beginning in the 1970s and 1980s, as the political emphasis on entrepreneurship and individual ambition rewarded those who "succeeded" in society and held those who did not responsible for the circumstances in which they found themselves. Often explanations for poverty were sought in the lifestyles of poor people, along with the attitudes and outlooks they supposedly espoused. Oscar Lewis (1968) set forth one of the most influential of such theories, arguing that a **culture of poverty** exists among many poor people. According to Lewis, poverty is not a result of individual inadequacies, but is a result of a larger social and cultural atmosphere into which poor children are socialized. The culture of poverty is transmitted across generations because young people from an early age see little point in aspiring to something more. Instead, they resign themselves fatalistically to a life of impoverishment.

The culture of poverty thesis has been taken further by the American sociologist Charles Murray. According to Murray, individuals who are poor through "no fault of their own"—such as widows or widowers, orphans, or the disabled—fall into a different category from those who are part of the **dependency culture**. By this term, Murray refers to poor people who rely on government welfare provision rather than entering the labor market. He argues that the growth of the welfare state has created a subculture that undermines personal ambition and the capacity for self-help. Rather than orienting themselves toward the future and striving to achieve a better life, those dependent on welfare are content to accept handouts. Welfare, he argues, has eroded people's incentive to work (Murray, 1984).

Theories such as these seem to resonate among the U.S. population. Surveys have shown that the majority of Americans regard the poor as responsible for their own poverty and are suspicious of those who live "for free" on "government handouts." Many believe that people on welfare could find work if they were determined to do so. Yet, as we have seen, these views are out of line with the realities of poverty.

A second approach to explaining poverty emphasizes larger social processes that produce conditions of poverty that are difficult for individuals to overcome. According to such a view, structural forces within society—factors like class, gender, ethnicity, occupational position, education attainment, and so forth—shape the way in which resources are distributed (Wil-

son, 1996). Writers who advocate structural explanations for poverty argue that the lack of ambition among the poor that is often taken for the dependency culture is in fact a *consequence* of their constrained situations, not a cause of it. Reducing poverty is not a matter of changing individual outlooks, they claim, but instead requires policy measures aimed at distributing income and resources more equally throughout society. Child-care subsidies, a minimum hourly wage, and guaranteed income levels for families are examples of policy measures that have sought to redress persistent social inequalities.

Both theories have enjoyed broad support, and we consistently encourage variations of each view in public debates about poverty. Critics of the culture of poverty view accuse its advocates of "individualizing" poverty and blaming the poor for circumstances largely beyond their control. They see the poor as victims, not as freeloaders who are abusing the system. Yet we should be cautious about accepting uncritically the arguments of those who see the causes of poverty as lying exclusively in the structure of society itself. Such an approach implies that the poor simply passively accept the difficult situations in which they find themselves.

Combating Poverty: Welfare Systems

Well-developed and systematically administered welfare programs, in conjunction with government policies that actively assist in keeping down unemployment, reduce poverty levels. But an economic and political price has to be paid for this. Such a society requires high levels of taxation; and the government bureaucracies needed to administer the complex welfare system tend to acquire considerable power, even though they are not democratically elected.

Being poor does not necessarily mean being *mired* in poverty. A substantial proportion of people in poverty at any one time have either enjoyed superior conditions of life previously or can be expected to climb out of poverty at some time in the future.

As we saw in the last section, critics of existing welfare institutions in the United States have argued that these produce "welfare dependency," meaning that people become dependent on the very programs that are supposed to allow them to forge an independent and meaningful life for themselves. They become not just materially dependent, but psychologically dependent on the arrival of the welfare check. Instead of taking an active attitude toward their lives, they tend to adopt a resigned and passive one, looking to the welfare system to support them.

Others deny that such dependency is widespread. "Being on welfare" is commonly regarded as a source of shame, they say, and most people who are in such a position probably strive actively to escape from it as far as possible.

However widespread it may be, tackling welfare dependency has become a main target of attempts at reform of American welfare institutions. Among the most significant of such reforms have been welfare-to-work programs, whose driving force is to move recipients from public assistance into paid jobs. Daniel Friedlander and Gary Burtless (1994) studied four different government-initiated programs designed to encourage welfare recipients to find paid work. The programs were roughly similar. They provided financial benefits for welfare recipients who actively searched for jobs as well as guidance in job hunting techniques and opportunities for education and training. The target populations were mainly single-parent family heads of households who were recipients of Aid to Families with Dependent Children, at the time, the largest cash welfare program in the country. Friedlander and Burtless found that the programs did achieve results. People involved in such programs were able either to enter employment or to start working sooner than others who didn't participate. In all four programs, the earnings produced were several times greater than the net cost of the program. The programs were least effective, however, in helping those who needed them the most—those who had been out of work for a lengthy period, the long-term unemployed (Friedlander and Burtless, 1994).

In 1996, Congress enacted and President Bill Clinton signed a law to "end welfare as we know it." The resulting program, Temporary Assistance for Needy Families (TANF), required that welfare recipients begin work after receiving benefits for two years. Families were cut off entirely after a cumulative five years of assistance. Prior to this reform, there were no time limits or work requirements imposed by the federal government for welfare recipients, many of whom are single mothers.

Although welfare-to-work programs succeeded in reducing welfare claims from 5.1 million families to 2.7 million families in its first three years (see Figure 8.6), some statistics suggest that the outcomes are not entirely positive. Among those who had left welfare for work, only 61 percent had found jobs, 20 percent relied on help from family members or private charities, and about 19 percent had no work or source of independent income. Among those working, the average wage was $6.61 an hour. For about half of this group, this amounted to less than what they had received from the welfare system. Only 23 percent had health insurance through their employer. In Wisconsin, the state that was one of the first to introduce welfare-to-work programs, two thirds of former welfare recipients live below the poverty line. Most have difficulty finding enough money for food and other essentials (Loprest, 1999).

Kathryn Edin and Laura Lein (1997) have shown that for low-income mothers, the costs of leaving welfare for work can outweigh the advantages. These mothers face expenses for food, rent, and other necessities that often exceed their income. Mothers who work must often pay for child care, so that their expenses surpass those of unemployed mothers. In addition, the jobs available to low-income mothers tend to be less stable and to pay less than welfare.

Because their expenses exceed their income, both working and welfare mothers must often find other sources of money. Mothers on welfare tend to rely on aid from charitable agencies or side work, which is likely to be unreported. (Reporting additional income can reduce or end welfare benefits.) Low-income working mothers also rely on support from people in their social networks, such as family members or boyfriends, to help pay the costs of daily life. Pointing to such findings, critics argue that the apparent success of the welfare-to-work initiatives in reducing the number of people on welfare conceals some troublesome patterns in the actual experiences of those who lose their welfare benefits. Moreover, even the most hopeful studies were conducted during a period of economic expansion. When growth slows—or declines—it will be increasingly difficult, if not impossible, for welfare recipients to find any jobs at all.

Social Exclusion

What are the social processes that lead to a large number of people's being marginalized in society? The idea of **social exclusion** refers to new sources of inequality—ways in which individuals may become cut off from involvement in the wider society. It is a broader concept than that of the underclass and has the advantage that is emphasizes *processes*—mechanisms of exclusion. For instance, people who live in a dilapidated housing project, with poor schools and few employment opportunities in the area, may effectively be denied opportunities for self-betterment that most people in society have. It is also different from poverty as such. It focuses attention on a broad range of factors that prevent individuals or groups from having opportunities that are open to the majority of the population.

Social exclusion can take a number of forms, so that it may occur in isolated rural communities cut off from many services and opportunities or in inner-city neighborhoods marked by high crime rates and substandard housing. Exclusion and inclusion may be seen in economic terms, political terms, and social terms.

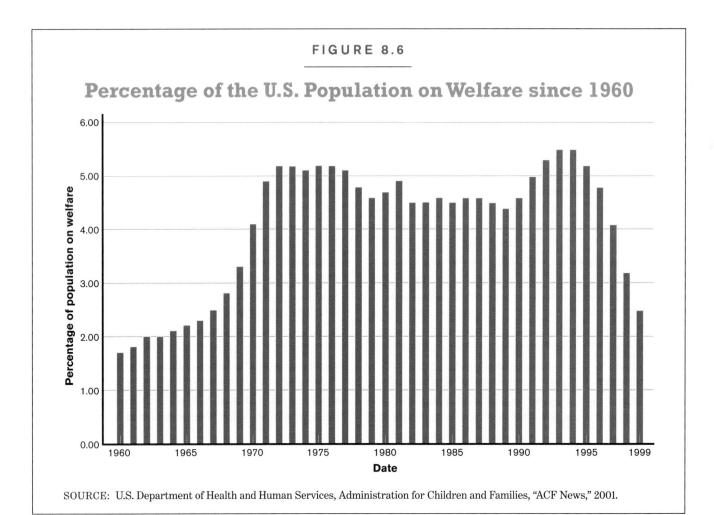

FIGURE 8.6

Percentage of the U.S. Population on Welfare since 1960

Percentage of population on welfare (y-axis: 0.00 to 6.00)

Date (x-axis: 1960 to 1999)

SOURCE: U.S. Department of Health and Human Services, Administration for Children and Families, "ACF News," 2001.

The concept of social exclusion raises the question of agency. After all, the word *exclusion* implies that someone or something is being shut out by another. Certainly in some instances, individuals are excluded through decisions that lie outside their own control. Banks might refuse to grant a current account or credit cards to individuals living in a certain zip code. Insurance companies might reject an application for a policy on the basis of an applicant's personal history and background. An employee laid off later in life may be refused further jobs on the basis of his or her age.

But social exclusion is not only the result of people's being excluded; it can also result from people excluding themselves from aspects of mainstream society. Individuals can choose to drop out of education, to turn down a job opportunity and become economically inactive, or to abstain from voting in political elections. In considering the phenomenon of social exclusion, we must once again be conscious of the interaction between human agency and responsibility on the one hand and the role of social forces in shaping people's circumstances on the other hand.

Forms of Social Exclusion

Sociologists have conducted research into the different ways in which individuals and communities experience exclusion. Investigations have focused on topics as diverse as housing, education, the labor market, crime, young people, and the elderly. We shall now look briefly at several examples of exclusion that have attracted attention in industrialized societies.

HOUSING AND NEIGHBORHOODS

The nature of social exclusion can be seen clearly within the housing sector. While many people in industrialized societies live in comfortable, spacious housing, others reside in dwellings that are overcrowded, inadequately heated, or structurally unsound. When entering the housing market, individuals are able to secure housing on the basis of their existing and projected resources. Thus, a dual-income childless couple will have a greater chance of obtaining a mortgage for a home in an attractive area, whereas a household whose adults are unemployed or in low-paying jobs may be restricted to less desirable options in the rented or public-housing sector.

Stratification within the housing market occurs at both the household and the community level. Just as disadvantaged individuals are excluded from desirable housing options, whole communities can be excluded from opportunities and activities that are norms for the rest of society. Exclusion can take on a spatial dimension: Neighborhoods vary greatly in terms of safety, environmental conditions, and the availability of services and public facilities. For example, low-demand neighborhoods tend to have fewer basic services such as banks, grocery stores, and post offices than more desirable areas. Community spaces such as parks, playing fields, and libraries may also be limited. Yet people living in disadvantaged places are often dependent on what few facilities are available. Unlike residents of more affluent areas, they may not have access to transportation (or funds) that would allow them to stop and use services elsewhere.

In deprived communities, it can be difficult for people to overcome exclusion and to take steps to engage more fully in society. Social networks may be weak; this reduces the circulation of information about jobs, political activities, and community events. High unemployment and low income levels place strains on family life; crime and juvenile delinquency undermine the overall quality of life in the neighborhood. Low-demand housing areas often experience high household turnover rates as many residents seek to move on to more desirable housing, while new, disadvantaged entrants to the housing market continue to arrive. Finally, since most public schools in the United States are financed with property taxes, poor neighborhoods are likely to have underfunded schools, which lowers the quality of education available to poor children.

RURAL AREAS

Although much attention is paid to social exclusion in urban settings, people living in rural regions can also experience exclusion. Some social workers and caregivers believe that the challenges or exclusion in the countryside are as large, if not larger, than those in cities. In smaller villages and sparsely populated areas, access to goods, services, and facilities is not as extensive as in more settled areas. In most industrial societies, proximity to basic services such as doctors, post offices, schools, houses of worship, libraries, and government services is considered a necessity for leading an active, full, and healthy life. But rural residents often have limited access to such services and depend on the facilities available within their local community.

Access to transportation is one of the biggest factors affecting rural exclusion. If a household owns or has access to a car, it is easier to remain integrated in society. For example, family members can consider taking jobs in other towns, periodic shopping trips can be arranged to areas that have a larger selection of shops, and visits to friends or family in other areas can be organized more readily. Young people can be fetched home from parties. People who do not have access to a car, however, are dependent on public transportation, and in rural areas such services are limited in scope.

SOCIAL EXCLUSION AT THE TOP

The examples of exclusion that we have considered thus far all concern individuals or groups who, for whatever reason, are unable to participate fully in institutions and activities used by the majority of the population. Yet, not all cases of exclusion occur among those who are disadvantaged at the bottom of society. In recent years, new dynamics of "social exclusion at the top" have been emerging. This means that a minority of individuals at the very top of society can opt out of participation in mainstream institutions by merit of their affluence, influence, and connections.

Exclusion at the top can take a number of forms. The wealthy might retreat fully from the realm of public education and health care services, preferring to pay for private services and attention. Affluent residential communities—the so-called gated communities located behind tall walls and security checkpoints—are increasingly closed off from the rest of society. Tax payments and financial obligations can be drastically reduced through careful management and the help of private financial planners. Particularly in the United States, active political participation among the elite is often replaced by large donations to political candidates who are seen to represent their interests. In a number of ways, the very wealthy are able to escape from their social and financial responsibilities into a closed, private realm largely separate from the rest of society. Just as social exclusion at the bottom undermines social solidarity and cohesion, exclusion at the top is similarly detrimental to an integrated society.

Crime and Social Exclusion

Some sociologists have argued that in industrialized societies such as the United States there are strong links between crime and social exclusion. There is a trend among late modern societies, they argue, away from inclusive goals (based on citizenship rights) and toward arrangements that accept and even promote the exclusion of some citizens (Young, 1998, 1999). Crime rates may be reflecting the fact that a growing number of people do not feel valued by—or feel they have an investment in—the societies in which they live.

Elliott Currie is a sociologist who has investigated the connections between social exclusion and crime in the United States, particularly among young people. Currie argues that American society is a "natural laboratory" that is already demonstrating the "ominous underside" of market-driven social policy: rising poverty and homelessness, drug abuse, and violent crime. He notes that young people are increasingly growing up on their own without the guidance and support they need from the adult population. While faced by the seductive lure of the market and consumer goods, young people are also confronted by diminishing opportunities in the labor market to sustain a livelihood. This can result in a profound sense of relative deprivation and a willingness to turn to illegitimate means of sustaining a desired lifestyle.

According to Currie, there are several main links between crime and social exclusion. First, shifts in the labor market and government taxation and minimum wage policies have led to an enormous growth in both relative and absolute poverty within the American population. Second, this rise in social exclusion is felt in local communities, which suffer from a loss of stable livelihoods, transient populations, increasingly expensive housing, and a weakening of social cohesion. Third, economic deprivation and community fragmentation strain family life. Adults in many poor families are forced to take on multiple jobs to survive—a situation that produces perpetual stress, anxiety, and absence from home. The socialization and nurturing of children is, as a result, weakened; the overall "social impoverishment" of the community means that there is little opportunity for parents to turn to other families or relatives for support. Fourth, the state has rolled back many of the programs and public services that could reincorporate the socially excluded, such as early childhood intervention, child care, and mental health care.

Finally, the standards of economic status and consumption that are promoted within society cannot be met through legitimate means by the socially excluded population. According to Currie, one of the most troublesome dimensions to this connection between social exclusion and crime is that legitimate channels are bypassed in favor of illegal ones. Crime is favored over alternative means, such as the political system or community organization (Currie, 1998).

THE HOMELESS

No discussion of social exclusion is complete without reference to the people who are traditionally seen as at the very bottom of the social hierarchy: the **homeless**. The growing problem of homelessness is one of the most distressing signs of changes in the American stratification system. The home-

With a sign for assistance strapped to his back, Rick Cathy, his wife, and their five-year-old daughter make their way to Sacramento. The family, originally from Buffalo, New York, was on the road continuously for more than eighteen months after losing their home.

less are a common sight in nearly every U.S. city and town and are increasingly found in rural areas as well. Two generations ago, the homeless were mainly elderly, alcoholic men who were found on the skid rows of the largest metropolitan areas. Today they are primarily young single men, often of working age. The fastest-growing group of homeless, however, consists of families with children, who make up as much as 40 percent of those currently homeless (Shinn and Weitzman, 1996). A study by the U.S. Conference of Mayors estimates that about a quarter of the urban homeless population are children under eighteen, while single men make up about half of the population, and single women about one-seventh. More than half of the homeless population is African American, and about a third is white. Very few homeless are Latino or Asian American immigrants, possibly because these groups enjoy close-knit family and community ties that provide a measure of security against homelessness (Waxman and Hinderliter, 1996). As many as 40 percent of homeless men are veterans, many of the Vietnam War (Rosenheck et al., 1996).

No one really knows how many homeless people there are, since it is extremely difficult to count people who do not have a stable residence (Appelbaum, 1990). Estimates of the number of homeless vary widely. The most recent estimate is that there are 462,000 homeless people in the United States on any given day, and that 2.3 million adults and children experience a spell of homelessness at least once during a year (Urban Institute, 2000). One survey of twenty-five cities, conducted by the U.S. Conference of Mayors in 2001, found a 17 percent increase in the number of homeless families applying for help over the previous year (Bernstein, 2001).

There are many reasons why people become homeless. One problem is that about a third of the homeless suffer from mental illness, and a third are substance abusers; as many as half have both problems (Blau, 1992; Burt, 1992). One reason for the widespread incidence of such problems among the homeless is that many public mental hospitals have closed their doors. The number of beds in state mental hospitals has declined by as many as half a million since the early 1960s, leaving many mentally ill people with no institutional alternative to a life on the streets or in homeless shelters. Such problems are compounded by the fact that many homeless people lack family, relatives, or other social networks to provide support.

The rising cost of housing is another factor, particularly in light of the increased poverty noted elsewhere in this chapter. Declining incomes at the bottom, along with rising rents, create an affordability gap between the cost of housing and what poor people can pay in rents (Dreier and Appelbaum, 1992). An estimated 5.4 million families spend more than half of their income on housing, leaving them barely a paycheck away from a missed rental payment and eventual eviction (NLIHC, 2000). The housing affordability gap has been worsened by the loss of government programs aimed at providing low-cost housing for the poor during the 1980s, which removed a crucial safety net just as poverty was increasing in the United States.

The sociological imagination enables us to understand how personal characteristics and larger social forces can combine to increase the risk of becoming homeless. Imagine two hardworking people with similar personal problems—for example, both struggle with alcoholism, depression, and family problems. One is an unskilled worker in a low-wage job, whereas the other is a doctor with a substantial income. Which one is more likely to become homeless?

The unskilled worker has little margin for mistakes, misfortunes, or economic changes that could threaten his or her job. During a time when American firms are moving their lowest-paying, least-skilled work overseas, the workers who hold such jobs are especially vulnerable to job loss and homelessness. A bout with too much drinking might be all that it takes to be thrown out of work. On the other hand, the doctor's job is unlikely to be threatened by globalization. Furthermore, he or she most likely has health insurance that covers counseling for personal problems and perhaps even costly treatment for alcoholism. There are likely other resources to fall back on as well: savings, investments, credit and loans, and friends and family who can afford to help out. This is not to say that only poor people run the risk of becoming homeless: If you have ever volunteered at a homeless shelter, you may have been surprised to encounter formerly middle-class families who "ran out of luck." But the people overwhelmingly at risk of becoming homeless are those who face a combination of low-paying jobs, poverty, and high housing costs along with a tangle of personal problems (Burt, 1992).

Theories of Stratification in Modern Societies

So far, we have examined closely types of class division, inequality, social mobility, poverty, and social exclusion. In this section, we step back and look at some broad theories by which thinkers have attempted to *understand* stratification. The most influential theoretical approaches are those developed by Karl Marx and Max Weber. Most subsequent theories of stratification are heavily indebted to their ideas.

Marx: Means of Production and the Analysis of Class

For Marx, the term *class* refers to people who stand in a common relationship to the **means of production**—the means by which they gain a livelihood. In modern societies, the two main classes are those who own the means of production—industrialists, or **capitalists**—and those who earn their living by selling their labor to them, the working class. The relationship between classes, according to Marx, is an exploitative one. In the course of the working day, Marx reasoned, workers produce more than is actually needed by employers to repay the cost of hiring them. This **surplus value** is the source of profit, which capitalists are able to put to their own use. A group of workers in a clothing factory, say, might be able to produce a hundred suits a day. Selling half the suits provides enough income for the manufacturer to pay the workers' wages. Income from the sale of the remainder of the garments is taken as profit.

Marx believed that the maturing of industrial capitalism would bring about an increasing gap between the wealth of the minority and the poverty of the mass of the population. In his view, the wages of the working class could never rise far above subsistence level, while wealth would pile up in the hands of those owning capital. In addition, laborers would daily face work that is physically wearing and mentally tedious, as is the situation in many factories. At the lowest levels of society, particularly among those frequently or permanently unemployed, there would develop an "accumulation of misery, agony of labor, slavery, ignorance, brutality, moral degradation" (1977).

Marx was right about the persistence of poverty in industrialized countries and in anticipating that large inequalities of wealth and income would continue. He was wrong in supposing that the income of most of the population would remain extremely low. Most people in Western countries today are much better off materially than were comparable groups in Marx's day.

Weber: Class and Status

There are two main differences between Weber's theory and that of Marx. First, according to Weber, class divisions derive not only from control or lack of control of the means of production, but from economic differences that have nothing directly to do with property. Such resources include especially people's skills and credentials, or qualifications. Those in managerial or professional occupations earn more and enjoy more favorable conditions at work, for example, than people in blue-collar jobs. The qualifications they possess, such as degrees, diplomas, and the skills they have acquired, make them more "marketable" than others without such qualifications. At a lower level, among blue-collar workers, skilled craft workers are able to secure higher wages than the semiskilled or unskilled.

Second, Weber distinguished another aspect of stratification besides class, which he called "status." *Status* refers to differences between groups in the social honor, or prestige, they are accorded by others. Status distinctions can vary independent of class divisions. Social honor may be either positive or negative. For instance, doctors and lawyers have high prestige in American society. **Pariah groups,** on the other hand, are negatively privileged status groups, subject to discrimination that prevents them from taking advantage of opportunities open to others. The Jews were a pariah group in medieval Europe, banned from participating in certain occupations and from holding official positions.

Possession of wealth normally tends to confer high status, but there are exceptions to this principle. In Britain, for instance, individuals from aristocratic families continue to enjoy considerable social esteem even after their fortunes have been lost. Conversely, "new money" is often looked on with some scorn by the well-established wealthy.

Whereas class is an objective measure, status depends on people's subjective evaluations of social differences. Classes derive from the economic factors associated with property and earnings; status is governed by the varying lifestyles that groups follow.

Weber's writings on stratification are important because they show that other dimensions of stratification besides class strongly influence people's lives. Most sociologists hold that Weber's scheme offers a more flexible and sophisticated basis for analyzing stratification than that provided by Marx.

Davis and Moore: The Functions of Stratification

Kingsley Davis and Wilbert E. Moore (1945) provided a functionalist explanation of stratification, arguing that it has beneficial consequences for society. They claimed that certain positions or roles in society are functionally more important than others, such as brain surgeons, and these positions require special skills for their performance. However, only a limited number of individuals in any society have the talents or experience appropriate to these positions. In order to attract the most qualified people, rewards need to be offered, such as money, power, and prestige. Davis and Moore determined that since the benefits of different positions in any society must be unequal, then all societies must be stratified. They concluded that social stratification and social inequality are functional because they ensure that the most qualified people, attracted by the rewards bestowed by society, fill the roles that are most important to a smoothly functioning society.

Davis and Moore's theory suggests that a person's social position is based solely on his innate talents and efforts. Not surprisingly, their theory has been met with criticism by other sociologists. For example, Melvin Tumin critiqued the theory for several reasons (Tumin, 1953). First, he argued that the functional importance of a particular role is difficult to measure and that the rewards that a society bestows on those in "important" roles do not necessarily reflect their actual importance. For instance, who is more important to society, a lawyer or a schoolteacher? If, on average, a lawyer earns four or five times the amount that a schoolteacher does, does that accurately reflect his or her relative importance to society? Second, Tumin argued that Davis and Moore overlooked the ways in which stratification limits the discovery of talent in a society. As we have seen, the United States is not entirely a meritocratic society. Those at the top tend to have unequal access to economic and cultural resources, such as the highest quality education, which help the upper classes transmit their privileged status from one generation to the next. For those without access to these resources, even those with superior talents, social inequality serves as a barrier to reaching their full potential.

Erik Olin Wright: Contradictory Class Locations

The American sociologist Erik Olin Wright has developed a theoretical position that owes much to Marx but also incorporates ideas from Weber (Wright, 1978, 1985, 1997). According to Wright, there are three dimensions of control over economic resources in modern capitalist production, and these allow us to identify the major classes that exist:

1. Control over investments or money capital.
2. Control over the physical means of production (land or factories and offices).
3. Control over labor power.

Those who belong to the capitalist class have control over each of these dimensions of the production system. Members of the working class have control over none of them. In between these two main classes, however, are the groups whose position is more ambiguous—the managers and white-collar workers mentioned earlier. These people are in what Wright calls **contradictory class locations,** because they are able to influence some aspects of production but are denied control over others. White-collar and professional employees, for example, have to contract their labor power to employers in order to make a living, in the same way as manual workers do. Yet at the same time they have a greater degree of control over the work setting than do most people in blue-collar jobs. Wright terms the class position of such workers "contradictory," because they are neither capitalists nor manual workers, yet share certain common features with each.

A large segment of the population—85 to 90 percent, according to Wright (1997)—falls into the category of those who are forced to sell their labor because they do not control the means of production. Yet within this population is a great deal of diversity, ranging from the traditional manual working class to white-collar workers. In order to differentiate class locations within this large population, Wright takes two factors into account: the relationship to authority and the possession of skills or expertise. First, Wright argues that many middle-class workers, such as managers and supervisors, enjoy *relationships toward authority* that are more privileged than those of the working class. Such individuals are called on by capitalists to assist in controlling the working class—for example, by monitoring an employee's work or by conducting personnel reviews and evaluations—and are rewarded for their "loyalty" by earning higher wages and receiving regular promotions. Yet, at the same time, these individuals remain under the control of the capitalist owners. In other words they are both exploiters and exploited.

The second factor that differentiates class locations within the middle classes is the *possession of skills and expertise.* According to Wright, middle-class employees possessing skills that are in demand in the labor market are able to exercise a specific form of power in the capitalist system. Given that their expertise is in short supply, they are able to earn a higher wage. The lucrative positions available to information

technology specialists in the emerging knowledge economy illustrate this point. Moreover, Wright argues, because employees with knowledge and skills are more difficult to monitor and control, employers are obliged to secure their loyalty and cooperation by rewarding them accordingly.

Frank Parkin and Social Closure

Frank Parkin (1971, 1979), a British author, has proposed an approach drawing more heavily on Weber than on Marx. Parkin agrees with Marx, as Weber did, that ownership of property—the means of production—is the basic foundation of class structure. Property, however, according to Parkin, is only one form of social closure that can be monopolized by one group and used as a basis of power over others. We can define as **social closure** any process whereby groups try to maintain exclusive control over resources, limiting access to them. Besides property or wealth, most of the characteristics Weber associated with status differences, such as ethnic origin, language, or religion, may be used to create social closure.

Two types of processes are involved in social closure. The first type, *exclusion*, refers to strategies that groups adopt to separate outsiders from themselves, preventing them from having access to valued resources. Thus, white unions in the United States have in the past excluded blacks from membership as a means of maintaining power and privilege. An emphasis on credentials is another major way by which groups exclude others in order to hold on to their power and privilege. In some U.S. school systems, for example, only those who have earned a secondary-school teaching certification in their subject, awarded by a school of education, are allowed to teach in the public schools.

The second type of processes involved in social closure, *usurpation*, refers to attempts by the less privileged to acquire resources previously monopolized by others—as where blacks struggle to achieve the rights of union membership.

The strategies of exclusion and usurpation may be used simultaneously in some circumstances. Labor unions, for instance, might engage in usurpatory activities against employers (going on strike to obtain a greater share of the resources or a position on the board of directors of a firm) but at the same time exclude ethnic minorities from membership. Parkin calls this dual closure. Here there is clearly a point of similarity between Wright and Parkin. Dual closure concerns much the same processes as those discussed by Wright with his concept of contradictory class locations. Both notions indicate that those in the middle of the stratification system in some part cast their eyes toward the top yet are also concerned with distinguishing themselves from others lower down.

Growing Inequality in the United States

Throughout this chapter, we have touched on the various ways in which changes in the American economy have affected social stratification, emphasizing the importance of both globalization and changes in information technology. We have pointed out that the global spread of an industrial capitalist economy, driven in part by the information revolution, has helped to break down closed caste systems around the world and replace them with more open class systems. The degree to which this process will result in greater equality in countries undergoing capitalist development will be explored in the next chapter.

What do these changes hold in store for you? On the one hand, new jobs are opening up, particularly in high-technology fields that require special training and skills and pay high wages. A flood of new products is flowing into the United States, many made with cheap labor that has lowered their costs. This has enabled consumers such as yourselves to buy everything from computers to automobiles at costs lower than you otherwise would have paid, thereby contributing to a rising standard of living.

But these benefits come with potentially significant costs. As you have read throughout this chapter, you live in a fast-paced world, in which you may find yourselves competing for jobs with workers in other countries who work for lower wages. This has already been the case for the manufacturing jobs that once provided the economic foundation for the working class and segments of the middle class. Companies that once produced in the United States—from automobiles to apparel to electronics—now use factories around the world, taking advantage of labor costs that are a fraction of those in the United States. Will the same hold true for other, more highly skilled jobs—jobs in the information economy itself? Many jobs that require the use of computers—from graphic design to software engineering—can be done by anyone with a high-speed computer connection, anywhere in the world. The global spread of dot-com companies will open up vastly expanded job opportunities for those with the necessary skills and training—but it will also open up equally expanded global competition for those jobs.

Partly as a result of these forces, inequality has increased in the United States since the early 1970s, resulting in a growing gap between rich and poor. The global economy has permitted the accumulation of vast fortunes at the same time that it has contributed to declining wages, economic hardship, and poverty in the United States. Homelessness is at least in part due to these processes, as is the emergence of an underclass of the new urban poor. Although the working class is especially vulnerable to these changes, the middle class is not exempt: A growing number of middle-class households experienced downward mobility from the late 1970s through the mid-1990s, until a decade of economic growth (now over) benefited all segments of American society. Although it is always hazardous to try to predict the future, global economic integration will likely continue to increase for the foreseeable future. How this will affect your jobs and careers—and stratification in the United States—is much more difficult to foresee.

The world today is undergoing a transformation as profound as the industrial revolution. The impact of that transformation will be felt well into the twenty-first century, touching our lives in every way. In the next chapter, we will further examine the impact of this transformation on stratification and inequality in other countries in the world, especially the poorer countries that have recently begun to industrialize.

Study Outline

www.wwnorton.com/giddens5

Social Stratification

- *Social stratification* refers to the division of people socioeconomically into layers, or strata. When we talk of social stratification, we draw attention to the unequal positions occupied by individuals in society. In the larger traditional societies and in industrialized countries today there is stratification in terms of *wealth*, property, and access to material goods and cultural products.

- Three major types of stratification systems can be distinguished: *slavery, caste,* and *class.* Whereas the first two of these depend on legal or religiously sanctioned inequalities, class divisions are not "officially" recognized but stem from economic factors affecting the material circumstances of people's lives.

Class Systems

- Classes derive from inequalities in possession and control of material resources and access to educational and occupational opportunities. An individual's class position is at least in some part achieved, for it is not simply "given" from birth. Some recent authors have suggested that cultural factors such as lifestyle and consumption patterns are important influences on class position. According to such a view, individual identities are now more structured around lifestyle choices than they are around traditional class indicators such as occupation.

- Class is of major importance in industrialized societies, although there are many complexities in the class system within such societies. The main class divisions are between people in the *upper, middle,* and *lower working classes,* and the *underclass.*

Inequality in the United States

- Most people in modern societies are more affluent today than was the case several generations ago. Yet the distribution of *wealth* and *income* remains highly unequal. Between the early 1970s and the late 1990s, partly as a result of economic globalization, the gap between rich and poor grew. Incomes at the top increased sharply, while many ordinary workers and families saw their incomes drop as higher-wage manufacturing jobs moved offshore to low-wage countries.

Social Mobility

- In the study of *social mobility,* a distinction is made between *intra-generational* and *intergenerational mobility.* The first of these refers to movement up or down the social scale within an individual's working life. Intergenerational mobility is movement across the generations, as when the daughter or son from a blue-collar background becomes a professional. Social mobility is mostly of limited range. Most people remain close to the level of the family from which they came, though the expansion of white-collar jobs in the last few decades has provided the opportunity for considerable short-range upward mobility.

Poverty

- Poverty remains widespread in the United States. Two methods of assessing poverty exist. One involves the notion of *absolute poverty,* which is a lack of the basic resources needed to maintain a healthy existence. *Relative poverty* involves assessing the gaps between the living conditions of some groups and those enjoyed by the majority of the population.
- Problems of declining income and poverty are especially pronounced among racial and ethnic minorities, families headed by single women, and persons lacking education. The *feminization of poverty* is especially strong among young, poorly educated women who are raising children on their own.

Social Exclusion

- Social exclusion refers to processes by which individuals may become cut off from full involvement in the wider society. People who are socially excluded, due to poor housing, inferior schools, or limited transportation, may be denied the opportunities for self-betterment that most people in society have. Homelessness is one of the most extreme forms of social exclusion. Homeless people lacking a permanent residence may be shut out of many everyday activities that most people take for granted.

Theories of Stratification

- The most prominent and influential theories of stratification are those developed by Marx and Weber. Marx placed the primary emphasis on class, which he saw as an objectively given characteristic of the economic structure of society. He saw a fundamental split between the owners of capital and the workers who do not own capital. Weber accepted a similar view, but distinguished another aspect of stratification, *status.* Status refers to the esteem, or "social honor," given to individuals or groups.

Key Concepts

absolute poverty (p. 228)
ascription (p. 221)
capitalist (p. 237)
caste society (p. 205)
caste system (p. 205)
class (p. 206)
contradictory class locations (p. 239)
culture of poverty (p. 232)
dependency culture (p. 232)
endogamy (p. 205)
exchange mobility (p. 221)
feminization of poverty (p. 230)
homeless (p. 236)
income (p. 208)
industrialism hypothesis (p. 221)
intergenerational mobility (p. 221)
intragenerational mobility (p. 221)
Kuznets curve (p. 207)
life chances (p. 206)
lower class (p. 216)
means of production (p. 237)
middle class (p. 215)
pariah group (p. 238)
poverty line (p. 238)
relative poverty (p. 228)
short-range downward mobility (p. 225)
slavery (p. 205)
social closure (p. 239)
social exclusion (p. 233)
social mobility (p. 220)

Review Questions

1. What is the difference between income and wealth?
   a. Income is the wages and salaries that you earn; wealth is what you are worth if you sell everything you own.
   b. Income is salary; wealth is the interest that accrues on investments.
   c. Income is money in the bank; wealth is locked up in physical assets.
   d. Income and wealth are the same thing.

2. What is the basis of Karl Marx's theory of class?
   a. Class is a byproduct of the Industrial Revolution.
   b. Modern societies are divided into those who own the means of production and those who sell their labor.
   c. People with power will always use it to protect their material interests.
   d. Class is a transitory system of stratification between feudal estates and the classlessness of communist society.

3. Which of the following is *not* true about the impact of globalization in the United States?
   a. Some manufacturing jobs have been lost.
   b. You may be competing for jobs with someone from a less-developed country.
   c. Inequality has declined as a result of globalization.
   d. Those with high skill levels are likely to get high compensation.

4. According to William Sewell and Robert Hauser, how does family background influence one's educational attainment?
   a. Family background determines the type of school children attended.
   b. Family background is a good indicator of family income, which had a direct impact on the economic resources parents could provide for their children.
   c. Family background influences one's educational aspiration.

   d. Family background influences educational attainment through its cultural capital.

5. What is the difference between intragenerational mobility and intergenerational mobility?
   a. Intragenerational mobility is about matters of social status, whereas intergenerational mobility is about matters of social class.
   b. Intragenerational mobility is the comparison of parents' class position with those achieved by their children, whereas intergenerational mobility is a person's movement up or down the socioeconomic scale in his or her working life.
   c. Intragenerational mobility is a person's movement up or down the socioeconomic scale in his or her working life, whereas intergenerational mobility is the comparison of parents' class position with those achieved by their children.
   d. Intragenerational mobility is a comparison of the occupational achievement of siblings, whereas intergenerational mobility is a comparison of parents' occupational achievement and with that of their children.

6. The feminization of poverty is highest among:
   a. Latino female-headed families.
   b. Asian American female-headed families.
   c. white female-headed families.
   d. all female-headed families.

7. Erik Olin Wright called the class positions of those who exploit and/or dominate but are also exploited and dominated
   a. dual closure points.
   b. contradictory class locations.
   c. pariah groups.
   d. the working class.

8. How does Murray explain the cause of the underclass in the inner cities?
   a. Murray maintains that racist barriers are the key to accounting for the urban underclass.
   b. Murray sees economic factors (class) as most important in accounting for the urban underclass.
   c. Murray argues that welfare dependence explains the existence of the urban underclass.
   d. All of the above.

9. What is the relationship between social exclusion and crime?
   a. Social exclusion reduces the crime rate.
   b. Social exclusion increases the crime rate.
   c. Social exclusion has no effect on the crime rate.
   d. No clear evidence is available.

10. Which of the following systems of stratification permits the least amount of mobility?
    a. Caste
    b. Class
    c. Slavery
    d. Clan

Thinking Sociologically Exercises

1. If you were doing your own study of status differences in your community, how would you measure people's social class? Base your answer on the textbook's discussion of these matters to explain why you would take the particular measurement approach you've chosen. What would be its value(s) and shortcoming compared with adopting alternative measurement procedures?

2. Using occupation and occupational change as your mobility criteria, view the social mobility within your family for three generations. As you discuss the differences in jobs among your grandfather, father, and yourself, apply all these terms correctly: *vertical* and *horizontal mobility, upward* and *downward mobility,* *intragenerational* and *intergenerational mobility.* Explain fully why you think people in your family have moved up, moved down, or remained at the same status level.

Data Exercises

www.wwnorton.com/giddens5
Keyword: Data8

• As you learned in Chapter 8, the stratification that exists among different groups of individuals is not only real, but has important consequences. These structured inequalities influence opportunities for achieving economic prosperity, referred to as *life chances* by sociologists. The data exercise for Chapter 8 explores the differences in social class at the community level.

Global Inequality: Differences Among Countries

Understand the systematic differences in wealth and power among countries.

Life in Rich and Poor Countries

Recognize the impact of different economic standards of living on people throughout the world.

Can Poor Countries Become Rich?

Analyze the success of the newly industrializing economies.

Theories of Global Inequality

Consider various theories explaining why some societies are wealthier than others, as well as how global inequality can be overcome.

Why Global Economic Inequality Matters to You

CHAPTER NINE

GLOBAL INEQUALITY

the past quarter century has seen the appearance of more global billionaires than ever before in history. In 2004, there were 587 billionaires worldwide—277 in the United States, 164 in Europe, 73 in Asia, 25 in Latin America, 17 in Canada, 24 in the Middle East, 5 in Australia, and 2 in Africa (*Forbes,* 2004). Their combined assets in 2004 were estimated at $1.9 trillion—greater than the total gross national income of 140 countries (calculated from World Bank, 2003). The success of America's high-technology economy, coupled with the financial crisis that struck Asia in the late 1990s, enabled the United States to lay claim to over half the world's billionaires.

As of 2004, the wealthiest person in the world was Microsoft Corporation's founder Bill Gates, with a net worth of $46.6 billion in that year—down from $63 billion in 2000, thanks to the decline in the stock market. Gates, whose fortune is based largely on ownership of his company's stock, would seem the personification of American entrepreneurialism: a computer nerd turned capitalist whose software provides the operating system for nearly all personal computers. During the late 1990s, Gates was the first person in history to have a net worth in excess of $100 billion. Shortly after achieving this mark, the lofty value of Microsoft's stock began to decline, leaving Gates's fortune greatly reduced but still sufficient to rank him number one in wealth in the world.

Gates was followed by the financier Warren Buffett, at $42.9 billion. Buffet is an investor and CEO of Berkshire Hathway, Inc., which owns companies such as Geico Direct Auto Insurance, Dairy Queen, and See's Candies. In 2003, Buffet became an adviser to California's governor,

Arnold Schwarzenegger. Next came Karl Albrecht, with $23 billion. Albrecht is the owner of the German discount supermarket chain Aldi and the American gourmet grocery store Trader Joe's. Fourth on the list is Prince Alwaleed Bin Talal Alsaud of Saudi Arabia, whose investments have established his worth at $21.5 billion. Now this nephew of the king is transforming himself from businessman to activist, calling for a range of reforms in his country: elections, women's rights, and job creation. Among the twenty-five richest people, thirteen were from the United States, five were from Europe, two were from Hong Kong, two were from Russia, one was from Canada, one was from Saudi Arabia, and one was from Mexico (*Forbes,* 2004). If Bill gates typifies the American high-tech entrepreneur, Hong Kong's Li Ka-shing—who was number 19 on the list and Asia's richest man—is the hero in a rags-to-riches story that characterizes the success of many Asian businessmen. Li (his surname) began his career by making plastic flowers; in 2004, his $12.4 billion in personal wealth derived from a wide range of real estate and other investments throughout Asia.

Globalization—the increased economic, political, and social interconnectedness of the world—has produced the opportunities for unthinkable wealth. Yet at the same time it has produced widespread poverty and suffering. Consider, for example, Wirat Tasago, a twenty-four-year-old garment worker in Bangkok, Thailand. Tasago—along with more than a million other Thai garment workers, most of whom are women—labors from 8 A.M. until about 11 P.M. six days a week, earning little more than $3 an hour working days that can last sixteen hours (Dahlburg, 1995). Billions of workers such as Tasago are being drawn into the global labor force, many working in oppressive conditions that would be unacceptable, if not unimaginable, under U.S. labor laws. And these are the fortunate ones: Those who remain outside the global economy are frequently even worse off.

In the previous chapter, we examined the American class structure, noting vast differences among individuals' income, wealth, work, and quality of life. The same is true in the world as a whole: Just as we can speak of rich or poor individuals within a country, so we can talk about rich or poor countries in the world system. A country's position in the global economy affects how its people live, work, and even die. In this chapter, we look closely at the systematic differences in wealth and power between countries in the late twentieth and early twenty-first centuries. We examine what differences in economic standards of living mean for people throughout the world. We then turn to the newly industrializing economies of the world to understand which countries are improving their fortunes and why. This will lead us to a discussion of different theories that attempt to explain why global inequality exists

and what can be done about it. We conclude by speculating on the future of economic inequality in a global world.

Global Inequality: Differences Among Countries

Global inequality refers to the systematic differences in wealth and power that exist among countries. These differences between countries exist alongside differences within countries: Even the wealthiest countries today have growing numbers of poor people, while less wealthy nations are producing many of the world's superrich. Sociology's challenge is not merely to identify all such differences, but to explain why they occur—and how they might be overcome.

One simple way to classify countries in terms of global inequality is to compare the wealth produced by each country for its average citizen. This approach measures the value of a country's yearly output of goods and services produced by its total population and then divides that total by the number of people in the country. The resulting measure is termed the *per-person gross national income (GNI),* a measure of the country's yearly output of goods and services per person. The World Bank (2003), an international lending organization that provides loans for development projects in poorer countries, uses this measure to classify countries as high-income (an annual 2002 per person gross national income of $9,076 or more, in 2002 dollars), upper-middle-income ($2,936–9,075), lower-middle-income ($736–2,935), or low-income (under $735). This system of classification will help us better understand why there are such vast differences in living standards between countries.

Figure 9.1 shows how the World Bank (2003) divides 132 countries, containing nearly 6 billion people, into the three economic classes. (There are 74 other economies in the world, encompassing about 178 million people, for which the World Bank did not provide data, either because the data were lacking or because the economies had fewer than 1.5 million people.) The figure shows that while 40 percent of the world's population lives in low-income countries, only 16 percent lives in high-income countries. Bear in mind that this classification is based on *average* income for each country; it therefore masks income inequality *within* each country. Such differences can be significant, although we do not focus on them in this chapter. For example, the World Bank classifies India as a low-income country, since its per-person gross national in-

FIGURE 9.1

Population and Per Capita Income in Low-, Middle-, and High-Income Countries, 2002

Like most countries, the world as a whole is highly unequal. Forty percent of the people in the world live in low-income countries, while 16 percent live in high-income countries. The average income of people in high-income countries is 63 times that of people in low-income countries. The remainder of the world's population—about 44 percent—live in middle-income countries. According to the World Bank, the world has become considerably more "middle class" in recent years: In 1999, the World Bank reclassified China from low-income to middle-income, moving its 1.3 billion people (22 percent of the world's population) into the latter category. Although China's average income has risen to global middle-class standards, the large majority of China's people remain distinctly low income.

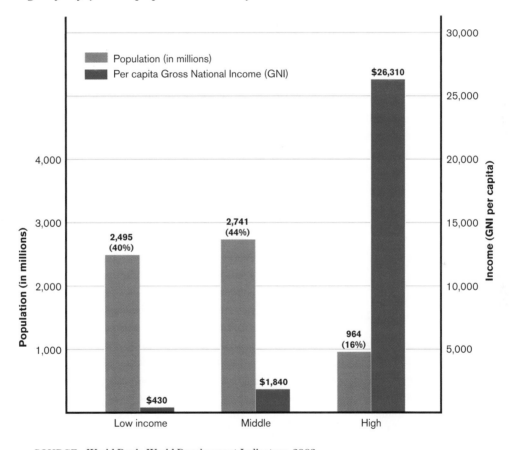

SOURCE: World Bank, World Development Indicators, 2003.

come in 2002 was only $480. Yet despite widespread poverty, India also boasts a large and growing middle class. China, on the other hand, was reclassified in 1999 from low- to middle-income, since its gross national income per capita in that year was $780 (recall the World Bank's lower limit for a middle-income country is $736). Yet even though its average income now confers middle-class status on China, it nonetheless has hundreds of millions of people living in poverty.

Comparing countries on the basis of economic output alone may be misleading, however, since gross national income includes only goods and services that are produced for cash sale. Many people in low-income countries are farmers or herders who produce for their own families or for barter, involving non-cash transactions. The value of their crops and animals is not taken into account in the statistics. Further, economic output is not a country's whole story: Countries possess unique and widely differing languages and traditions. Poor countries are no less rich in history and culture than their wealthier neighbors, but the lives of their people are much harsher.

High-Income Countries

The *high-income countries* are generally those that were the first to industrialize, a process that began in England some two hundred fifty years ago and then spread to Europe, the United States, and Canada. About thirty years ago, Japan joined the ranks of high-income, industrialized nations, while Singapore, Hong Kong, and Taiwan moved into this category only within the last decade or so. The reasons for the success of these Asian latecomers to industrialization are much debated by sociologists and economists. We will look at these reasons later in the chapter.

High-income countries account for only 16 percent of the world's population (roughly 965 million people)—yet lay claim to almost 81 percent of the world's annual output of wealth (derived from World Bank, 2003b). High-income countries offer decent housing, adequate food, drinkable water, and other comforts unknown in many parts of the world. Although these countries often have large numbers of poor people, most of their inhabitants enjoy a standard of living unimaginable by the majority of the world's people.

Middle-Income Countries

The *middle-income countries* are primarily found in East and Southeast Asia and also include the oil-rich countries of the Middle East and North Africa, the Americas (Mexico, Central America, Cuba and other countries in the Caribbean, and South America), and the once communist republics that formerly made up the Soviet Union and its East European allies (see Global Map 9.1). Most of these countries began to industrialize relatively late in the twentieth century and therefore are not yet as industrially developed (nor as wealthy) as the high-income countries. The countries that the Soviet Union once comprised, on the other hand, are highly industrialized, although their living standards have eroded during the past decade as a result of the collapse of communism and the move to capitalist economies. In Russia, for example, the wages of ordinary people dropped by nearly a third between 1998 and 1999, while retirement pensions dropped by nearly half: Millions of people, many of them elderly, suddenly found themselves destitute (CIA, 2000).

In 2002, middle-income countries included 44 percent of the world's population (2.7 billion people) but accounted for only 16 percent of the wealth produced in that year. Although many people in these countries are substantially better off than their neighbors in low-income countries, most do not enjoy anything resembling the standard of living common in high-income countries. The ranks of the world's middle-income countries expanded between 1999 and 2000, at least according to the World Bank's system of classification, when China—with 1.3 billion people (22 percent of the world's population)—was reclassified from low- to middle-income because of its economic growth. This reclassification is somewhat misleading, however. China's average per-person income of $940 per year is barely above the cutoff for low-income countries ($736), and a large majority of its population in fact is low income by World Bank standards.

Low-Income Countries

Finally, the *low-income countries* include much of eastern, western, and sub-Saharan Africa; Vietnam, Cambodia, Indonesia, and a few other East Asian countries; India, Nepal, Bangladesh, and Pakistan in South Asia; East and Central European countries such as Georgia and Ukraine; and Haiti and Nicaragua in the Western Hemisphere. These countries have mostly agricultural economies and are only recently beginning to industrialize. Scholars debate the reasons for their late industrialization and widespread poverty, as we will see later in this chapter.

In 2002, the low-income countries included over 40 percent of the world's population (2.5 billion people) yet produced only 3.4 percent of the world's yearly output of wealth. What is more, this inequality is increasing. Fertility is much higher in low-income countries than elsewhere, where large families provide additional farm labor or otherwise contribute to family income. (In wealthy industrial societies, where children are more likely to be in school than on the farm, the economic benefit of large families declines, so people tend to have fewer children.) Because of this, the populations of low-income countries (with the principal exception of India) are growing more than three times as fast as those of high-income countries (see Table 9.1).

In many of these low-income countries, people struggle with poverty, malnutrition, and even starvation. Most people live in rural areas, although this is rapidly changing: Hundreds of millions of people are moving to huge, densely populated cities, where they live either in dilapidated housing or on the open streets (see Chapter 19).

Growing Global Inequality: The Rich Get Richer, the Poor Get Poorer

During the last thirty years, the overall standard of living in the world has slowly risen. The average global citizen is today better off than ever before (see Table 9.2). Illiteracy is down, infant deaths and malnutrition are less common, people are living longer, average income is higher, and poverty is down. Since these figures are averages, however, they hide the substantial differences among countries: Many of these gains have been in the high- and middle-income countries, while living standards in many of the poorest countries have declined. Overall, the gap between rich and poor countries has widened.

From 1988 to 2002, average per-person GDP rose 34 percent in low-income countries and 54 percent in high-income countries, widening the global gap between rich and poor (see Figure 9.2). (Average income in middle-income countries remained largely unchanged.) By 2002, the average person in a typical high-income country earned $26,310, sixty-one times as much as the roughly $310 earned by his or her counterpart in a low-income country. Some 1.5 billion people—about a quarter of the world's population at that time—were estimated to live in poverty (World Bank, 2000–2001).

TABLE 9.1

Differences in Fertility and Population Growth: Low-, Middle-, and High-Income Countries

| | INCOME LEVEL | | |
	LOW	MIDDLE	HIGH
Annual births per woman, 2002	3.5	2.1	1.7
Average yearly percent population growth, 1990–2002	1.6	1.3	.06

NOTE: No data for 1997.

SOURCE: World Bank, World Development Indicators, 2003.

TABLE 9.2

The Global Quality of Life Has Risen During the Past 30 Years

QUALITY OF LIFE INDICATORS	1968	1998
Percentage illiterate	53	30
Average number of children per woman	6	3
Number of children who die in first year	1 in 4	1 in 8
Number of infants who die each year	12 million	7 million
Number of people suffering from malnutrition	4 out of 10	2 out of 10
Life expectancy at birth	50 years	61 years
Annual per person income	roughly $700	roughly $1,100
Percentage living on less than $1/day	roughly 50	roughly 25

SOURCE: Salter, 1998.

Rich and Poor Countries: The World by Income, 2002

Like individuals in a country, the countries of the world as a whole can be seen as economically stratified. In general, those countries that experienced industrialization the earliest are the richest, while those that remain agricultural are the poorest. An enormous—and growing—gulf separates the two groups.

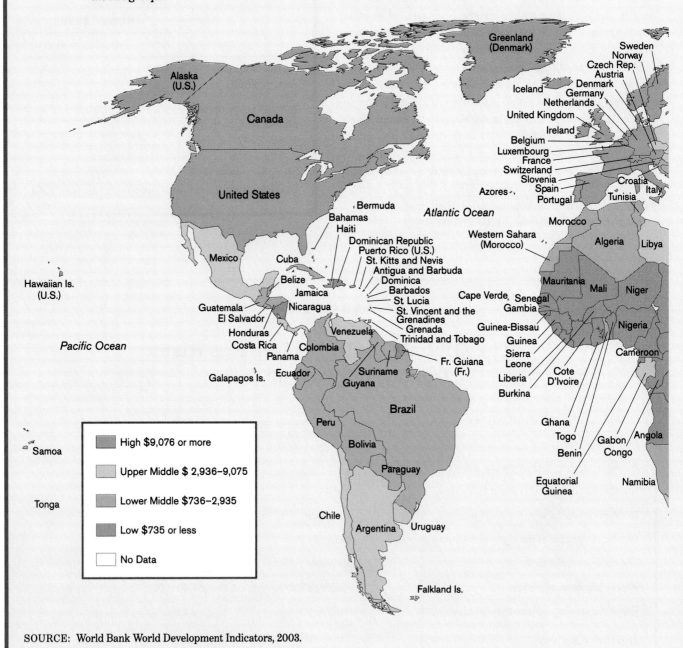

High $9,076 or more

Upper Middle $ 2,936–9,075

Lower Middle $736–2,935

Low $735 or less

No Data

SOURCE: World Bank World Development Indicators, 2003.

Finland
Estonia
Latvia
Lithuania
Poland
Belarus
Slovakia
Hungary
Ukraine
Serbia & Montenegro
Bosnia/Herzegovina
Moldova
Romania
Georgia
Bulgaria
Turkey
Greece
Albania Cyprus
Lebanon
Syria
Iraq
Iran
Libya
Egypt
Israel
Jordan
Chad
Eritrea
Sudan
Cent.
African
Rep.
Uganda
Democratic
Rep. of
Congo
Burundi
Zambia
Botswana
South Africa
Lesotho
Swaziland
Malawi
Mozambique
Zimbabwe
Madagascar
Mauritius
Kenya
Rwanda
Tanzania
Seychelles
Somalia
Ethiopia
Djibouti
Yemen
Oman
U.A.E
Saudi
Arabia
Kuwait
Bahrain
Qatar Pakistan
Afghanistan
Armenia
Azerbaijan
Turkmenistan
Uzbekistan
Tajikistan
Kyrgyzstan
Kazakhstan
Russia
Mongolia
People's Republic of
China
N. Korea
S. Korea
Japan
Taiwan
Bhutan
Nepal
Bangladesh
India
Myanmar
Laos
Thailand
Cambodia
Vietnam
Philippines
Brunei
Malaysia
Singapore
Sri Lanka
Maldives
Indonesia
East Timor
Australia
New
Zealand
Papua
New
Guinea
Palau
Mariana
Islands
(U.S.)
Guam (U.S.)
Federated
States of
Micronesia
Marshall
Islands
Kiribati
Nauru
Solomon Is.
Tuvalu
Vanuatu
Fiji
New
Caledonia
(Fr.)

NOTE: The map presents economies classified according to World Bank estimates of 2003 GNI per capita.
Not shown on the map because of space constraints are French Polynesia (high income); American Samoa
(upper middle income); Kiribati and Tonga (lower middle income); and Tuvalu (no data).

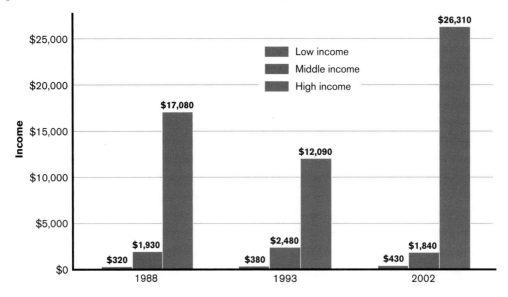

FIGURE 9.2

GDP per Person in Low-, Middle-, and High-Income Countries, 1988, 1993, and 2002

Despite overall growth in the global economy, the gap between rich and poor countries has not declined in recent years. Between 1988 and 2000, per-person GDP in low-income countries increased an average of 1.4 percent a year, far less than in high-income countries (2.2 percent). As a consequence, the average person in a high-income country earned roughly 61 times as much as the average person in a low-income country. Average per-person GDP in middle-income countries remained unchanged.

SOURCE: World Bank, 1990, 1995, 2000–2001.

Life in Rich and Poor Countries

An enormous gulf in living standards separates most people in rich countries from their counterparts in poor ones (*Harvard Magazine*, 2000). Wealth and poverty make life different in a host of ways. For instance, about one third of the world's poor are undernourished, and almost all are illiterate and lack access to even primary-school education. Although most of the world is still rural, within a decade there are likely to be more urban than rural poor (World Bank, 1996). Many of the poor come from tribes or racial and ethnic groups that differ from the dominant groups of their countries, and their poverty is at least in part the result of discrimination (Narayan, 1999).

Here we look at differences between high- and low-income countries in terms of health, starvation and famine, and education and literacy.

Health

People in high-income countries are far healthier than their counterparts in low-income countries. Low-income countries generally suffer from inadequate health facilities, and when they do have hospitals or clinics, these seldom serve the poorest people. People living in low-income countries also lack proper sanitation, drink polluted water, and run a much greater risk of contracting infectious diseases. They are more likely to suffer malnourishment, starvation, and famine. All of these factors contribute to physical weakness and poor health, making people in low-income countries susceptible to illness and disease. There is growing evidence that the high rates of HIV/AIDS infection found in many African countries are due in part to the weakened health of impoverished people (Stillwagon, 2001).

Because of poor health conditions, people in low-income countries are more likely to die in infancy and less likely to live to old age than people in high-income countries. Infants are eleven times more likely to die at birth in low-income countries than they are in high-income countries, and—if they survive birth—they are likely to live on average eighteen years fewer (see Table 9.3). Children often die of illnesses that are readily treated in wealthier countries, such as measles or diarrhea. In some parts of the world, such as sub-Saharan Africa, a child is more likely to die before the age of five than to enter secondary school (World Bank, 1996). Still, conditions have improved in low- and middle-income countries: Between 1980 and 2002, for example, the infant mortality rate dropped from 97 (per thousand live births) to 81 in low-income countries and from 60 to 29 in middle-income countries. AIDS, and growing poverty in some regions of the world, have contributed to the increase in infant mortality in the poorest countries in recent years.

During the past three decades, some improvements have occurred in most of the middle-income countries of the world and in some of the low-income countries as well. Throughout the world, infant mortality has been cut in half, and average life expectancy has increased by ten years or more because of the wider availability of modern medical technology, improved sanitation, and rising incomes.

TABLE 9.3

Differences in Infant Mortality and Life Expectancy: Low-, Middle-, and High-Income Countries, 2002

	INCOME LEVEL		
	LOW	MIDDLE	HIGH
Annual infant deaths per 1,000 live births	81	29	5
Life expectancy at birth (years)	59	70	78

SOURCE: World Bank, World Development Indicators, 2003.

Hunger, Malnutrition, and Famine

Hunger, malnutrition, and famine are major global sources of poor health. These problems are nothing new. What seems to be new is their extent—the fact that so many people in the world today appear to be on the brink of starvation (see Global Map 9.2). A recent study by the United Nations World Food Program (2001) estimates that 830 million people go hungry every day, 95 percent of them in developing countries. The program defines "hunger" as a diet of 1,800 or fewer calories a day—an amount insufficient to provide adults with the nutrients required for active, healthy lives.

According to the World Food Program study, 200 million of the world's hungry are children under five, who are underweight because they lack adequate food. Every year hunger kills an estimated 12 million children. As one ten-year-old child from the west African country of Gabon told researchers from the World Bank, "When I leave for school in the mornings I don't have any breakfast. At noon there is no lunch, in the evening I get a little supper, and that is not enough. So when I see another child eating, I watch him, and if he doesn't give me something I think I'm going to die of hunger" (Narayan, 1999). Yet more than three quarters of all malnourished children under the age of five in the world's low-

and middle-income countries live in countries that actually produce a food surplus (Lappe et al., 1998).

Most famine and hunger today are the result of a combination of natural and social forces. Drought alone affects an estimated 100 million people in the world today. In countries such as Sudan, Ethiopia, Eritrea, Indonesia, Afghanistan, Sierra Leone, Guinea, and Tajikistan, the combination of drought and internal warfare has wrecked food production, resulting in starvation and death for millions of people. In Latin America and the Caribbean, 53 million people (11 percent of the population) are malnourished—a number that rises to 180 million (33 percent) in sub-Saharan Africa, and 525 million (17 percent) in Asia (UNWFP, 2001).

The AIDS epidemic has also contributed to the problem of food shortages and hunger, killing many working-age adults. One recent study by the United Nations Food and Agricultural Organization (FAO) predicts that HIV/AIDS–caused deaths in the ten African countries most afflicted by the epidemic will reduce the labor force by 26 percent by the year 2020. Of the estimated 26 million people worldwide infected with HIV, 95 percent live in developing countries. According to the FAO, the epidemic can be devastating to nutrition, food security, and agricultural production, affecting "the entire society's ability to maintain and reproduce itself" (UN FAO, 2001).

Hunger Is a Global Problem

Hunger is a global problem, although it is disproportionately found in the poorest regions of the world. The world's great concentrations of hunger are in central and sub-Saharan Africa, followed by the Indian subcontinent. Although somewhat less widespread, significant amounts of hunger are also found in parts of Asia, Russia, and other republics of the former Soviet Union, South America, Central America, and Mexico. It is estimated that at any given time, 830 million people are hungry, 200 million of whom are children.

Legend:
- <2.5% Extremely low
- 2.5–4% Very low
- 5–19% Moderately low
- 20–34% Moderately high
- >35% Very high
- No data

SOURCE: UNWFP, 2001.

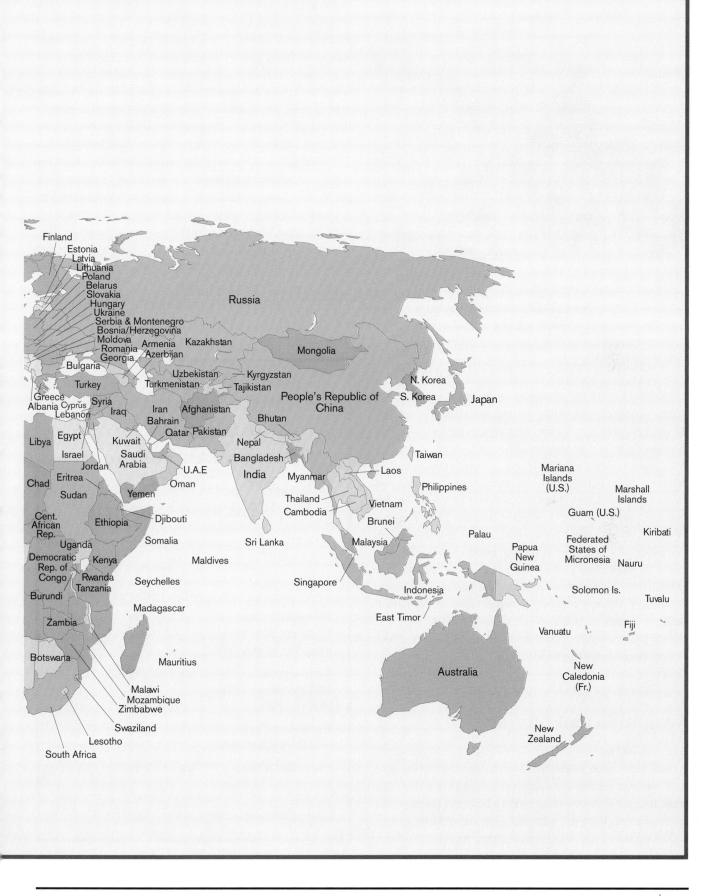

An Afghan shepherd leads his herd in search of water in Kabul. Four years of harsh and successive drought in many areas of land-locked Afghanistan has caused the water level to drop drastically. Hundreds of people and tens of thousands of animals have died due to drought-related problems in various parts of the country.

The countries affected by famine and starvation are for the most part too poor to pay for new technologies that would increase their food production. Nor can they afford to purchase sufficient food imports from elsewhere in the world. At the same time, paradoxically, as world hunger grows, food production continues to increase. Between 1965 and 1999, for example, world production of grain doubled. Even allowing for the substantial world population increase over this period, the global production of grain per person was 15 percent higher in 1999 than it was thirty-four years earlier. This growth, however, is not evenly distributed around the world. In much of Africa, for example, food production per person declined in recent years. Surplus food produced in high-income countries such as the United States is seldom affordable to the countries that need it most.

Education and Literacy

Education and literacy are important routes to economic development. Here, again, lower-income countries are disadvantaged, since they can seldom afford high-quality public education systems. As a consequence, children in high-income countries are much more likely to get schooling than are children in low-income countries, and adults in high-income countries are much more likely to be able to read and write (see Table 9.4). While virtually all high school–age males and females attend secondary school in high-income countries, in 1997 only 71 percent did so in middle-income countries and only 51 percent in low-income countries. Thirty percent of male adults and almost half of female adults in low-income countries are unable to read and write. One reason for these differences is a sizable gap in public expenditures on education: High-income countries spend a much larger percentage of their gross domestic product on education than do low-income countries (World Bank, 2000–2001).

Education is important for several reasons. First, as noted, education contributes to economic growth, since people with advanced schooling provide the skilled workers necessary for high-wage industries. Second, education offers the only hope for escaping from the cycle of harsh working conditions and poverty, since poorly educated people are condemned to low-wage, unskilled jobs. Finally, educated people are less likely to have large numbers of children, thus slowing the global population explosion that contributes to global poverty (see Chapter 19).

TABLE 9.4

Differences in Education and Literacy: Low-, Middle-, and High-Income Countries

	INCOME LEVEL		
	LOW	MIDDLE	HIGH
Percentage of high-school-age youth in secondary school, 1997	51	71	96
Public expenditure on education as percentage of GNP, 1997	3.3	4.8	5.4
Percentage of males over 15 illiterate, 1998	30	10	0
Percentage of females over 15 illiterate, 1998	49	20	0

SOURCE: World Bank, 2000–2001.

Can Poor Countries Become Rich?

As we saw in Chapter 3, by the mid-1970s a number of low-income countries in East Asia were undergoing a process of industrialization that appeared to threaten the global economic dominance of the United States and Europe (Amsden, 1989). This process began with Japan in the 1950s but quickly extended to the **newly industrializing economies (NIEs),** that is, the rapidly growing economies of the world, particularly in East Asia but also in Latin America. The East Asian NIEs included Hong Kong in the 1960s and Taiwan, South Korea, and Singapore in the 1970s and 1980s. Other Asian countries began to follow in the 1980s and the early 1990s, most notably China, but also Malaysia, Thailand, and Indonesia. Today, most are middle income, and some—such as Hong Kong, South Korea, Taiwan, and Singapore—have moved up to the high-income category.

Figure 9.3 compares the economic growth of seven East Asian countries (including Japan) with the United States from 1980 to 1999. These are all places that were poor only two generations ago. The low- and middle-income economies of the East Asian region as a whole averaged 7.7 percent growth a year during that period, a rate that is extraordinary by world standards (World Bank, 2000–2001). By 1999, the gross domestic product per person in Singapore was virtually the same as that in the United States. China, the world's most populous country, has one of the most rapidly growing economies on the planet. At an average annual growth rate of 10 percent between 1980 and 1999, the Chinese economy doubled in size.

Economic growth in East Asia has not been without its costs. These have included the sometimes violent repression of labor and civil rights, terrible factory conditions, the exploitation of an increasingly female work force, the exploitation of immigrant workers from impoverished neighboring countries, and widespread environmental degradation. Nonetheless, thanks to the sacrifices of past generations of workers, large numbers of people in these countries are prospering.

How do social scientists account for the rapid economic growth in the East Asian NIEs, especially from the mid-1970s through the mid-1990s? The answer to this question may hold some crucial lessons for those low-income countries elsewhere that hope to follow in the steps of the NIEs. Although the NIEs' success is partly due to historically unique factors, it is also due to factors that could lead to a rethinking of the causes of global inequality. To understand the rapid development of this region, we need to view these countries both historically and within the context of the world economic system today (So and Chiu, 1995).

The economic success of the East Asian NIEs can be attributed to a combination of factors. Some of these factors are historical, including those stemming from world political and economic shifts. Some are cultural. Still others have to do with the ways these countries pursued economic growth. Following are some of the factors that aided their success:

1. **Historically, Taiwan, South Korea, Hong Kong, and Singapore were once part of colonial situations that, while imposing many hardships, also helped to pave the way for economic growth.** Taiwan and Korea were tied to the Japanese Empire; Hong Kong and Singapore were former British colonies. Japan eliminated large landowners who opposed industrialization, and both Britain and Japan encouraged industrial development, constructed roads and other transportation systems, and built relatively efficient governmental bureaucracies in these particular colonies. Britain also actively developed both Hong Kong and Singapore as trading centers (Gold, 1986; Cumings, 1987). Elsewhere in the world—for example, in Latin America

Singapore, along with Taiwan, South Korea, and Hong Kong, was transformed from a low-income country to a relatively prosperous, newly industrialized country.

FIGURE 9.3

Percentage Growth in GDP in Selected East Asian Countries, the United States, and the World as a Whole, 1980–1990 and 1990–1999

The East Asian economies grew at historically unprecedented rates during 1980s and 1990s. The economies of the low- and middle-income countries in the region as a whole grew nearly 150 percent over the period, or an average of 7.7 percent a year. By way of comparison, the U.S. economy grew only 61 percent, or 3 percent per year—only slightly more than the economies of Japan, the other high-income industrial countries of the world, and the world as a whole. China, the world's largest economy, was also one of the fastest growing, growing by an average of over 9 percent a year and doubling in size. By 2000, GDP per capita was higher in Japan ($44,830) than in the United States ($31,966), and almost as high in Singapore ($28,229). Economic growth was somewhat slower during the 1990s than the 1980s, in East Asia as well as throughout the rest of the world. The East Asian economic crisis of 1998–1999 briefly halted the rapid economic growth of the region, which since has largely recovered.

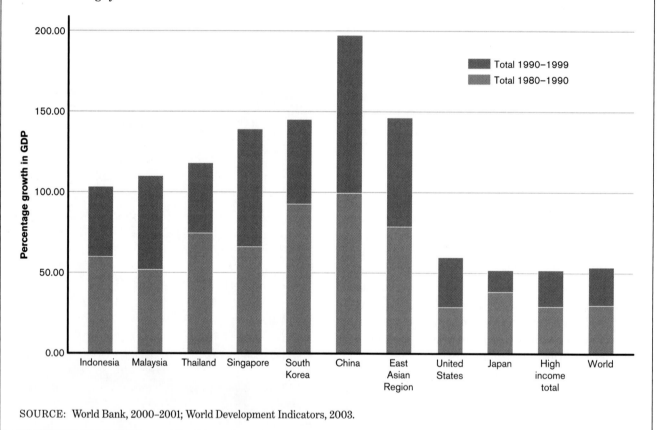

SOURCE: World Bank, 2000–2001; World Development Indicators, 2003.

and Africa—countries that are today poor did not fare so well in their dealings with richer, more powerful nations.

2. **The East Asian region benefited from a long period of world economic growth.** Between the 1950s and the mid-1970s, the growing economies of Europe and the United States provided a big market for the clothing, footwear, and electronics that were increasingly being made in East Asia, creating a "window of opportunity" for economic development. Furthermore, periodic economic slowdowns in the United States and Europe forced businesses to cut their labor costs and spurred the relocation

of factories to low-wage East Asian countries (Henderson and Appelbaum, 1992).

3. **Economic growth in this region took off at the high point of the cold war, when the United States and its allies, in erecting a defense against communist China, provided generous economic and military aid.** Direct aid and loans fueled investment in such new technologies as transistors, semiconductors, and other electronics, contributing to the development of local industries. Military assistance frequently favored strong (often military) governments that were willing to use repression to keep labor costs low (Mirza, 1986; Cumings, 1987, 1997; Deyo, 1987; Evans, 1987; Amsden, 1989; Henderson, 1989; Haggard, 1990; Castells, 1992).

4. **Some sociologists argue that the economic success of Japan and the East Asian NIEs is due in part to their cultural traditions, in particular, their shared Confucian philosophy.** Nearly a century ago, Max Weber (1977) argued that the Protestant belief in thrift, frugality, and hard work partly explained the rise of capitalism in Western Europe. Weber's argument has been applied to Asian economic history. Confucianism, it is argued, inculcates respect for one's elders and superiors, education, hard work, and proven accomplishments as the key to advancement as well as a willingness to sacrifice today to earn a greater reward tomorrow. As a result of these values, the Weberian argument goes, Asian workers and managers are highly loyal to their companies, submissive to authority, hard working, and success oriented. Workers and capitalists alike are said to be frugal. Instead of living lavishly, they are likely to reinvest their wealth in further economic growth (Berger, 1986; Wong, 1986; Berger and Hsiao, 1998; Redding, 1990; Helm, 1992).

   This explanation has some merit, but it overlooks the fact that businesses are not always revered and respected in Asia. Students and workers throughout the East Asian NIEs have opposed business and governmental policies they felt to be unfair, often at the risk of imprisonment and sometimes even their lives (Deyo, 1989; Ho, 1990). Furthermore, such central Confucian cultural values as thrift appear to be on the decline in Japan and the NIEs, as young people—raised in the booming prosperity of recent years—increasingly value conspicuous consumption over austerity and investment (Helm, 1992).

5. **Many of the East Asian governments followed strong policies that favored economic growth.** Their governments played active roles in keeping labor costs low, encouraged economic development through tax breaks and other economic policies and offered free public education.

Whether the growth of these economies will continue is unclear. In 1997–1998, a combination of poor investment decisions, corruption, and world economic conditions brought these countries' economic expansion to an abrupt halt. Their stock markets collapsed, their currencies fell, and the entire global economy was threatened. The experience of Hong Kong was typical: After thirty-seven years of continuous growth, the economy stalled and its stock market lost more than half its value. It remains to be seen whether the "Asian meltdown," as the newspapers called it in early 1998, will have a long-term effect on the region or is merely a blip in its recent growth. Once their current economic problems are solved, many economists believe, the newly industrializing Asian economies will resume their growth, although perhaps not at the meteoric rates of the past.

Theories of Global Inequality

What causes global inequality? How can it be overcome? In this section we shall examine four different kinds of theories that have been advanced over the years to explain global inequality: market-oriented, dependency, world-systems, and state-centered theories. These theories each have strengths and weaknesses. One shortcoming of all of them is that they frequently give short shrift to the role of women in economic development. By putting the theories together, however, we should be able to answer a key question facing the 85 percent of the world's population living outside high-income countries: How can they move up in the world economy?

Market-Oriented Theories

Forty years ago, the most influential theories of global inequality advanced by American economists and sociologists were **market-oriented theories.** These theories assume that the best possible economic consequences will result if individuals are free, uninhibited by any form of governmental constraint, to make their own economic decisions. Unrestricted capitalism, if allowed to develop fully, is said to be the avenue to economic growth. Government bureaucracy should not dictate which goods to produce, what prices to charge, or how much workers should be paid. According to market-oriented theorists, governmental direction of the economies of low-income countries results only in blockages to economic development. In this view, local governments should get out of the way of

What Can You Do About Child Labor?

Does child labor still exist in the world today? According to the United Nations International Labor Organization, more than 250 million boys and girls between the ages of five and fourteen are working in developing countries, about one out of every four children in the world. Some 50 to 60 million children between the ages of five and eleven work under hazardous conditions. Child labor is found throughout the developing world—in Asia (61 percent of the children are engaged in labor), Africa (32 percent), and Latin America (7 percent). They are forced to work because of a combination of family poverty, lack of education, and traditional indifference among some people in many countries to the plight of those who are poor or who are ethnic minorities (ILO, 2000; UNICEF, 2000).

Two thirds of working children labor in agriculture, with the rest in manufacturing, wholesale and retail trade, restaurants and hotels, and a variety of services, including working as servants in wealthy households. At best, these children work for long hours with little pay and are therefore unable to go to school and develop the skills that might eventually enable them to escape their lives of poverty. Many, however, work at hazardous and exploitative jobs under slavelike conditions, suffering a variety of illnesses and injuries. The International Labor Organization provides a grisly summary: "wounds, broken or complete loss of body parts, burns and skin diseases, eye and hearing impairment, respiratory and gastro-intestinal illnesses, fever, headaches from excessive heat in the fields or factories" (ILO, 2000).

A United Nations report provides several examples:

In Malaysia, children may work up to 17-hour days on rubber plantations, exposed to insect and snake bites. In the United Republic of Tanzania, they pick coffee, inhaling pesticides. In Portugal, children as young as 12 are subject to the heavy labor and myriad dangers of the construction industry. In Morocco, they hunch at looms for long hours and little pay, knotting the strands of luxury carpets for export. In the United States, chil-

dren are exploited in garment industry sweatshops. In the Philippines, young boys dive in dangerous conditions to help set nets for deep-sea fishing.

Conditions in many factories are horrible:

Dust from the chemical powders and strong vapors in both the storeroom and the boiler room were obvious. . . . We found 250 children, mostly below 10 years of age, working in a long hall filling in a slotted frame with sticks. Row upon row of children, some barely five years old, were involved in the work. (UNICEF, 1997)

One form of child labor that is close to slavery is "bonded labor." In this system children as young as eight or nine are pledged by their parents to factory owners in exchange for small loans. These children are paid so little that they never manage to reduce the debt, condemning them to a lifetime of bondage. One recent case of bonded labor that attracted international attention was that of Iqbal Masih, a Pakistani child who, at age four, was sold into slavery by his father in order to borrow six hundred rupees (roughly $16) for the wedding of his firstborn son. For six years, Iqbal spent most of his time chained to a carpet-weaving loom, tying tiny knots for hours on end. After fleeing the factory at age ten, he began speaking to labor organizations and schools about his experience. Iqbal paid a bitter price for his outspokenness: At age thirteen, while riding his bicycle in his hometown, he was gunned down by agents believed to be working for the carpet industry (Free the Children, 1998; India's Tiny Slaves, 1998).

Abolishing exploitative child labor will require countries around the world to enact strong child-labor laws and be willing to enforce them. International organizations, such as the United Nations' International Labor Organization (ILO), have outlined a set of standards for such laws to follow. In June 1999, the ILO adopted Convention 182, calling for the abolition of the "Worst Forms of Child Labor." These are defined as including:

- all forms of slavery or practices similar to slavery, such as the sale and trafficking of children, debt bondage and serfdom, and forced or compulsory labor, including forced or compulsory recruitment of children for use in armed conflict;
- the use, procuring, or offering of a child for prostitution, for the production of pornography, or for pornographic performances;
- the use, procuring, or offering of a child for illicit activities, in particular for the production and trafficking of drugs as defined in the relevant international treaties; and
- work that, by its nature or the circumstances in which it is carried out, is likely to harm the health, safety, or morals of children. (ILO, 1999)

Countries must also provide free public education and require that children attend school full time (UNICEF, 2000). But at least part of the responsibility for solving the problem lies with the global corporations that manufacture goods using child labor—and, ultimately, with the consumers who buy those goods. Here are two things that you can do right now:

1. **Check the Label.** Mind what you are buying. Begin by looking at the label. When you purchase clothing, rugs, and other textiles, the label will tell you where it was made, if unionized labor was used, and, in a few cases, whether it is certified to be "sweatshop free." Avoid buying garments made in countries with known human rights abuses, such as Myanmar (Burma). If the product has a label indicating it was made with union labor, it is likely to be free from child labor. "Sweatshop free" labels, although still rare, are likely to become more common in coming years, as labor and consumer groups pressure the U.S. government to more closely monitor imported goods. In one well-publicized campaign that grew out of Iqbal's tragic experience, Indian human rights activists developed the "Rugmark" label, which certifies that the carpet is free of child labor. The U.S. Department of Labor is also working toward a way of certifying goods that are sold in the United States to be "sweatshop free," although at this time there is no way to do so reliably: The millions of factories around the world involved in making consumer goods are too vast and dispersed to monitor.

2. **Join Up.** Join (or start) an antisweatshop campaign at your own college or university. There is a national campaign, organized by United Students Against Sweatshops, to require schools to engage in "responsible purchasing" when they buy or sell clothing, athletic equipment, and other goods that carry the school logo. Schools are urged to sign agreements with all their vendors that require full disclosure of the names and locations of the factories where the goods are made, certifying that the goods are free from child labor and other forms of exploitation. School sales are a multibillion-dollar business, and if schools set a high standard, manufacturers will be forced to take notice.

In a global economy, you can choose what you buy, as well as influence others to make informed and ethical choices about the products they consume. Be a smart shopper—it can make a difference.

development (Rostow, 1961; Warren, 1980; Berger, 1986; Ranis and Mahmood, 1992; Ranis, 1996).

Market-oriented theories reflect the belief that "any country can make it if it does it 'our way' "—that is, like the United States and other similar high-income countries. These theories inspired U.S. government foreign-aid programs that attempted to spur economic development in low-income countries by providing money, expert advisers, and technology, paving the way for U.S. corporations to make investments in these countries.

One of the most influential early proponents of such theories was W. W. Rostow, an economic adviser to former U.S. president John F. Kennedy, whose ideas helped shape U.S. foreign policy toward Latin America during the 1960s. Rostow's explanation is one version of a market-oriented approach, termed "modernization theory." **Modernization theory** argues that low-income societies can develop economically only if they give up their traditional ways and adopt modern economic institutions, technologies, and cultural values that emphasize savings and productive investment.

According to Rostow (1961), the traditional cultural values and social institutions of low-income countries impede their economic effectiveness. For example, many people in low-income countries, in Rostow's view, lack a strong work ethic: They would sooner consume today than invest for the future. Large families are also seen as partly responsible for "economic backwardness," since a breadwinner with many mouths to feed can hardly be expected to save money for investment purposes.

But to modernization theorists, the problems in low-income countries run even deeper. The cultures of such countries, according to the theory, tend to support "fatalism"—a value system that views hardship and suffering as the unavoidable plight of life. Acceptance of one's lot in life thus discourages people from working hard and being thrifty to overcome their fate. In this view, then, a country's poverty is due largely to the cultural failings of the people themselves. Such failings are reinforced by government policies that set wages and control prices and generally interfere in the operation of the economy. How can low-income countries break out of their poverty? Rostow viewed economic growth as going through several stages, which he likened to the journey of an airplane:

1. **Traditional stage.** This is the stage just described. It is characterized by low rates of savings, the supposed lack of a work ethic, and the so-called fatalistic value system. The airplane is not yet off the ground.

2. **Takeoff to economic growth.** The traditional stage, Rostow argued, can give way to a second one: economic takeoff. This occurs when poor countries begin to jettison their traditional values and institutions and start to save and invest money for the future. The role of wealthy countries, such as the United States, is to facilitate this growth. They can do this by financing birth-control programs or providing low-cost loans for electrification, road and airport construction, and starting new industries.

3. **Drive to technological maturity.** According to Rostow, with the help of money and advice from high-income countries, the airplane of economic growth would taxi down the runway, pick up speed, and become airborne. The country would then approach technological maturity. In the aeronautical metaphor, the plane would slowly climb to cruising altitude, improving its technology, reinvesting its recently acquired wealth in new industries, and adopting the institutions and values of the high-income countries.

4. **High mass consumption.** Finally, the country would reach the phase of high mass consumption. Now people are able to enjoy the fruits of their labor by achieving a high standard of living. The airplane (country) cruises along on automatic pilot, having entered the ranks of high-income countries.

Rostow's ideas remain influential. Indeed, the prevailing view among economists today, **neoliberalism,** argues that free-market forces, achieved by minimizing governmental restrictions on business, provide the only route to economic growth. Neoliberalism holds that global free trade will enable all countries of the world to prosper; eliminating governmental regulation is seen as necessary for economic growth to occur. Neoliberal economists therefore call for an end to restrictions on trade and often challenge minimum wage and other labor laws, as well as environmental restrictions on business.

Sociologists, on the other hand, focus on the cultural aspects of Rostow's theory: Whether and how certain beliefs and institutions hinder development (Davis, 1987; So, 1990). These include religious values, moral beliefs, belief in magic, and folk traditions and practices. Sociologists also examine other conditions that resist change, particularly the belief local cultures have that moral decay and social unrest accompany business and trade.

Dependency Theories

During the 1960s, a number of theorists questioned market-oriented explanations of global inequality such as modernization theory. Many of these critics were sociologists and economists from the low-income countries of Latin America and Africa who rejected the idea that their countries' economic underdevelopment was due to their own cultural or institutional faults. Instead, they build on the theories of Karl Marx, who argued that world capitalism would create a class of countries manipulated by more powerful countries just as capitalism within countries leads to the exploitation of workers. The **dependency theorists,** as they are called, argue that the poverty of low-income countries stems from their exploitation by wealthy countries and the multinational corporations that are based in wealthy countries. In their view, global capitalism locked their countries into a downward spiral of exploitation and poverty.

According to dependency theories, this exploitation began with **colonialism,** a political-economic system under which powerful countries establish, for their own profit, rule over weaker peoples or countries. Powerful nations have colonized other countries usually to procure the raw materials needed for their factories and to control markets for the products manufactured in those factories. Under colonial rule, for example, the petroleum, copper, iron, and food products required by industrial economies are extracted from low-income countries by businesses based in high-income countries. Although colonialism typically involved European countries establishing colonies in North and South America, Africa, and Asia, some Asian countries (such as Japan) had colonies as well.

Even though colonialism ended throughout most of the world after World War II, the exploitation did not: Transnational corporations continued to reap enormous profits from their branches in low-income countries. According to dependency theory, these global companies, often with the support of the powerful banks and governments of rich countries, established factories in poor countries, using cheap labor and raw materials to maximize production costs without governmental interference. In turn, the low prices set for labor and raw materials prevented poor countries from accumulating the profit necessary to industrialize themselves. Local businesses that might compete with foreign corporations were prevented from doing so. In this view, poor countries are forced to borrow from rich countries, thus increasing their economic dependency.

Low-income countries are thus seen not as underdeveloped, but rather as misdeveloped (Emmanuel, 1972; Amin, 1974; Frank, 1966, 1969a, 1969b, 1979; Prebisch, 1967, 1971). With the exception of a handful of local politicians and businesspeople who serve the interests of the foreign corporations, people fall into poverty. Peasants are forced to choose between starvation and working at near-starvation wages on foreign-controlled plantations and in foreign-controlled mines and factories. Since dependency theorists believe that such exploitation has kept their countries from achieving economic growth, they typically call for revolutionary changes that would push foreign corporations out of their countries altogether (Frank, 1966, 1969a, 1969b).

Whereas market-oriented theorists usually ignore political and military power, dependency theorists regard the exercise

Although Nigeria is the world's eighth largest producer of oil, the overwhelming majority of the profits generated in the energy trade go to oil companies and the military government, providing no benefit to the country's poverty-stricken inhabitants. These women are protesting Royal Dutch Shell's exploitation of Nigeria's oil and natural gas resources.

of power as central to enforcing unequal economic relationships. According to this theory, whenever local leaders question such unequal arrangements, their voices are quickly suppressed. Unionization is usually outlawed, and labor organizers are jailed and sometimes killed. When people elect a government opposing these policies, that government is likely to be overthrown by the country's military, often backed by the armed forces of the industrialized countries themselves. Dependency theorists point to many examples: the role of the CIA in overthrowing the Marxist governments of Guatemala in 1954 and Chile in 1973 and in undermining support for the leftist government in Nicaragua in the 1980s. In the view of dependency theory, global economic inequality is thus backed up by force: Economic elites in poor countries, backed by their counterparts in wealthy ones, use police and military power to keep the local population under control.

The Brazilian sociologist Enrique Fernando Cardoso, once a prominent dependency theorist, argued twenty years ago that some degree of **dependent development** was nonetheless possible—that under certain circumstances, poor countries can still develop economically, although only in ways shaped by their reliance on the wealthier countries (Cardoso and Faletto, 1979). In particular, the governments of these countries could play a key role in steering a course between dependency and development (Evans, 1979). Today, as the immediate past president of Brazil, Cardoso has changed his thinking, calling for greater integration of Brazil into the global economy.

World-Systems Theory

During the last quarter century, sociologists have increasingly seen the world as a single (although often conflict-ridden) economic system. Although dependency theories hold that individual countries are economically tied to one another, **world-systems theory** argues that the world capitalist economic system is not merely a collection of independent countries engaged in diplomatic and economic relations with one another but rather must be understood as a single unit. The world-systems approach is most closely identified with the work of Immanuel Wallerstein and his colleagues. Wallerstein showed that capitalism has long existed as a global economic system, beginning with the extension of markets and trade in Europe in the fifteenth and sixteenth centuries (Wallerstein, 1974a, 1974b, 1979, 1990, 1996a, 1996b; Hopkins and Wallerstein, 1996). The world system is seen as comprising four overlapping elements (Chase-Dunn, 1989):

- a world market for goods and labor;
- the division of the population into different economic classes, particularly capitalists and workers;
- an international system of formal and informal political relations among the most powerful countries, whose competition with one another helps shape the world economy; and
- the carving up of the world into three unequal economic zones, with the wealthier zones exploiting the poorer ones.

World-systems theorists term these three economic zones "core," "periphery," and "semiperiphery." All countries in the world system are said to fall into one of the three categories. **Core countries** are the most advanced industrial countries, taking the lion's share of profits in the world economic system. These include Japan, the United States, and the countries of Western Europe. The **peripheral countries** comprise low-income, largely agricultural countries that are often manipulated by core countries for their own economic advantage. Examples of peripheral countries are found throughout Africa and to a lesser extent in Latin America and Asia. Natural resources, such as agricultural products, minerals, and other raw materials, flow from periphery to core—as do the profits. The core, in turn, sells finished goods to the periphery, also at a profit. World-systems theorists argue that core countries have made themselves wealthy with this unequal trade, while at the same time limiting the economic development of peripheral countries. Finally, the **semiperipheral countries** occupy an intermediate position: These are semi-industrialized, middle-income countries that extract profits from the more peripheral countries and in turn yield profits to the core countries. Examples of semiperipheral countries include Mexico in North America; Brazil, Argentina, and Chile in South America; and the newly industrializing economies of East Asia. The semiphery, though to some degree controlled by the core, is thus also able to exploit the periphery. Moreover, the greater economic success of the semiperiphery holds out to the periphery the promise of similar development.

Although the world system tends to change very slowly, once-powerful countries eventually lose their economic power and others take their place. For example, some five centuries ago the Italian city-states of Venice and Genoa dominated the world capitalist economy. They were superseded by the Dutch, then the British, and currently the United States. Today, in the view of some world-systems theorists, American dominance is giving way to a more "multipolar" world where economic power will be shared among the United States, Europe, and Asia (Arrighi, 1994).

An important offshoot of the world systems approach is a concept that emphasizes the global nature of economic activities. **Global commodity chains** are worldwide networks of labor and production processes yielding a finished product. These networks consist of all pivotal production activities that form a tightly interlocked "chain" extending from the raw materials needed to create the product to its final consumer (Gereffi, 1995; Gereffi, 1996; Hopkins and Wallerstein, 1996; Appelbaum and Christerson, 1997).

The commodity-chain approach argues that manufacturing is becoming increasingly globalized. Manufactures accounted for approximately three quarters of the world's total economic growth during the period 1990–1998. The sharpest growth has been among middle-income countries: Manufactures accounted for only 54 percent of these countries' exports in 1990, compared with 71 percent just eight years later. Yet the high rate of increase of manufactures as a share of world exports has since slowed; in 2002, 75 percent of world exports were manufactures (World Trade Organization, 2003). China, which has moved from the ranks of low- to middle-income countries in part because of its role as an exporter of manufactured goods, partly accounts for this trend. Yet the most profitable activities in the commodity chain—engineering, design, and advertising—are likely to be found in the core countries, while the least profitable activities, such as factory production, usually are found in peripheral countries.

One illustration of the global commodity chain can be found in the manufacture of Barbie, the most profitable toy in history. The forty-something teenage doll sells at a rate of two per second, bringing the Los Angeles–based Mattel corporation well over a billion dollars in annual revenues. Although she sells mainly in the United States, Europe, and Japan, she can also be found in 140 countries around the world. She is a truly global citizen (Tempest, 1996). Barbie is global not only in sales, but in

Barbie, the quintessentially American doll, has never actually been produced in the United States. Since she was first made in Japan in 1959, rising wages in Asia have moved Barbie production from one low-wage country to another. The four factories that currently make Barbie are located in southern China, Indonesia, and Malaysia.

terms of her birthplace as well. Barbie was never made in the United States. The first doll was made in Japan in 1959, when that country was still recovering from World War II and wages were low. As wages rose in Japan, Barbie moved to other low-wage countries in Asia. Her multiple origins today tell us a great deal about the operation of global commodity chains.

Barbie is designed in the United States, where her marketing and advertising strategies are devised and where most of the profits are made. But the only physical aspect of Barbie that is "made in the U.S.A." is her cardboard packaging, along with some of the paints and oils that are used to decorate the doll.

Barbie's body and wardrobe span the globe in their origins:

- Barbie begins her life in Saudia Arabia, where oil is extracted and then refined into the ethylene that is used to create her plastic body.
- Taiwan's state-owned oil importer, the Chinese Petroleum Corporation, buys the ethylene and sells it to Taiwan's Formosa Plastic Corporation, the world's largest producer of polyvinyl chloride (PVC) plastics, which are used in toys. Formosa Plastics converts the ethylene into the PVC pellets that will be shaped to make Barbie's body.
- The pellets are then shipped to one of the four Asian factories that make Barbie—two in southern China, one in Indonesia, and one in Malaysia. The plastic mold injection machines that shape her body, which are the most

expensive part of Barbie's manufacture, are made in the United States and shipped to the factories.
- Once Barbie's body is molded, she gets her nylon hair from Japan. Her cotton dresses are made in China, with Chinese cotton—the only raw material in Barbie that actually comes from the country where most Barbies are made.
- Hong Kong plays a key role in the manufacturing process of the Chinese Barbies. Nearly all the material used in her manufacture is shipped into Hong Kong—one of the world's largest ports—and then trucked to the factories in China. The finished Barbies leave by the same route. Some 23,000 trucks make the daily trip between Hong Kong and southern China's toy factories.

So where is Barbie actually from? The cardboard and cellophane box containing the "My First Tea Party" Barbie is labeled "Made in China," but as we have seen, almost none of the materials that go into making her actually originates in that country. Out of her $9.99 retail price, China gets only about 35 cents, mainly in wages paid to the 11,000 peasant women who assemble her in the two factories. Back in the United States, on the other hand, Mattel makes about $1 in profits.

What about the rest of the money that is made when Barbie is sold for $9.99? Only 65 cents is needed to cover the plastics, cloth, nylon, and other materials used in her manufacture. Most of the money goes to pay for machinery and

Women and Economic Development

Although the theories of economic development reviewed in this chapter largely ignore women, women in fact play a key role in the global economy (Blumberg, 1995; Scott, 1995). Even where women contributed to revolutionary social change—such as in Vietnam, where more than a quarter of a million female soldiers died on behalf of communism during the Vietnam War—their economic role has not been fully acknowledged (Tétreault, 1994).

Today, women make up a major part of the work force in the world's factories. Yet studies that stress cheap factory work in the global economy often fail to examine the central importance of women's labor. In export-processing zones throughout the world, young women assemble clothing, electronics, and other components into finished products for sale in Europe and North America. The jobs in these factories pay little and offer few opportunities for advancement. They are repetitive, monotonous, and frequently hazardous. These factories often employ women as young as fourteen or fifteen years old, who work long hours for low wages.

Women make up a large portion of the world's work force for two very different sorts of reasons (Fernández Kelly, 1987;

Tiano, 1994). First, many are compelled to work in factories by their husbands or parents who need additional income. Second, many women view these jobs—however unsatisfactory—as preferable to unpaid work at home, since wage earning provides them with a measure of economic stability and financial independence.

Women are often the most exploited of workers. Because they are seen as less likely to protest than men, from the standpoint of employers they are "ideal" workers who will take a lot of abuse. The following accounts are from four women who work in giant Mexican denim factories, where they sew stonewashed jeans for major U.S. manufacturers for forty-eight to sixty hours a week. They spoke to a U.S. human rights delegation under conditions of secrecy, fearful that they would lose their jobs for speaking out:

Cristina:

I've worked there for five years. I earn 280 pesos a week [U.S. $35]. I pay 72 pesos a week [U.S. $9] to get a ride

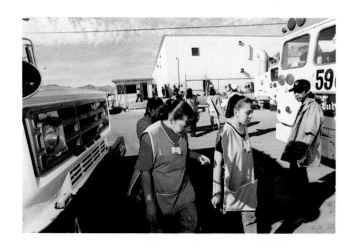